Routledge Research in Finance and Banking Law

Available

Law and Finance after the Financial Crisis
The Untold Stories of the UK Financial Market
Abdul Karim Aldohni

Microfinance and Financial Inclusion
The challenge of regulating alternative forms of finance
Eugenia Macchiavello

Law and Regulation of Mobile Payment Systems
Issues arising 'post' financial inclusion in Kenya
Joy Malala

Management and Regulation of Pension Scheme
Australia: A Cautionary Tale
Nicholas Morris

The Regulation and Supervision of Banks
The post crisis Regulatory Responses of the EU
Chen Chen Hu

Regulation and Supervision of the OTC Derivatives Market
Ligia Catherine Arias-Barrera

Value Added Tax Fraud
Marius-Cristian Frunza

Trust and Distrust in Digital Economies
Philippa Ryan

Credit and Creed
A Critical Legal Theory of Money
Andreas Rahmatian

For more information about this series, please visit: www.routledge.com/Routledge-Research-in-Finance-and-Banking-Law/book-series/FINANCIALLAW

Credit and Creed

A Critical Legal Theory of Money

Andreas Rahmatian

Routledge
Taylor & Francis Group
LONDON AND NEW YORK

First published 2020
by Routledge
2 Park Square, Milton Park, Abingdon, Oxon OX14 4RN

and by Routledge
605 Third Avenue, New York, NY 10017

Routledge is an imprint of the Taylor & Francis Group, an informa business

British Library Cataloguing-in-Publication Data
A catalogue record for this book is available from the British Library

Library of Congress Cataloging-in-Publication Data
Names: Rahmatian, Andreas, 1967– author.
Title: Credit and creed : a critical legal theory of money / Andreas Rahmatian.
Description: Abingdon, Oxon ; New York, NY : Routledge, 2019. | Series: Routledge research in finance & banking law | Includes bibliographical references and index.
Identifiers: LCCN 2019041890 (print) | LCCN 2019041891 (ebook)
Subjects: LCSH: Money—Law and legislation.
Classification: LCC K4431 .R34 2019 (print) | LCC K4431 (ebook) | DDC 343/.03201—dc23
LC record available at https://lccn.loc.gov/2019041890
LC ebook record available at https://lccn.loc.gov/2019041891

ISBN: 978-0-367-18103-1 (hbk)

Typeset in Galliard
by Apex CoVantage, LLC

Contents

Quotes on Money and Credit

Remember that Credit is Money. If a man lets his money lie in my hands after it is due, he gives me the interest, or so much as I can make of it during that time. This amounts to a considerable sum where a man has good and large credit, and makes good use of it.

Benjamin Franklin, *Advice to a Young Tradesman* (1748)[1]

The use of money produced a great alteration in the human heart. Money having at command the goods of fortune, introduced inequality of rank, luxury, and artificial wants without end. No bounds are set to hoarding, where an appetite for artificial wants is indulged: love of money becomes the ruling passion: it is coveted by many, in order to be hoarded; and means are absurdly converted into an end.

Henry Home, Lord Kames, *Sketches of the History of Man* (1778)[2]

We are dealing with a systemic crisis, with a dictatorship of the financial markets. The big private banks, funds, insurances and hedge funds stop at nothing, break down all remaining dams and break all taboos. They do not have the strength and the courage to finally do something about it. But that is urgently needed. This is not just about countries like Greece, Portugal, Spain or Ireland; it's about the core countries of capitalism. The United States, France and Italy are also under attack. Private American rating agencies dependent on large banks downgraded the US. Come on! That does not matter to them anymore; they have meanwhile become so powerful. I have heard from you for years: 'We need a public rating agency in Europe'. Where is it? It is high time to create it. It is not the Left but the financial markets that are destroying capitalism from within. The rating agencies are now even toppling governments, as in Ireland and Portugal. Nobody gets upset about it. Once upon a time, there was a voting right of the population; today it's completely different. Even if you do not want to admit it: we have to deal with a crisis of democracies all over the world because we are dictatorially dominated by the financial markets.

Dr Gregor Gysi MP, German Bundestag, 7 September 2011[3]

1 Franklin (1961: 306). See Bibliography for details.

2 Henry Home, Lord Kames, *Sketches*, Vol. III, Appendix, 'Sketch I (Scotch Entails)', (2007: 907).

3 Dr. Gregor Gysi, Die Linke, Plenary protocol 17/123, 123rd session, Wednesday, 7 September 2011, pp. 14474–14745.

The methods of money production in society today are profoundly corrupting in ways that would matter to everyone if they were clearly understood. . . .

How is it done? The process is so simple that the mind is repelled. It is this:

'Whenever a bank makes a loan, it simultaneously creates a matching deposit in the borrower's bank account, thereby creating new money'.

I have been told many times that this is ridiculous. . . . The explanation is taken from the Bank of England article 'Money creation in the modern economy', and it seems to me it is rather hard to dismiss.

. . . something about which I get incredibly frustrated is the use of that word 'capital'. I have heard economists talk about capital when what they really mean is money, and typically what they mean by money is new bank credit, because 97% of the money supply is bank credit. That is not capital; capital is the means of production. . . .

. . . there is a categorical difference between earning money through the sweat of one's brow and making money by just creating it when lending it to someone in exchange for a claim on the deeds to their house. Those two concepts are fundamentally, categorically different, and this goes to the heart of how capitalism works.

Steve Baker MP, Debate in the UK House of Commons on 'Money Creation and Society', 20 November 2014[4]

4 The Right Hon. Steve Baker, Conservative Party, MP for Wycombe, Hansard, House of Commons, Debate: 'Money Creation and Society', HC 20 November 2014, Vol. 588, col. 434, 437–438.

Preface

This book is about a legal theory of money. It considers a matter of private law and property theory, not one of economics. This is deliberate: in fact this book argues that money is a concept of law which economics relies on; it is not an economic or sociological notion as such, although it obviously has great importance in sociology and economics and will also be discussed in this context. In my research as a commercial lawyer I soon noticed that the legal concept of money is, unlike in the nineteenth century, entirely outside academic lawyers' research interests today. This is astonishing, since the most important legal transaction in commercial law is the contract of sale, which necessarily and by legal definition involves money, otherwise it is a barter – a distinction economists are not normally prepared to make.[1]

I had to realise that academics and non-academics generally have little interest in the concept of money. Admittedly, the system of money is complex and, for some at least, mysterious. This has always invited cranks[2] and conspiracy theorists to add their unwanted comments. If conspiracy theorists were open to rational argument, they would have to acknowledge that the large majority of the human population under the present monetary system, how undesirable it may be, is complicit in that system, and not necessarily unwillingly or unwittingly, which makes several billion conspirators. The methods and devices with which money charlatans (esoteric crackpots as well as agents luring people to invest in dubious financial products) spread their wisdom are the same by which one can obtain solid information about money and its effects. The electronic media have made access to useful material, whether academic writings, legislation or government material of various jurisdictions, more convenient than ever before. This allows for astonishing transparency, inadvertent or not. In fact, much more material is available than could possibly have been used in this work. Some themes may appear surprising at first sight: when a section in this book is devoted to alchemy and money,[3] it is not the indulgence in some occult falderal but the

1 This will be discussed in detail in Chapters 1 and 3.
2 See the comment on those by Keynes (2013b: 193).
3 See Chapter 4.

demonstration of alchemistic philosophical concepts which greatly influenced Renaissance philosophy and the emerging concepts of money. Also the system of double-entry bookkeeping, developed in the Italian Renaissance and central for the creation of bank money through loans, was an expression of the Renaissance ideals of balance, symmetry and proportion.[4] In several places this book will deal with such parts of the intellectual history of money concepts.

For this book, legislative material, academic publications and documents, available on the internet or elsewhere, but no insider knowledge of the banking business, have been used. Furthermore, no interviews or projects with banks have been carried out. Apart from the fact that banks would have been very tight-lipped in relation to requests for such interviews or the participation in studies,[5] this kind of empirical research would have necessitated grant funding, and that may have given the impression that this study may not have been entirely impartial. Although external grant funding bodies very rarely exercise an active influence over the conduct and outcome of a funded study, the impression of 'he who pays the piper calls the tune' can never be brushed aside completely in such situations. Since the theme of this study, the concept of money, is of fundamental importance to the economy, it is beneficial to adopt a pronouncedly detached and disinterested approach, contrary to the current trend in academia to seek external grant funding for every substantial study. The idea of the disconnected, and critical, academic who obtains credibility because he/she is not, and does not even appear to be, involved in some other interests, still has its merits. Anyone who therefore regards this and similar studies as unworldly ivory-tower research concedes implicitly that the study is actually relevant. Otherwise the work would simply be ignored. This confirms Kant's viewpoint that practice without theory means ignorance, but if theory appears not to be useful in practice, the theory is still insufficient and has to be completed.[6]

A book like this invariably contains interlinked concepts which come together only at the end, like the keystone of a vault, with some repetitions that buttress the arch until it holds itself. I have provided many cross-references to make 'anticipatory reading' easier. Chapter 1 discusses the legal concept of money as an application of the more general concept of dematerialised property in property theory, and it emphasises that money is a legal, not an economic, creature. The chapter also contains definitions of the forms of money, such as cash and bank money. Chapter 2 explores the creation of cash and bank money and its legal basis. This includes a discussion of the janiform nature of money as loan-debt and as circulating credit which the method of money creation reveals. The chapter finishes with electronic money and cryptocurrencies as new technological applications of long-standing concepts. Chapter 3 gives an overview of the economists'

4 See Chapter 2.

5 See Werner (2014b: 13) for an account of trying to get banks to carry out an empirical project with him to prove the phenomenon of bank money creation out of nothing by way of credit.

6 Kant, *Über den Gemeinspruch . . .* (2017: 127–128).

approach to money – in fact an absence of money in the microeconomic market model – and a critique in relation to those elements of the economists' conceptions that are relevant to the jurist. The chapter also comprises a discussion of the reasons for the suppression of money in classical and neo-classical economics, and looks at these underlying conceptions of Friedman's modern quantity theory of money which are important for a legal theory of money, although my conclusions will diverge widely from Friedman's intentions. In contrast to the economists' static concept of money as examined in the previous chapter, Chapter 4 discusses a dynamic, time-based, legal theory of money. It first sets out the social space or framework of relations that money designs, the four 'cases' of money, and then explores philosophical conceptions of alchemy which are still relevant for the role of money as a 'transmuting' agent that transforms commodities of lesser liquidity into objects of higher liquidity and of exchange value only. In the economy, the exchanges enabled by money occur in an alienation cycle with two components: the externalisation/transfer cycle and the estrangement cycle, which describes common sociological effects of that transfer. Chapter 5 deals with the religious and historical origin of the underlying belief system that guarantees the operation of money, as well as the practical implementation or backing of this belief today: the legal enforceability of the debt that money constitutes, in its Janus-faced characteristics. The remaining sections discuss the almost unassailable powers of banks as 'strong debtors' which have been entrenched further by recent bank rescuing measures of the EU. The chapter finishes with a short outline of alternative concepts of money.

'Brexit' hardly features in this book, and important as the departure of the UK from the EU is politically and economically, it is unlikely that the laws and the legal concept of money will be affected by it. The EU did not invent any new concepts of money and banking, and in the modern economy these have become international anyway. English common law and practice of banking were probably the makers of the modern banking and monetary system, though perhaps more by historical accident than by design, and so it is appropriate that the present discussion uses English law as a basis. Other legal systems are, however, occasionally referred to.

'Brexit', whenever it happens, may have taken place culturally already in any case. Britain's withdrawal from the EU is likely to reduce considerably the importance of Britain and English law in the world in political, commercial and legal respects, and certain bizarre political events in the British government and Parliament between summer 2018 and spring 2019 may have reinforced this impression. However, the legal concepts remain: these concepts continue to exist in many other jurisdictions, similar to concepts of Roman law lingering on after the Romans had long gone. In the areas of banking and finance law it is unlikely that this situation will change soon, and its future will rather be a kind of internationally harmonised law shaped by practices in the financial centres of the world. 'Brexit' can become a nightmare for textbook writers, but a monograph dealing with the legal concepts of money is unaffected by it, as it distils general principles from a particular legal system and thereby transcends a specific local jurisdiction.

This book can be considered, or criticised, as being rather continental European in its approach because of its theoretical abstractions, and indeed it probably has continental European features. 'Brexit' may have emphasised the idea of a difference in the way of thinking in England (less so in Scotland) in comparison to the European continent: a disdain for principles, systems and concepts, a suspicion of philosophies and ideologies, particularly in the field of the common law. During the eighteenth and nineteenth centuries England became more pragmatic compared to the sixteenth and seventeenth centuries, and philosophies gave way to 'getting on with it': the average Englishman makes money, he does not think much about it. This cliché is actually unfounded and wrong, as essential sources from English writers of the nineteenth century in this book show, but it still seems to be a generally accepted self-image in England, also among many lawyers.

Therefore it is no surprise that this book, written in English, the Latin of the scientists in the twenty-first century, came into existence in France, where I was fortunate to have had a wonderful year at the Institut d'études avancées (IEA) in Nantes in 2014–15 as a fellow and where large parts of Chapters 1 and 3 were written. Later in Glasgow I wrote some parts of Chapters 2 and 4, but it was only in Paris in spring 2018 where I assembled my rather disjointed writings over a long period of time and could merge them into one coherent book which I could subsequently complete in Scotland. I had additional inspiring sojourns at the University of Alcalá near Madrid in October–November 2018 and IDC Herzliya near Tel Aviv in March–April 2019, where I taught courses based on sections of this book, enriched by good discussions with students.

Friends and colleagues, mainly in France, helped me a lot to clarify my thoughts, although – or perhaps because – many of them are neither lawyers nor economists. I would like to express my thanks particularly to (in alphabetical order) Selçuk Demirel, Mamadou Diawara, Svante Fischer, Judy Fudge, Marco Goldoni, Samuel Jubé, Giuseppe Longo, Pierre Musso, Guido Nicolosi, Boris Samuel, Matteo Solinas, Carlos Sonnenschein, Ana Soto, Alain Supiot and Bruno Théret. Some will be surprised to find their names mentioned here, because I may not have spoken with them about my book specifically. But they helped me thinking outside the boundaries of my own specialisation in many unexpected ways, and with conviviality and friendship. A book on a legal theory of money is necessarily a Renaissance-like project across many disciplines. My friends and colleagues helped me connecting these diverse disciplines in multifaceted ways; I have learned very much from them. Thank you to all of you.

Stirling (Scotland), July 2019
A. R.

1 The *legal* concept of money

1. Money as a *legal* concept of property as opposed to an *economic* concept of a medium of exchange

(a) *The disappearance of money from law*

Sometime around the turn of the last century, the lawyers handed the research and conceptualisation of the phenomenon of money over to the economists. That was a quiet, unspectacular and probably not even conscious change, but it had the effect that from the early twentieth century onwards, textbooks and academic research in commercial law are strangely silent about money. Money is indispensable in all commercial transactions, the very subject matter of commercial law. However, law students these days hear next to nothing about money in their commercial law courses. The old legal theories on money in the nineteenth century, such as by Savigny,[1] which presuppose commodity money and a gold standard, are outdated and no longer applicable to the modern monetary system without substantial modifications.[2] Today, lawyers specialised in banking and commercial law discuss the legal technicalities of money transfers, such as the contractual relations and ownership in the money before/after such transfers, but they do not dwell on the essence of money in law.[3] Money is presumed to be a form of property[4] – which it is indeed – but there is no discussion about the peculiar properties of this property, nor how this property has come into existence and what its effects are.

1 Savigny, *Obligationenrecht I* (1851: 440–508).

2 See below under sec. 6.

3 Compare the typical approach in modern commercial law and banking law textbooks, for example. Cranston et al. (2017: 362–371) has a useful practical overview of money with no discussion of the concept of money. McKendrick (2016: 488) has, commendably, a separate chapter on money, but largely discusses payment, payment systems and legal claims to money (personal and proprietary) from pp. 489 onwards, while, for example, Ellinger et al. (2011) on banking law has no chapter devoted to money specifically.

4 Mann (1992: 8), defines money as 'chattel personal', the term for tangible (choses in possession) and intangible (choses in action) moveable property in English law, see also Bridge (2015: 13–14, 21).

While lawyers have gradually forgotten what money is, economists have never really understood money in the first place. They presuppose money diffusely as a social reality, a calculation and transaction device that is generally neutral in its effects,[5] especially in the microeconomic treatment of market mechanisms.[6] Hence in microeconomics money is disregarded and disappears entirely from the market model of supply and demand. The price at the intersection of the supply and demand curves is the equilibrium price (the quantity being the equilibrium quantity), that point where that clearing of the market occurs.[7] 'Price' is defined as the quantity ratio of goods exchanged, e.g. the price for one sheep is one-third of a cow (barter), or £600 (sale). That price is expressed in money, but money as a notionally separate entity vanishes in the price. It is trite to say that economists have always been aware of the problematic nature of this simplifying equation of price, supply and cost of production which partly determine the price, and money as the neutral yardstick or tool of measuring. Marshall remarks:[8]

> When considering costs from the point of view of the capitalist employer, we of course measure them in money. . . . But when considering costs from the social point of view, when inquiring whether the cost of attaining a given result is increasing or diminishing with changing economic conditions, then we are concerned with the real costs of efforts of various qualities, and with the real cost of waiting. If the purchasing power of money, in terms of effort has remained about constant, and if the rate of remuneration for waiting has remained about constant, then the money measure of costs corresponds to the real costs: but such a correspondence is never to be assumed lightly.

However, cautionary comments by some economists concerning the 'variation in the medium in which value is estimated or price expressed',[9] that is, the variation of the medium of money, have had little practical effect. In macroeconomics, to the extent to which it is monetary theory, economists seek to explain what money

5 Compare the definition of money by Mankiw (2013: 80): 'money is the stock of assets that can be readily used to make transactions'.

6 'Market' is understood in the way Jevons defines this term: '[T]he word has been generalised, so as to mean any body of persons who are in intimate business relations and carry on extensive transactions in any commodity', Jevons, quoted by Marshall, *Principles*, V, 1, § 2 (2013: 270).

7 Compare the discussion of the market equilibrium in the microeconomics sections in the usual economics textbooks: e.g. Marshall, *Principles*, V, 3, §§ 3–6 (2013: 283–289), and at § 6 (at 287): 'When demand and supply are in equilibrium, the amount of the commodity which is being produced in a unit of time may be called the ***equilibrium-amount***, and the price at which it is being sold may be called the ***equilibrium-price***'; Mankiw (2012: 77), Bofinger (2011: 65–68), Streissler (1984: 30–31).

8 Marshall, *Principles*, V, 3, § 7 (2013: 291).

9 Ricardo, *Principles*, chapter 1, vii (2004: 30).

does, not what money is.[10] Often the existence of money is explained with the anthropologically unsound reason that money has developed as a medium of exchange to facilitate barter.[11] This is reflected in the old story that commerce originated from barter, most prominently put forward in the Scottish Enlightenment by Adam Smith in the opening chapters of his *Wealth of Nations* (1776): 'a certain propensity in human nature . . . to truck, barter, and exchange one thing for another'.[12] David Hume[13] and Lord Kames[14] adopted the same narrative. The argument that barter is flawed and unwieldy for developed commercial transactions is much older; it was already the jurist Paulus in Ancient Rome who made such a point in favour of money.[15] Before, Aristotle made a similar claim in his *Politics.*[16] However, there does not seem to be any anthropological proof that in the development of human societies barter was indeed at the beginning of commerce and money.[17]

Economists also assume that what lawyers call a sale is just a form of barter (one good against money, which is just another good). Most economics textbooks presuppose that tacitly, without further explanation,[18] with the effect that the absence of money in the microeconomic supply and demand model is justifiable and not perceived as a shortcoming. It will be shown later that the exchange which involves the transfer of money against goods is not the same as barter. Thus one will agree with Lord Kames (1774): while Kames stressed that barter was deficient in commercial dealings which necessitated the introduction of money, he, being a lawyer, also stressed the difference between barter and sale, not only in technical law but also for the *economic* analysis of commercial transactions.[19] A sale, that is, the exchange of goods against money expressing a certain price is a *sale* in economics, too, not only in law. Thus the economic perspective requires a distinction between sale and barter as well. Money cannot be eliminated from the transaction as if the exchange were a true barter of two commodities, such as wheat against beer. Money influences the characteristics of the exchange substantially; it is not a non-entity, not a medium of exchange that

10 See e.g. the short passage in Mankiw (2013: 79–84), 'What Is Money?' as an illustration, and even this section mostly deals with types of money and the control of the quantity of money.

11 Crowther (1946: 14–16), Mankiw (2012: 620), and critically Heinsohn and Steiger (2013: 18).

12 Smith, *Wealth of Nations*, book 1, chapter 2 (2000: 14).

13 Hume, *Of Money* (2003: 122–123).

14 Kames, *Sketches*, I, iii (2007: 74).

15 Paulus, *Commentary on the Edict*, book 33, D 18, 1, 1, pr.

16 Aristotle, *Politics*, book 1, chapter 9 [1257a–b].

17 See Humphrey (1985: 48), Graeber (2011: 21, 43), Heinsohn and Steiger (2013: 6–7), and Chapter 3, sec. 5 on the problematic historical narrative about barter.

18 An exception is Streissler (1984: 2), who stresses the wider meaning of barter in economics, when compared to law, but this is also an economics textbook for lawyers.

19 Kames, *Sketches*, I, iii (2007: 76). See also Commons (1924: 245): '[B]usiness is not an *exchange* of commodities – it is a *purchase* and *sale* of commodities' (original emphasis).

acts as a transparent and neutral transmitter,[20] and therefore it cannot be factored out in microeconomic analysis.

Money is entirely a creature of the law;[21] it is born by and dies through the law, as any other property,[22] and the nature and essence of money must be understood in legal categories and concepts first. Only the study of the *effects* of money in the market, especially at macroeconomic level, can be carried out meaningfully with the scientific methods of economics, and even then these methods presuppose necessarily, but typically unintentionally, the law as the originator and framework of the object of research. So it is law and legal theory that are the scientific basis and paradigm for a study of the nature of money. It is interesting to note that a legal discussion of the concept of money and the mechanism of the monetary system benefits greatly from social philosophy and sociology, but little from modern economics.[23] Thus in unavoidable opposition to the prevalent economic approaches to money nowadays, this book will focus on law, legal theory and social philosophy in the treatment of money. A brief cautionary comment for the moment: money is entirely a creature of the *law*, not necessarily of the *state*, particularly not with regard to the modern systems of money which are increasingly detached from any individual nation state. The state only appears as an enforcer of the law, which in turn gives legal effect to money.

The shift of emphasis away from economics firmly on law has immediate repercussions. It undermines the fundamental simple market model of supply and demand in microeconomics,[24] which models an exchange (supposedly a barter) of goods we experience in the real world as a sale between sellers and buyers in almost all cases. Since the economist interprets the sale in law as a barter, the economic model restructures the sale as a transaction that is rare in reality and has no relevance in the modern economy. If, under the influence of a legally informed theory, money is postulated in economics as property with certain qualities, that means money has important effects on the transaction. So it becomes apparent that the economists' elimination of money in the supply-demand model is artificial and misleading.

At the beginning of this study, perhaps a few words should be said about the currently ubiquitous discipline of law-and-economics,[25] which can then be discarded for good. Law-and-economics is a seemingly interdisciplinary research approach that actually seeks to transform legal institutions and concepts into

20 Ingham (2004: 22–23).

21 Knapp (1924: 1). This position is in fact much older. Hugo Grotius says, with reference to Aristotle, in *The Freedom of the Seas* (*Mare Liberum*), chapter 8 (1916: 62): 'the universal laws of all contracts, namely exchange, is derived from nature, but some particular kinds of exchange, and the money payment itself, are derived from law'. Economists may jump to the conclusion that the position taken here is a Chartalist view of money – it is not, see below under sec. 3(b)(iv). On a historical account of why money is a legal institution, see Desan (2016: 21).

22 Bentham (1891: 111).

23 A similar point was made by Mann (1992: 5) and note 12.

24 E.g. Mankiw (2012: 67–78), Bofinger (2011: 65–73), and above.

25 An orthodox explanation of law-and-economics, e.g. by Cooter and Ulen (1997: 3–7).

economic concepts, so as to turn law into a ready tool for the unrestrained realisation of market-fundamentalism ('neo-liberalism').[26] A justification of this approach is displayed by a mathematisation of artificial reductions of legal and social relations which are then postulated to have been ascertained empirically.[27] For economists, law-and-economics is superfluous, because they presuppose legal institutions and concepts as the framework of markets (such as contract and property), but legal concepts are not the focus of their interest. For lawyers, law-and-economics is utterly destructive, not only because it reinterprets law in such a distorting way that it is not even recognisable in its disfigured image to the traditional legal specialist, but also because it deprives law of its essential regulatory and remedial functions. These regulatory and invasive features of the law are obviously objectionable to free-market fundamentalists. But that disregard of the authoritative regulative power of law means that law-and-economics is entirely inappropriate for the study of a legal theory of money: this starts with the fact that money is a creature of the law, not of markets.

(b) The current definition of money by economists

An emphasis on the legal nature of money requires some qualification of the usual definition of money that economists use. According to the economists' definition, money has three functions in the economy. Money is (1) a *medium of exchange*, that is, an asset that buyers and sellers use to trade for goods and services rather than for consumption; money acts as an intermediary which splits the theoretical direct barter into two sales – instead of goat against corn, it is goat against money, money against corn;[28] (2) a *unit of account*, that is, a standard yardstick to express prices (Walras's *numéraire*),[29] a generally accepted measure individuals use to set prices and make economic calculations; (3) a *store of value*, that is, a means for the transfer of purchasing power from the present to the future, or, put differently, a means of holding purchasing power over time.[30] While a lawyer would not disagree with this economic definition of the functions of money as such,[31] he will have to add that these functions do not only operate differently in different circumstances, and not always simultaneously,[32] but they can also operate in a way which economists do not seem to realise or do not regard as relevant. These are some effects of the fact that money is *dematerialised property*. This legal conception must now be explained.

26 On the difference between historical neo-liberalism (ordoliberalism) and market fundamentalism which is now generally called 'neo-liberalism', see Chapter 3.
27 For an unsympathetic critique, Rahmatian (2013: 193–196).
28 See Mises, *Theory of Money*, § 2 (1953: 30).
29 Walras, *Monnaie* (1886: 12, 15).
30 Crowther (1946: 15–16), Krugman and Wells (2015: 855–856), Mankiw (2012: 621), Streissler (1984: 317–319), Jarchow (2010: 1–3).
31 Compare Mann (1992: 5), Bridge (2015: 21), Savatier (1979: 100, 218). Proctor (2012: 10) adds that money also acts as a standard for contractual obligations.
32 That point has also been made by economists, see e.g. Streissler (1984: 319–320).

2. The legal conceptions of 'property' and 'dematerialised property'

(a) The legal conception of dematerialised property in general

(i) Meaning of the term 'property'

Money is one of the most important examples of *dematerialised property*, but for the moment we leave aside the aspect of dematerialisation. In broad outline, there is general agreement among lawyers about what 'property' is: property rights confer exclusive rights in objects or 'things', such as a house, a car, an apple, that are enforceable against the whole world (*erga omnes*); everyone is bound to observe these rights. This is in contrast to contractual rights which bind the parties to the contract only (privity of contract, but there are exceptions), or other personal rights arising from tort or other obligations.[33] In Roman law–based jurisdictions these exclusive property rights are often summarised as the *ius utendi, fruendi, et abutendi*: the right to use and exploit the object, to reap the fruits or other benefits of its use, and to dispose of it.[34] The objects which these exclusive rights attach to are commonly referred to as 'property', and the objects may be tangible (corporeal) or intangible (incorporeal), moveable or immoveable, fungible or non-fungible, things for consumption and so on. The exact classification of property objects depends on the national legal system in question and differs considerably.[35]

Generally, the conceptual differences in the various property systems are much greater than in other areas of private law, which is one reason why harmonising this area of the law across the European Union is very difficult.[36] However, there are a few criteria of property that are accepted by all Western property law systems. Apart from the absoluteness or exclusivity of the right *erga omnes*, property is characterised by being identifiable, by being able to be transferred and by having a certain duration[37] or permanence in principle.[38] Furthermore, one assumes

33 Generally and for the German legal family in particular, e.g. Bydlinski (1996: 171–174). For French law, Reboul-Maupin (2010: 111–112). For English law, e.g. Bridge (2015: 2–3), McKendrick (2016: 31).

34 Reboul-Maupin (2010: 154–160) for French law, Prütting (2008: 113–114) for German law with regard to ownership; Nicholas (1975: 154) for Roman law.

35 The biggest difference is between the common law of England and the common law countries, and Continental European civil law systems. In this regard Scotland has a Roman law–based civil law system and follows Continental European jurisdictions in its system of property law. See, for England, e.g. Bridge (2015: 10–20), and from a comparative law perspective between England and Germany, Rahmatian (2008: 198, 200–203).

36 Sparkes (2007: 95) with regard to immoveable property (land) where that would be particularly difficult to achieve; Rahmatian (2008: 198).

37 Roman law–based systems stress the perpetual nature of property rights, see e.g. Reboul-Maupin (2010: 162), but even these legal systems have to allow for the exception of intellectual property rights, and in English law there is no general idea of a perpetual nature of property in any case, see Rahmatian (2011a: 44–45).

38 In English law this rule of thumb for identifying property rights has been stated by Lord Wilberforce in *National Provincial Bank v. Ainsworth* [1965] AC 1175, 1247G–1248A. See, for the similar criteria in French law, Reboul-Maupin (2010: 160–167).

a closed and exhaustive list of property rights generally (*numerus clausus*), so that parties to a contract cannot invent new property rights by agreement or alter the nature of existing property rights.[39] There are several considerable qualifications to these criteria which depend on the type of property and on the national jurisdiction in question.

Lawyers, especially practitioners (and here academics concentrating on the black-letter law of property are considered as practitioners), usually operate on a practical rough-and-ready understanding of property and property rights but are little concerned about the concepts of property from the perspective of legal theory. Therefore they focus on the unquestionably great differences in the details of the national property laws. However, for the theme of this book only the underlying property theory and the principles of property are relevant, and these apply across the different legal systems, so that one can adopt a generalising approach that is not attached too closely to a specific jurisdiction and national property system.

A more theoretically informed examination of the nature of property in law[40] will immediately notice that the term 'property' has in fact several meanings. Property means (1) the sum of 'assets'[41] (in French '*patrimoine*', in German '*Vermögen*'),[42] (2) property right or real right/proprietary right, the subjective right to a thing, and (3) property object or thing or *res* (in the following, mostly the latter term will be used), the object which the property right refers to and which it attaches to. A fourth meaning is common but imprecise and will not be used here: 'property' often also denotes 'ownership', a special, and the most extensive, type of property right. The present terminology is generally assumed, but there is hardly ever a systematic presentation of the different meanings of property by lawyers in common law systems.[43] The property right appears as a relation between a person and an object, but it is really a social and legal relation between persons in respect of an object or objects. Thus this is a relational concept of property:[44] the property right of ownership, for example, is enforced by a person, the owner, against another person, such as a thief or a trespasser, in relation to a specific object, for example a ring or a garden.

39 Rudden (1987: 244) for English law; Reboul-Maupin (2010: 117) for French law; Prütting (2008: 8) for German law.

40 For this section the emphasis is on the idea of property in *law*, not in political philosophy or sociology.

41 The assets minus the liabilities in tangible and intangible form, which constitute the person's estate, usually expressed in a price as money for accounting purposes, as it typically happens in the cases of succession and insolvency.

42 Reboul-Maupin (2010: 13) with a discussion of the theories concerning the *patrimoine* in French law. Köhler (2003: 336–337) for German law: 'Als Vermögen bezeichnet man im allgemeinen die Summe aller geldwerten Rechte und Güter einer Person' (the sum of all rights of monetary value and goods of a person).

43 The exception is the Scottish jurist and philosopher Lord Kames (Henry Home), (1696–1782), from whom the account presented here is taken, with a slightly modernising adaptation, see Rahmatian (2015: 224).

44 See Rahmatian (2015: 225). This relational concept of property dates back to at least the eighteenth century. See, very clearly, Kant (1977: 371–372).

(ii) Property object (res) *created by the property right*

The aspect of property denoting a person's *assets* (being a natural or legal person, such as a company), is not problematic, but the notions of *property right* and *property object* (*res*) are important here and will have to be discussed. The property rights attach to the property object and confer its protection, the entitlement being enforceable against everybody, which is the essence of the idea of 'property right'. But in fact the property rights create the property object for the purpose of the law. This is a constructivist approach to the idea of property. A physical object in the real world, such as a car or an apple, is not 'naturally' an object of property. It is an abstract legal (that is, normative) conception which effects that the real right turns the physical thing into a legal *res* and makes it recognisable by the law. The apple becomes 'property' through the legal conception of the property *right*; in that way the law (private and commercial law) recognises conceptually the physical thing and incorporates it into its abstract framework. The legal concept of property obviously does not change the material qualities or 'properties' of the object that is subject to the property right. Real rights in an object of the material world do not exist physically; what exists is only a certain social behaviour of human beings in relation to other humans with regard to a certain object. The social behaviour manifests the right in the object claimed, such as the entitlement shown by exercising possession, use, acceptance by the others, and so on.

The content of the real right determines the social behaviour, and this content has two sides. The internal side of the real right is the right to use, while the external side is the right to exclude. The prototype and most far-reaching real right is ownership.[45] The social behaviour that enforces and, through that, effectively creates, the property right,[46] this *performance*, enforced or instigated by the law (and its sanctions in case of non-compliance) translates the normative idea of a real right, the 'ought', into a reality, a material 'is'.[47] A purchase and ownership transfer of a car is therefore a change of behaviour of the persons involved.[48] Property rights are therefore human behavioural patterns in relation to objects, or relations between persons with regard to things as the law imagines and organises them.[49] The aspect of behaviour or performance, which turns the concept into a reality, not too dissimilar to the performance of a theatre play according

45 More discussion in Rahmatian (2011b: 366–367), Rahmatian (2015: 227–228) with further references to the academic literature.

46 There is obviously a proximity to the Scandinavian Realist School of this argumentation. See Freeman (2008: 1057–1062) with extracts from Karl Olivecrona, *Law as Fact* (1939). See recently about the usefulness and limits of Scandinavian Legal Realism for the discussion of practical legal implications of conceptualisations of phenomena as property, Rognstad (2018: 7). On money in particular, Olivecrona, *The Monetary Unit* (1971: 297).

47 Rahmatian (2011b: 365). On the logical problem of concluding from 'ought' to 'is' (Hume's law, naturalistic fallacy), see the classical statement by Hume, *Treatise*, book 3, part 1, section 1 (1984: 521).

48 Rahmatian (2015: 232–234).

49 Rahmatian (2011b: 365–366).

to the instructions (text) of the playwright, will return in the discussion of the nature of money.

It has become apparent that the property objects or *res* are the creation of the real rights attached to them. This means that 'property' and property rights are not natural rights but conventional rights; they are invented, not reflected by the law, and can be changed at will in whichever form. This positivist view adopts the position of Hume[50] and Bentham.[51] It also means that a property object or *res* only 'exists' in law because it is the product of a legal concept; it has no existence in law beyond that, and it does not exist in the eyes of the law if it is not conceptualised as '*res*'. In this way the law typifies the individual object as a '*res*' and incorporates the object into the normative world. Thus the apple, the car, the garden all become *res* by virtue of the reductionist abstraction of property law. One can call this conceptual transformation, succinctly but inelegantly, *propertisation.*

(iii) Dematerialised property and social reifier

It does not matter how the legal concept '*res*' is 'filled': either with physical objects of whichever kind, such as land or a car, or with abstract concepts that are themselves creations of the law, such as a copyright.[52] This is the essence of the idea of *dematerialised property*: it is conceptually insignificant for the law whether the object of the real right is an object of the material world or an abstract object as conceptualised by the law. It follows that a physical object represents, but does not constitute, the *res*, the legal concept. The physical object acts as a 'social reifier'. The reification is a representation in the material world of an abstract legal concept, for example, the *res* is represented by the reifier 'bag of rice' in a given case. Since the *res* are the creation of the real rights attached to them, one can use the terms 'property *right*' (real right) and 'property' or 'property-object' (*res*) interchangeably in principle.[53] With regard to tangible property one will rather say 'property' to refer to the material reifier of the *res*, and 'property right' to emphasise the rights to the object as realised through the human behavioural patterns. However, with regard to conceptual, intangible property, such as intellectual property, there is no merit in distinguishing between intellectual property and intellectual property *right.* But in either case – that is, with regard to material and incorporeal/conceptual objects – the real right creates the thing for the purpose of the law.

In relation to intangible and abstract objects,[54] the reifier is also material but it is not necessarily the physical object which is the aim of the property rights

50 Hume, *Treatise*, book 3, part 2, section 2 (1984: 542–543).
51 Bentham (1891: 111–113).
52 Rahmatian (2011a: 13).
53 Rahmatian (2011b: 369).
54 This is not exactly the same. English law, for example, distinguishes between intangible property, such as gas, and pure intangibles which are legal concepts, such as debts and intellectual property rights. See Bridge (2015: 13–16).

that attach to it; thus the reification is *indirect* or one step removed.[55] The most important case in point here is intellectual property.[56] The intellectual property right 'copyright' in a novel is a right that attaches to a legal concept, the copyright-property, an instance of a *res*. That is not different from a personal (moveable) property right to an apple in principle. However, in the case of personal tangible property, the *res* is reified *directly* by the very object that is the aim of property protection, the apple, while in the case of copyright, the copyright-object is only *indirectly* reified by the book. A paper copy of a book is really the reifier of two different *res*. The physical book itself is the *direct* material reifier of the personal/moveable property right to the *res*, exemplified by the physical copy of the book. Furthermore, that physical copy of the book, or indeed any other copy of the book, or a copy of the text on the internet, is the *indirect* reifier of the copyright-property right in relation to the 'literary work' which the text of the novel constitutes.[57]

The different *res* and the different roles of the reifier become particularly apparent, for example, when a painting is sold. That leads to a partial change of entitlement to the *res* and its real rights. The new owner of the painting obtains real rights in relation to the personal/moveable property *res*, exemplified by the canvas, colours and so on, while the copyright-property to the artistic work, the actual copyright protection of the painting, rests with the artist as the author of the work.[58] But the copyright-*res* 'artistic work' is also represented by the physical painting, so the concrete entitlement (or change of entitlement) only becomes apparent in the behavioural patterns of the persons involved. There is a further complication in the case of musical works because the physical object, the score, is not even a reifier of the copyright-*res* 'musical work' itself, but only a kind of 'building instruction' to create the musical work.[59] But there is an interesting parallel: as the real right comes into existence through *performance*, a behavioural pattern, so does music. The difference is that music, when performed, becomes an acoustical reality in the material world, while legal rights remain abstract conceptions. Legal rights become a reality not directly, but only sociologically as behaviour in society following legal rules.[60] In a similar vein, the social reifier for patent rights (or patent-*res*) is the text of the patent application as granted, while in the case of trademarks the sign as reifier denotes the business goodwill that exemplifies the *res* in question.[61]

55 Rahmatian (2011b: 369–372).
56 On the intangible nature of intellectual property (IP) rights as opposed to other property, see e.g. Rognstad (2018: 46–51).
57 Rahmatian (2011a: 15–16).
58 This is unless a special assignment of copyright has also been made in those countries where the assignment of copyright is legally possible at all (in the UK and the United States, but not in Germany). For further discussion, see Rahmatian (2011a: 203–205).
59 More discussion of this complicated issue in Rahmatian (2011a: 18) with further references.
60 Rahmatian (2005: 279–281).
61 Rahmatian (2011b: 375, 377) for further details which are not relevant in the present context.

(iv) Propertisation – commodification – monetisation

As said, the conceptualisation of all physical and notional matters as *res*, created by the real rights in property law, can be termed *propertisation*. This transformation of things in all shapes and varieties, physical objects or abstract ideas, whether moveable or immoveable, whether food or other necessaries, cultural goods and achievements, such as poems and music, ideas and concepts, creates an exchangeability, a notional homogenisation or standardisation, which can be referred to as *commodification*. The dangerous social consequences of this conceptualisation and intellectual reduction, if that conceptualisation is not only regarded as a limited technical device, but as a means to promote an ideology, will be discussed later.[62]

One can speak of *propertisation* if one emphasises the transformation of factual objects of any kind into a legal *res*, or of *commodification* if one stresses the interchangeable, fungible and standardising nature which the transformation into a *res* brings about. One can also term this process *monetisation*, in that these standardised (notional) commodities or *res* can come close to, or can indeed operate as, forms of money, at least for conceptual and modelling purposes. Two phenomena present particularly good examples of this notional standardising commodification and interchangeability which the idea of the *res* produces: company shares and debts. They will also be important for the way to a concept of money in law and legal theory.

(b) Specific applications of the concept of dematerialised property: company shares and debts (including debts formalised in writing)

(i) Company shares

The company share is already a largely symbolic reification of the *res*, since the 'share' denotes certain rights in relation to a company. The reification is effected by a formalised *text* on paper, at least with classical share certificates. Nowadays, however, shares are often dematerialised, so that the shares are only denoted as account entries in databases in a computer settlement system,[63] which facilitates the transfer of shares in the share trade, especially on the stock exchange. Certificated shares can be turned into dematerialised shares, and these can be reconverted into certificated paper shares. The share certificate denotes something intangible, a legal concept, not a physical object that is fit for use or consumption, such as a car or a loaf of bread.

The rights that company shares represent are not easy to ascertain. The discussion here is confined to the modern public limited company (plc), the incorporated limited company with separate legal personality which grew out of the joint stock company,[64] and which is characterised by an unrestricted transferability of

62 See Chapter 4.

63 Solinas (2014: 57–60), with discussion of the CREST system in the UK.

64 A short overview of the historical development in Solinas (2014: 71–78).

its shares that are often also listed on the stock exchange. These types of companies exist in very similar form in all jurisdictions, such as the *Societé Anonyme* in France[65] or the *Aktiengesellschaft* in Germany,[66] while other types of companies limited by shares can assume significantly different forms in different jurisdictions.[67] A share in a public limited company (and its equivalents in the respective national jurisdictions) does not confer on the shareholder a property right in the company's assets;[68] this is an effect of the company being a separate legal entity and therefore owner of its assets. The share only gives the shareholder membership in the company and represents a proportionate stake measured by a sum of money 'for the purpose of liability . . . and of interest'.[69] This 'stake' is a financial claim on the company, most typically the claim to a dividend on the shares, but includes also voting rights and so on. The shareholder's exact rights against the company are determined by the company's constitution; often a company will issue shares of different classes with different types of shareholders' rights.[70] The shareholder has no property right in the company and no right to any item of property owned by the company. The shareholder has only a claim to a share in the profits while the company carries on business and a share in the distribution of the surplus assets when the company is wound up.[71] That is what the *res* consists of, and the *res* is (symbolically) reified by a share certificate or, if the share is dematerialised, by an electronic entry in accounts within a computer settlement system.

Company shares are a bundle of rights and obligations between the company and the shareholder, but the link between the shareholders and 'their' company is tenuous: for example, there is no direct correlation between the nominal share value and the actual monetary value of the legal interest of the shareholder in the company at a given time. Furthermore, there is no true correlation between the estimated monetary value of the 'share' – being the shareholder's notional fractional interest (though not property right) in the company's assets – and the share price on the stock exchange. The share represents an entitlement, but the value of the entitlement is not reflected by the value of the corresponding fraction of the assets of the company. In addition, the value of the entitlement and the price for it on the stock exchange have no discernible connection, because the factors which determine the price on the stock exchange are different ones: broadly, they are expectations of the price development which may or may not be influenced

65 E.g. Cannu and Dondero (2009: 417–421) for the principles of the *Société Anonyme.*
66 Hueck and Windbichler (2008: 266–272, 278–282, 287).
67 See Rahmatian (2002: 252–253) for a discussion of the differences between the private limited company (Ltd) in the UK and the *Gesellschaft mit beschränkter Haftung* (GmbH) in Germany.
68 For English law: *Bligh v. Brent* (1837) 160 ER 397.
69 *Borland's Trustee v. Steel Brothers & Co. Ltd.* [1901] 1 Ch. 279 at 288.
70 For further discussion of these matters see the usual textbooks on company law, for example Kershaw (2012: 709).
71 *Macaura v. Northern Assurance Company* [1925] AC 619.

by actual values of the entitlement or the interest in the company.[72] For present purposes one can say, in a somewhat reductionist fashion, a company share is a *res* which is a form of ***debt***, and that *res* is represented by a share certificate as a social reifier, particularly for the visualisation of the entitlement and transfer.

(ii) Debts in general

Debts in general arise out of contract or from extra-contractual obligations (tort, unjustified enrichment broadly understood). The contractual debts are the relevant ones here. The debt can be, to give two examples among many, a debt in money or for the delivery of a commodity, such as in a sale the debt (obligation) of the seller to deliver the goods sold and the buyer to pay the purchase price in money.[73] Because the contract underlying the microeconomic market model is effectively only the sale (or barter in the economists' conception), we disregard debts arising out of other types of contract (except for the loan, which we will deal with later). The seller is creditor in relation to the buyer's money debt for the payment of the purchase price, while the buyer is insofar debtor; the buyer is, however, creditor in relation to the delivery of the goods, while the seller is insofar debtor. English legal language is here less precise than the terminology in German or French law. The underlying debts or obligations of such a sale are not named in a distinguishing way in English law, while in German and French law the debt from the creditor's perspective is called ***Forderung*** and ***créance***, respectively, while the debt from the debtor's perspective is named ***Schuld*** (or ***Verbindlichkeit***) and ***obligation*** or, mainly if it is a monetary debt, ***dette***.[74] Although this is uncommon in English contract law, in this book it will often be necessary to refer to debts from the position of the creditor as ***claims*** and from the debtor's perspective as ***debts*** for the purpose of differentiation.

The debt or obligation is also a *res*, because debts are also property, at least in most jurisdictions.[75] But the debt is often not reified by a physical object. In a sale, the seller's debt to deliver is not reified by the subject matter of delivery, say, three kilograms of apples: the apples are the social reifier of the property object-*res*, not the debt-*res*. In some cases it is, however, necessary to have a social reification to make the entitlements visible and ascertainable. This is typically so with the ***assignment***, the transfer of the creditor's claims ('debts') to a new creditor, in which case the old creditor is replaced by the new creditor. Here it is necessary to see what exactly the rights of the new right holder attach to. Transferability is

72 E.g. Keynes, *General Theory* (1964: 158–162) on speculation.

73 For the UK see e.g. Sale of Goods Act 1979, ss. 27, 28, 37.

74 For Germany, see e.g. Medicus (2003: 3–4). For France, see e.g. Savatier (1979: 13–14): *créance* (= côté actif); obligation, *dette* (= côté passif).

75 E.g. for France, Savatier (1979: 61, 64–65). An exception is German law, where debts (claims) are not property (*Sachen*), see § 90 BGB. The historical reasons for this unusual situation (ultimately a legacy of Pandectism in Germany) cannot be discussed here. From a legal theorist's (and especially from an economist's) perspective, debts are always property and form part of a person's assets.

also an indication of the proprietary nature of the debt, since a central feature of property is transferability, at least in principle. However, in a transfer of a debt the reification is often replaced by certain overt acts of humans, by performances, instead of a representation by physical objects which denote the legal *res* in the material world. Many jurisdictions therefore require notification of the debtor or some other formal act to effect an assignment of a claim (debt) and make the assigned claim enforceable by the new creditor against the debtor.[76] Socially it is the debtor's behaviour, particularly not to dispute the claim against him,[77] which translates the normative idea of the property object (here the debt), the 'ought', into a reality, a material 'is'. The behavioural element is important for all types of property, but with a debt, where the property object is an abstract legal concept, the performative aspect of property right enforcement as the actual property right *creation* (and property object creation) becomes particularly apparent. The term of English law for debts, 'choses in action',[78] underlines this idea nicely. However, the law often resorts to stronger behavioural requirements, formality rules, which effectuate the reification. These may be for the purpose of evidence,[79] but they may also be constitutive for the valid transfer, such as the writing requirement for the transfer of an equitable interest or trust at the time of the transfer (disposition) in English law.[80]

(iii) Negotiable instruments

There are debts which are reified in form of a corporeal reifier, and these bring us close to the concept of money. Debts can be reified in the form of documentary intangibles:[81] these are documents/instruments that are so much identified with the obligation embodied in them that this obligation can only be performed/

76 This question does not depend on whether the legal system is a common law or civil law jurisdiction. For England, see Treitel (2003: 676), for Scotland, see Reid, para. 656 (1996: 530) (intimation). For Germany, see e.g. Medicus (2003: 360) on § 407 BGB; for France, see Savatier (1979: 323) on the principles of art. 1690 of the Code Civil. The legal techniques are, however, quite different in each legal system.

77 I deliberately distinguish here 'not disputing' from an 'acknowledgement' of the debt which has a different legal quality.

78 That means, abstract property objects of this kind cannot be possessed (in fact, there is no physical object that represents the *res*), and entitlement is only effected by bringing legal action in court. See e.g. Bridge (2015: 14–15). The *res* is represented by the human behaviour of suing. The English law term 'chose in action' is, however, not more precise than 'debt', so it is not used in the following.

79 In England, e.g. Law of Property Act 1925, s. 53(1)(b): writing requirement for the declaration of a trust of land. On the evidentiary function, the cautionary function and the channelling function of legal formalities, see Fuller (1941: 800).

80 Law of Property Act 1925, s. 53(1)(c). If that formality requirement is not complied with, the disposition is void. On that provision, see e.g. Gardner (2011: 101).

81 The term of English law is used here, but the principle exists, under different names, in all other jurisdictions.

enforced or transferred through the medium of the document.[82] Examples are bills of lading, insurance policies or company shares (if not dematerialised). The most important case is, however, the formalised paper of a ***negotiable instrument***, particularly the ***bill of exchange*** and its more specialised version, the ***cheque***, as well as the simpler cousin of the bill of exchange, the ***promissory note***. In a bill of exchange, the drawer gives the drawee an unconditional order in writing to pay an exact sum of money, either on demand or at a determinable future date, to a payee who is either specified or the bearer of the bill.[83] Or payment has to be made to the order of the payee, that is, to the indorsee, being the transferee (and new creditor) of the claim to payment of the sum of money stated in the bill which the payee (and original creditor) has held in his hands. The 'negotiation of the bill', being the transfer of the payee's claim to the indorsee,[84] effected by the formality rules of indorsement and delivery,[85] is therefore a formalised assignment of a debt (claim). If the drawee consents to the drawer's order by written (formal) acceptance, then he creates an independent obligation to the payee (or, subsequently, indorsee) to perform this payment, although there was typically no relationship before between the drawee/acceptor on whom the bill of exchange is drawn and the payee as the envisaged recipient of the sum of money by order of the drawer.

If the bill of exchange is drawn on a banker or bank, it is a cheque.[86] A promissory note ('IOU') involves a bipartite relationship only. It is an unconditional order in writing by the promisor to pay to the promisee a specified sum of money on demand or at a determinable future date.[87] A bill of exchange can emulate the promissory note, namely, if the drawer and the drawee are the same person, and in this case the law allows the holder of the instrument to decide whether to treat it as a bill of exchange or as a promissory note.[88] Both promissory notes and

82 Bridge (2015: 19). The same concept can be found in all jurisdictions, e.g. Savatier (1979: 54, 76) for France.

83 For the UK, see Bills of Exchange Act 1882, s. 3, and the usual textbooks, e.g. Ellinger et al. (2011: 386). English law has been used here as a basis, but the principles of the law of bills of exchange and of cheques are much the same in all jurisdictions. See, e.g. for Germany, Zöllner (1987: 56–57, 65–66).

84 That can carry on until maturity of the bill, so from payee to indorsee 1, who negotiates as indorser to indorsee 2, and so on.

85 That means, the payee writes on the bill the name of the new creditor or indorsee and signs (indorsement), and hands over the bill to the indorsee (delivery). A bearer bill, that is, a bill which does not specify a payee (or indorsee in case of an indorsement in blank), is negotiated by delivery (handing over) only. For the UK, see Bills of Exchange Act 1882, ss. 31(2) and (3), and s. 32, and e.g. Ellinger et al. (2011: 438–442). The situation essentially the same in other jurisdictions. See e.g. for Germany Zöllner (1987: 89–91), for France e.g. Savatier (1979: 77).

86 For the UK, see Bills of Exchange Act 1882, s. 73. The cheque also has to be payable on demand, while a normal bill of exchange need not be, but that is not relevant for the present discussion.

87 For the UK, see Bills of Exchange Act 1882, s. 83.

88 Bills of Exchange Act 1882, s. 5(2).

cheques can be bearer instruments[89] and are, theoretically,[90] negotiable (transferable), like the normal bill of exchange. There are other negotiable instruments. For example, in Germany share certificates of company shares are negotiable instruments.[91] In Britain, share warrants to bearer[92] are negotiable instruments but not share certificates.[93]

Common to all these negotiable instruments is that they 'embody', that is, reify, debts. Negotiable instruments and company shares have in common the symbolic and standardising reification. The monetisation through the concept of the *res* is also reflected by the fungible quality of the reifier. There is no reference to concrete things but only to exchangeable/fungible concepts themselves: company shares or debts as expressed in money, and money is the most negotiable and fungible of all forms of property.[94] In case of a bill of exchange, the creditor's (payee's) claim, created ultimately by the formal acceptance of the drawee, obtains a social reifier in form of a paper on which a text is written that has to comply with strict formality rules to be legally valid.[95] The same applies to the promissory note: the debt is represented by a paper, indeed it is embodied in it, that is, the performance or transfer of the obligation must be through the medium of the paper. But while an apple, for example, is a material and concrete social reifier of the concept 'property right' and '*res*', the paper as material reifier only refers to an abstract creation of the law, the debt that is otherwise not reified, and the paper itself as material reifier only acts as a sign and symbol for a *res*; it has no value in itself. The paper is only a symbol for effectively an entitlement, a claim (that is someone else's debt), that is, an expectation that this abstract entitlement will be transformed into something of genuine value sometime in the future, such as an apple one can eat, clothes one can wear and so on.

The transformation from a valueless sign and symbol to something valuable in the future by virtue of an entitlement or an expectation that operates by way of human performance (like in a theatre play, here the discharge of a debt in law) – all these aspects are also the ingredients of the concept of money: we have a kind of 'alchemistic' transformation from a base 'substance' or condition (expectation) to a precious one (object of intrinsic value). More generally, the

89 That is, anyone who holds the instrument in his hands is (on the face of it) entitled.
90 In reality the cheque is practically never negotiable in the UK. See the legal basis for preventing negotiation in Bills of Exchange Act 1882, ss. 81, 81A, which banks in the UK always opt for. See also Ellinger et al. (2011: 415).
91 German Aktiengesetz, § 68. See also Rahmatian (2002: 254).
92 Their legal basis is in UK Companies Act 2006, s. 779(1). Unlike in the case of a share certificate, the identity of the holder of the share warrant is not declared on the company's register of members when the share warrant is issued, nor is a record of the owner made when the warrant is transferred.
93 Solinas (2014: 111–112).
94 E.g. McKendrick (2016: 489).
95 For the UK, Bills of Exchange Act 1882, s. 3(1) and (2). The strict formality rules are characteristic of negotiable instruments in all legal systems.

performance is the assertion of the power of art over nature.[96] The entitlement to such a transformation in the future is symbolised as an expectation, whereby the symbols are *per se* valueless social reifiers in form of signs (text, numbers); the human performance (enforced by, as well as creating, legal rules) that acts on the promise that the symbol not be empty but filled with substance, though at a future date, transforms the symbol into genuine value. This mechanism prompts a kind of belief system and even an eschatology: the debts are repaid in the end. The parallel to the imagination as well as the *imaginaire* of the Christian religion is not accidental.[97] It is also not accidental that this virtual nature of a regress of entitlements from one debt to another (e.g. a cheque to bank money to cash),[98] representing always – perhaps in the future – another debt (claim) in relation to a physical object of real value one can use and enjoy (in practical terms: food, clothing and shelter), has grown enormously in the post-industrialist and computer age where products and services merge into a 'cervofacture' (Hervé Serieyx).[99] The electronic devices of computers, databases and the internet with their virtual imagery that can blend with the world of imagination provided by the entertainment industries are not only the means but, to a significant extent, also the makers of the modern system of money.

(iv) Banknotes

The banknote, to take the most conspicuous symbol of money, was historically a special kind of promissory note,[100] and in some countries banknotes are still made out today in a form as if they were promissory notes. Thus the banknotes issued by the Bank of England still bear the text: 'I promise to pay the Bearer on Demand [Ten] Pounds', and the banknotes issued by the three Scottish banks who have preserved the privilege to issue banknotes have an equivalent text.[101] Banknotes are no longer promissory notes in a commercially practical sense today, even when the text of a promissory note appears on them;[102] they fulfil another function as reifiers, to denote circulating central bank money[103] (besides central

96 See Chapter 4 for further discussion.

97 See Chapter 5, sec. 1.

98 The differences will be explained below under sec. 3.

99 See e.g. Musso (2014: 36–39) for a brief discussion.

100 McKendrick (2016: 489) and note 7. Morgan (1965: 23–24). In the UK Banking Act 2009, s. 208, 'banknote' is defined as a 'promissory note, bill of exchange or other document which (a) records an engagement to pay money, (b) is payable to the bearer in demand, and (c) is designed to circulate as money'.

101 A Scottish £10 banknote, for example of the Royal Bank of Scotland, says, 'The Royal Bank of Scotland plc promise to pay the Bearer on Demand Ten Pounds Sterling at their Head Office here in Edinburgh by Order of the Board'. On this point see also Rahmatian (2014: 225–226). In Scotland the Bank of Scotland, the Royal Bank of Scotland and the Clydesdale Bank have retained the right to issue banknotes, see UK Banking Act 2009, s. 214(2).

102 See Chapter 2.

103 Bank of England (2014b: 7).

bank reserves, unless also held in form of banknotes), which is not necessarily the function the general public believes it to be.

The banknote emerged in the seventeenth century and so appeared later on the scene than other negotiable instruments, namely the bill of exchange (fourteenth century at the latest)[104] and the cheque (early seventeenth century). The promissory note was recognised in England as a negotiable instrument by the early eighteenth century.[105] Banknotes gained significant importance in England and in Scotland in the last third of the eighteenth century, and Adam Smith devotes much discussion to this then fairly new phenomenon in the *Wealth of Nations.*[106] The banknote then spread quickly in Europe with the need to finance the Napoleonic Wars. At that time, and throughout the nineteenth century, the banknote was indeed a promissory note of the issuing bank in question, and the promise was directed at the ultimate convertibility of the banknote into gold.[107] We can leave aside this interesting discussion in the present context, as this is only of historical interest in the light of the modern monetary system.

Though not promissory notes anymore in reality, banknotes are still negotiable instruments in that a reification of the debt in the form of a formalised paper is required to effect constitutively entitlement to and transfer of the debt, whereby it is the bearer of the instrument who obtains entitlement. It will be examined later what kind of debt banknotes embody.[108] The banknote is, however, only one symbol and representation of a certain type of money (cash), which is nowadays economically of minor importance compared to bank money. For an examination of the legal concept of money, it will first be necessary to define and classify the types of money. These definitions often differ substantially from an economist's idea of money.

3. Classification of money

(a) Introductory comments

Money today is a form of debt. That will be discussed in more detail later.[109] As has already been mentioned, any attempt at formulating a *legal* theory of money is characterised by the fact that lawyers currently seek refuge in the technicalities of black-letter law without confronting the problem of a definition directly. An

104 Ellinger et al. (2011: 386).

105 *Williams v. Williams* (1693) Carth. 269, *Potter v. Pearson* (1702) 2 Ld. Raym. 759.

106 Smith, *Wealth of Nations*, book 2, chapter 2 (2000: 317–319, 326–329, 333–335).

107 E.g. Crowther (1946: 29), also on the fact that the convertibility into gold was suspended in the UK between 1797–1819 and from 1914 onwards. For a historical account, see e.g. Smith, *Wealth of Nations*, book 2, chapter 2 (2000: 326): 'The whole paper money of every kind which can easily circulate in any country never can exceed the value of the gold and silver, of which it supplies the place, or which (the commerce being supposed the same) would circulate there, if there was no paper money'.

108 See Chapter 2.

109 See Chapter 2.

example of the traditional approach, from Mann, *The Legal Aspect of Money*,[110] highlights the difficulty. This is probably still the standard text on the law of money in the English-speaking world, and unquestionably a most impressive work, despite the criticism voiced here. Mann says:[111]

> What are the characteristics in virtue of which a thing is called money? What is the intrinsic nature of the phenomenon described by the word 'money'? In answering these two questions economic theory is unlikely to assist the lawyer to any appreciable extent. . . . [S]uch problems as monetary policy, the management and supply, the quantity and soundness of money are no concern of the lawyer. . . . As a rule, . . . the economist's view that everything is money that functions as money is unacceptable to lawyers. Bank accounts, for instance, are debts, not money, and deposit accounts are not even debts payable on demand. Similarly, bills of exchange are not money; on the contrary, they require the drawee to pay 'a sum certain in money'. Debts are contracted in terms of money, not in terms of bank accounts or bills. In the absence of the creditor's consent, . . . debts cannot be discharged otherwise than by the payment of what the law considers as money, namely legal tender. . . . Money is not the same as credit. Nor is the law of money identical with the law of credit. Nor does the fact that 'bank money' largely functions as money prove that in law it necessarily and invariably is money.

This approach is too narrow, even though the right questions have been put, and legal theory will have to keep a distance from black-letter law as well as from economics if it wants to achieve a satisfactory result. In particular, one needs to acknowledge that 'credit' has several forms, one of them being money, an idea which accommodates 'bank money' as well as cash. Since money in a modern monetary system is a form of debt, such a conclusion is inevitable, also in law. The new author of the current edition of Mann's work on the law of money correctly seeks to widen the definition of money and proposes a functional approach,[112] while Mann himself maintained that there is 'no room in a book on the law of money for a discussion of such problems as bank accounts, deposits . . . or negotiable instruments'.[113]

Mann's approach, already obsolete in the 1990s, is too much entangled in the technical mechanisms and rules of concrete legal phenomena to serve as a basis for a legal theory that explains the conceptual framework of money. It does not allow for a flexibility either that can accommodate future developments. Banknotes, coins, bank money, negotiable instruments, digital currencies, cryptocurrencies (Bitcoin etc.) are subject to specific and different rules as to the details but are all

110 Reference is made to the fifth edition of 1992, which was the last prepared by Mann himself.
111 Mann (1992: 5–6).
112 Proctor (2012: 10–13).
113 Mann (1992: 6), note 20.

instances of a higher-ranking category, that of dematerialised property, of which money forms a sub-category. What is more, they can function as money, not only from an economist's perspective but also for the purpose of the law. For illustration, one can draw a parallel to the taxonomy for the animal kingdom in zoology: banknotes and coins are species of the genus 'cash', while cash and bank money (and arguably also cryptocurrencies) are genera of the family 'money in a narrow sense'; the families 'money in a narrow sense' and 'money in a wider sense' (with the genus negotiable instruments in particular) are within the order of 'dematerialised property'.[114] This is what a theoretical approach should start from.

(b) Definitions of forms of money

The first step towards a legal concept of money is a set of definitions in relation to the terms 'cash', 'bank money', 'legal tender' and so forth which will be used in the following discussion.

(i) Cash

Cash are coins and banknotes, nowadays without either having any significant intrinsic value. They are physical money, and fully negotiable, that is, anyone who receives coins or banknotes in good faith and for value obtains a good title to them even if the transferor's title has been defective, for example, because he has stolen them (exception from the *nemo dat quod non habet* rule).[115] Although coins and banknotes are chattels,[116] they are not the subject matter of a sale but act as a medium of exchange to enable the sale: coins and banknotes are not bought or exchanged themselves.[117] Where a coin or banknote is itself subject matter of a sale, as a curio or collector's item, it does not operate as money but is an ordinary commodity; in that case there is no negotiability either and the transferee in good faith does not obtain good title if the transferor's title is defective (no exception from the *nemo dat quod non habet* rule).[118]

Cash is this form of money which cannot be converted into a more liquid or fungible form and is the most basic type of money. As banknotes and coins, it is also the most visible form for the general public. This representational function of

114 This classification metaphor should be taken as what it is: a metaphor for the illustration of a principle. In reality, the sub-categories are by no means clear-cut: regional private currencies and (digital) cryptocurrencies may be a form of cash or bank money or closer to cheques (negotiable instruments), for example. The boundaries between the categories are necessarily blurred, also because of the fact that one category can be transformed into another category (a cheque paid into a bank account becomes bank money) and ultimately, into the basic category (cash), at least in theory, which makes it more appropriate to concentrate on the superior category, that of dematerialised property.

115 *Miller v. Race* (1758) 2 Kenyon 189 (1 Burr 452), 96 ER 1151.

116 That is, *res* represented by a physical object in the conception of dematerialised property.

117 McKendrick (2016: 489).

118 In the UK: *Moss v. Hancock* [1988] 2 QB 117 (in this case the commodity was a coin).

cash for a country's currency makes it an important symbol of a polity's integrity and unity, despite the fact that this 'printed money' is neither a source of revenue for the government nor an instrument of monetary policy today.[119] There is now a trend towards the abolition of cash in the traditional format of banknotes and coins, and its replacement by digital currency or electronic money,[120] perhaps by means of blockchain technology used by cryptocurrencies, such as Bitcoin.[121] Strictly speaking, this does not necessarily abolish cash as such but only its traditional physical reifiers (paper notes and metal) that are then replaced by mere accounting entries on computers, so that there is almost no reification at all. In reality, however, the difference between bank money and digital cash can hardly be made out, given that digital money is processed, and even issued, by commercial banks rather than by central banks.[122] That makes it in no way different from usual bank money, created by commercial banks through credit to customers.[123] Since cryptocurrencies are a combination of new electronic payments systems with new currencies that are not issued by a central bank, they are a kind of commercial/private bank money and not 'cash' in a traditional sense, issued by a central bank, like notes and coins. A central bank could theoretically issue its own digital currency or cryptocurrency, which would be the electronic equivalent of traditional cash or money in physical form. The Bank of England has been researching the possibility of launching its own digital currency to rival bitcoin, but it has no current plans to pursue this because of fears about the impact on the wider financial system.[124] The Bank for International Settlement (BIS) has recently warned against the issuing of cryptocurrencies by central banks because of the stability risk to the global financial system.[125]

Although cash forms a very small percentage of all circulating money today, it is still the reference point for all types of money and for many lawyers still the only 'money proper' or 'State money',[126] a category from which bank money and credit

119 Cranston (2002: 111).

120 Proctor (2012: 50). The EU Directive 2009/110/EU on the taking up, pursuit of and prudential supervision of the business of electronic money institutions (superseding EU Directive 2000/46/EC) defines in Art. 2(2) 'electronic money' as electronically, including magnetically, stored monetary value as represented by a claim on the issuer which is issued on receipt of funds for the purpose of making payment transactions and which is accepted by a natural or legal person other than the electronic money issuer.

121 Pilkington (2016: 225–227).

122 The EU Directive 2009/110/EC provides in Art. 10 that any natural or legal person that is not an electronic money issuer is prohibited from issuing electronic money. An electronic money issuer is under Art. 1(1) in particular (a) a credit institute as defined in Art. 4 pt. 1 of the EU Directive 2006/48/EC (in short: a bank), (b) a post office giro institution, (c) a central bank (if not acting in its capacity as monetary authority). So this new form of cash issued – electronic money – would be a form of bank money.

123 See Chapter 2, and Rahmatian (2019: 115).

124 David Thorpe, 'Bank halts crypto-currency plans over stability fears', *FT Adviser*, 4 January 2018.

125 Claire Jones, Hannah Murphy, 'Central bank cryptocurrencies pose stability risk, says BIS', *Financial Times*, 12 March 2018.

126 Two terms borrowed from Keynes (2013a: 5).

in particular are excluded.[127] This interpretation of money as being cash only is too narrow for the modern lawyer, but the idea behind it is that ultimately only cash is the form of money which is able to discharge a debt.[128] Most payment is made in form of bank money by bank transfer today, but since the ready and unrestricted conversion to cash is secured in a normal economic situation, bank money and cheques are for practical purposes treated as the equivalent of cash. An actual conversion of bank money to cash (and typically a subsequent reconversion to bank money) is unnecessary in ordinary business, an approach similar to forms of constructive delivery in property law for the transfer of possession and potentially ownership.[129]

In commercial and banking practice, very liquid assets that can easily be turned into cash are often referred to as cash themselves, for example bank money, cheques and even other very liquid financial instruments or marketable securities. Practical for the financial market and pragmatic this approach undoubtedly is, that broad definition has not been adopted here for a good basis of a legal theory of money, although even the courts sometimes consider such instruments, for example cheques, 'as good as cash'.[130] However, conceptually it is necessary to distinguish between *cash proper* and the *equivalent of cash* or 'as good as cash'. In particular, the terms 'cash' and 'money' should not be used interchangeably: cash is a form of money, but not all money is cash.

Although cash is typically legal tender, this is not inevitably so; these two terms do not coincide.[131] Legal tender will be discussed below.[132] The UK provides some good examples for the difference. Banknotes issued by the Scottish banks which have retained the privilege to issue their own banknotes[133] are unquestionably cash, but not legal tender, either in Scotland or in England.[134] Banknotes of the Bank of England are not legal tender in Scotland;[135] only coins issued by the Royal Mint are.[136] In England, banknotes of the Bank of England are legal tender,[137] but they became legal tender only in 1833;[138] before that time they

127 Mann (1992: 5–6).
128 McKendrick (2016: 490).
129 E.g. McKendrick (2016: 289, 468).
130 For example, according to the Scottish case *The Glasgow Pavilion v. William Motherwell* (1903) 6 F 116, IH, at 119, payment by cheque may be referred to as payment in cash. The court's argument was that since banknotes are (or were in the early 1900s) promissory notes of the banks and must be considered as cash, so must the (very fungible) cheques be. The additional twist is here that banknotes issued by Scottish banks were, and technically still are, classical promissory notes, not legal tender.
131 Mann (1992: 42).
132 See below under (iv).
133 Banknotes (Scotland) Act 1845, largely repealed by the Banking Act 2009, s. 214(2). The legal regime for Northern Ireland is similar, see Banking Act 2009, s. 214(1).
134 *The Glasgow Pavilion v. William Motherwell* (1903) 6 F 116, IH, at 119.
135 Except for banknotes of denominations of less than five pounds, see Currency and Bank Notes Act 1954, s. 1(2). But such banknotes have not been issued.
136 Coinage Act 1971, s. 2, as amended by the Currency Act 1983, s. 1(3).
137 Currency and Bank Notes Act 1954, s. 1(2).
138 Bank of England Act 1833, s. 6.

were just cash, not also legal tender.[139] Coins issued by the Royal Mint are legal tender in the whole of the UK up to a certain amount, depending on the denomination in question.[140] Beyond that amount they are cash, but not legal tender.

(ii) Bank money

About 97% of all circulating money is bank money.[141] Bank money[142] (*monnaie scripturale* in French,[143] *Buchgeld* in German – these terms better indicate its nature) is a monetary debt that is based on the special contractual bank-customer relationship. The relevant criterion for establishing a bank-customer relationship is the existence of an account with the bank.[144] It is irrelevant whether the account is in credit or overdrawn and what type of account it is. There is some discussion if and under which circumstances somebody can be customer of a bank if he does not have an account with that bank,[145] but this is unimportant here: there is only bank money where there is a bank account. Bank money is a debt held in a bank account, the amount of which is expressed in figures in the books of the bank, nowadays exclusively in the bank's computer system. Bank money is of course an exemplary form of dematerialised property. We will see later that 'bank money' is also the principal example of 'credit': they are the same.[146]

The main difference between bank money and money 'in specie' or cash (notes and coins) is that cash does not presuppose a contractual relationship between the holder of the cash and a bank, while bank money does. Otherwise the difference in the nature of these two types of money is very slight: both are debts, only that cash is notionally a debt of the government to its central bank,[147] while bank

139 *Wright v. Reed* (1790) 3 TR 554 (100 ER 729). See also discussion in *Miller v. Race* (1758) 2 Kenyon 189 (1 Burr 452), 96 ER 1151, at 1154 with the distinction between 'current specie' or 'ready money' or 'cash' and paper money or banknotes. But Lord Mansfield said: 'by usage, and the common course of business, these notes are become the same as cash'.
140 Coinage Act 1971, s. 2(1A) and (1B).
141 Bank of England (2014a: 15) for December 2013. This phenomenon is not new, see Keynes (2013a: 27) who presumed (in 1930) that 90% of the aggregate of current money was bank money.
142 Mann (1992: 5).
143 E.g. Savatier (1979: 216).
144 *Great Western Railway v. London & County Banking Co. Ltd.* [1901] AC 414, at 425 (HL); *Iskandar v. Bank of America National Trust & Savings Association* [1998] 1 SLR 37 (Singapore).
145 Ellinger et al. (2011: 116–117).
146 See below under (iii).
147 For the historical development of the Bank of England set up as an entity lending to government, see Clapham (1944: 17–18), Morgan (1965: 114). For the UK, see Currency and Banknotes Act 1928, s. 3, and the limit for cash issue backed by government securities under s. 2 of the Currency Act 1983 (fiduciary note issue). For the general restriction of the treasury to borrow from the Bank of England, see s. 12(7) of the National Loans Act 1968. For the eurozone, see the principal prohibition for governments to borrow from the European Central Bank, see Art. 123(1) TFEU (ex 101(1) TEC), and Art. 21 of the Protocol (No. 4) on the Statute of the European System of Central Banks and of the European Central Bank.

money is a debt of the bank to its customer, and the social reifier of cash is printed paper and metal, and in case of bank money an accounting entry, a line printed on a bank account statement, so hardly any reifier at all: it is 'scripted money'[148] or 'book money'. But the legal relevance of the statement of account underlines its function as social reifier and proof of the debt in question.[149]

Bank money is effectively electronic money; no bank records deposits and loans in paper accounts by hand nowadays. As has been said in the discussion of cash before, it can become difficult to separate e-money or digital cash and cryptocurrencies from bank money; such a separation has to be a conceptual one, enforced by law and regulators, because the electronic basis in information technology systems is the same. If e-money is defined as monetary value represented by a claim on the issuer which is stored in an electronic device and accepted as a means of payment by undertakings other than the issuer,[150] then it is hard to see how the handling of this money is distinguished from bank money in the case of bank transfers (effectively electronically), and payment by bank transfer is practically the only method of settlement for more than small sums.[151]

The way in which bank money arises is determined by the nature of the bank-customer relationship, and its principles have been set out by the landmark case of *Foley v. Hill*.[152] When a customer deposits money – for this example we assume cash – in his bank account, the banker becomes owner of the banknotes and at the same time the customer's debtor, the amount of the debt equalling the sum deposited in cash. The customer, in turn, becomes unsecured creditor of the banker in relation to the sum held in the bank account.[153] The banker is not trustee[154] of the customer with regard to the money paid in; the relationship is only a contractual one:[155]

> The money placed in the custody of a banker is, to all intents and purposes, the money of the banker, to do with it as he pleases; he is guilty of no breach of trust in employing it; he is not answerable to the principal if he puts it into jeopardy, if he engages in a hazardous speculation; he is not bound to keep it or deal with it as the property of his principal, but he is of course answerable to the principal, when demanded, a sum equivalent to that paid into his hands.

148 The double meaning of 'scripted' is appropriate: the text and the numbers are normative, requiring a certain (legally enforceable) behaviour of the actors involved, similar to a playwright's text addressed at actors on a stage. See Rahmatian (2014: 224–225), and Chapter 2, sec. 6.
149 Ellinger et al. (2011: 233).
150 That is the definition in Art. 2(2) of the EU E-Money Directive 2009/110/EC as amended by Directive 2015/2366 on payment services in the internal market. See also Proctor (2012: 50).
151 McKendrick (2016: 490).
152 *Foley v. Hill* (1848) 2 HLC 28.
153 *Foley v. Hill* (1848) 2 HLC 28, at 36–37.
154 *Foley v. Hill* (1848) 2 HLC 28, at 43–44.
155 *Foley v. Hill* (1848) 2 HLC 28, at 36–37.

It follows from this rule that the bank is entitled to commingle its customers' deposits with its general funds and is entitled to use the amount accumulated. Thus the bank, not being a trustee of the customer but a simple party to the contract, has no duty to keep customers' funds in a separate trust account. The bank-customer contract entitles the bank to use deposits for its own purposes, with the corresponding obligation to repay an amount equal to that deposited, either on demand (typically: current account) or at a fixed time (typically: savings account), with or without interest. A bank is a reservoir of money: that applies to the individual bank and to the banking network as a whole.[156]

When a customer overdraws his account (with the bank's permission), then the creditor-debtor relationship reverses: the customer becomes the bank's debtor, and the bank the customer's creditor. An overdrawn account is simply a bank loan. Generally, when the lending bank pays out a loan it credits a customer's account with the loan money as a deposit: theoretically it is the bank's obligation to honour withdrawal in cash, as with any money deposited, although with larger loans that very rarely happens (if it is contractually possible at all). At the same time the bank credits itself, because the customer-borrower is indebted to the bank as a result of the loan granted to him.[157] This fact, as well as the fact that there is no duty of the bank to keep separate trust accounts for customers depositing money, are essential for the money creation by commercial banks. This process will be discussed in Chapter 2. Here one cannot avoid noting that many economists are usually ignorant of these essential legal principles of banking. Unencumbered by legal knowledge, they could then establish concepts of money supply which have little relevance to banking reality.

Foley v. Hill, handed down in the mid-nineteenth century, obviously did not invent but only reflected and enforced existing banking methods. The decision is one of English law, but banking practice is the same worldwide, so this case can serve as a basis for general legal principles of money and money creation, independent of a particular jurisdiction.

(iii) Credit

Cash gets transformed into bank money when deposited in a bank account. With the deposit, a debt of the bank (debtor) is created, that is, a corresponding claim of the customer (creditor) is created. This claim is credit, that is only a different term for the same type of dematerialised property. This commonplace statement should not surprise anyone, but economists differentiate incorrectly between money or cash and credit,[158] and lawyers are not precise enough either or make similar erroneous distinctions, for example Mann: 'Bank accounts . . . are debts,

156 Ellinger et al. (2011: 120, 215).
157 Bank of England (2014a: 16).
158 Schumpeter (1954: 1087) rightly criticises this.

not money. . . . Money is not the same as credit'.[159] One wonders why not.[160] H. D. Macleod was much more perceptive in the 1880s;[161] in particular, he said, with a premonition of the concept of dematerialised property:[162]

> [T]hese Bank Credits, or Deposits, are a mass of Property, just like so much corn or timber; they are *Pecunia*, *Bona*, *Res*, *Merx*; they are now, though, of course, legally only debts, for all practical purposes the current coin of commerce: and the great medium of payment of the country: and specie is now only used occasionally, and as a supplement to payments in Credits of different forms.

Macleod also pointed out that 'Money and Credit . . . are both of the same nature: they are each a Right or Title to demand something to be paid or done by someone else'.[163] The idea is clear: bank money and cash are debt or credit (depending on the perspective). When somebody hands over a banknote, he negotiates the debt of the government vis-à-vis the Bank of England embodied in the banknote as negotiable instrument[164] and entitles the transferee and new bearer to this debt as new creditor. The reality is, however, that this debt embodied in a banknote has no practical significance today. Neither does it entitle the bearer to the government's debt, nor does it entitle him to claim payment in gold of the denominated sum on the banknote as technically a promissory note (IOU). With the abolition of the gold standard, the promise expressed through (and in England: *on*)[165] the banknote is nugatory: what the bearer can get is, for example, two £10 notes in exchange for his £20 note. The debt expressed in bank money is, however, very real, and non-payment ultimately leads to its legal enforceability. This bank money-debt can also be transferred, in theory either by way of an assignment or through a negotiable instrument, such as the cheque.

159 Mann (1992: 5 and 6).

160 Historical banking practice, for example the idea behind the issuing of banknotes by John Law in France in the 1710s confirms that money was considered as credit from early on, see e.g. Schumpeter (1954: 321). See also John Law himself in his *Money and Trade Considered* (1705): 'But no laws can make [money] go further, nor can more people be set to work without more money to circulate so, as to pay the wages of a greater number. They may be brought to work on credit, and that is not practicable, unless the credit have a circulation, so as to supply the workman with necessaries; if that is supposed then that credit is money, and will have the same effects on home and foreign trade', quoted in Murphy (1997: 88), and on John Law's ideas in this regard, Murphy (1997: 81–82, 89).

161 Macleod (1886: 307–310), discussing some nineteenth-century court decisions affirming that 'ready money' is credit. This matter is long settled and needs no further discussion.

162 Macleod (1886: 311).

163 Macleod (1883: 45). He then proceeds to equate money with legal tender and gives examples which presuppose the gold standard, so that is a historical discussion.

164 McKendrick (2016: 489), note 7.

165 This is the specific statement on English banknotes beside the image of the monarch: 'I promise to pay the bearer on demand the sum of £20'. This promise is irrelevant in practical terms today. Euro banknotes, for example, do not carry such a statement.

The cheque is technically a bill of exchange drawn on a banker (that is, in relation to the credit in the customer's/drawer's account) payable on demand,[166] and in theory negotiable, so that the customer's bank money-claim can be transferred to a new cheque holder. However, in modern banking practice cheques have effectively lost their negotiability,[167] and in many countries cheques have been phased out altogether.[168]

Today, however, the transfer of an amount of bank money is mostly by way of a money transfer order (bank giro credit transfer), which does not transfer the credit itself, and it does not transfer the entitlement to the credit sum either. The money order rather extinguishes (or reduces) the credit with the transferor and creates the equivalent credit with the transferee, usually held at a different bank.[169] This is a reason why the law of assignment probably does not apply to money transfer orders. That opinion depends on the legal system in question; it is the majority view in the UK.[170] An assignment, however, would transfer the credit itself as an object of dematerialised property. This distinction is commercially not very relevant but legally important. In *R. v. Preddy*,[171] the House of Lords identified a sum of money in a bank account as property. When a money transfer is effected, the transferor's account is debited and the transferee's account credited. But that, the court held, is not a transfer of property, that is, a transfer of the debt or chose in action in question (being the sum in the customer's bank account owed to the customer-transferor by his bank). That debt or chose in action is rather extinguished or reduced *pro tanto*, and a chose in action is brought into existence representing a debt in an equivalent sum owed by a different bank to the transferee.[172]

A cheque, now typically deprived of negotiability, would (after clearing) effectively operate similar to a money transfer order when paid into the payee's bank account. If the cheque is cashed,[173] the bank money represented by the cheque is converted into cash and then reconverted into bank money when that cash is deposited.

166 For the UK, see Bills of Exchange Act 1882, s. 73.

167 Ellinger et al. (2011: 389).

168 For example in Germany and Austria after the introduction of the euro. In France, also a euro country, cheques are still in use.

169 See *Libyan Arab Foreign Bank v. Bankers Trust Co* [1989] QB 728, at 750.

170 Ellinger et al. (2011: 593, 597–599). A reason for this view is the particularly complicated system of statutory and equitable assignment in England. In Scotland, the legal regime of assignations (assignments) is different, so theoretically opinions could differ on this issue.

171 [1996] AC 815.

172 [1996] AC 815, at 834, per Lord Goff. The discussion in this criminal law case was the preliminary question in civil law whether the transferred funds were indeed 'property belonging to another' dishonestly obtained, so that the deception provision of the Theft Act 1968, s. 15(1) could be applied. The extinction and recreation of the debt during the money transfer order is not 'obtaining' and not 'belonging to another', a ruling which led to a reform of English criminal law (enactment of Theft Act 1968, s. 15A).

173 Today cheques are usually crossed, so payment in cash is prevented. The printed standard cheque forms in the UK are crossed.

(iv) Legal tender; fiat money; distinction between theories of money: Chartalism, institutional and functional theories of money

The differences between cash and legal tender have been discussed earlier.[174] Legal tender or compulsory tender is the quality conferred on certain things or *res* (objects of dematerialised property, reified in some material form, a moveable) by the law to operate as money, particularly in its function as medium of exchange. If the law declares a certain *res* as being legal tender, then this *res*, by order of law, *must* be accepted by a creditor in full and final satisfaction of the debt owed to him.[175] In the framework of relations money creates, this is the first case or *casus nominativus.*[176] The law has provided that cash (within limits) is legal tender, that is, banknotes and coins. Particular statutes proclaim that banknotes and coins have the status of legal tender, for example for the UK,[177] for the euro in the EU,[178] or for Germany, as a euro country restating the relevant EU legislation.[179]

A common term for legal tender is *fiat money*, particularly among economists,[180] which emphasises the legal command ('*fiat*') to accept an intrinsically worthless token for perhaps a valuable commodity in exchange, for instance, a bundle of intrinsically worthless banknotes for a new car. Fiat money (paper money) is not convertible to any other asset, for example gold or silver.[181]

The notion of legal tender still attaches to the physicality of a token, however worthless, so there must be paper or metal, a *res* reified socially by a chattel, the *res* itself being the debt the central bank money constitutes. With the drive towards dematerialisation in banking business, the idea of legal tender becomes increasingly outdated in its present form. Bank money is not – or not yet – legal tender, but upper limits for cash payments exist in several countries, which effectively makes bank money legal tender for higher sums of payment.[182] The withdrawal

174 See above under (i).
175 Mann (1992: 42–43).
176 See Chapter 4.
177 The present legal basis for banknotes as legal tender in England is the Currency and Bank Notes Act 1954, c. 12, s. 1(3), for coins as legal tender in the whole UK the Currency Act 1983, c. 9, s. 1(3) amending Coinage Act 1971, c. 24, s. 2. On the historical predecessor of the Elizabethan case of *The Case of the Mixt Monies* (1604), see Desan (2016: 27–28).
178 Art. 128(1) TFEU states: 'The banknotes issued by the European Central Bank and the national central banks shall be the only such notes to have the status of legal tender within the Union', see also EU Regulation EC/974/98, Art. 10. The euro coins are regulated in Art. 128(2) TFEU, but it is EU Regulation EC/974/98, Art. 11, which designates euro coins as being legal tender.
179 Section 14 Bundesbankgesetz 1992.
180 E.g. Mankiw (2012: 622).
181 Bank of England (2014b: 8).
182 See the recent consultation of the EU Commission 'EU initiative on restrictions on payments in cash', 27 February 2017–31 May 2017, available at: https://ec.europa.eu/info/consultations/eu-initiative-restrictions-payments-cash_en (visited 28 April 2018).

of high-denomination banknotes, such as in the EU[183] or in India,[184] has a similar effect. Whatever the official justifications for such actions are (tackling counterfeiting or money laundering etc.), at least one principal effect is that the supply of money is shifted more from central bank money to bank money created by commercial banks,[185] which privatises money supply further and brings that process increasingly into the influence of the commercial banks. The withdrawal of such high-denomination banknotes reduces, however, the ability for commercial banks to hoard large amounts of central bank money in form of these banknotes as collateral for the commercial banks' own liabilities in case of possible liquidity shortages. Low-denomination banknotes for the same sums take up substantially more storage space in bank safes, so that problems of logistics, cost and efficiency arise. The emergence of electronic money and general tendencies to abolish cash, at least in part, are likely erode the concept of legal tender in the future.[186]

The law not only decrees which chattels are legal tender but also *by whom* these tokens must have been issued to function as legal tender. This emphasis on where the 'money' must originate from in order to be money denotes the second case or *casus genitivus* among the cases or aspects of money.[187] Therefore Monopoly money and forged banknotes are not legal tender. (The workings of the concept of dematerialised property in this context can be demonstrated well with the example of an unauthorised banknote as opposed to an authorised banknote.)[188] Money, not only money as legal tender, is crucially based on the fact that some persons or institutions have an authority to issue a text with normative effect (most visibly but not necessarily in form of a sheet of printed paper, the banknote), while others have not. This is the general principle that money is not more than a normative text.[189] Paul Valéry identified the problem quite accurately in *Tel quel*:[190]

> Ce qui distingue un billet faux d'un billet vrai, ne dépend que du faussaire.
>
> Un homme passait en justice accusé de faux, et deux billets portant les mêmes numéros étaient sur la table du juge. Il fut absolument impossible de les distinguer.
>
> – De quoi m'accusez-vous? disait-il . . . Où est le corps du délit?

183 Withdrawal of the €500 banknote by the European Central Bank until the end of 2018, see press release of the ECB of 4 May 2016, available at: www.ecb.europa.eu/press/pr/date/2016/html/pr160504.en.html (visited 28 April 2018).

184 For example the sudden withdrawal of the 500- and 1,000-rupee banknotes in India in late 2016, see the press statement of the Reserve Bank of India of 8 November 2016, available at: https://rbi.org.in/Scripts/BS_PressReleaseDisplay.aspx?prid=38520 (visited 28 April 2018).

185 Discussed in Chapter 2.

186 Proctor (2012: 12 nn 33, 51).

187 See Chapter 4.

188 See below under sec. 4, discussing the *Banco de Portugal* case.

189 Rahmatian (2014: 221).

190 Valéry (2008: 100).

The actual normative text that confers the quality of money (or even legal tender) on a token or, more precisely, a *res* represented by a token, is rather clear in relation to cash, but can be difficult to ascertain for bank money.[191]

Without preempting further discussions, it is worth clearing up a common misconception at this stage. We will see later that what makes a *res* to money is the legal enforceability of the fungible and transferable ('liquid') debt the *res* constitutes,[192] so that all money is a creation of the law, but not all money is therefore legal tender. In particular, bank money is not, but the enforceability of the debt that it constitutes makes it to money. Especially economists jump to the conclusion that whenever money is postulated as a creature of the law, this must be a Chartalist theory of money,[193] following G. Knapp,[194] and then perhaps criticise the perceived narrowness of this conception, because money is supposed to be based on a social convention which makes it operational: money is what it does – an asset that can easily be used to purchase goods and services.[195] Economists are typically unaware that any property or any debt is the result of the law, so must also money be – property in form of a debt. They often also wrongly think that lawyers consider money and legal tender as being synonymous,[196] and conclude, for instance, from that erroneous premise: 'The concept of money as a creature of law and the state is clearly untenable. It is not justified by a single phenomenon of the market' (Mises).[197] Apart from that, the phenomena of the market are not the primary interest of the lawyer.

Money issued by the State through its central bank can indeed be described as 'Chartal money'; this is also the idea on which Knapp's theory of money is founded.[198] Such money issued by the State is also legal tender, at least within limits prescribed by law: for example, one thousand 1p coins for the discharge of a £10 debt are not legal tender and need not be accepted by the creditor.[199] However, bank money is not 'Chartal money', not issued by a State authority and not legal tender, but money, made to that by enforcing the debt which bank money constitutes. Legal tender is *res* made to money by the law *directly* through the command of taking the *res* (its reifier) as discharge of the debt; bank money is *res* made to money by the law *indirectly* through enforceability of the debt (*res*) and uninhibited ability to convert into cash or legal tender. Hence the categorisation in 'Chartalist', 'societary' or 'functionalist' theories of money[200] is of no use for a legal theory of money. If at all, the present legal theory comes closest to an

191 Discussed in Chapter 2, sec. 6.
192 Discussed in Chapter 2, sec. 4 and Chapter 5, sec. 2.
193 Proctor (2012: 16).
194 Knapp (1924: 1).
195 Krugman and Wells (2015: 854).
196 E.g. Mises (1953: 69–71). See the discussion by Schumpeter (1954: 1090) for a good illustration of the eventual incompatibility of the legal and economic approach.
197 Mises (1953: 69).
198 Knapp (1924: 24–25).
199 UK Coinage Act 1971, s 2(1A)(b).
200 Discussion in Proctor (2012: 15–25).

institutional theory of money,[201] but only if one stresses that this 'institution' is a normative or legal creation. Furthermore, the conventional institutional theory focuses too much on the central banks (despite their dwindling importance in the money supply), so that this theory is too narrow and misleading. These two reasons make the category of an 'institutional theory' rather redundant again. One has to concede, however, that some of the economists' muddled thinking was the consequence of a too narrow conception of money by lawyers, such as Mann, who really equates money with legal tender and so has a genuine Chartalist view.[202] There is not much merit either in labelling the approach taken in the present book as 'nominalism',[203] although the idea that money is a normative text is effectively a nominalist one.[204]

(v) Central bank money, narrow money and broad money; categorisations of money (M1–M4)

Monetary economics and banking business distinguish between different categories of money. These categories are not entirely consistently applied – that depends particularly on the jurisdiction and the central bank in question – and they are generally of fairly insignificant importance to the lawyer.

The Federal Reserve of the United States divides the money supply into M1 and M2 (M3 was abolished in 2006). M1 is money in the narrow sense, the really fungible, convertible, and most liquid asset: cash (currency in circulation), traveller's cheques, deposits in current accounts payable on demand ('chequable deposits'). M2 comprises M1 *plus* 'near-moneys': savings deposits, small-denomination time deposits (those issued in amounts of less than $100,000), and retail money market mutual fund shares. These are less liquid financial assets that are not directly usable as a medium of exchange but can quickly be converted into cash or on-demand deposits (including savings accounts with a later maturity date which nevertheless allow withdrawal any time before that date, perhaps on payment of a penalty).[205]

The Bank of England distinguishes between 'base money' or 'central bank money' and 'broad money'.[206] 'Central bank money' comprises currency (about 94% banknotes and about 6% coin in the UK) and central bank reserves (deposits by commercial banks with the central bank, that is, liabilities of the central bank vis-à-vis the commercial banks), sometimes also labelled M0.[207] M1 consists of M0 plus non-interest bearing sight deposits held by the non-bank private sector;

201 Proctor (2012: 25–30) with further references, especially to Sáinz de Vicuña who formulated this theory.
202 Mann (1992: 8, 14, 22–23).
203 Mann uses this term for his theory of money, see Mann (1992: 90).
204 Compare discussion in Olivecrona (1971: 299) about the monetary unit.
205 See Federal Reserve, available at: www.federalreserve.gov/faqs/money_12845.htm (visited 29 April 2018); Krugman and Wells (2015: 857–858).
206 Bank of England (2014b: 7).
207 Bank of England (2014a: 23), Bank of England (2014b: 7).

M2 comprises M0, M1 and all retail deposits (including time deposits) held by the non-bank private sector; M3 includes, broadly, less liquid assets; M4 also includes certificates of deposit, repos and securities with a maturity of less than five years held by the non-bank private sector – to list the most important monetary aggregates.[208]

The European Central Bank defines M1 as the sum of currency in circulation and overnight deposits. M2 comprises M1 plus deposits with an agreed maturity of up to two years and deposits redeemable at notice of up to three months; and M3 is M1 and M2 plus repurchase agreements, money market fund shares/units and debt securities with a maturity of up to two years.[209] The categorisations of the monetary aggregates by the German Central Bank, being in the eurozone, are very similar.[210]

The notions of 'narrow money' with highest liquidity and 'broad money' with less high liquidity are sufficient for the present discussion. The concept of dematerialised property circumvents this categorisation because all types of money are *res* (that is, fungible credit or debt), with different reifiers, so that there is effectively a notional monetisation not only of all forms of money but potentially also of all sorts of other assets through their conceptualisation as a *res*, distinguished only by a different level of liquidity.[211] The exact level of liquidity is essential for the banker and the economist but has little conceptual relevance for the legal theorist.

(vi) Definitions of money by the English courts

There are some statements in English court cases that provide a definition of money; the latest of them are from the nineteenth century, still at the time of the gold standard and of commodity money. They were, however, sufficiently pragmatic to be able to survive into the time of a modern system of money. The standard definition of money in English law is still in *Moss v. Hancock*:[212]

> [Money is] that which passes freely from hand to hand throughout the community in final discharge of debts and full payment for commodities, being accepted equally without reference to the character or the person who offers it and without the intention of the person who receives it to consume it or apply it to any other use than in turn to tender it to others in discharge of debts or payment for commodities.

208 Bank of England (2014a: 23). There are further categories MZM, M4ex, ibid.

209 ECB website, see: www.ecb.europa.eu/stats/money_credit_banking/monetary_aggregates/html/index.en.html (visited 29 April 2018).

210 Deutsche Bundesbank website, see: www.bundesbank.de/Redaktion/DE/Glossareintraege/G/geldmenge.html (visited 29 April 2018).

211 On the concept of monetisation or 'monetarisation' (a rather uncommon word in English), see Chapter 3, sec. 4 and Chapter 4, sec. 4.

212 *Moss v. Hancock* [1899] 2 QB 111, at 116, per Darling J.

This definition, taken over from Francis A. Walker's *Money in Its Relations to Trade and Industry* (1889), p. 4, focuses on money as a means for the discharge of debts. From the viewpoint of the practical lawyer, including the academic concentrating on black-letter law, this is usually satisfactory.[213] This definition has primarily money in mind that is represented physically in form of banknotes and coins ('passes freely from hand to hand'). The case concerned a coin and the question whether it was used as a mere commodity or performed the function of money ('coin of currency'). However, the decision also leaves room for money not represented by specific types of chattels, so that bank money should be covered if one interprets the expression 'passing from hand to hand' metaphorically. Legal practice certainly does this anyway.

As early as in 1758, Lord Mansfield was even more pragmatic in *Miller v. Race*:[214]

> It has been ingeniously argued on the part of the defendant; but the fallacy lies in comparing the note to things substantially different: it is neither goods, nor security for money, nor any document of a debt, but as much money as a guinea is, which appears by the receipts given by bankers, on your paying bank notes into their hands: their receipt is not for the specific bank-notes, but for so much money: which is so well understood, that they are commonly called paper money. Money, properly speaking, is whatever common consent has fixed upon as a sign denoting a certain value; and though, commonly, of gold, or silver, yet, sometimes, of mixed metals: and leather stamped has been used; so may paper; seeing, whatever the material is, common consent may make it money, to all intents, and purposes; and that banknotes are so received, and not considered as documents of a debt, or securities for money only, appears from many determinations.

Lord Mansfield arrived at this conclusion at a time when there was still the gold standard and commodity money, and banknotes were not yet legal tender. The decision shows an understanding of money as credit (and the nature of bank money) and the banknote as the social reifier ('sign') of the *res*, being 'money' or 'credit' or 'debt' itself, not just the certification of a debt.

Lord Mansfield also said that banknotes 'are become the same as cash; and any thing that would check, or interrupt their currency, would be of the worst consequence'.[215] (Today English banknotes *are* cash, and they are legal tender now, too.) A parallel view was expressed almost 150 years later in the Scottish case *Glasgow Pavilion v. Motherwell*, highlighting also the difference between cash and legal tender: A creditor may refuse to accept Scottish banknotes and insist on payment in coin, but if he accepts banknotes as payment he cannot deny

213 Payment is also the focus of McKendrick (2016: 490): the crucial question is not what constitutes money but what constitutes payment.

214 *Miller v. Race* (1758) 2 Kenyon 189 (also 1 Burr 453), 96 ER 1151, at 1154.

215 Ibid.

that he would be held, 'according to our law and practice', to have been paid in cash.[216] (Scottish banknotes were not, and still are not, legal tender.)

The emphasis of *Miller v. Race* on the social acceptance ('common consent') of what functions as money and on commercial expediency will find favour with economists and sociologists. However, one should not forget that if something becomes socially accepted to operate as money, then that is because this operation as money is legally enforced, for example through court judgments like *Miller v. Race*, even if this enforcement only appears as a definition or declaration of a state of affairs.

A modern broad definition of money has been provided by the Supreme Court of Canada:[217]

> [I]n ordinary speech, bank credit implies a credit which is convertible into money. But money as commonly understood is not necessarily legal tender. Any medium which by practice fulfils the function of money and which everybody will accept in payment of a debt is money in the ordinary sense of the words even although it may not be legal tender.

For the legal theorist, this definition is adequate but not sufficient. One may now wish to look at the adjacent discipline of economics for further guidance.

(vii) The limited use of money definitions by economists

The legal definitions of money by English judges are realistic and pragmatic, and they recognise the role that money plays in the economy. One would expect corresponding definitions by economists, but that is not the case. Mostly economists presuppose money as a social reality without being aware that it is the law which creates this social reality and therefore has to be defined by the law in order to be created, so that the law delineates economic definitions. Economists often sidestep the question by stating that 'money is that money does' – a definition by Francis A. Walker[218] and echoed by current economics textbooks[219] – and immediately lunge at the functions of money,[220] as if these were beyond any doubt, especially the store of value function.

If one looks at Keynes's classification of money in his *Treatise on Money* (1930), to take a prominent example of detailed definitions of money by an economist, then one will soon realise that such an effort is of little assistance to the lawyer. Keynes distinguishes between money and money of account. Money of account 'comes into existence along with debts' and is 'that in which debts and prices

216 *The Glasgow Pavilion v. William Motherwell* (1903) 6 F 116, IH, at 119.
217 *Reference re Alberta Legislation* [1938] 2 DLR 81, [1938] SCR 100, at 116, para. 39.
218 Schumpeter (1954: 1086). F. A. Walker, *Money in Its Relation to Trade and Industry* (1889), p. 1: 'To parody a familiar proverb: Money is that Money does'.
219 Krugman and Wells (2015: 854).
220 Mankiw (2012: 621).

and general purchasing power are expressed'; it is 'the *description* or *title*' while 'money is the *thing* which answers to the description'. Furthermore, money itself 'derives its character from its relationship to the money of account, since debts and prices must first have been expressed in terms of the latter'. The delivery of money itself leads to the discharge of debt contracts and price contracts, and 'in the shape of [money] a store of general purchasing power is *held*'.[221] Why there should be a distinction between money and debt ('money of account') is unclear, given that it has been accepted that money is a form of debt itself ('title') and not just an expression of existing debts, measured in prices ('description') and its objectification as a 'thing'. But at least it hints at an idea of dematerialised property with its concept of the *res*, the debt that money constitutes (for the discharge of another debt, for example payment in a sales contract) and the reifier, for example the banknote as a physical thing. However, the joy about a possible appreciation of a notion of dematerialised property is short-lived, because 'money' is not 'the thing which answers to the description' that is at the same time title, thus claim arising from an obligation, as Keynes says. 'Money' is rather a form of *res*. There is no merit either in lumping together in one term ('money of account') normative *res* (debts) and factual prices and general purchasing power (probably perceived as factual but also normative in part as the whole market model is, despite economists' contrary opinion). Keynes's muddled approach does not take us further.

There are more confusions. Keynes says, for example, that 'money of account gives rise to two derived categories – offers of contracts, contracts and acknowledgements of debt, which are in terms of it, and money proper, answering to it',[222] a classification lawyers can hardly find useful, also because of the foggy understanding of contract law (what are offers of contracts compared with contracts?), and it is presumably not beneficial for economists either. It then goes on: 'Bank money is simply an acknowledgement of a private debt, expressed in the money of account',[223] which raises the question why bank money is not a debt itself. One may presume that there is no sufficient appreciation of the difference between a debt to be paid in money arising out of a contract, such as a sale, and money (e.g. bank money), itself a debt, to discharge the contractual debt expressed in the purchase price: in case of bank money, the money-debt is the debt the bank owes its customer who has deposited a sum in the bank account with the bank. However, it is not even clear how Keynes uses the term 'bank money': 'The bank money may represent no longer a private debt . . . but a debt owing by the State; and the State may then use its chartalist prerogative to declare that the debt itself is an acceptable discharge of a liability'.[224] This indicates an understanding of a necessary conceptual distinction between cash and legal tender, but labelling central bank money and cash as 'bank money' (i.e. commercial bank money) and at the same time apparently recognising that this 'bank

221 Keynes (2013a: 3). Emphasis in original.
222 Keynes (2013a: 5).
223 Keynes (2013a: 5).
224 Keynes (2013a: 5).

money' is *itself* a debt and not just an acknowledgement of it (in that case a debt owed by the State) is just perplexing. Keynes's tendency not to get sidetracked by precision in his endeavour to present an elegant exposition of the subject does not help either. H. D. Macleod's concept of money as credit is infinitely more workable,[225] and the fact that he was a lawyer may well have been advantageous.

There are economic theories on money, influenced by Keynes, of which at least one recognises accurately the central importance law has for the understanding of money, and, in connection, the relevance of the legal concept of property rights for an analysis of the operation of money. Heinsohn and Steiger put forward a theory of money in which legal enforcement of debts and security rights play a principal role for the explanation of money in economic terms.[226] The authors cannot be blamed for representing a marginal, heterodox view that is presumably disregarded entirely by mainstream economists. However, what can be held against them is their inadequate understanding of property law[227] and a too close dependence on Keynes's deficient conceptualisation of money ('money of account and money proper'),[228] both of which provide a questionable basis for their own conception of money. As a result, Heinsohn and Steiger postulate that money is created through credit without becoming credit itself.[229] This erroneous view – since money *is* credit (or: a debt)[230] – derives from the idea that in order to create money or to have something operating as money, it is necessary to grant a security right over someone's assets.[231] Money creation requires[232]

> the willingness to burden property as a safeguard against potential redemptions (money-issuing creditor) and the willingness to hypothecate[233] property (credit-receiving debtor). Only such a risky loss of the free disposition over property generates money.

This theory rightly acknowledges that money is not neutral and must be a creation of the law, in that money itself must have some debt-like character. Therefore it is

225 Sympathetic discussion also in Schumpeter (1954: 718–719, 1115 and n 7).
226 Heinsohn and Steiger (2013: 54–55).
227 For example, the discussion of *de jure* and *de facto* possession, see Heinsohn and Steiger (2013: 5–15). The editor of Heinsohn's and Steiger's book, Frank Decker, also shows this insufficient familiarity with property law and concepts of security rights over property in his introduction when he seeks to explain the originally German property law for the common law reader, see Heinsohn and Steiger (2013: xxiv). A critique of the various imprecisions and inaccuracies of their description of ownership, possession, pledge, hypothec, charge and other security rights would be extensive but irrelevant for the arguments advanced here.
228 Heinsohn and Steiger (2013: 66).
229 Heinsohn and Steiger (2013: 70).
230 This has been explained above under 3(b)(ii) and (iii) and will be discussed in greater depth in Chapter 2.
231 This has also been expressed by the somewhat convoluted argument that '[bank] notes imply claims against the property of the issuer as soon as they are originated via the credit contract document', see Heinsohn and Steiger (2013: 59).
232 Heinsohn and Steiger (2013: 69).
233 In this context to be understood more generally as to 'grant a security right over it'.

the law which enforces this kind of debt, secured by (tangible?) property as collateral of some sort. However, there are several flaws in this theory. First, there does not seem to be sufficient understanding of the legal quality of a debt which money itself also constitutes – money is not just a medium *to* a collateralised debt or credit (from the creditor's perspective). The debt 'money' is enforceable,[234] and in the enforcement or execution procedure implemented by the law the debt turns into (physical) assets or 'real commodities',[235] and that is independent of whether or not this monetary debt has been collateralised before by the parties (that is, a security right granted over the debtor's or a third person's property which is available to the creditor in case of the debtor's default). Second, money does not need to be backed by (physical) assets as security at all, and that applies to central bank money (especially cash) and money created by commercial banks ('bank money') alike. A loan can be unsecured,[236] and yet, if granted by a commercial bank, perfectly creates money,[237] that is, an enforceable debt, regardless of any possible security rights.

This theory still seems to contain a lingering idea of a gold standard, emulated by backing assets in form of *jura in re aliena* (security rights) created over them. Furthermore, the theory does not appear to have an appreciation of the concept of dematerialised property, and particularly not of the trite reality that property objects are often not physical but mere legal concepts – in banking business that is the rule. It is the enforcement by law of the debt which money constitutes that makes a *res* operate as money, not a possible prior collateralisation to which that money may relate.[238]

In contrast, lawyers know and appreciate (generally) the underlying property concepts. Nevertheless, many lawyers' ideas of money are often either too narrow[239] or too inexact and even circular in their argument: if that which constitutes money is determined by what payment is,[240] then one has to ascertain first how the law confers on something the quality to be able to act as (a means of) payment. The legal and the economic interpretations of money are ultimately incompatible because they have different objectives. As Mises said:[241]

> Of course, in law as well as in economics, money is only the common medium of exchange. But the principal, although not exclusive, motive of the law for concerning itself with money is the problem of payment. When it seeks to

234 Thus the debtor satisfies the money debt (e.g. purchase price of £10) with money (e.g. a £10 note) as a debt *per se* (because of the way money is created); and if he defaults, the creditor can seek judgment against the debtor in court and start enforcement proceedings if payment of the judgment debt is not forthcoming, see Chapters 2 and 5.
235 See Chapter 4 for this term.
236 The credit card debt is a practical example of this situation.
237 See discussion in Chapter 2.
238 See Chapter 2, sec. 4 and Chapter 5, sec. 2 for further discussion.
239 Such as the one by Mann (1992: 6).
240 That is the argument in McKendrick (2016: 490).
241 Mises (1953: 35–36).

> answer the question, What is money? it is in order to determine how monetary liabilities can be discharged. For the jurist, money is a medium of payment. The economist, to whom the problem of money presents a different aspect, may not adopt this point of view if he does not wish at the very outset to prejudice his prospects of contributing to the advancement of economic theory.

That does not prevent lawyers from establishing their own theories of money[242] which may well inform economic models. However, in this *Streit der Fakultäten* (Kant) or, more prosaically, turf war between the disciplines, economists will not be inclined to admit that the lawyers necessarily set out the frame in which the economists can then develop their theories of money. Faced with the possible prerogative of law in many areas, it is no surprise that particularly law-and-economics theorists of the Chicago School try to subvert law by reconceptualising legal notions as economic ones (with the idea of externalities to explain property rights, for example) to create a new normative artifice (that they may call 'law') as a basis for the fiction of the free market unencumbered by legal regulation.[243]

(viii) Historical forms of money: commodity money and commodity-backed money

The oldest form of money, and in use well into the beginning of the twentieth century, was commodity money. In that case, money is a commodity with an intrinsic value, particularly gold or silver.[244] The scarcity of precious metals which could also be transported and measured easily, as well as human psychology that induces the idea that money must be valuable itself if it represents value, made gold and silver the perfect commodity for playing the role of money.[245] Human psychology is important in attributing value to gold, for example – with the effect of initiating the invasions and colonisation of Africa and South America by Spain and Portugal in the search for gold from the 1450s onwards[246] – because gold, apart from its use for jewellery, became practically important only in the twentieth century in the computer industry and nanotechnology and for medical equipment. Before that time, iron, for instance, was industrially and commercially infinitely more important (and it still is) than the extremely soft metal gold, but iron was not valued for its utility as such.[247] When the state issued money in form of gold and silver coins it typically charged seignorage for coinage. Seignorage (or seignoriage), the fixing of the nominal value of the coin above the intrinsic value of the metal the coin consists of, was an important source of income for the states and rulers. The classical

242 On historical legal theories of money, see below under sec. 6.
243 Rahmatian (2013: 192–196, 226–227).
244 E.g. Mankiw (2012: 621).
245 Crowther (1946: 18).
246 Vilar (1984: 46–52).
247 Lord Kames pointed that out in the eighteenth century, actually a truism, but strangely never stated, see Kames, *Sketches*, I, iii (2007: 78).

authors, like Adam Smith[248] or David Ricardo,[249] devoted considerable discussion to the charge of seignorage, but today it has no more economic relevance for the issuance of any form of currency, whether as coin or as paper money.[250] The theories of money presupposing commodity money, such as by the theoretical metallists,[251] are of interest to the economic historian only. Classical legal theories of money,[252] based on commodity money, also have merely limited importance today.

Commodity-backed money is money without any intrinsic value, particularly paper money, but backed by a valuable commodity of equivalent value to the nominal value stated on the money (banknote). The 'backing' was in fact a guaranteed promise that the money could always be converted into valuable commodity on demand,[253] and if the backing commodity was gold, then the currency operated under a gold standard.[254] Other assets, for example the land of a country, can be used as backing assets, as it happened with the German Rentenmark in 1924.[255] In the UK the gold standard was finally abolished in 1931,[256] together with most other countries around this time.[257]

After the Second World War, the Bretton Woods system provided some tenuous backing of paper money by gold. The Bretton Woods Agreement of 1944 stipulated that the par value of the currency of each member of the agreement shall be expressed in terms of gold as a common denominator or in terms of the US dollar of the weight and fineness in effect on 1 July 1944 (0.888671 grams per dollar), so that the US dollar was a reserve currency linked to the price of gold. Between 1968 and 1973 the Bretton Woods system was put to an end, particularly after US President Nixon abolished the convertibility of dollar into gold on 15 August 1971, presumably in breach of the treaty, but with the effect that the terms of the Bretton Woods Agreement were universally disregarded and the currencies 'floated', that is, they no longer observed any fixed parities.[258] From then on, this system was entirely replaced by the present fiat money system.

4. Money as dematerialised property: a legal conception

In the light of the forgoing discussion, one can now summarise the nature of money as dematerialised property, being a *res* in form of a debt.

248 Smith, *Wealth of Nations*, book 4, chapter 6 (2000: 593–598).
249 Ricardo, *Principles*, chapter 27 (2004: 238).
250 Cranston (2002: 111).
251 Schumpeter (1954: 288, 699).
252 An outline below under sec. 6.
253 Krugman and Wells (2015: 856).
254 Mann (1992: 32) for a short outline of the history. There is obviously also a gold standard in place if a country uses (almost only) gold coins as money. In the UK, for example, certain gold coins can still be legal tender (Coinage Act 1971, s. 2(1)), but this exceptional use has no practical importance for the present currency system as a fiat money system.
255 Crowther (1946: 19).
256 Gold Standard (Amendment) Act 1931, s. 1.
257 For the history of the end of the gold standard, see e.g. Crowther (1946: 354–362).
258 Mann (1992: 31, 36).

(a) Money as dematerialised property

Money is a form of dematerialised property. The basic conception of dematerialised property is that property rights and property objects ('things') are creations of the law; there is no 'natural' property (right), so this is a normative, constructivist idea of property. The property right that attaches to the property object or *res* really creates the property object for the purpose of the law: only the features of the property right – especially enforceability against everybody – make the object an object of property or *res* in law. The *res* is the abstract normative property object by virtue of the property right set down by law; it can be, but need not be, represented by a physical object, such as an apple or table, being a reification of the *res*. From the perspective of private law, the apple or table represents the *res* or property object in law: the law perceives the apple or table and turns them into a *res* or property, and the property rights in the *res* are represented by the apple or table as a social reifier. For non-lawyers and even for some property lawyers, it is difficult to grasp the idea that 'property' is conceptually never a relationship to a physical object and may be represented only socially by such a tangible, corporeal thing, however without this being a theoretical requirement. But the concept of dematerialised property has no difficulties in accommodating land, chattels, intellectual property rights and all varieties of debts as forms of property, as these are only different *versions* of the *res*, sometimes physically represented (e.g. a car), sometimes hardly doing that at all (e.g. accounting entries stating a debt).[259] Modern instances of *res* can easily be incorporated in the concept of dematerialised property, such as existing and future types of trade instruments (financial derivatives etc.) or different kinds of electronic money.[260]

Money is a debt. That becomes apparent when the money creation mechanism is examined,[261] and this is true of the obvious case of bank money created by commercial banks as well as of the less obvious one of money supplied by central banks. A debt constitutes a form of *res*. This debt itself can then be represented or reified by paper, as is the case with documentary intangibles, such as negotiable instruments – bills of exchange, cheques and promissory notes. The banknote is – formally still and historically in substance – a special version of a promissory note. However, it is ambiguous what the social reifier of the paper note represents. First, the paper represents the *res* in form of 'chattel', since a sheet of paper is tangible moveable property (technically: it represents the reified version of the *res*

259 The terminology is arbitrarily chosen but seeks to emphasise conceptual differences. A *version of reification* of the *res* is through tangible objects (chattels, land), intangibles (electricity) and pure intangibles (debts, intellectual property rights), an *instance of reification* of the *res* are, e.g. this type of chattel or another, for example, this or the other apple, see also Rahmatian (2018a: 210). Since the *res* is an abstract, therefore necessarily intangible, concept, this distinction is not required, but helpful, because in reality we are interested in the practical manifestations of the *res* (reifications) which are also the object of contracts and property transfers.

260 See above under sec. 3(b)(ii) and Chapter 2, sec. 7.

261 See Chapter 2.

'tangible moveable property object'). Second, the paper also embodies the debt which money itself constitutes. Thus the physical banknote represents two different *res* at once: the physical chattel-*res* and the incorporeal money obligation-*res*. In special situations these two *res* can identifiably separate from one another.[262] With bank money the reification reduces itself to a mere accounting entry, so that there is hardly any physicality or reification of the *res* at all.

The distinction between chattel-*res* and money obligation-*res* represented by the same object of a banknote appears to be a hair-splitting exercise. But the rare situation in the House of Lords decision of *Banco de Portugal v. Waterloo & Sons*[263] shows that this analysis is applied in reality. In this case the Bank of Portugal ordered a British printer to print 600,000 banknotes, each with a face value of 500 escudos. The banknotes were delivered and put into circulation by the Bank of Portugal. Then a fraudster who successfully posed as a representative of the Bank of Portugal ordered 580,000 notes of the same type from the printer which were then delivered to the fraudster's criminal gang. The gang put the notes into circulation, which forced the Bank of Portugal to withdraw the whole issue of the 500 escudos notes. This second batch of notes was printed from the original plates by the same printer who believed to have been authorised by the Bank of Portugal, so the notes were not actual forgeries, but unauthorised issues.[264] The Bank of Portugal sued the British printer for breach of contract because of the delivery of the further 580,000 notes. The question was whether damages were to be measured only by reference to the cost of the printing and production of the new notes, or whether damages could additionally be claimed for the exchange value in sterling of the Portuguese currency given in exchange for the unauthorised notes, thus taking account of the notes' face value.

The House of Lords decided in favour of the latter by a 3:2 majority. Before banknotes are issued, they have no legal effect as promissory notes.[265] If they are destroyed before issue, damages would be the paper and printing costs only. When the notes are put into circulation, they become operative promissory notes: the bank undertakes an obligation to pay the bearer of the banknote on demand 500 escudos, and that obligation is not affected by the question whether a gold standard applies or whether there is a paper currency, in which case the central bank has no obligation to pay the equivalent in gold. What matters is the obligation undertaken by the bank after issue, denoted by the face value of the banknote. The issued banknote has the quality of legal tender and possesses purchasing power to the amount indicated on its face. Hence damages comprise the face value of the notes, not only the cost of paper and printing.[266]

262 See discussion of the case of *Banco de Portugal v. Waterlow* immediately below.

263 *Banco de Portugal v. Waterloo & Sons* [1932] AC 452, HL.

264 This is an example of the second case or *casus genetivus* of money, the case of origin, see Chapter 4.

265 This is the general rule for promissory notes, see Bills of Exchange Act 1882, ss. 21, 84: Bills of Exchange and promissory notes have legal effect only if they are delivered (handed over) to the payee.

266 *Banco de Portugal v. Waterloo & Sons* [1932] AC 452 at 478, 483–484, 487, 510.

The decision does not use the terminology of dematerialised property, but that can be supplied easily. The mere printed paper represents the personal property-*res* or chattel-*res* (which is in this regard not different to an old banknote as a collector's item or monopoly money), and, at the same time, represents the debt/money obligation-*res*, denoted by the face value. Damages for the destroyed chattel-*res* are the printing costs, while damages for the money obligation-*res* are the damages for the lost currency value of the note.[267]

Since money is a form of debt (*res* as debt), money is credit – 'credit' only denotes the perspective of the creditor in relation to the obligation (claim or credit/*créance* corresponding to the debt/*dette*). Although economists in particular (with a few exceptions) deny that money is credit and try to make a distinction between money and credit, the only tenable view is that money *is* credit because this is the only interpretation that is in accordance with established banking law[268] and everyday commercial practise. H. D. Macleod's early summary of the legal categorisation of money, already stated before, is still valid: 'bank credits, or deposits, are a mass of property . . . they are *pecunia*, *bona*, *res*, *merx*' and 'legally only debts' which are 'for all practical purposes the current coin of commerce' and the principal payment method.[269] By contrast, Mises says:[270]

> We may give the name *commodity money* to that sort of money that is at the same time a commercial commodity; and the name *fiat money* to money that comprises things with a special legal qualification. A third category may be called *credit money*, this being that sort of money which constitutes a claim against any [*irgendeine*][271] physical or legal person. But these claims must not be both payable on demand and absolutely secure; if they were, there could be no difference between their value and that of the sum of money to which they referred.

From a juristic perspective, one is hard-pressed to see the difference between 'normal' money and credit money, particularly in relation to bank money: why is bank money not payable on demand and 'secure', as far as anything is secure in the banking system? And is there not a claim against a physical or legal person, in theory at least, both with regard to cash and bank money? With bank money the claim is very real if the bank's customer and account holder is debtor, but much more theoretical if the customer is creditor of his bank.[272]

267 See also Rahmatian (2018a: 213).
268 *Foley v. Hill* (1848) 2 HLC 28, and discussion above under sec. 3(b)(ii) and (iii) and in Chapter 2.
269 Macleod (1886: 311).
270 Mises (1953: 61).
271 From the German original: 'any' in this context is not to be understood as 'every person', but as 'no matter which person', which is a legally important distinction.
272 See Chapter 5, sec. 3.

(b) Expectation, not entitlement through money

The nature of money as a debt and *res* can be shown in an analysis of the role of money in the transaction of the sale.

When the seller hands over a commodity under a contract of sale, he obtains no real value in return from the buyer by being given another commodity of intrinsic value, as would be the case in a proper barter. What he obtains is money: a *res* that has been granted the quality of money by having been conferred legal enforceability of the debt (credit) that this *res* constitutes.[273] Money has no intrinsic value itself but carries the expectation that at a later date this imaginary commodity can be exchanged to a commodity of real and intrinsic value.[274]

Therefore money operates not as a medium of exchange but as a medium of exchange *delay*, because the anticipated exchange is that of *real* commodities. A *real commodity* in this context is a commodity that has an intrinsic or contemplative value which arises primarily through its use and enjoyment or consumption (food, apartment etc.),[275] while an *imaginary commodity* defines its value through its exchange value only, that is, its value is realised in its transfer: money in particular is such a case.[276] Yet, in contrast to prevalent neo-classical economic doctrine, money is not a neutral token, but as a debt, it is a *res* or an object of property itself, with consequences (the other tangible moveable property-*res*, if any, such as a metal coin or paper, is disregarded). Like any other kind of property, money can be, and often is, the object of markets and speculations (currency speculations), so a (possibly rising) value is bestowed on money itself. Money is therefore not a value-free medium or item of exchange but an independent property with its own market.[277]

When money functions as a unit of account, it is not a detached reference point of a fixed quantity but is mutable:[278] it is a *res* that operates as a representation of expectation and has itself exchange value. In addition, unlike most other forms of property, money also attracts interest because money is created as a (loan) debt or credit that is in reality never interest-free.[279] Thus money is a non-neutral medium of *exchange delay*, a medium which is itself a *res* that (a) has a changing exchange value, and (b) attracts interest (and a rise in exchange value). The non-neutral medium money |M| is interposed between two transactions (A/seller – B/

273 See Chapter 2, sec. 4 and Chapter 5, sec. 2.

274 See e.g. Keynes, *General Theory* (1964: 293): '[T]he importance of money essentially flows from its being a link between the present and the future'.

275 In case of payment for services, the service is not a 'real commodity' with a contemplative value as such, but an activity that is designed to lead ultimately to a real commodity, such as food, clothing, housing (in the widest sense). The service is an interpolation.

276 For this terminology, see Chapter 4, sec. 3(c).

277 See Binswanger (2013: 39): 'Money is a market product like any other. Money is also produced for the purpose of making profits'.

278 Köhler (2013: 896–897).

279 That applies particularly to commercial bank money, the economically vastly more important form of money, compared to cash, see Chapter 2.

buyer |M| B/buyer – C/new seller), which could be[280] one genuine barter but for the intervention of money. Money transforms the direct exchange into an indirect exchange.[281] The money involved in both sales influences the prices in these transactions, contrary to the economists' orthodox view.[282] The concept of dematerialised property facilitates such an analysis.

Although money is a debt, it gives *no entitlement to any specific real commodity* in exchange for the money. The seller only obtains an expectation and takes the money trusting that it will be convertible to any real commodity in the future. For this reason, the 'store of value' function of money is doubtful: a real store of value requires existing value, not an unspecific and legally unenforceable expectation. The debt 'money' or money-*res* is not a debt of which he is a creditor entitling him to a specific real commodity. Because of the fact that the money-*res* is transferable (for example embodied in a banknote as promissory note), it can serve as a medium of exchange, but its transferability also means that it is detached from the original obligation it derives from in the money creation process. It is also unrelated to the obligation in which it is supposed to operate as a means of payment. For example, in a sale the buyer hands over to the seller a banknote of £20, a debt (*res*) embodied in (reified by) the banknote, to discharge the monetary debt of £20 which has arisen from the contract of sale between him and the seller. Since the banknote is legal tender, the seller has to accept this other debt (money debt-*res* reified by the banknote) as a full discharge of his claim from the sales contract (sales debt-*res* which may not be reified at all). In the case of payment by bank money, the seller could theoretically refuse such a giro credit transfer (money transfer order) and insist on cash, unless contractually agreed otherwise. However, the English courts are unlikely to allow such a refusal and tend to draw an inference that bank money transfers can be made, particularly if a bank money transfer is commercial practice in the given circumstances or the amounts are substantial.[283] In such a case bank money effectively assumes the role of legal tender. The difference between cash and bank money is that in case of cash the *res* (money-debt) originates from the central bank, in case of bank money the *res* originates from a commercial bank having granted credit (a loan).[284]

The transferability of the money debt-*res* is also the reason why money is separate, non-neutral property and can be the object of speculation. First, transferability as such is an indicator that something is private property.[285] Second, because the money debt-*res* is independent of the obligation it originates from (cash:

280 That depends on whether a direct exchange is possible. It is not if A holds commodity x and B holds commodity y but needs commodity z, held by C who may need x or y, and other combinations, see Mises (1953: 30).

281 Mises (1953: 30–33), but Mises does not discuss the non-neutrality of money.

282 See Chapter 2, sec. 3(d) and Chapter 3.

283 *Homes v. Smith* [2000] Lloyd's Rep. Bank 139, at para. 23, *The Laconia* [1976] QB 835, at 846–847, 850, 855, *The Chikuma* [1981] 1 WLR 314, at 320.

284 See Chapter 2.

285 *National Provincial Bank v Ainsworth* [1965] AC 1175, 1247G–1248A, per Lord Wilberforce.

central bank, bank money: commercial bank), it can assume an exchange value that is detached from the question if, when and how this debt can be discharged by the original debtors, that is, the central or commercial banks. The English courts have recognised this very early. Lord Mansfield said in *Miller v. Race*:[286]

> Money . . . is whatever common consent has fixed upon as a sign denoting a certain value . . . whatever the material is, common consent may make it money . . . and that banknotes are so received, and *not considered as documents of a debt*, or *securities for money only*, appears from many determinations.

This sets out the role of the banknote: not just documentary title of the debt (money), but embodiment of the debt itself and reifier of the *res*, the *res* being debt, but also separate value as such, able to operate as a medium of exchange, that is, money. Today bank money has largely assumed the same role as cash. The trust in the theoretical redeemability of the debt that money constitutes seems to suffice to satisfy the markets. If the money-debt were not transferable it could not become an object of a separate market and of speculation, but then it could not operate as a medium of exchange, that is, as money, either.

5. The concept of money as dematerialised property and the judicial reality

The *Banco de Portugal* case[287] indicates that the concept of dematerialised property is in effect applied by the courts in relation to money. It must be stressed, however, that the courts may only have some notion as to how the concept of dematerialised property operates in practice; there is no conscious appreciation and no express explanation of such a concept in the *Banco de Portugal* case or other decisions of the courts. There are no judicial pronouncements that use the concept of dematerialised property as the legal theory to frame the notion of money. However, the concept of dematerialised property is a useful theoretical device to understand money in law and it is easily compatible with the actual decisions of the courts. For example, the pragmatic willingness of the courts to consider bank money and even cheques[288] as an equivalent of cash indicates a notion of a *res* as a separate object of property that money constitutes and that can manifest itself and be realised in different ways.[289] Whether the courts will once explicitly refer to the concept of dematerialised property remains to be seen.

In other legal systems, for example in Germany, the courts occasionally engage in a more abstract examination about the nature of money, but not necessarily

286 *Miller v. Race* (1758) 2 Kenyon 189 (1 Burr 452), 96 ER 1151, at 1154, emphasis added.

287 *Banco de Portugal v. Waterloo & Sons* [1932] AC 452. See above under sec. 4.

288 *Miller v. Race* (1758) 2 Kenyon 189 (1 Burr 452), 96 ER 1151, at 1154; *The Glasgow Pavilion v. William Motherwell* (1903) 6 F 116, IH, at 119.

289 In the case of cheques this approach presupposes complete convertibility into cash or bank money which is indeed the normal situation in practice.

with an entirely satisfactory outcome. In a decision about whether money would benefit from constitutional protection as 'property'/ownership (*Eigentum*) under Art. 14 of the German Constitution,[290] the German constitutional court[291] commingled different functions and features of money: money as physical property (paper money, coins), money as a debt/claim, money as constituting exchange value/monetary value *per se*. This complicates the assessment as to what exactly is supposed to enjoy constitutional protection; according to academic opinion apparently only money in a physical form (*Sacheigentum*) is, or should be, protected.[292] This view may have been influenced by the unusual situation that in German private law only corporeal objects are regarded as property or things (*Sachen*).[293] The concept of dematerialised property could have been of assistance in this decision, and one could have distinguished more easily between the corporeal reifiers paper and coin, (bank) money as debt (*res*) itself, and the monetary debt from a sales contract, to be discharged with (bank) money. This could have given stronger contours to the constitutionally protected and unprotected aspects of money. Furthermore, in German academic literature one finds discussions about the (supposedly) different nature of debts discharged by payment of money and debts discharged by delivery of commodities (e.g. no impossibility in case of a monetary debt),[294] but not much awareness[295] that money, which discharges that monetary debt, is itself a debt, a fact that could have influenced the findings. Academic discussion with a more analytical approach to property and contract law could give guidance to the courts in such instances.

Generally, however, the judiciary, particularly in common law systems, is not fond of elaborating on the possible theoretical underpinnings of their concrete decisions, but focuses on the case at issue with no great ambition to set out a general system beyond it. Such a task is primarily left to academic lawyers.

6. Historical legal theories of money: a short outline

Before the mechanism of money supply, or more accurately, money creation, is examined in Chapter 2, an outline of some older legal theories of money should be given. It was emphasised earlier that in the eighteenth and nineteenth centuries lawyers were willing to devote much discussion to the legal side of money,

290 In Germany, assets in general ('*Vermögen*') are not protected by the constitutional right to property, only identifiable items of property are, see Lepsius (2002: 313, 319).

291 Entscheidungen des Bundesverfassungsgerichts (BVerfGE), Vol. 97, p. 350, at 370–371.

292 Lepsius (2002: 314–315, 317).

293 Section 90 German Civil Code (BGB).

294 Kähler (2006: 821, 823). In English law impossibility or frustration of an obligation to pay money is accepted in principle, see *Ralli Brothers v. Compañia Naviera Sota y Aznar* [1920] 2 KB 287, at 296, 304.

295 Köhler (2013: 912, 916), is an exception. See ibid. at p. 912: 'However, [money] circulates no longer in the simple form of coins of precious metal, but in the changed form of representation as bank money and basis for circulating credit (*Zirkulationskredit*)' (Own translation).

and a brief sample is presented here. Today almost all of it is of historical interest only, because the authors based their treatment of money in law on commodity money operating under a gold standard (Britain) or a silver standard, at least a partial one (German States). Furthermore, any analysis of the most important form of money, bank money, though at the time already of great commercial relevance, was far too brief to be significant. This short sketch may therefore serve primarily as a demonstration that the nature of money *can* be discussed in legal terms and need not be a subject reserved solely to economists. Some of the old concepts are, however, still important.

William Blackstone (1723–1780) stressed the quality of (commodity) money as necessarily being issued by the state under the king's prerogative. One would see this today as a 'Chartalist' view of money. The function of money as a 'medium of commerce' or 'common standard' (i.e. medium of exchange and unit of account) seems to derive from the king's authority as the issuing body.[296] The stamping of the coin as the determination of its denomination is also an act of the king's prerogative powers or sovereign powers of the states.[297] Blackstone then set out a crude quantity theory of money, probably under the influence of Hume,[298] to whom he also referred, but in a different context.[299]

Friedrich Carl v. Savigny (1779–1861) was, as one would expect, more theoretical in his approach. He said that the question of what a money debt is must lead to an analysis of the concept of money.[300] That is essentially the approach taken in the present book, against the pragmatic, and ultimately too superficial, idea that the relevant point is not what the concept of money is, but whether payment of a debt can be effected with it.[301] The most important features of Savigny's discussion of money are that he was not a 'Chartalist' but had a functional approach to money, and he also described money, seemingly loosely, as conferring on the owner 'asset power' ('*Vermögensmacht*').[302] Money appears in this asset power 'as an abstract means for dissolving all forms of assets into mere quantities',[303] which is an outmoded way of describing monetisation and commodification as features of the dematerialised property conception discussed above.[304] According to Savigny, it is not the state which founds and creates money and fixes its (market) value, but the state is only an intermediary which seeks to bring about a certain faith ('*Glaube*') by issuing coins in a considerate way, for example. The belief consists in the willingness to accept money because one can expect that everybody

296 Blackstone, *Commentaries*, Vol. 1 (1800: 276).
297 Blackstone, *Commentaries*, Vol. 1 (1800: 277–278).
298 Hume, *Of Money* (2003: 121–122), and Chapter 3.
299 Blackstone, *Commentaries*, Vol. 1 (1800: 276–277) and note 17, refers not to Hume's essays on money and interest but to Hume's *History of England*, but it is unlikely that Blackstone was not familiar with Hume's essays.
300 Savigny, *Obligationenrecht I* (1851: 404).
301 This is the approach, e.g. by McKendrick (Goode), see McKendrick (2016: 490).
302 Savigny, *Obligationenrecht I* (1851: 405–406, 408).
303 Savigny, *Obligationenrecht I* (1851: 405).
304 See above under sec. 2(a)(iv).

else will accept that money for the same value later. It is public opinion, sustained by a responsible financial policy of the state, which decides whether something is money and to what extent it operates as money.[305] Savigny was confronted with the phenomenon of several currencies extending beyond several principalities among the German States well before German unification in 1871.[306] In contrast, Blackstone could proceed from the unitary state of Britain. Savigny's functionalist (or economists') theory of money and the description of the system of money as a belief system make this theory appear quite modern, although it still presupposes the old metal money system. However, Savigny did not maintain his functionalist theory of money consistently when he discussed paper money[307] and the withdrawal of currency which, as he says, must happen by a legal (i.e. 'Chartalist') act of the state.[308]

Savigny did not grasp completely the phenomenon of paper money, and certainly not that of bank money. He did stress the importance of the faith in the convertibility of paper money (and that faith can only be maintained by the government if there is no excessive issuance of paper money), but he did not consider paper money as 'real money' ('*wirkliches Geld*'), like gold or silver coins.[309] Savigny regarded issued banknotes as (a) a means that can operate as if they were money, and, at the same time, as (b) an interest-free loan to the state ('*unverzinsliche Staatsschuld*').[310] In this context he made an important observation. He equated excessive issuance of paper money with excessive issuance of divisional coin[311] and explained that in a historical example from Prussia in the second half of the eighteenth century when there was a too extensive issuance of divisional coins. Although their value fell in fact because of the increase in volume, these divisional coins were accepted for a long time still for their increasingly excessive nominal value, and 'notably almost the whole grain trade was carried out with this money'. Only after the war of 1806 there was a dramatic fall in the value of the currency.[312] Here Savigny (inadvertently) described phenomena of the modern paper money and bank money system and the important question of the convertibility of imaginary or anticipated commodities (mediated by money) to real commodities with an intrinsic value (grain). His concept of the 'asset power' of money also alludes to this idea. We will come across a similar thought in the discussion of the externalisation cycle in Chapter 4.

305 Savigny, *Obligationenrecht I* (1851: 407–408).

306 Savigny, *Obligationenrecht I* (1851: 407): 'with the increase of monetary transactions well beyond the borders of a single state . . . to which the power and influence of the governing force is restricted'.

307 Savigny, *Obligationenrecht I* (1851: 413): The belief in the value of the metal is absent in case of paper money, and so 'the faith can only be founded in the faith in the government'.

308 Savigny, *Obligationenrecht I* (1851: 451).

309 Savigny, *Obligationenrecht I* (1851: 413).

310 Savigny, *Obligationenrecht I* (1851: 414).

311 '*Scheidemünze*' in German; usually copper coins of small denomination that cannot be properly made as precious metal coins because their value is smaller than the monetary unit.

312 Savigny, *Obligationenrecht I* (1851: 416).

Savigny's idea of faith as a constituent factor for money to operate as a medium of exchange has in some ways a predecessor in Adam Müller (1779–1829), a major representative of the philosophy of economics in the Romantic period in Germany. His *Elemente der Staatskunst* (*Elements of Statecraft*, 1809) are to some extent a 'wild work' for economists and lawyers alike, but certain aspects should not be discarded. Müller claimed that the value of money is not just the exchange value, but particularly the willingness of society to accept (metal) money as a suitable representative of individual and societal values in general.[313] In fact, in every sale the seller and buyer develop a notion of 'invisible money' or 'living money' beside, and connected with, the commodity and the metal money.[314] For the real abstraction and anticipation of products of an economy is *credit*, and that goes beyond mere (metal) money.[315] We have come across this anticipatory function of money already[316] and will discuss it further in Chapter 4. Müller understood 'credit' primarily as 'trust', as was typical for the late 1700s and early 1800s,[317] but the connotation with (bank) money is already there. Müller also described briefly 'real arithmetic money' ('*wirkliche Rechenmünze*') or 'standard money' used between banks in particular, which is an early (1809!) reference to bank money.[318]

Levin Goldschmidt (1829–1897), the father of the discipline of commercial law in Germany, provided probably the most extensive discussion of money in law and, rooted in principles of Roman law and Pandectism, had left the Romantic period well behind. He had a clearer idea of bank money and credit and cited, among other authors, H. D. Macleod.[319] He took over from Savigny the notion of money as an 'asset power',[320] but he had a narrower, more 'Chartalist' and less 'functionalist' approach to money than Savigny. However, he criticised not only Savigny but also too nominalist notions or 'state theories' of money.[321] But he came close to Savigny when he said that 'things [chattels] that are generally recognised and used as money within a state or across several states are also money in a legal sense for these territories'. The law that recognises such things as money is either customary law or, preferably, a statute.[322] Goldschmidt shared Savigny's view that only precious metal money is 'complete' or 'real' money; divisional coins and paper money in a broad sense (banknotes and negotiable IOUs) are 'imperfect money'. He also stated that a 'combined legal theory for all so-called money [coins, notes, bank money] does not exist'.[323] Goldschmidt did not see

313 Müller (2006: 271–272).
314 Müller (2006: 276).
315 Müller (2006: 257).
316 See above under sec. 4.
317 See Chapter 2 on the credit creation theory of money.
318 Müller (2006: 285).
319 Goldschmidt, *Handbuch des Handelsrechts I* (1868: 1060), note.
320 Goldschmidt, *Handbuch des Handelsrechts I* (1868: 1067).
321 Goldschmidt, *Handbuch des Handelsrechts I* (1868: 1079–1080), note 28.
322 Goldschmidt, *Handbuch des Handelsrechts I* (1868: 1069).
323 Goldschmidt, *Handbuch des Handelsrechts I* (1868: 1069–1071).

the money creation–power of bank money or credit. For him, the banker is only the intermediary for the circulation of money; he does not create it.[324] Furthermore, Goldschmidt stated that credit does not create money but only facilitates its circulation and distribution, and it does not replace money; there is rather a difference between money and credit.[325] He was therefore a representative of what would later be called the financial intermediation theory of money.[326] Otherwise he was remarkably modern for his time, because he even discussed the giro transfer (bank money transfer order) in some detail.[327]

Bernhard Windscheid (1817–1892), the principal representative of Pandectism in Germany, followed Goldschmidt[328] in his famous textbook of private law (*Lehrbuch des Pandektenrechts*): paper money (IOUs and banknotes) is not 'real money' because it merely represents, but does not contain, metal money (gold and silver). Only metal money discharges a debt, but the law can order that banknotes have to be accepted as full payment,[329] which points towards a predecessor of the modern fiat money system.

While all these theories are no longer directly useful because they were based on the obsolete system of commodity money, certain ideas are still relevant and will recur in the following discussions.

7. Conclusion

This chapter has shown that the legal concept of money ought to be an essential research subject in commercial law, but money has hardly concerned lawyers since the beginning of the twentieth century, much in contrast to the eighteenth and nineteenth centuries. The chapter has discussed the concept of dematerialised property and its major applications for analytical examination: company shares, debts and money as a special form of debt. Then definitions of the various types of money, in the light of the concept of dematerialised property and of judicial practice, have been presented. The discussion has also shown that money definitions by economists prove to be unsatisfactory for legal analysis. The criticism of the economists' incomplete understanding of money in juridical terms in this chapter and elsewhere may be perceived as beside the point – economics is surely a different science with objectives different from law. That may be so, but since money is a creature of the law, economists have to operate within a legal understanding of money as a starting point for their economic studies. Admittedly, this approach may be unpopular with economists.

324 Goldschmidt, *Handbuch des Handelsrechts I* (1868: 1068).

325 Goldschmidt, *Handbuch des Handelsrechts I* (1868: 1190, 1193). In this regard Goldschmidt clearly did not follow H. D. Macleod.

326 See Chapter 2.

327 Goldschmidt, *Handbuch des Handelsrechts I* (1868: 1186–1187).

328 Windscheid also followed Goldschmidt in his criticism of Savigny's functional theory of money, see Windscheid, *Lehrbuch des Pandektenrechts* (1963: 49) and note 17.

329 Windscheid, *Lehrbuch des Pandektenrechts* (1963: 53) and note 34.

Both lawyers and economists have, with some exceptions, tended to consider money and credit as two different matters. This chapter has shown that money is credit, as it is a debt in law, 'credit' being the debt only from the creditor's perspective. This credit theory of money is not only in accordance with current and long-standing banking law, it is also strongly vindicated by the money creation system of central bank money and commercial bank money. This will be discussed in Chapter 2.

2 The creation of money and its legal basis[1]

1. Theories of money creation or money supply

Creation of money, or more broadly, money supply, is usually seen as a fairly straightforward affair by the general public. In a layperson's view 'money', first and foremost cash, comes particularly from central banks in form of banknotes, and commercial banks record the (cash) deposits by their customers as bank money in their accounts[2] – these deposits out of which the commercial banks then grant loans. This incorrect opinion, generally held by laypeople, including politicians, can then lead to unfortunate economic policy decisions as a result of insufficient understanding of the true situation. To the credit of the non-specialists, however, one has to emphasise that the interpretation of the money supply process has long been controversial, and if one looks at economics textbooks, many economists still do not seem to comprehend it fully. Lawyers, in turn, do not attempt an appreciation of the money supply process because they regard that issue as part of the domain of economics.[3]

Three theories have been advanced for the explanation of the money supply process: (a) the financial intermediation theory of money, (b) the fractional reserve theory, and (c) the credit creation theory of money.[4]

(a) Financial intermediation theory of money

The financial intermediation theory of money comes closest to the layperson's view sketched out above. According to this theory, banks obtain deposits from customers and lend these to borrowers. Thus banks borrow from their depositors with short-term maturities and lend to other customers in form of long-term loans. In such an arrangement banks are only financial intermediaries and

1 This chapter is based on Rahmatian (2018a: 205–236) and follows this article to a large extent.

2 See e.g. the amusing story by Hudson (2013: 893) for an illustration of his own belief as a boy.

3 See discussion of this problem in Chapter 1.

4 See also literature review on these theories by Werner (2014b: 2–12) and Werner (2016: 362–370).

do not differ from other non-bank financial institutions. Banks supply money; they do not create it. This view is plausible to non-specialists, but economists should realise that such an organisation of banks' lending practice could soon lead to liquidity problems of banks or even their collapse if banks are really just intermediaries. And lawyers should notice that the idea that banks are not different from non-bank financial institutions would simply be against the law: as will be detailed below, non-banks taking a deposit or client money have to keep it in a separate client account while banks do not have this legal requirement. Nevertheless, prominent economists have supported the financial intermediation theory,[5] for example Keynes, at first more tentatively in his *Treatise on Money* (1930):[6]

> A banker is in possession of resources which he can lend or invest equal to a large proportion (nearly 90 per cent) of the deposits standing to the credit of his depositors. In so far as his deposits are savings deposits, he is acting merely as an intermediary for the transfer of loan capital. In so far as they are cash deposits, he is acting both as a provider of money for his depositors, and also as a provider of resources for his borrowing customers.

And further:[7]

> What is the true criterion of a creation of credit which shall be non-inflationary? . . . We have found the answer to lie in the preservation of a balance between the rate of saving and the value of investment. That is to say, bankers are only entitled to create credit, without laying themselves open to the charge of inflationary tendencies, if the net effect of such credit creation on the value of new investment is not to raise the value of such investment above the current savings of the public; and, similarly, they will lay themselves open to the charge of deflationary action unless they create enough credit to prevent the value of new investment from falling below the amount of current savings.

This indicates that bankers are not just intermediaries but can create credit. However, they are very much restrained by an equilibrium through self-regulation or being imposed by the monetary policy of central banks, and by a fractional reserve to be maintained and controlled by the central banks. In fact, inflation is not kept low by restraints on lending – and there is not much restriction anyway, otherwise the financial crisis of 2008–9 would have unravelled differently – but because the money created largely does not leave the inter-banking sector; only

5 Detailed overview with quotes by Werner (2014b: 9–12), Werner (2016: 362–364). Werner's specialist account goes beyond the needs for the present discussion.

6 Keynes (2013b: 191).

7 Keynes (2013b: 197).

when it does and a conversion (retransformation) of loan or deposit money into 'real commodities'[8] takes place does it become relevant for inflation.

In his *General Theory* (1936), Keynes abandons any qualifications:[9]

> It is supposed that a depositor and his bank can somehow contrive between them to perform an operation by which savings can disappear into the banking system so that they are lost to investment, or, contrariwise, that the banking system can make it possible for investment to occur, to which no saving corresponds. . . . The notion that the creation of credit by the banking system allows investment to take place to which 'no genuine saving' corresponds can only be the result of isolating one of the consequences of the increased bank-credit to the exclusion of others. . . . No one can be compelled to own the additional money corresponding to the new bank-credit, unless he deliberately prefers to hold more money rather than some other form of wealth. . . . Thus the old-fashioned view that saving always involves investment, though incomplete and misleading, is formally sounder than the new-fangled view that there can be saving without investment or investment without 'genuine' saving.

Keynes's dominance in economics after the Second World War has dwindled away since the 1980s, but his opinion on this point, though inaccurate, has been convenient for the banking sector and has been maintained by most economists. Contrary to Keynes's suggestion, it is of course possible, and indeed inevitable, to save and to have separate unrelated investments, carried out in relation to the same bank, without any connection between the saving deposit and the investing loan. Even if the bank were a financial intermediary only, the customer would have no right to decide whether, of which amount, and to whom a loan out of his deposit is to be granted; the contrary view would presuppose that the deposit is the customer's own money which would contradict well-established banking law.[10] Deposit-investment and loan-investment are necessarily separate, and the depositor cannot 'contrive' anything with his bank.

(b) Fractional reserve theory of money

The fractional reserve theory of money, which the first extract from Keynes (2013a) from 1930 has already mentioned, is a considerable qualification of the financial intermediation theory. One could be tempted to see it as a bridge to the credit creation theory, but it is still a species of the financial intermediation theory because it also presupposes banks as essentially financial intermediaries, however with the ability to create money by way of loans. According to this theory it is not the individual bank but the banking sector as whole from a

8 On this point and on this term, see Chapter 4, discussing the alienation cycle.

9 Keynes (1964: 81–83).

10 *Foley v. Hill* (1848) 2 HLC 28.

macroeconomic perspective which creates money through the mechanics of the fractional reserve system. C. A. Phillips said in 1920: 'What is true for the banking system as an aggregate is not true for an individual bank that constitutes only one of many units in that aggregate'.[11] Before his *General Theory* (1936), Keynes also described approvingly the fractional reserve system in his *Treatise on Money* (1930):[12]

> A bank must . . . first of all decide what amount of reserves it will be prudent to aim at . . . each bank fixes in its own mind on a certain proportion of its deposits (e.g. 10 per cent) which it will aim at keeping in reserve. . . . Having fixed on this proportion, the bank will then be as unwilling to see its reserves rise above it, since this generally means that it is doing less profitable business than it might, as to see them fall below it. Consequently it will be actively creating deposits by lending and investing on a small or on a larger scale, according to its reserves. . . .
>
> We now perceive that there exists, not only the check on individual banks that they must keep step, but also a check on the banks as a whole. For if the banks as a whole are creating deposits at a rate which will cause the reserves as a whole to fall too low, some bankers will find their reserve ratios deficient and will, therefore, be compelled to take a step backwards; whilst if the aggregate deposits are below their normal ratio to reserves, some banks will find their reserve ratios excessive and will be stimulated to take a step forwards. Thus it is the aggregate of the reserve resources which determines the 'pace' which is common to the banking system as a whole. . . .
>
> There can be no doubt that, in the most convenient use of language, all deposits are 'created' by the bank holding them. . . . But it is equally clear that the rate at which an individual bank creates deposits on its own initiative is subject to certain rules and limitations; – it must keep step with the other banks and cannot raise its own deposits relatively to the total deposits out of proportion to its quota of the banking business of the country. . . . the 'pace' common to all the member banks is governed by the aggregate of their reserve resources.

Thus according to Keynes, banks also withdraw from their deposits at the central bank ('reserve resources') in order to lend money, though with caution in order not to upset the equilibrium between aggregate deposits and aggregate reserves. Only a 'multiple deposit expansion' (Paul Samuelson)[13] allows the banks in aggregate to create money; an individual bank is unable to do that: the size of its loans is still confined to its deposits received. The fractional reserve system with its 'money multiplier' approach is typically discussed at length in economics textbooks, so that a brief outline suffices for present purposes, particularly since

11 Quoted in Werner (2016: 364).
12 Keynes (2013a: 25–26).
13 Werner (2014b: 8).

the legal theory of money put forward in this book does not accept the fractional reserve theory of money anyway, and even the Bank of England has rejected it fairly recently.[14]

Money creation through bank credit will be explained in detail below.[15] The fractional reserve theory claims that money creation is restricted by the operation of the money multiplier. If customer A deposits cash, say 100, in a bank account, this does not have an effect on the money supply because the cash has been converted into a claim of customer A against the bank to pay out on demand.[16] Then, according to the fractional reserve theory, the bank retains a certain amount of A's deposit, say, 10% as reserves and lends out the rest, that is, 90, to B, by way of a cash payment. At this stage, the money supply is increased because in addition to the 100 as debt of the bank against A, 90 in form of cash are put into circulation. B can then use the cash to buy goods from C, and C may then deposit the received 90 in cash in his bank account (with the same or another bank). The bank holding C's account can then take 90% of the 90 (10% are retained as a reserve) to lend these 81 to D, paying out in cash, and D can buy goods for 81, so that the recipient of 81 in cash can deposit that amount with his bank, which, in turn has 90%, or 72.9 available for a new loan. And so forth: 100 – 10% = 90 – 10% = 81 – 10% = 72.9 – 10% = 65.61 – 10% = 59.049. Thus the money supply has been increased from 100, the initial deposit, to 100 + 90 + 81 + 72.9 + 65.61 + 59.049.[17]

The calculation of the money supply is more complicated in reality,[18] but the present simplified sketch explains the principles sufficiently well. Information brochures of central banks use very similar examples.[19] If we assume that the required fraction of the deposits in reserve is 10%, this means that a loan of 100 does not make available an amount of 100 for further loans that can be deposited with this or another bank, but only 90. The reserve ratio is therefore 10% or 1/10, or put differently, the money multiplier is 10, being the reciprocal of the reserve ratio of 1/10 in the present example. According to the fractional reserve theory of money, central banks supposedly influence the amount of money created by changing the reserve ratio: the higher it is, the less banks can lend, and the smaller the money multiplier, so that the money supply is decreased.[20] Economics textbooks still describe the process of money creation and the assumed influence of the central bank in this way.[21] The Bank of England itself, however, has recently called such a power of the central bank a 'common misconception'.[22]

14 Bank of England (2014a: 15).
15 See below under secs. 2 and 3.
16 *Foley v. Hill* (1848) 2 HLC 28.
17 Krugman and Wells (2015: 864–867); Mankiw (2015: 628–631).
18 Krugman and Wells (2015: 867–869).
19 See e.g. the instructive examples by the Deutsche Bundesbank, ch. 4 (2008: 61) and by the Federal Reserve Bank of Chicago (1994: 5–11).
20 Mankiw (2012: 629, 630, 634).
21 Mankiw (2012: 627–632), Krugman and Wells (2015: 864–868).
22 Bank of England (2014a: 15).

Furthermore, the stated reserve of 10% in the preceding example is a rather arbitrary assumption. Capital adequacy rules do require that commercial banks must hold a fraction of their total deposits with the central bank, either as sight deposits of the commercial bank with the central bank, or as cash which is also a debt of the central bank owed to the commercial bank or to whoever who holds the notes (historically to be redeemed in gold before the abolition of the gold standard).[23] In reality, the obligatory minimum reserve is often well below 10% and depends on the type of liability. In the EU (eurozone), under Regulation (EC) 1745/2003, the required reserve ratio is 2%, but for deposits with agreed maturity over two years or redeemable at notice over two years it is 0%.[24] The capital adequacy requirements in the EU follow, and go beyond, the Basel Accord (now Basel III).[25] They have been criticised as ineffective because they are based on the theory that banks are financial intermediaries,[26] that is, banks lend out of their customers' deposits, which the fractional reserve theory also presupposes.

The narrative of money creation with fractional banking is still predominant among economists, and even the Bank of England, despite having endorsed the credit creation theory of money (see below) in 2014,[27] still seems to have adherents of the financial intermediation theories (simple and fractional reserve) among its staff.[28] However, not all economists have supported the fractional reserve banking conception but have considered it as removed from reality and misleading, even before the financial crisis of 2008, for example Howells and Bain.[29] They criticise that this model presupposes that the central bank sets the quantity, but in fact it sets the price. Since the central bank sets the rate of interest (the price of reserves), it must then supply the reserves that banks require and that depends on the demand for new loans and deposits at the going rate of interest which is, in turn, determined by the state of the economy, not by the central bank. The Bank of England has taken the same view and added that 'neither are reserves a binding constraint on lending, nor does the central bank fix the amount of reserves that are available'.[30] Keynes's idea of an equilibrium between aggregate deposits and aggregate reserves also appears to be artificial

23 Crowther (1946: 48), Binswanger (2013: 40) and note 3.

24 Regulation (EC) 1745/2003 of the European Central Bank on the application of minimum reserves of 12 September 2003 (ECB/2003/9) OJ L 250/10 (as amended by Regulation (EU) No 1376/2014 of the European Central Bank of 10 December 2014 amending Regulation (EC) No 1745/2003, OJ L 366/79), Art. 4. The minimum reserves are to be held with the respective national central bank of each EU member state according to Art. 6. See also European Central Bank: www.ecb.europa.eu/ecb/legal/1002/1015/html/index.en.html (visited 21 April 2018).

25 Basel Committee on Banking Supervision, *Basel III: A global regulatory framework for more resilient banks and banking systems*, pp. 55–56, Pt. 129, 131. See also Cranston et al. (2017: 45–49) for more detail.

26 E.g. Werner (2014a: 76).

27 Bank of England (2014a: 14–15).

28 Werner (2016: 370).

29 Howells and Bain (2005: 241).

30 Bank of England (2014a: 15).

theory, although the idea of an equilibrium is generally very much in the toolkit of the economist's trade. The fractional reserve system has a certain relevance in banking practice,[31] but it does not explain properly the money creation process and should not be given too much emphasis.

(c) Credit creation theory of money

The credit creation theory of money denies any correlation between money in depositors' deposits and money provided by loans and therefore emphasises that banks do not use customers' deposits to grant loans. In contrast, banks create money by giving credit: 'Whenever a bank makes a loan, it simultaneously creates a matching deposit in the borrower's bank account, thereby creating new money'.[32] Banks are not financial intermediaries at all, neither individually (financial intermediation theory) nor in aggregate (fractional reserve theory). Schumpeter describes the money creation process in this way:[33]

> It is much more realistic to say that the banks 'create credit', that is, that they create deposits in their act of lending, than to say that they lend deposits that have been entrusted to them. . . . The theory to which economists clung so tenaciously makes [depositors] out to be savers when they neither save nor intend to do so; it attributes to them an influence on the 'supply of credit' which they do not have.

The credit creation theory is not the newest of the three theories of money supply; it can rather be traced back to the nineteenth century and was only eclipsed by the other two theories, particularly after the Second World War. In the eighteenth century, 'credit' was still associated with moral ideas of 'trust' and 'confidence' between businessmen, not just with legal claim or debt, for example in the *Essay on Credit* by Pelatiah Webster of Philadelphia (1786):[34]

> A *bank* is a large repository of cash, deposited under the direction of proper officers . . . for the purpose of establishing and supporting a great and extensive credit, to be made use of in every case where an established credit will answer in exchange or payment, as well as cash, or better than cash, as in many circumstances will manifestly and undoubtedly be the case.

It is not without irony that the credit creation theory relies on the trust by the public for its functioning, but once this theory of money creation is explained, that trust may be waning. This presumably did not endear it to economists; Schumpeter was rather an exception. In the late nineteenth century, H. D. Macleod was

31 See e.g. Crowther (1946: 45). See also below under sec. 3(b).
32 Bank of England (2014a: 14). Further discussion below under sec. 3.
33 Schumpeter (1954: 1114).
34 Webster (1786: 9–10), see also p. 3 on a definition of credit in the commercial context.

one of the first who put forward the conception of the credit creation theory. First, he postulated that *money is credit* – the *credit theory* of money:[35]

> Money and Credit . . . are both of the same nature: they are each a Right or Title to demand something to be paid or done by someone else. . . . when . . . a person has voluntarily exchanged anything for Money, it is in reality only Credit; because he only takes it because he thinks that he can exchange it away again.

Then Macleod set out the credit *creation* theory of money. He said about banks specifically:[36]

> Nothing can be more unfortunate or misleading than the expression which is so frequently used that banking is only the 'Economy of Capital', and that the business of a banker is to borrow money from one set of persons and lend it to another set. Bankers, no doubt, do collect sums from a vast number of persons, but the peculiar essence of their business is, not to lend that money to other persons, but on the basis of this bullion to create a vast superstructure of Credit; to multiply their promises to pay many times: these Credits being payable on demand and performing all the functions of an equal amount of cash. Thus banking is not an Economy of Capital, but an increase of Capital; the business of banking is not to lend money, but to create Credit: and by means of the Clearing House these Credits are now transferred from one bank to another, just as easily as a Credit is transferred from one account to another in the same bank by means of a cheque. And all these Credits are in the ordinary language and practice of commerce exactly equal to so much cash or Currency.

It is appropriate to quote this passage in full, because it contains the essence of the argument in the present book. A lawyer may add that credits and the amounts of cash or currency which they correspond to are debts or instances of dematerialised property,[37] the method by which law incorporates these phenomena into its own system.

Macleod's analysis of money as credit has had a predecessor in Henry Thornton from 1802,[38] and even in the eighteenth century Richard Cantillon had a clear understanding of the notion of banks' credit.[39] Nevertheless, the idea that

35 Macleod (1883: 45).

36 Macleod (1886: 311).

37 See Chapter 1.

38 Arnon (2011: 104), Schumpeter (1954: 719).

39 Cantillon writes in his *Essai sur la Nature du Commerce en Général* (1755) in Part 3, chapter 6: 'In the national Banks of Venice and Amsterdam payment is made only in book credit, but in that of London it is made in credit, in notes, and in money at the choice of the individuals, and it is today the strongest Bank'.

money is simply credit granted by a bank has not been accepted easily. In 1914, A. M. Innes, a follower of the credit theory of money, saw the need to reinforce and elucidate the concept of 'credit':[40]

> The present writer [Innes] is not the first to enunciate the Credit Theory of money. This distinction belongs to that remarkable economist H. D. Macleod . . . [who] alone saw that money was to be identified with credit. . . . Macleod wrote in advance of his time and the want of accurate historical knowledge prevented his realising that credit was more ancient than the earliest use of metal coins. . . . he was unable to formulate the basic theory that a sale and purchase is the exchange of a commodity for a credit and not for a piece of metal or any other tangible property. In that theory lies the essence of the whole science of money.

Innes's and Macleod's definition of money as credit has been adopted for the legal theory of money expounded in this book,[41] both in relation to the concept of dematerialised property with money as one practical example,[42] in respect of the credit *creation* theory of money which presupposes Innes's view,[43] and with regard to the conceptualisation of the exchange between commodity and money in a contract of sale.[44] Schumpeter has accepted the credit creation theory;[45] Keynes, as we have seen, has not.

The following discussion proceeds on the basis of the credit creation theory of money. The *ex nihilo* creation of money that ensues from the credit creation theory[46] may have been unsettling, which has presumably contributed to the rejection of this theory by most economists, possibly even until today. However, the credit creation theory of money is the only theory that is in agreement with banking law, in the UK at least since 1848.[47] It has also been confirmed as the only correct theory by the Bank of England in 2014 (which disapproved of both the financial intermediation theory and the fractional reserve theory),[48] and, following the Bank of England, by the British Parliament in a debate devoted to money creation.[49] Hence a lawyer cannot actually speak of a credit (creation) *theory* of

40 Innes (1914: 159).
41 See also Commons (1924: 246) on Macleod.
42 See Chapter 1.
43 See below under secs. 2 and 3.
44 See Chapter 3, sec. 1 and particularly Chapter 4.
45 Schumpeter (1954: 1113–1115), and footnote 5 at pp. 1114–1115.
46 See below under sec. 3(b).
47 *Foley v. Hill* (1848) 2 HLC 28, and the discussion further below.
48 Bank of England (2014a: 15).
49 Hansard, House of Commons, Debate: 'Money Creation and Society', HC 20 November 2014, Vol. 588, col. 434.

money, because it is not just a theory: money *is* (circulating) credit, or – which is the equivalent – a debt.[50]

2. The creation of money by central banks

Less than 5% of all money in the economy is created by central banks, but it is that form of money which the general public would usually associate with the term 'money', that is, cash. A central bank, such as the Bank of England, is the banks' bank because a commercial bank needs to have operational accounts with the central bank, in order to keep reserves (as the fractional reserve theory of money prominently stresses), and to settle debts by netting payments due to other banks against those to itself.[51] Netting, a form of set-off, is usually done among the banks via their accounts with the central bank. In addition, settlement (transfer of value to discharge a payment obligation) between banks within one jurisdiction can be done across the books of the central bank since both banks involved maintain accounts with the central bank.[52] The central bank is also the government's banker in that the central bank performs the bank services for the government that commercial banks provide for their customers.[53]

Furthermore, the central bank is lender of last resort by providing extra reserves to a bank in difficulties or to avoid a breakdown of the banking system as a whole in an economic crisis.[54] For example, as a first step towards the government bail-out of the failing Royal Bank of Scotland (RBS) during the financial crisis in 2008–9, the Bank of England provided Emergency Liquidity Assistance (ELA) to RBS, thus acting as a lender of last resort.[55] However, whether the use of the Bank of England's Emergency Lending Facility is really lending of last resort, and what that term actually means, has been controversial among experts.[56]

50 See particularly under sec. 3 below. On the historical basis of money as credit, see Desan (2014: 331).

51 Cranston (2002: 111), Crowther (1946: 59).

52 On settlement and netting in general, see Cranston et al. (2017: 349–350). See also Crowther (1946: 58–59). Definition of netting in EU Directive 98/26/EC on Settlement Finality in Payment and Securities Settlement Systems, OJ L 166/45, Art. 2(k): '"netting" shall mean the conversion into one net claim or one net obligation of claims and obligations resulting from transfer orders which a participant or participants either issue to, or receive from, one or more other participants with the result that only a net claim can be demanded or a net obligation be owed'.

53 Cranston (2002: 111–112).

54 Bagehot, chapter 7, section 2 (1873: 187–207); Cranston (2002: 110–111).

55 Financial Services Authority, *The Failure of the Royal Bank of Scotland. Financial Services Authority Report*, December 2011, p. 94, para. 111; Chris Giles, Norma Cohen, Patrick Jenkins, 'Bank secretly lent RBS and HBOS £61.6bn', *Financial Times*, 24 November 2009.

56 A. Milne, 'Can Central Bank Provision of Market Liquidity Create a Problem of Moral Hazard?', in Franco Bruni and David T. Llewellyn (eds.) (2009), 'The Failure of Northern Rock: A Multi-Dimensional Case Study', SUERF – The European Money and Finance Forum Vienna, p. 176, available at www.suerf.org/docx/s_5d6646aad9bcc0be55b2c

The principal practical purpose of central banks today is exercising monetary policy (especially ensuring monetary stability),[57] a central aspect for bankers and economists[58] but little relevant for the legal concept of money that is discussed here.

The most important role of the central bank in the present context is the central bank's privilege to issue banknotes,[59] or more generally, currency. The right to issue coins may also be given to central banks, or, as in Britain, to a special body, the Royal Mint with the Chancellor of the Exchequer as its master.[60] In the Eurozone, the European Central Bank exclusively authorises the issue of banknotes and approves the quantity of coins issued by the EU member states.[61] Since coins are not conceptually different from other money created by central banks and since they play an insignificant role in economic terms (only about 6% of the currency in circulation), they are disregarded in the further discussion.

A banknote issued by the central bank represents a debt of the issuing central bank expressed by the face value. With the abolition of the gold standard, conversion into gold or any other commodity of value is no longer possible. That makes the debt self-referential because the promise to pay is redeemed with further promises to pay.[62] Therefore the debt is never repaid but 'eternal'.[63] Cash (banknotes), whether circulating or held by commercial banks, as well as deposits of the commercial banks with the central bank are all liabilities of the central bank.[64] Banknotes and coins (currency) and bank deposits of customers with commercial banks are sometimes referred to as 'broad money',[65] while currency and central bank reserves (debts of the central bank to the commercial banks keeping deposits with the central bank) are usually called 'base money' or 'central

---

82f69750387_2141_suerf.pdf (visited 28 April 2018). The example here was the lending facility provided to the UK Northern Rock bank which it faced a bank run in August 2007. Since discretionary loans by central banks or governments are always a possibility, the label 'lender of last resort' has little distinguishing power. On the various 'myths' about the lender of last resort, see Goodhart (2002: 229, 234, 241).

57 Cranston (2002: 115–122).

58 Bank of England (2014a: 20), Mankiw (2012: 632).

59 In England the Bank of England alone is authorised to issue banknotes, see Currency and Bank Notes Act 1954, s. 1. Three Scottish banks have preserved their right to issue their own banknotes which are, however, not legal tender in Scotland (only coins are), see Bank Notes (Scotland) Act 1845, c. 38 (8 & 9 Vict.), now largely repealed by the Banking Act 2009, s. 214 (2). See for the relationship between the central bank (Bank of England) and the Scottish banks with regard to the currency, Rahmatian (2012: 338–339). A similar privilege to issue separate banknotes exists for Northern Ireland, see Banking Act 2009, ss. 210, 214(1).

60 UK Coinage Act 1971, ss. 1 and 4.

61 Art. 128(1) TFEU: 'The European Central Bank shall have the exclusive right to authorise the issue of euro banknotes within the Union. The European Central Bank and the national central banks may issue such notes'. Art. 128(2) TFEU: 'Member States may issue euro coins subject to approval by the European Central Bank of the volume of the issue'.

62 Crowther (1946: 62–63), Bank of England (2014b: 8), Mann (1992: 40–41).

63 Binswanger (2013: 40).

64 Crowther (1946: 59–60).

65 See also Chapter 1 for the definitions of money.

bank money'.[66] Here we are concerned with central bank money. When commercial banks need additional banknotes, for example to pay customers withdrawing from their accounts, or to pay out in cash a loan granted, they reduce their credit balance with the central bank (central bank reserves) and increase their liability, provided the commercial banks obtain that cash from the central bank directly and not from other banks on the money market.[67] Since payments in and out of a bank in central bank money tend to coincide over a given period of time, the bank only needs to hold a small amount of central bank money to maintain its liquidity. Hence commercial banks can function with much reduced cash balances compared to non-bank enterprises. Commercial banks can also counteract peaks in payment by purchasing central bank money, and the central bank can always provide additional money to the commercial banks, usually through repurchase agreements which operate as credits to the banks. As central bank money is an eternal, non-redeemable debt, the central bank can always act as a lender of last resort if a commercial bank faces liquidity difficulties and requires central bank money.[68]

The central bank can increase or reduce the quantity of money issued to the public.[69] The money supply can be regulated or, more accurately, influenced by changing the quantity of reserves (purchase/sale of government bonds, lending of reserves to banks) or through changes of the reserve ratio of banks with the central bank. Economics textbooks still stress these interventions as principal regulatory measures for central banks.[70]

It follows from the foregoing discussion that central bank money is also 'credit', both in relation to currency or cash (notes and coins) and in relation to central bank reserves. With regard to currency, the creditor is the holder of the banknote[71] (which he may use to pay another debt), but the quality as credit has become academic because a meaningful discharge never occurs and is not even systemically intended. Nobody is entitled to repayment of the debt in gold or otherwise, and realistically the central bank cannot seek repayment from the ministry of finance or the state either (since the central bank's cash debt/liability

66 Bank of England (2014b: 7).

67 Crowther (1946: 47), Binswanger (2013: 40) and note 3. Binswanger (2009: 118), note 1. The German original is clearer than the English translation of Binswanger (2013: 40). There are further ways in which a bank can increase its cash holding, such as by selling secondary liquid assets, for example rediscountable bills and securities. A rise in demand of banknotes is often levelled out through the inter-banking clearing system because payments in and payments out tend to counterbalance over any one period.

68 Binswanger (2013: 40) and note 3 with a quote from the dissertation (1977) of Binswanger's well-known former PhD student, Josef Ackermann, CEO of the Deutsche Bank until 2012. See also Goodhart (2002: 233–234).

69 Crowther (1946: 62). In the UK restrictions on the increase for the Bank of England by the Currency Act 1983, s. 2 (fiduciary note issue, i.e. the issue of banknotes is backed by securities deposited with the Bank of England by the government).

70 E.g. Mankiw (2012: 632–635).

71 See e.g. Ugolini (2017: 172).

to the cash holder is ultimately a credit to the state, usually backed by securities deposited with the central bank).[72]

Although the debt of the central bank represented by a banknote and expressed by its face value is self-referential and nugatory in commercial terms, there are rare occasions when it is not. This was the case in the *Banco de Portugal* decision,[73] already discussed.[74] The damages did not constitute the paper and printing costs of the issue of banknotes which the central bank later had to withdraw; they amounted to the face value of the banknotes that had to be withdrawn after they had been issued as a result of a fraud, though the banknotes were not forgeries themselves. Thus the damage lies in the destroyed debt represented by the banknotes that had to be withdrawn, and therefore the debt in this case is not nugatory but gives rise to an equivalent damages claim. That is irrespective of whether the actual debt has to be redeemed in gold or in other paper currency – the debt as such remains. The House of Lords made that quite clear:

> The Bank . . . is bound to pay on its note; but it need only pay its note in currency, i.e. in its own notes; and if it will not or cannot so pay, it can be sued for the face value of the note.[75]

There is no theoretical reason why issued and circulating currency must be conceptualised as a debt/credit, but the Bank of England was set up in 1694 as an entity whose subscribers financed credit to be given to the government – a loan of £1,200,000 to the government at 8% interest.[76] This model of central banking seems to have been copied in most other states. Moreover, the Bank of England – different from the earlier Bank of Genoa and Bank of Amsterdam which were models to some extent – took deposits (and gave bills/promissory notes in return)[77] for no other purpose than that of trading with them. 'It coined, in short, its own credit into paper money'.[78] The paper money of the Bank of England became legal tender only in 1833,[79] but the principal idea existed right from the beginning, and one can see the difference when one compares 'paper credit' (cash) with a usual loan between private parties. In case of an ordinary loan the potential lender can decide whether or not to lend in the first place, and a trade with/transfer of the credit that the loan constitutes is not normally

72 In the UK this is regulated by the Currency Act 1983, s. 2, and a statutory instrument by the Treasury (fiduciary note issue).

73 *Banco de Portugal v. Waterloo & Sons* [1932] AC 452.

74 Chapter 1, sec. 4.

75 *Banco de Portugal v. Waterloo & Sons* [1932] AC 452, at 487–488 per Lord Atkin.

76 Bank of England Act 1694 (actually Tunnage Act 1694 which contained the sections on the foundation of the Bank of England), s. 18 (repealed), on the authorisation to take subscriptions for £1,200,000, subsequently to be lent to the English government, i.e. the Exchequer, see Clapham (1944: 17–20), Richards (1929: 145), Desan (2014: 304–308).

77 On the exact historical types of notes of the Bank of England, see Clapham (1944: 21–22).

78 Rogers (1887: 9). See also Desan (2014: 304).

79 Bank of England Act 1833, s. 6.

envisaged, but rather repayment of the loan is intended. A transfer can however be made with a negotiable instrument, such as a bill of exchange, but then the potential recipient of the instrument can decide whether he wants to become holder and new creditor of the loan, and if he transfers further, he incurs secondary liability through indorsement of the bill, unless it is a bearer bill. In contrast, the holder of a banknote has no choice but to become creditor,[80] and furthermore, creditor of a credit never to be repaid: this is the effect of the fiat money system.

Another form of central bank money besides currency (banknote or coin) are the central bank reserves, that is, the credit balance commercial banks hold with the central bank. This is 'actual credit': a debt which the central bank *must* settle – by way of cash. In this situation the credit in the deposit is exchanged by the credit the banknotes represent[81] (unless the commercial bank wants to obtain the cash on the money market and not from the central bank). The creditor of this different debt is any one holder of the banknote (initially the commercial bank withdrawing from its actual credit with the central bank), but he cannot seek effective settlement of this debt, as it is fiat money. If the commercial banks withdraw from their central bank reserves, the commercial banks' credit in the deposit with the central bank is reduced by the amount of the withdrawal in cash. The central bank reserves balance, an electronic record that is adjusted according to the amount of reserves swapped for cash,[82] is conceptually only a form of bank money.[83] This is the parallel situation to customers withdrawing cash from their bank accounts with their commercial banks. However, in contrast to the credit of central bank money, the credit or debt that commercial bank money constitutes is very real.

3. The creation of money by commercial banks

(a) The creation of bank money in the banks' accounts

The legal starting point is the House of Lords decision of *Foley v. Hill*,[84] which was already discussed when the concept of bank money was explained.[85] When a customer deposits money (cash or bank money) in his bank account, it becomes the bank's money, and the customer becomes creditor of the bank, the amount of the credit being the amount of the money deposited. The bank's debt consists in

80 However, he cannot incur any secondary liability in relation to the debt embodied in the banknote because the banknote is a bearer instrument. Furthermore, he is creditor of a credit already granted, he does not grant credit himself; the claim out of the existing credit is only transferred to him, see Mises (1953: 272).

81 Bank of England (2014b: 11).

82 Bank of England (2014b: 11).

83 That bank money is 'transferred' between the commercial banks' central bank reserves to settle their debts between them (netting). On the 'transfer' of bank money in general, see Chapter 1, sec. 3(b)(iii).

84 *Foley v. Hill* (1848) 2 HLC 28.

85 See Chapter 1, sec. 3.

the repayment of the sum deposited (plus interest, if stipulated), and with a current account that entails the obligation to repay on demand. The requirement of a demand for payment out of a bank account makes the difference to an ordinary loan[86] whereby the bank as debtor would have to find its customer (creditor) to arrange repayment of the money.[87] Otherwise loan and bank account deposit/credit are conceptually the same, especially in economic terms. After deposit and before repayment, the bank can deal with the money as it sees fit and the customer is unsecured creditor of his bank in relation to the money debt owed to him. In particular, the bank is not trustee of the customer in relation to the money deposited. As Atkin LJ put it (following the principles of *Foley v. Hill*) in *Joachimson v. Swiss Bank Corporation*:[88]

> The bank undertakes to receive money and to collect bills for its customer's account. The proceeds so received are not to be held in trust for the customer, but the bank borrows the proceeds and undertakes to repay them. [The contract] includes a promise to repay any part of the amount due against the written order of the customer addressed to the bank at the branch. . . . it is necessarily a term of such contract that the bank is not liable to pay the customer the full amount of his balance until he demands payment from the bank at the branch at which the current account is kept.

Thus there is only a debtor-creditor relationship between bank and customer and the bank is not the customer's trustee. Because of that, the bank need not hold the customer's money in separate trustee accounts as would normally be required for trustees. This is essential for the creation of money by commercial banks.[89]

When a bank grants a loan, it credits the customer's bank account (either an existing one or a newly opened one) with the loan amount as a deposit. In this way the bank also indebts itself to the customer-borrower at the same time, because this amount appears like a customer's deposit as if the customer pays money into his bank account. The difference is that in case of a loan the amount does not come from the customer, but is created by the bank: this amount is the new money, created by the bank giving the loan. Or, to repeat the statement by the Bank of England: 'Whenever a bank makes a loan, it simultaneously creates a matching deposit in the borrower's bank account, thereby creating new money'.[90] As we have seen already in the discussion of the credit creation theory of money,[91] this is really new money *created* by the bank, not existing money provided by the bank, for example from savings deposits. This money is bank

86 *Joachimson v. Swiss Bank Corporation* [1921] 3 KB 110 (CA), at 127–128 per Atkin LJ (as he then was).

87 *Bradford Old Bank Ltd. v. Sutcliffe* [1918] 2 KB 833, at 848–849.

88 *Joachimson v. Swiss Bank Corporation* [1921] 3 KB 110 (CA), at 127.

89 See below under (b).

90 Bank of England (2014a: 14).

91 See above under sec. 1.

money, and the way in which it comes into existence is a result of the legal principles of the bank-customer relationship in *Foley v. Hill* and of general principles of accounting. Under *Foley v. Hill*, payment into an account makes the bank debtor and the customer unsecured creditor.[92] The loan money is credit and the borrower is creditor in that he can dispose of the money, for example by way of giro transfer, when he wants to pay a seller. In principle he can also make a cash withdrawal (depending on the conditions of the loan). The bank has to honour the obligation to effect a money (giro) transfer order or to pay out in cash. Since the money in the bank account has not originally been provided by the customer but lent by the bank, the customer-borrower is at the same time debtor under the loan agreement and the bank-lender is creditor. Thus as account holder the customer is creditor; as borrower he is debtor; the bank is debtor as account provider and creditor as lender.

This combination of creditor-debtor relations is invariably reflected in the system of accounting. Money, also bank money, is credit (that is, a claim in law[93] from the creditor's perspective) or a debt (from the debtor's perspective). Accordingly are the accounting entries: when the loan is agreed, the loan amount appears on the liability side of the bank's balance sheet because the loan has not yet been made available to the borrower, but the bank has the obligation to do so under the loan contract. When the loan sum is then made available by the bank, it appears on the assets side of the bank's balance sheet because the borrower incurs the obligation to repay the loan. But the liability side of the bank's balance sheet remains unchanged because the bank remains debtor in relation to the loan amount, as the loan is paid into the borrower's bank account and therefore must appear as credit in the borrower's bank account (i.e. the application of *Foley v. Hill*). This means that making available the loan money does not discharge the bank's liability. The bank cannot discharge its liability because its liability is the customer's loan appearing as credit in his bank account, otherwise there is no loan money.[94] This shows again that money is a debt: anyone who is in credit (savings, loan money) must necessarily have a debtor, here the bank. From the position of the bank, bank assets and liability increase by the same amount, so this is only a lengthening of the bank's balance sheet.[95] No funds from elsewhere are made available; the amount by which the balance sheet has been lengthened is the new money. The credit money does not come from existing customer's deposits,[96] and a recent empirical study of the accounting entries of a real loan

92 *Foley v. Hill* (1848) 2 HLC 28, at 36–37.

93 On the terminology used here – claim (from the creditor's side) and debt (from the debtor's side) under an obligation, modelled upon French and German law, but uncommon in English law, see Chapter 1, sec. 2(a)(ii).

94 Consequently, if the loan is repaid, the deposit that the loan money constitutes is destroyed and therefore the money is destroyed, see Bank of England (2014a: 16).

95 Werner (2014a: 74), Lautenbach (1952: 45).

96 A relatively early clear statement in Federal Reserve Bank of Chicago (1994: 6): '[Banks] do not really pay out loans from the money they receive as deposits. If they did this, no additional money would be created' (original version 1961).

contract with a smaller German bank has also confirmed this apparently controversial fact.[97] Nor does the aggregate quantity of central bank reserves directly constrain the volume of lending/deposit creation of the commercial banks.[98] Thus the simplified balance sheet of a commercial bank before making the loan may look like this:

Assets	*Liabilities*
Loans Reserves with Central Bank (including cash held by commercial bank) Securities (shares, negotiable instruments etc.)	Deposits by non-banks Loans by other banks Own capital

After the loan (of 100) has been made available, the simplified account of the bank/lender is:

Assets	*Liabilities*
Loan to borrower +100	Borrower deposit +100

The account of the customer/borrower is:

Assets	*Liabilities*
Loan deposit +100	Loan from bank +100

The balance sheet of the bank does not change when the loan amount is made available (or 'paid out'), no balance is drawn down when the borrower's account is credited with the loan money. The crediting of the borrower's account is the new money, because, in contrast to a non-bank,[99] that credit does not correspondingly reduce the balance of any other accounts of the bank from which the lent funds would derive: the money (in form of bank money) is indeed created 'out of nothing', through accounting entries ('fountain pen money').[100] The bank's balance sheet remains lengthened.[101]

97 Werner (2014b: 13–16) with the exact accounts.
98 Bank of England (2014a: 16).
99 This difference is discussed below under (b).
100 Tobin (1963: 1): '[A] long line of financial heretics have been right in speaking of "fountain pen money", money created by the stroke of the bank president's pen when he approves a loan and credits the proceeds to the borrower's checking account'.
101 Werner (2014a: 74).

Thus banks grant credit by indebting themselves, and the borrower pays his debts with the debts of the bank.[102] The present description of the accounts is a simplified outline because it does not state the exact accounting entries and phases of the double-entry accounting events, and it also disregards the usual interest payment obligation on the loan.[103]

The treatment of bank money creation in the accounts – or one may say, through the accounts – is ultimately also the outcome of the system of double-entry accounting,[104] or the Venetian style of bookkeeping which had been practised in Venice probably from the late 1300s.[105] It became the principal method of bookkeeping after the publication of the first textbook on bookkeeping by the Renaissance mathematician Luca Pacioli (or Paciolo) in 1494, the *Summa de Arithmetica, Geometria, Proportioni et Proportionalita*, which contains the bookkeeping treatise. In line with Renaissance thinking of his time, Pacioli believed in the interrelatedness of disciplines and the special importance of harmony and balance, proportion and symmetry, as expressed in the sciences, arts and architecture,[106] and he also wrote *De Divina Proportione* (1497) for which Leonardo da Vinci helped prepare the drawings.[107] Hence the books must balance to give effect to the harmony, symmetry and proportion of the world order.[108] In relation to cash and bank money payments, that appears as follows:[109]

> If you put money in the bank, debit the bank . . . and credit cash. . . . [Now] suppose that you are the banker. . . . When you pay, debit the particular person to whom payment is made and credit your cash. If your creditor (without withdrawing money) should order payment to somebody else, say in the Journal: 'Debit that particular creditor, credit the person to whom the money was assigned, etc.'. In this manner, make the transfer from one creditor to another, while still remaining debtor.

102 See Bank of England (2014a: 3), Crowther (1946: 50–52), Binswanger (2013: 41–44), Howells and Bain (2005: 235–239), Deutsche Bundesbank (2017: 75–82), Eucken (1959: 163), Werner (2014a: 71–74).

103 A rather detailed step-by-step description by Werner (2014a: 72–74). Other presentations of the accounts, simplified but more detailed than here, e.g. by Bank of England (2014a: 3), Binswanger (2013: 41–43), Jarchow (2010: 14–17).

104 In the double entry system, each accounting event is recorded twice, so that the accounting equation Assets = Liabilities + Owners' Equity remains in balance, see e.g. Ainsworth and Deines (2007: 181).

105 Chatfield (1977: 36–38, 41–42).

106 Hale (1971: 269–270).

107 Chatfield (1977: 45).

108 Pacioli, chapter 1 (1963: 26): 'How to keep accounts and books will be illustrated in order that each thing can easily be found in its proper place. . . . As the saying goes, "Where there is no order, there is chaos."' In the context of a Renaissance mathematician, 'chaos' can be understood in its (neo)platonic and biblical sense.

109 Pacioli, chapter 24 (1963: 76, 78).

This does not describe a bank loan but a cash deposit/withdrawal from a bank account and a (bank) money transfer. However, the kernel of the accounting entries for a bank loan is already visible. If the loan were provided in cash (nowadays never), the banker would credit the customer-borrower and debit his own cash (the exact opposite of Pacioli's scenario). If the loan were provided as bank money by transfer, from an account of the lending bank to an account of the customer-borrower, as it were, the bank (transferor) would have to be debited and the customer (transferee) credited because he would receive the money. But in relation to whom is the banker creditor since he has credit (subsequently reduced) on his own bank account? In case of cash, it would be the credit (subsequently reduced) in form of the banker's own gold coins. But in case of bank money, the credit probably comes from nowhere. If the banker does not have a genuine debtor, such as another bank, the banker will have to create the fiction of being his own debtor and creditor, because one can only have credit in an account if there is a debtor (and if he were indeed debtor and creditor in relation to the *same obligation*,[110] then in law that would mean *confusio*: claim and debt of an obligation being united in one person, which extinguishes the obligation).[111] The banker can then only debit his account (when paying out the loan) if he has an account in credit which requires a corresponding debtor. Otherwise the books cannot balance. Anything else is incompatible with the system of double-entry bookkeeping and the harmony, proportion and balance it should present.

The new money, in the form of bank money on the customer's bank account as the loan amount, enters the economy as circulating money with a money transfer order to a third party, or with a cash withdrawal in which case the bank money is transformed into cash. This new money operates as any other cash or bank money: in its nature being credit (and as credit it has come into existence), it has the money functions of medium of exchange, unit of account, means of holding purchase power over time (store of value), at least in a buoyant economy. Once the borrower has obtained the loan, she will pay, for example, the seller of the car sold to her and thereby discharge the debt arising from the contract of sale. However, the debt which the loan-credit *res* also constitutes, stays and is not discharged, including the interest that it incurs,[112] and it remains with her as borrower-debtor of her lending bank, despite the fact that the debt-*res* as money

110 The janiform nature of money (see below under sec. 4) makes it difficult to decide whether there is the same obligation: money is created as a debt through a loan and is that loan contract's debt, but at the same time money operates as circulating credit/debt. So one can see two obligations: the loan obligation and the money-debt obligation. The bank is creditor of the loan obligation (repayment) and debtor of the money payment obligation (account payable regarding the payment of the loan money to the borrower). Technically these are *two* obligations in the hand of one person initially (the bank) where that person is debtor in relation to one and creditor in relation to the other obligation, both 'embodied' in the money. This is not the merger of claim/credit and debt of the *same* obligation in one person which would be the situation of *confusio*.

111 A general legal principle, for example in Roman law as the basis for modern laws: D 46, 3, 75. See Zimmermann (1996: 759).

112 On the issue of interest, see below under sec. 5.

has long been transferred to others. This is a real, enforceable debt that has to be satisfied;[113] it is not like the technical self-referential debt of cash as fiat money (legal tender). This commercial bank debt-*res* or money, either subsequently converted to cash or remaining (hardly) reified as bank money in the accounts of the bank, continues to exist and is, and operates as, money, fully fungible (transferable) and conferring purchase power on any holder at any one time. Schumpeter was correct and straight to the point:[114]

> [A] deposit,[115] though legally only a claim to legal-tender money, serves within very wide limits the same purposes that this money itself would serve. . . . The theory of 'credit creation' not only recognises patent facts without obscuring them by artificial constructions; it also brings out the peculiar mechanism of saving and investment that is . . . the true role of banks in capitalist evolution.

The car seller will deposit the purchase money received in his bank account, either directly (bank money transfer) or after conversion from cash (paying into the account). This deposit is not entirely irrelevant for his bank, in that the creation of money through credit (lending) is subject to some very limited restrictions imposed on the bank,[116] and these capital adequacy requirements also rely in some measure on the amount of money deposited, although this precaution rather serves as a practical psychological measure to maintain public trust in the banks. There is no conceptual legal or accounting connection between customers' deposits and money lent by the bank, as however the fractional reserve theory of money suggests.[117] The car seller's bank can, effectively independent of the car seller's deposit, create new money again by way of giving a loan, either to the car seller, or to another person or company, and the process repeats itself: that new money no. 2 is also added to the quantity of money in the economy in the way described above. Keynes's statement is therefore beside the point: 'No one can be compelled to own the additional money corresponding to the new bank-credit, unless he deliberately prefers to hold more money rather than some other form of wealth'.[118] When someone is handed over cash, he is invariably creditor of a nominal debt reified by the banknote,[119] and when someone deposits money in his bank account, that deposit is separate from any loan/credit the bank may

113 See discussion in Chapter 5, sec. 2 on the enforcement of the money debt.

114 Schumpeter (1954: 1114).

115 The deposit in this context is the loan amount, being a new and independent deposit in the bank account of the borrower.

116 On the reserve requirement and the practical aspects of the fractional reserve theory (money multiplier), see above under sec. 1 and below under (c).

117 See above under sec. 1 and, on the practical relevance of the fractional reserve system, below under sec. 2(c).

118 Keynes, *General Theory* (1964: 81, 83).

119 That *res* is necessarily a debt that itself cannot be discharged meaningfully as it is fiat money, and the recipient can only hope that it will translate later into a real commodity when it operates as a medium of exchange.

grant. The depositor cannot own, or be compelled to own, additional money because there is no correspondence to the new bank credit; that money is freely available on the market as bank money, initially at least.

There is no effective legal regulatory limit to the creation of bank money through loans, and the economic limit is what market confidence is prepared to tolerate. However, the amount of money created through credit does not rise without any restrictions. In particular, loans are not only granted but are also constantly paid back in the economy, often by using newly created money to repay outstanding bank loans. Any discharge of a loan debt means that money is destroyed.[120] Keynes's comment that the amount of credit which banks can create must not upset an equilibrium has some relevance from a practical perspective:

> How much credit has to be created in order to preserve equilibrium . . . depends upon how the credit is being used and upon what is happening to the other monetary factors . . . the test can always be found in the stability or instability of the price level output as a whole.[121]

But there is no real regulatory or conceptual boundary, and the test (if it is one) cannot always be found. The massive increase of the quantity of money created by loans, also with the banking crisis of 2008, has so far not yet influenced substantially the price levels,[122] only that one gets practically no more interest on money deposited on savings accounts, partly because there is an abundance of (bank) money in the economy (together with deflationary tendencies resulting from austerity policy), and partly because the banks do not actually need the customers' deposits for lending, so that there is at first glance no incentive to reward customers.

However, banks will still seek to convince a customer to deposit with them even if they do not need the deposit for granting loans. If, for example, a customer changes the bank, the old bank has to transfer the customer's credit in his account to the account of the new bank. Since this is not a loan to the customer, the old bank cannot create new money, but has to pay the money from its reserves with the central bank. Hence banks will seek to have a similar volume of deposits, so that bank money transfers between them largely even out and their reserves do not become substantially reduced[123] but stay broadly the same overall after netting. In any case, markets can be irrational enough to pretend or ignore

120 Bank of England (2014a: 20).
121 Keynes (2013b: 197).
122 See Chapter 4, sec. 4 on the externalisation cycle.
123 If a commercial bank needs to increase its reserves, for example because of a very high amount of withdrawals/transfers from its accounts, then it has to pay interest for that loan the central bank gives to increase the commercial bank's reserves. This interest rate is at present (2019) very low, but the commercial bank's transfer of money to another commercial bank must ideally be for free, so that there is always a loss for the transferring bank.

Keynes's postulated equilibrium, or the banks may deceive the markets successfully with obfuscating financial products.

(b) The problem of money creation 'out of nothing': the banks' privilege of not being required to hold clients' accounts

The preceding discussion may give the impression that whenever a loan is granted, also by non-banks, this could lead to a creation of new money. This is not the case; only banks create (bank) money by making loans; non-banks, such as companies and private persons, are not able to do so. That difference can be seen in the way in which the grant of a loan appears in the accounts of a non-bank, as opposed to a bank. The reason for this difference goes back to the legal principle that banks do not hold the deposited money in trust for the customer.[124]

When a non-bank makes a loan, the loan funds credited to the borrower must come from the lender's own funds, either own money or a loan from a third party. The loan amount shifts from the lender to the borrower. When the loan contract is made, the lender undertakes the obligation to pay the loan money to the borrower. Once he does that, this obligation is discharged and disappears from the non-bank's liability account. At the same time, the non-bank's cash/deposit balance is reduced, as the loan money is transferred to the borrower, and the non-bank obtains a claim for repayment of the loan. So there is no lengthening of the balance sheet: no new money is created, only existing money is transferred.[125]

In the case of banks, the customer deposit, that is the loan money paid into the customer's account, does not correspond to a reduction of the balance in any of the bank's asset accounts. The bank retains its liability to pay the loan, since it does not actually pay out the loan funds but rather invents a fictitious customer deposit with which the bank credits the customer's account. This is the creation of money 'out of nothing'.[126] Real customer deposits and fictitious loan deposits look the same in accounting and monetary terms and play the same role: credit that operates as money. Since the assets side (claim being the borrower's liability to repay the loan) is matched by the liability side (customer deposit, borrower's

124 *Foley v. Hill* (1848) 2 HLC 28, at 36, 43–44, *Joachimson v. Swiss Bank Corporation* [1921] 3 KB 110 (CA), at 127.

125 Werner (2014a: 74).

126 Mises (1953: 271): 'the loans [by banks who undertake current account business for their customers] are granted out of a fund *that did not exist before the loans were granted*' (original emphasis). Schumpeter (1954: 320): 'Banks are no longer said to "lend their deposits" or "other people's money", but to "create" deposits or bank notes: they appear to manufacture money rather than to increase its velocity or to act – which is a completely unrealistic idea – on behalf of their depositors'. The latter passage presupposes that commercial banks could also issue their own banknotes, which they did indeed in the past. However, with the possibility of the giro transfer (bank money transfer) a reification of the *res* (credit/debt) in form of paper money is no longer necessary for the transfer. Conceptually Schumpeter's account is still valid.

claim/bank's liability being the amount of the loan granted), and since there is no balance drawn down when the loan is paid (in bank money) to the borrower (so the bank's liability remains), the bank's balance sheet is lengthened.

The bank makes available the loan funds in form of an accounting measure: the bank, which technically still owes the money, re-classifies its liability when it 'pays out' the loan; the bank's 'accounts payable' obligation (the bank's liability to the borrower to pay out the loan because of the loan agreement) is reduced by the loan amount and at the same time re-classified as 'customer deposit' of the borrower with the bank, although neither the customer-borrower nor the bank deposited any funds.[127] This new 'customer deposit' is the new money created through credit, and it is money according to the understanding of money in banking practice:[128] it is a new money obligation or *res*. Since a *res* is an abstract legal notion according to the concept of dematerialised property, there is no need for an already existing *res*, perhaps represented by a physical reifier. A money obligation-*res* can be created out of nothing as any other obligation or as a work of copyright, for example. Since the bank has created a legally enforceable claim through the accounting entries for granting the loan, and since this claim can ultimately be transformed into physical assets in the enforcement process, the bank has created an expectation value as creditor by virtue of an act of writing. The bank's accounting entries are therefore a normative text,[129] similar to the text of a bill of exchange or cheque[130] made out in accordance with the legal formality requirements.[131] The possible legal basis for the normative quality of the accounting entries will be discussed later.[132]

Non-banks cannot re-classify their liabilities. The reason is that when non-banks obtain customer/client money, they have to keep them in separate accounts as trust accounts, segregated from their own business accounts. This prevents the creation of money by way of giving credit, apart from the fact that non-banks do not regularly hold customer deposits. The liability which a client's deposit constitutes for the non-bank (company, lawyer etc.) has to be held in trust by the non-bank. Solicitor's accounts are a typical practical example: solicitors' conduct rules require that client money paid to the solicitor must be held in separate trust accounts (client accounts).[133] Banks are not required to, and do not, hold depos-

127 Werner (2014a: 74).

128 See Bank of England (2014b: 10, 12).

129 Rahmatian (2014: 224–225, 229). This definition of (bank) money has a nominalist/Scandinavian realist flavour, see Olivecrona (1971: 299–303), and at 303: 'Without reference to the rules, promises and payments would be meaningless sounds and gestures. The rules are not only such rules as those we call legal. These rules are supplemented by social rules, and in some connections only social rules may be relevant. But rules there must be'.

130 BoEA 1882, s. 3(2), s. 89(1).

131 The present passage largely follows Rahmatian (2018a: 220–221).

132 See below under sec. 6.

133 E.g. for England and Wales, see Solicitors Regulation Authority (SRA), Code of Conduct 2011, version 19, 2017, part 2: Client money and operation of a client account, rule 13 et seq. (with the express prohibition of the provision of banking facilities in rule 14.5).

its in trust, according to *Foley v. Hill*.[134] That applies to 'real' customer deposits on customers' (current and savings) accounts as well as to the 'fictitious' deposits created when the bank advances the loan money and credits the customer's account correspondingly. So the bank's liability to advance the loan can be re-classified as customer deposits which are also debts/bank's liabilities. There is no duty to keep customer deposits (real or fictitious/created) in trust and separate from other liabilities of the bank.

Financial regulation provisions reflect the banks' privileged position when compared to non-banks: banks are exempt from the standard client money rules. The CASS (Client Asset Sourcebook) rules (CASS 7) of the Financial Conduct Authority (FCA) in the UK may be given as a representative example. Normally, a firm receiving client money must hold this deposit in separate accounts to segregate the client money from the firm's own funds.[135] However, this does not apply to banks. According to the rules of the FCA Handbook, the following is not client money: any deposits within the meaning of the CRD held by a CRD credit institution,[136] and 'the money held for that client is held by the firm as banker and not as a trustee under the client money rules'.[137] This exception effectively restates *Foley v. Hill* that a banker taking deposits does not hold the money as a trustee but is only party to the contract with the customer.[138] It is, however, this exception from the normal client money rules which enables banks to create money through credit by mixing or re-classifying different liabilities.[139] This is also an implementation of the economic concept of a bank as a reservoir of money.[140] The English courts recognise that deposited funds are not specifically segregated but are commingled with the bank's other funds.[141] Since the deposited money is under the control of the banker and the banker's money,[142] segregation of accounts would not make sense. Accordingly, the money paid into the bank account cannot be traced ('tracing' means here the equitable remedy *in rem* for breach of trust) and the customer is unsecured creditor.[143]

The practical difference between client money and unsegregated money deposited with a bank became apparent in the UK Supreme Court decision of *Lehman*

134 *Foley v. Hill* (1848) 2 HLC 28, at 36.

135 FCA Handbook CASS 7.13.1 and 3, 'Client Money Rules: Segregation of Client Money' (version: release 28, June 2018), see www.handbook.fca.org.uk (visited 1 July 2018).

136 A full CRD credit institution is, for present purposes, a bank authorised under relevant EU regulations (abbreviated as CRD): it is defined as an undertaking whose business is to receive deposits or other repayable funds from the public and to grant credits for its own account and that has its registered office (or, if it has no registered office, its head office) in an EEA state.

137 FCA Handbook CASS 7.10.16 and 7.10.19 (1), 'Client Money Rules: Credit Institutions and Approved Banks' (version: release 28, June 2018).

138 *Foley v. Hill* (1848) 2 HLC 28, at 36, 43–44; Ellinger (2011: 120–122).

139 Werner (2014a: 74–75).

140 Ellinger (2011: 215).

141 *Azam v. Iqbal* [2007] EWHC 2025 (Admin), [2008] BusLR 168, paras. 15–17, 27–29.

142 *Foley v. Hill* (1848) 2 HLC 28, at 36.

143 *Sinclair v. Brougham* [1914] AC 398, at 419. See also Ellinger (2011: 120).

Brothers International (Europe) v. CRC Credit Fund Ltd.[144] Although the insolvent firm in question, Lehman Brothers International (Europe) (LBIE), was a trading subsidiary in the UK of the US holding company as part of the (then also insolvent) Lehman Brothers investment bank group, this firm did *not* operate as a bank. It was authorised by the Financial Services Authority (FSA), as it then was, to take and handle client money, but not to keep deposits.[145] The firm was therefore subject to client money rules under Chapter 7 of the Client Assets Sourcebook (CASS 7), issued by the FSA under s. 138 of the Financial Services and Markets Act 2000 and giving effect to the EU Markets in Financial Instruments Directives (MiFiD).[146] The CASS 7 rules required LBIE to segregate the client money and to keep it in separate accounts. Since under normal English trust law the segregation of clients' money alone is not sufficient to establish a proprietary (equitable) interest in the clients' funds[147] because the necessary declaration of trust is usually lacking (no certainty of intention), and a declaration of trust without segregation is not sufficient either (no certainty of subject matter),[148] CASS 7 created a statutory trust which did not have to be interpreted according to the criteria of ordinary trust law.[149] Under the CASS 7 rules, the LBIE could (1) either pay received client money immediately into a segregated client account (normal approach) or (2) it could instead pay incoming client money into the firm's own account with the duty to segregate client money in a client bank account on a daily basis after a reconciliation of records and accounts of the entitlement of each client for whom the firm holds client money with the firm's existing client accounts (alternative approach).[150] LBIE opted for the alternative approach, but failed 'on a truly spectacular scale' to identify and segregate

144 *In the matter of Lehman Brothers International (Europe) v. CRC Credit Fund Ltd.* [2012] UKSC 6, also reported as: *Lehman Brothers International (Europe) (in administration) v. CRC Credit Fund Ltd. and others* (Financial Services Authority intervening) [2012] Bus LR 667. On the following passage, see Rahmatian (2018a: 222–226).

145 *Lehman Brothers v. CRC Credit Fund*, para. 24.

146 Directive 2004/39/EC of the European Parliament and of the Council of 21 April 2004 on Markets in Financial Instruments (OJ 2004 L145, p. 1) and the Commission Directive 2006/73/EC of 10 August 2006 implementing Directive 2004/39/EC of the European Parliament and of the Council as regards organisations requirements and operating conditions for investment firms and defined terms for the purposes of that Directive (OJ 2006 L241, p. 26). On the implementation of these Directives in Civil law jurisdictions who do not have the division into legal and equitable ownership under English trust law, see Gruyaert and van Loock (2014: 225).

147 The equitable interest is the basis for the protection of clients' (investors') funds from the firm's creditors in case of the firm's insolvency, because equitable ownership ensures that the clients do not part with ownership and the clients' funds do not become part of the insolvent firm's assets. That equitable ownership can only be effected with a trust.

148 *Lehman Brothers v. CRC Credit Fund*, para. 186.

149 *Lehman Brothers v. CRC Credit Fund*, para. 110. Especially the distribution rules of the trust (client) money under the trust do not follow general trust law, but the CASS 7 rules, *Lehman Brothers v. CRC Credit Fund*, para. 121.

150 The rules are set out in detail in *Lehman Brothers v. CRC Credit Fund*, para. 39.

client money according to the corresponding rules.[151] When LBIE became insolvent, the problem was whether participation in the client money pool also applies to client money held in non-segregated accounts.

The Supreme Court held unanimously that the statutory trust arises when the client's money is received.[152] Otherwise the opinions were split 3:2. The majority held that the clients can participate in the client money pool even when no actual segregation has taken place but ought to have taken place,[153] so that the client money rules are also applied to client money in LBIE's own accounts. This generous interpretation is, in the majority view, in line with the rationale of the MiFiD to ensure investor protection.[154] The minority view was of the opinion that clients can only avail themselves of the client money protection if their funds have actually been segregated in client accounts.[155] The majority position would have a curious effect:

> Where money is received from a client . . . it would be unnatural, and contrary to the primary purpose of client protection, for the money to cease to be the client's property on receipt, and for it (or its substitute) to become his property again on segregation.[156]

Indeed, the majority view seems to change the contractual claims concerning the *non-segregated* client money to proprietary claims (equitable ownership under a statutory trust) on which the client protection in case of non-compliance of the firm with the rules was based.[157] However, that scenario would be rather similar to the situation when money is deposited with a real bank which is not the customer's trustee and need not keep segregated customers' trust accounts. The money paid in becomes the bank's property, so the customer's proprietary claim changes into a contractual one for repayment; when withdrawal occurs, the customer's contractual claim changes into a proprietary one in relation to the money paid out. But since LBIE was a non-bank, it *was* fixed with the client account trust rules which it however breached.[158] The duty to segregate client money stands against the creation of new money through loans and (fictitious) matching deposits as accounting devices. Only banks have the privilege of re-classifying liabilities (loan to be disbursed becomes deposit credited to the customer's

151 *Lehman Brothers v. CRC Credit Fund*, para. 27.
152 *Lehman Brothers v. CRC Credit Fund*, paras. 15, 62, 111, 128, 171.
153 The failure to segregate was in breach of the client money rules in CASS 7, *Lehman Brothers v. CRC Credit Fund*, paras. 27, 80–81.
154 *Lehman Brothers v. CRC Credit Fund*, paras. 109–110, 167–169, 171, 196.
155 *Lehman Brothers v. CRC Credit Fund*, paras. 18, 23, 85.
156 *Lehman Brothers v. CRC Credit Fund*, para. 63, per Lord Walker (one of the two dissenting judges).
157 Gruyaert and van Loock (2014: 249).
158 A more extensive discussion of *Lehman Brothers v. CRC Credit Fund* in Rahmatian (2018a: 222–226) and Gruyaert and van Loock (2014: 217–228, 244–249).

account). If there were a duty to hold clients' deposits (real or fictitious ones) on trust, such a re-classification would be a breach of trust.

(c) The practical relevance of the fractional reserve system

It has already been pointed out that the fractional reserve theory of money with the fractional reserve system and the instrument of the money multiplier at its heart is not an accurate representation of the money creation process, although it is still the commonly found explanation for the money supply in economics textbooks.[159] The fractional reserve system was described in the early eighteenth century already by Richard Cantillon in France as a common practice at least among English bankers.[160] The fractional reserve theory maintains that banks create money when they lend out excess reserves which generates a multiplier effect on the money supply.[161] The amount of the reserves is supposed to be a binding constraint on lending, whereby the central bank directly determines the amount of reserves. This 'common misconception' (in the words of the Bank of England),[162] has also been adopted by eminent writers, such as Crowther:[163]

> In England the Bank of England does not, by custom, lend to the Member Banks. . . . What it does is to lend money to all comers (or buy their bills – either operation will increase its assets), but to charge such a stiff rate of interest that the borrowers will hasten to repay the loan as soon as they can. In this way . . . [the Bank of England] knows – and every one else knows – that a reduction, and a consequent stringency of cash and restriction of credit, is in the immediate offing. The Bank of England is virtually the dictator of conditions in the Money Market, and hence of the size of the Member Banks' cash reserves.

However, the Bank of England does not claim such a role for itself, at least not today. Reserves are normally supplied on demand by the Bank of England to commercial banks in exchange for other assets on their balance sheets: 'In no way does the aggregate *quantity* of reserves directly constrain the amount of bank lending or deposit creation'.[164] We have seen that banks create money individually by granting loans, not in aggregate determined by the effect of the money multiplier, being the amount of money the whole banking system generates with each unit of the reserves held. But Crowther also highlighted an important reason for the fractional reserve system in banking practice. Keeping cash reserves,

159 The textbooks used here are Mankiw (2012: 628–631), Krugman and Wells (2015: 864–869). See discussion above under sec. 1.
160 Vilar (1984: 251) with quote from Cantillon.
161 Krugman and Wells (2015: 869).
162 Bank of England (2014a: 15).
163 Crowther (1946: 197).
164 Bank of England (2014a: 16).

although actually not operating as a restriction on lending, maintains customers' confidence in the banks for the functioning of the banking system:[165]

> 'Creating' money involves an increase in the bank's deposit liabilities, and the bank cannot afford to let its cash reserve fall below 10 per cent. of its total deposit liabilities. It might, indeed, be safe to let the cash ratio fall to 8 or even 6 per cent. But the public has grown so accustomed to the existing ratio that it would begin to look askance at a bank which allowed its cash ratio to fall below the usual figure. . . . [A banker's] whole business depends upon the confidence of the public in his ability to meet his liabilities on demand. If his reserves are enormous, nobody will question his ability to pay on demand. But if they are falling below the figure to which the public is accustomed, nervous depositors will begin to wonder whether the banker could after all meet all his liabilities, and they will begin to draw their deposits out in cash, just to be sure. There are many paradoxes in the banking business. No banker could pay all his liabilities in cash on demand, if they were all to be presented at once. In that sense, every banker is always insolvent. But the banker's whole business depends absolutely upon his reputation for solvency.

The reason why Crowther's old text from the 1940s has been cited repeatedly at length is that newer authors either do not express these interrelations at all or much more coyly. Nobody today would state the truism so openly that every bank is technically insolvent, provided one equates insolvency with illiquidity: this is appropriate in case of a bank which does not produce and deliver goods or tangible commodities or services, but money, the most liquid *res.*[166] However, the bank rests its operation on the customers' belief that it is not insolvent or illiquid. This creed, in part sustained by the keeping of cash reserves (or deposits with the central bank) as the fractional reserve theory stipulates, is an essential part in the functioning of the modern monetary system. The trust in the bankers' reputation is also reinforced by the banks' ability to create own capital through lending which is, in turn, a reason for the phenomenon of price making through lending.

(d) Bank money creation: increase of banks' own capital and price making through lending

Banks create bank money by granting loans and they credit accordingly the customer-borrower's account with a deposit as the loan sum; this is the new money. In the course of the inter-banking transfer or through other intermediate

165 Crowther (1946: 45).

166 On the dubiousness in practical terms of a distinction between liquidity and solvency of a bank, also in the context of an emergency loan by a central bank as a lender of last resort, see e.g. Goodhart (2002: 229, 231–232).

transactions, a bank can also create money to increase its own capital, as long as it finds borrowers, including other banks. One way is to lend money to an investor who can then buy shares in the bank with the borrowed money, either directly or through intermediary firms or banks, and so increase the bank's capital.[167] After the 2008 banking crisis, this was a method to shore up a bank's financial position if it was not willing to obtain government (taxpayers') funds for that.[168] The prohibition for normal public companies to provide financial assistance for the purchase of the company's own shares[169] could be circumvented in this way, but it is doubtful whether this prohibition applies to banks at all,[170] because it presupposes that funds are transferred from elsewhere in the company to purchase the company's shares, as would indeed be the situation with loans by non-banks. But in the case of a bank, the funds are created *ex nihilo* and come from nowhere.[171] So that does not cover the rationale of the prohibition of a pretended increase of the company's capital by shifting the same capital. With a bank the new funds in form of bank money, initially at least, are really here, only that banks alone have the privilege of inventing them.

In the same way, through lending, banks can obtain, and initially create, funds to pay fines imposed by the regulator or damages ordered by the courts. If a bank has to pay such fines, the money cannot come from elsewhere but has to be provided by creating money through credit. A bank cannot take its customers' deposited money to meet these payments. It is possible that the money comes from another bank as a loan, but it must have been created before by some bank, in most cases the lending bank. If the central bank's emergency lending facility is not used (its use could be a reputational issue for the bank), that other bank is always another commercial bank.

Another phenomenon is related to the banks' ability to increase their own capital through lending. Banks can indirectly increase prices by instigating overpayment because of their willingness to make available (additional) loan money to meet higher payments. Residential and commercial properties are usual examples. If an object is valued at, say, £400,000, the willingness of a bank to finance the purchase with a (higher) loan, so that the property can be acquired for £500,000 (perhaps after a revaluation), that leads to an increase of new money which has

167 Thus the bank (a) obtains the liability to pay out the loan, then (b) this liability is re-classified as customer deposit bank liability, and then (c) this liability is transformed into the bank's equity (own capital) – all different positions on the liability side of the bank's balance sheet.

168 Werner (2014a: 76).

169 In the UK: Companies Act 2006, s. 678.

170 In the UK, there seems to be an express exception from the prohibition for banks, Companies Act 2006, s. 678(5), and s. 682(1): s. 682 makes an exception to s. 678 if the company giving the assistance is a private or public company and 'the company has net assets that are not reduced by the giving of the assistance'; s. 682(2) says, 'The transactions to which this section applies are, [. . .] where the lending of money is part of the ordinary business of the company, the lending of money in the ordinary course of the company's business'. That should cover banks.

171 See above under (b).

been created with the corresponding credit (the high prices in such cases prevent cash payments). That at the same time increases the market price for comparable objects. This may not be in line with the economists' market equilibrium model, but it is the reality. Money, here bank money, is not a neutral medium of exchange in the sales transaction at all and it is not a unit of account that denotes the prices impartially; it rather influences the prices fundamentally, and it typically will do so, because a bank which refuses to lend in principle cannot exist. Overpayment of this kind allows the expanded creation of new money, and more widespread and increased indebtedness in general: in relation to private individuals, companies, local authorities and government bodies, and the state. Such overpaid objects can also be acquired by companies which are related to the banks, through shareholding etc. which increases the capital appearing in the books, either of the banks themselves or its subsidiaries. In this way banks can exercise economic and political powers in large segments of society.

The creation of new money and of the loan debt, including interest, is important, what is less relevant is the actual repayment of the loan (capital). Interest repayment secures the *rentier* effect of capitalism, which Keynes too optimistically declared as a transitional phase that will disappear.[172] Besides, the new money is added to the quantity of money in the economy. Repayment of loan capital (including interest) would destroy money[173] and the debt from which it derives, and is therefore not a major aim. Repackaged existing debts, perhaps securitised, can also be resold as an investment product. The sub-prime mortgage crisis in 2008 in the United States can partly be explained because of that.[174] This crisis also showed that banks do not need to be too concerned about liquidity and bad loans, because the collapse of one bank would usually be considered as a danger that this leads to a systemic failure of the financial system. That needs to be averted at all cost. States will then step in with emergency loans financed by taxes and subsequent economic austerity, since banks are for the most part perceived as 'too big to fail'. The rescue of the banks can drive states to *de facto* insolvency and a sovereign debt crisis, although the debts were initially not held by the states themselves.[175] The rescue measures nevertheless allow banks to continue to operate as before.[176] In a monetary system based on bank money that is

172 Keynes, *General Theory* (1964: 376).

173 Bank of England (2014a: 16), Jarchow (2010: 13), Eucken (1950: 121).

174 United States: Financial Crisis Inquiry Commission (2011: 88–90).

175 E.g. Ireland in 2008–9, see Pilkington (2017: 150–157). See also Chapter 5.

176 This is not surprising because a proper rescue of a bank should understandably avert its insolvency if at all possible, see e.g. Recital 5 of the Directive 2014/59/EU of 15 May 2014, Establishing a Framework for the Recovery and Resolution of Credit Institutions and Investment Firms: 'A regime is therefore needed to provide authorities with a credible set of tools to intervene sufficiently early and quickly in an unsound or failing institution so as to ensure the continuity of the institution's critical financial and economic functions, while minimising the impact of an institution's failure on the economy and financial system'. And Recital 8: 'Resolution of an institution which maintains it as a going concern may, as

conceptualised as debt and created by commercial banks through credit, alternatives are hard to imagine.

4. The enforcement of the debt that money constitutes: legal enforcement makes the *res* to money. The janiform nature of the money-debt *res*

The following discusses an aspect that is entirely absent from any definitions of money by economists which lawyers then adopt. Medium of exchange and unit of account can be achieved by issuing tokens, whether or not of intrinsic value, and the noting of prices referring to a *numéraire*. But the store of value function of money is much more difficult to explain. How can money represent value? Why is an intrinsically worthless banknote 'money'? Why is a set of accounting entries 'money'? The answer comes from the law. While money certainly has a historical and socio-economic origin, it is the law which turns these tokens and acts of writing into money.

The money creation process has shown that money is a debt in law. That applies to cash (money issued by the central banks or – sometimes in the case of coins – the state directly)[177] and bank money (created by commercial banks when making loans).[178] The difference between the cash/central bank debt and the bank money debt is that cash is created by a central bank, thus in a (legally) closed monopoly, while commercial bank money is created in competition or, more accurately, in an oligopoly of the commercial banks.[179] Either debt is enforceable in law, but in relation to cash this enforceability is notional, while in case of bank money it is very real. The bank money debt is enforceable according to the relevant enforcement provisions in the respective jurisdictions.[180] What is enforced is the creditor's claim that arises out of the credit that has created, and is, the money. Money has therefore two components: the loan from which the new bank money is generated and the credit that this loan constitutes which operates as medium of exchange (and unit of account to express prices). The money-debt *res* is janiform: (1) It stays between the bank as lender and creditor and the customer as borrower and debtor (theoretically the bank could assign its claim for loan repayment to a new creditor, but that is ignored here). (2) It gets transferred as a fungible *res* indefinitely between different actors on the market; thus it *circulates* entirely detached from the obligation that has originally brought the debt into existence, so a repayment of the loan at some point does not affect the validity of

---

a last resort, involve government financial stabilisation tools, including temporary public ownership'.

177 See above under sec. 2.

178 See above under sec. 3.

179 Eucken (1950: 120–121).

180 For example, in England: Civil Procedure Rules, Part 70, Part 83 et seq.; Insolvency Act 1986, Second Part, ss. 251A et seq. In Scotland: Bankruptcy and Diligence (Scotland) Act 2007, Parts 4–11, Bankruptcy (Scotland) Act 2016, ss. 78, 109. The details are not relevant here.

this specific circulating money-debt. With regard to (2), the money *res* operates like a debt embodied in a bill of exchange or promissory note, detached from any underlying obligation and not subject to a defence arising out of such an obligation.[181]

The enforcement of this janiform debt that the money-*res* constitutes occurs (1) as ***loan debt*** against the borrower (so the borrower must keep up repayment of the loan, otherwise execution/attachment ensues) and (2) as ***circulating money debt***, that is, as a claim against a bank (the originating bank or any other one) which is debtor in relation to the account in which the money-*res* appears in credit for the customer and account/deposit holder, so that the customer as creditor has an enforceable claim against the bank and can withdraw the money. Independent from (2) is the question of payment for which the money is used, for example payment of a purchase price from a contract of sale; that is a separate debt discharged with the money payment. The janiform nature of money is reflected by the way in which the grant of a loan and, at the same time, the creation of new bank money appear in the books of the bank, as has been discussed before.[182] When the loan is granted, the bank's balance sheet is lengthened because of an increase of its assets and its liabilities by the same amount:[183] the bank is creditor in relation to the loan sum granted (aspect 1 or 'face 1' of the Janus face of money: loan debt), while at the same time the bank is debtor in relation to the new money created, being the loan amount, which stands to the credit of the borrower's account (aspect 2 or 'face 2' of money: circulating money debt). Hence banks grant credit by indebting themselves and the borrowers pay their debts with the banks' debts. This janiform nature of money may be a reason why most economists and many lawyers baulk at acknowledging money as being credit or as a debt with a dual quality.

The store of value function of money – if one insists on this term[184] – derives from the fact that an intrinsically worthless *res* (and its representative, respectively) establishes a generally reasonable expectation, though not strictly an entitlement, to real commodities of intrinsic value, such as food, clothing and other (ultimately physical) objects, in the future.[185] This expectation is, however, not brought about by social or economic conventions alone, as economists and sociologists often claim, but is most fundamentally the result of the legal enforceability of the debt which money constitutes. And it is this dual enforceability – as loan-debt and money-debt at the same time – which makes people accept money as the medium of exchange and means of payment. It is true that, when

181 McKendrick (2016: 564–565).

182 See above under sec. 3.

183 Lautenbach (1952: 45). The German term is '*Bilanzverlängerung*'. The German term appears more common than the English equivalent.

184 Put more precisely, money itself does not store value as such but enables the expectation to value in the future.

185 This is certainly not a new insight: one can find such an analysis already with Wicksell, see Arnon (2011: 346).

considering the historical development of the law, commercial and social practices will have been the source of legal rules that enforce circulating debts and thereby make them to operative money today. (In relation to bank money, the exact legal rules are rather mysterious anyway.)[186] But that does not change the principle: nobody would consider an accounting entry denoting credit in one's account or the handing over of a banknote as functioning money and accept payment with it if the law did not ultimately provide the enforcement of the dual debt which money constitutes. This legal enforcement is notional for cash provided by central banks (almost always legal tender), and it is practical reality for bank money provided by commercial banks. The actual effect of the enforcement of bank money debt, as a transfer of real value, will be discussed later.[187]

Thus it is the enforcement by law which turns a *res* into operative money. For that reason, any distinction between Chartalist and non-Chartalist (institutional, functional) money concepts that can commonly be found in academic literature, is futile.[188] A conventional Chartalist view (State theory of money) would probably reduce money to cash and legal tender only, and would understand the statement 'money is a creature of law' in this limited way,[189] and that is indeed too narrow. The various forms of money, cash and bank money, are nonetheless made to be money by the law, through the legal enforcement of the debt they embody. The present perspective is different from the traditional Chartalist position: here the emphasis is on the *enforcement* of circulating debt by the law which makes the *res* to money; with the Chartalists the emphasis is on the authoritative declaration by the law of certain *res* as money. Nevertheless, money remains a creature of law.

The few economists who do recognise the legal-contractual and proprietary element on which money is founded still consider the proprietary aspect of money as extraneous and are apparently unable to see money itself as a *res* in the form of a debt. Thus the idea that money itself is not credit (but created through credit), and therefore money is not the same as bank deposits (demand deposits) because these deposits are only claims on money, is wrong.[190] Furthermore, any emphasis on the securitisation of the loan through a collateral by the debtor (in form of a security without the requirement of the creditor's possession, a hypothec, mortgage/charge etc.) for the explanation of the nature of money is beside the point.[191] That approach nevertheless stresses at least the element

186 See below under sec. 6.

187 See Chapter 4 on the alienation (externalisation) cycle and Chapter 5, sec. 2 on the enforcement.

188 See discussion in Chapter 1.

189 As Knapp (1924: 1) did, a view which Mann (1992: 14) shared.

190 This is however the view of Heinsohn and Steiger (2013: 70–71). These authors also seem to struggle with the janiform debt that money constitutes when they distinguish between the interest-bearing document or credit contract and the non-interest-bearing document, the money note or money proper, an unsatisfactory conception. It seems to echo Keynes's distinction between money of account and money proper.

191 For Heinsohn and Steiger (2013: 55–56, 69–71), this is however a central element in their conception of money and credit that creates money.

of enforceability as a constitutive element of money, but it also suggests incorrectly that the enforcement of the debt only happens if it is a secured debt. In fact, the security only guarantees a greater likelihood of a practical realisation of the enforcement: if a loan is secured with a house (in form of a hypothec, mortgage/charge) it is more likely that the loan (which has created bank money with its grant) will be enforced successfully with the sale or auction of the house and the creditor's outstanding debt will be satisfied. However, the loan can perfectly well be unsecured, and yet it is still the source of new bank money, and it is enforceable in law. Even if the loan is secured by property, for example by a house, that house may not have a direct connection with the loan, that is, it has not been purchased with the loan sum. It may not be owned by the loan debtor either, as 'ownership economists' however appear to presume, but can belong to a third party whose liability is confined to the property object only, unlike the unlimited personal liability of the debtor himself. These different possibilities of securitisation/collateral are entirely irrelevant to the concept of money itself. 'Ownership economists' seem to have an inadequate understanding of private law concepts, which offsets their otherwise commendable recognition of the importance of law for the concept of money, in contrast to mainstream economics.

5. The problem of interest

The numerous economic theories of interest[192] are of no relevance in the present context. What matters is that not only the obligation of the repayment of the capital lent but also the stipulated interest can be enforced.[193] The growth of interest payments has enormous and potentially devastating effects in the economy. Commercial banks could grant interest-free loans, but that never happens in practice. When a bank makes a loan, it creates the loan sum but not the interest. Only the credit the loan constitutes adds to the circulating quantity of money. The payable interest has to come from elsewhere, from funds which were created from other loans or from increased productivity. This additional payment obligation is very substantial but usually underestimated by the general public. There are different ways in which loan interest can be calculated: the full amount to be repaid – loan sums plus interest payments – depends on the duration and interest rate, the type of the loan (repayment mortgage etc.), the amount, number or

192 See e.g. Keynes, *General Theory* (1964: 165, 175) for his own and for classical theories of the rate of interest. See also Jarchow (2010: 217). For historical theories of interest, see Schumpeter (1954: 327).

193 See e.g. *Commissioners of Inland Revenue v. Sir H. C. Holder and another* [1931] 2 KB 81, CA, at 98–99, on the conversion of interest by the bank to payable capital (accepted by the court), so that this does not count as compound interest that could be regarded as too high or usurious. Interesting is the comment by Romer LJ at 100: 'It is true that the reason that originally induced the banks to keep accounts in this way has disappeared with the repeal of the usury laws. But that repeal cannot, as it seems to me, have changed the nature and effect of accounts that continue to be kept in the same way as before'.

frequency of repayments, and other costs which the individual loan agreement would stipulate.

For the present analysis a simple calculation of interest and compound interest of an investment suffices: an investment of 100 over 10 years with 10% interest yields a sum of 259.37, according to the formula: $M = P \times (1 + i)^n$, whereby M is the final amount, P the principal sum, i is the interest rate per year and n the number of years. Thus $100 \times (1 + 0.1)^{10} = 259.37$, that is an increase of almost 160% (the assumption is compound interest once a year). The interest rises exponentially. The gain of almost 160 is an asset which must have a corresponding liability somewhere (debt), so if that sum is deposited on a bank account, the bank will be debtor, but will make itself creditor with the grant of (unrelated) loans which have to be serviced mainly by non-banks. For a loan, this figure of 259.37 will not be the same because of the different calculation methods depending on the specific loan stipulations, but the figure still gives good guidance.

Individual persons and enterprises may be able to meet the interest repayments, but it is obvious that the economy as a whole cannot possibly do that. The debtors may have longer working hours or take on additional jobs, be driven to increased productivity and efficiency, and can hope for windfall profits, for example because of a legacy. Enterprises can also hope for an extraordinary profit because of a successful product innovation which outstrips the repayment obligations; otherwise enterprises will have to reduce employees' salaries and to produce more cheaply to cut costs so that they can meet the increasing interest payments. The need for economic growth is particularly important to cope with loans and interest: the result is an ever quicker production of goods of progressively lower quality and durability, a destructive exploitation of natural resources, and a permanent damage to the environment and climate.[194] With salaried employees a disproportionate gain is far less likely in any case because salaries rise only steadily, if at all. Both for enterprises and workers, a rollover of one loan to the next one is the most likely solution, whereby the new loan is necessarily increased, because a substantial part of the capital sum has hardly ever been repaid which would have diminished the interest accordingly. The new loan will provide new money again, but not the interest to be repaid. The state and local governments also operate on this basis. History is full with examples of states obtaining new natural resources and manpower through colonialism, slavery and warfare to address their indebtedness.

Repayment of loan *capital* is quite clearly of secondary importance. Banks are happy to obtain the interest as a steady income (and usually interest will be repaid before capital).[195] If a borrower defaults on the loan, they can obtain real assets from the borrower with the enforcement of the outstanding debt (residential or commercial properties, plant and machinery, know-how etc). If a debtor's real assets are less lucrative for the banks, they can grant a new loan instead of insisting on the enforcement of the outstanding debt and so retain a *rentier* relationship.

194 This argument is not new, see e.g. Binswanger (2013: 155–156).

195 Hence banks often stipulate in the loan agreement that the early repayment of the loan will attract a penalty, or the opportunity of early repayment comes with an increased interest rate.

This permanent indebtedness becomes a modern form of feudal dependence. In many instances, repayment of the loan is unattractive for the banks: not only would money be destroyed, the continual income from interest payments would also be terminated. States, as debtors to banks, could theoretically reduce their indebtedness fairly easily by raising taxes and cutting expenses, for example in the social sector. In that case they invariably shift their indebtedness to enterprises and private individuals, because otherwise there would be no debt and no money: repayment of debts destroys assets and money: savings accounts, pension funds and so on. The balance sheet of a state after such an austerity program may look fine, but that of its citizens and enterprises may be disastrous, and that may have dangerous consequences for the state's economy.

The problem of the rise of interest and its ethical ramifications has preoccupied thinkers for a long time. Interest, according to Marshall, is the supply price of capital[196] or the price paid for the use of capital in any market,[197] and this echoes what Locke had already said about interest: 'the price of the hire of money'.[198] Locke saw interest as a purely monetary phenomenon and took the supply side of money for granted, as it is related to the total supply of money in circulation,[199] which was the usual approach in the seventeenth and eighteenth centuries.[200] Locke also denied the possibility to regulate interest by law.[201]

Interest, especially usurious interest, was however always a concern.[202] Aristotle's moral disdain for interest is well known,[203] as is the prohibition of charging interest by the Church to avoid usury.[204] However, the thinkers of the late-scholastic Salamanca School in the sixteenth century provided a monetary theory that could serve as a preparation for a modern capitalist society.[205] They developed Aristotle's[206] and medieval scholastic definitions of exchange and money further[207] and concentrated on the exchange, the price of goods and the

196 Marshall, *Principles*, IV, 12 § 12 (2013: 261).
197 Marshall, *Principles*, VI, 2 § 4 (2013: 443).
198 Locke, *Some considerations of the consequences of the lowering of interest and raising the value of money* (1991: 211). A similar, near contemporary definition of interest as 'use or price of money on loan', see Anon., *Some Thoughts on the Interest of Money in General* (1738: 21).
199 Vickers (1960: 47).
200 Schumpeter (1954: 329).
201 Locke, *Some considerations of the consequences of the lowering of interest and raising the value of money* (1991: 211–212, 227).
202 Schumpeter (1954: 103).
203 Aristotle, *Politics* [1258b]: 'For money was intended to be used in exchange, but not to increase at interest. And this term interest [gr. τόκος, 'offspring'], which means the birth of money from money, is applied to the breeding of money because the offspring resembles the parent'. See also [1259a].
204 MacCulloch (2009: 369, 419).
205 Grice-Hutchinson (1952: 40, 47), Schumpeter (1954: 95, 328–329).
206 Aristotle, *Politics* [1257b]: 'coin is the unit of exchange and the measure or limit of it'.
207 Grice-Hutchinson (1952: 47–48). On the theological (Thomist) meanings of the donation as a predecessor to the exchange and commerce in the late Middle Ages, see Todeschini (2017: 167).

role of money. Doctor Navarrus (Martín de Azpilcueta) was concerned about veiled usury hidden in exchange transactions, including insurance arrangements, whereby the term 'exchange' did not only mean to him the usual sale with goods against money but also money against money, the loan, the deposit and every other contract of money.[208] In particular,[209]

> in order for this contract to be licit, it is necessary to give a just salary to the exchanger for conferring a document that makes someone else give money to its holder in another place, and it is necessary that he not take more than what is due. . . . unjust exchanges that are mortally evil are those where the exchanger takes more than his fair salary, even if he sells on credit to the person who does not have any money and will give it back at a later date. The more he takes for having to wait for longer periods of repayment, the worse these exchanges are.

This indicates a prohibition of all credit business if interest is charged beyond a 'salary' for the lender.[210] Luis de Molina follows Doctor Navarrus largely in this regard.[211]

The Jesuit theologian Leonardus Lessius, who lived in the then Spanish-ruled Netherlands, emphasised that, following long-standing learned opinion, 'interest' appears in two forms: (a) compensatory interests on the fruits that the seller should have reaped, which are allowed, and (b) lucrative interests, that is, usury, which is prohibited.[212] Lessius permitted the seller to ask for compensation (interest on the price) from the buyer if the seller obtains payment at a later stage and the risk falls on him in the meantime, not on the buyer.[213] He was also more lenient in relation to stipulations by a buyer that the seller has to buy back the good sold at a higher price after a time period, which he did not regard as usurious, although he conceded a possible suspicion of usury, depending on the

208 Azpilcueta, *On Exchange*, secs. 1–4, 14 (2014: 7–12, 34–35).

209 Azpilcueta, *On Exchange*, secs. 23–24 (2014: 56). This is in context of a bill of exchange contract but applies to money generally, since the paper note (banknote) is also a negotiable instrument embodying a debt (and the promissory note from which banknote derives is effectively a simple version of a bill of exchange); whether central bank money or commercial bank money is reified by the paper (or appears as a ledger entry) is conceptually irrelevant. Bank money – not central bank money specifically – was already recognised by the Scholastic doctors in the sixteenth century, see Molina, *De iustitia et iure*, Argument 409 (2015: 119–120), discussing the ways in which bankers can pay debts 'without utilising currency', that is, by way of giro transfer of bank money.

210 When the writers of the Salamanca School name an act as 'mortally evil' or declare that the actors 'mortally sin', see e.g. Molina, *De iustitia et iure*, Argument 408 (2015: 113), this act is for them not a 'sin' only because it infringes a law or a divine injunction, but because it is by its rational nature bad for man, so there is the idea of an underlying rational natural law, see with regard to Gabriel Vázquez (1549–1604), Mandrella (2016: 139).

211 Molina, *De iustitia et iure*, Argument 404 (2015: 82–84).

212 Lessius, *De iustitia et iure*, book 2, ch 21, question 13 (2016: 83).

213 Lessius, *De iustitia et iure*, book 2, ch 21, question 13 (2016: 89–90).

circumstances.[214] Lessius was generally more approving of non-excessive interest than his fellow Scholastic doctors,[215] and his texts have contributed to the argument that modern capitalist thought started already in Catholicism, not in Protestantism according to Max Weber's account.[216] In any case, Lessius is one of the important early theorists of the emerging discipline of economics.[217]

For the theologians, money grows and 'begets' interest abnormally quickly: after lending, interest starts accruing immediately. That interest obtained is then itself lent and attracts further interest and begins to accrue and so on. This 'procreation' of money is unnaturally fast and increases exponentially.[218] These objections and the analysis of interest or usury follow Aristotle: 'For the most hated sort, and with the greatest reason, is usury, which makes a gain out of money itself, and not from the natural object of it [i.e. exchange]'.[219] Today, charging interest is perfectly lawful, while claiming usurious interest is not.[220] Modern legal systems have their prohibitions of usury in principle,[221] but no clear indication as to when an interest rate becomes usurious. As a rule, the courts do not regard usual interest rates in banking practice as usurious, even where these rates are high (20%–25%), particularly for unsecured loans, such as credit card loans and bank overdrafts.

6. The legal basis for the creation of money by central and commercial banks

(a) The normative text of money and the presumed legal sources

Bank credits and the interest which accrues are enforced by law, and that enforcement ultimately enables the transfer of real commodities with an intrinsic value.[222] This is the basis for bank credits (debts from loans granted) being able to be transferred and accepted as payment, that is, they can act as money or medium of exchange. A debt from a contract of sale is also enforceable in law, such as the seller's debt to deliver the goods and the buyer's debt to pay the purchase price.[223] But neither the seller nor the buyer, as non-banks, can draw up accounts

214 Lessius, *De iustitia et iure*, book 2, ch 21, question 14 (2016: 97–98).
215 Van Houdt (1995: 24–26).
216 Weber (2001: 15, 53).
217 Todeschini (2017: 356).
218 Van Houdt (1995: 13).
219 Aristotle, *Politics* [1258b]. See also Schumpeter (1954: 105).
220 The Anglican Church, true to religious tenets, has started an initiative against 'loan sharks' fairly recently, see Hannah Kuchler and George Parker, 'Church of England to take on payday lenders', *Financial Times*, 25 July 2013.
221 E.g. UK Consumer Credit Act 1974, s. 140A, § 138 (2) German BGB, § 879 (2) ss. 4 Austrian ABGB, Art. 1792-6 French Code Civil, Art. 514-1 French Code monétaire et financier, Art. L314-6 French Code de la consummation.
222 See Chapter 5, sec. 2.
223 E.g. for the UK: Sale of Goods Act 1979, s. 27.

and create entries which become new bank money, that is, enforceable debt, as has been demonstrated before. The enforceability of the bank loan and the new bank money with which the loan sum is provided means that the accounting entries amount to a normative text,[224] an ought, recognised and enforced by law. Non-banks can imitate the accounting entries, but no money can be created because there is no legal enforcement; such activities would be similar to the printing of Monopoly money. This privilege of the commercial banks to create bank money, that is, enforceable debt capable of circulating and therefore being a medium of exchange, must have been conferred by norms, to make the banks' actions normative and enforceable. What are these legal norms?

With regard to central bank money, more precisely, cash or circulating currency in form of banknotes and coin, we have at least clear indirect legal provisions, because cash is now almost always[225] designed as legal tender by law,[226] which presupposes the creation of such legal tender by the central banks. There is legislation with legal tender rules, for instance, for the currency in the UK,[227] the euro in the EU,[228] or the euro in Germany, as a euro country that reflects the relevant EU law.[229] Thus the coming into existence and circulation of cash as legal tender created by central banks has a legal basis, as one would expect.

The situation is much more mysterious with regard to commercial bank money, that type of money that constitutes at least 95% of all money. The debt quality of the *res* that makes it to money is much more alive with bank money than with cash/legal tender, where the debt is only a historical formality. There are two questions: to what extent is the credit (or claim/debt) that bank money constitutes enforceable, and where are the legal rules authorising commercial banks to create such enforceable debts that can then circulate as (bank) money?

The first question deals with the perspective of the customer-depositor who pays money into his bank account. He is unquestionably creditor of his bank with regard to the amount deposited that is bank money on his account, and if it is a current account, he can claim the money in cash on demand at any time.[230] Every customer has this claim against his bank, but not all customers; in fact only a small proportion has it at once, otherwise there is a bank run and a collapse of

224 Rahmatian (2014: 225, 229).

225 For the exceptions (e.g. Scottish banknotes), see Chapter 1, sec. 3(b).

226 On legal tender, see Chapter 1, sec. 3(b).

227 For England, see the Currency and Bank Notes Act 1954, c. 12, s. 1(3), for coins as legal tender in the whole UK the Currency Act 1983, c. 9, s. 1(3) amending Coinage Act 1971, c. 24, s. 2.

228 Art. 128 (1) TFEU and EU Regulation EC/974/98, Art. 10. The euro coins are regulated in Art. 128 (2) TFEU, and their designation as legal tender by EU Regulation EC/974/98, Art. 11.

229 Section 14 Bundesbankgesetz 1992.

230 *Foley v. Hill* (1848) 2 HLC 28, at 36, 43–44, *Joachimson v. Swiss Bank Corporation* [1921] 3 KB 110 (CA), at 127, *Libyan Arab Foreign Bank v. Bankers Trust Co* [1989] QB 728, at 760–761, 764: There can be an express or implied term that the customer is not entitled to demand cash, but that was not so in this case.

the bank and/or a suspension of payments imposed by the regulatory authorities. It is hard to define the legal quality of a right which one has but one can only exercise in accordance with systemic expediency, although one has little insight in, and no control over, that system. A law that always applies in general but can never be taken for granted to apply in any one of the individual cases seems to be a legal version of Zeno's paradox:[231] there cannot be motion, because at any given point in time the supposedly moving arrow occupies an equal space and therefore stands still.[232] One may want to leave any further discussion about the legal nature of such a right to rights theorists in legal philosophy and may hope that a confrontation with a practical problem will not lead to a meltdown of their otherwise splendid reasoning faculties. An analysis of the phenomenon of the 'strong debtor' and the 'weak creditor' does not seem to exist as yet.[233] For instance, if all worried pensioners ('weak creditors') were to withdraw 'their' money from their bank accounts at the same time, count the cash to check 'if it is still there', and then pay the withdrawn amount back in immediately, this would cause a complete breakdown of the banking system within a few hours. But that shows the essence of the banking business.

The second question deals with the perspective of the commercial bank as lender-creditor and creator of bank money in form of circulating debt/credit. A search for legal rules authorising this creation of bank money becomes difficult, as the examples of the UK and Germany show.

(b) Examples: UK and Germany

In the UK, the only statutory rules regarding money are the central bank money and legal tender provisions referred to before. There are no express rules in relation to the practice and creation of bank money as such. However, the acceptance of bank money by the law is beyond any doubt.[234] There has also been case law for a long time that clearly presumes bank credit as being able to operate as money. Lord Mansfield's frequently stated observation in *Miller v. Race*, that banknotes are not just documents of debt and that 'whatever the material is, common consent may make it money',[235] opens up to bank credit as a version of money, where the 'material' is only a legal-conceptual *res* as a result of common consent or custom recognised by law – an application of the concept of dematerialised property with hindsight. More modern decisions allow, or even presume, payment by bank money in satisfaction of an outstanding debt,[236] which also con-

231 Rahmatian (2018a: 232).
232 See Aristotle, *Physics*, book 6 [239b], as one major source for Zeno's paradoxes.
233 See Chapter 5, sec. 3, for the discussion of this concept.
234 For example, the ruling in *Foley v. Hill* (1848) 2 HLC 28, is underpinned by such an understanding.
235 *Miller v. Race* (1758) 2 Kenyon 189 (1 Burr 452), 96 ER 1151, at 1154.
236 E.g. *The Laconia* [1976] QB 835, at 846–847, 850, 855, *The Chikuma* [1981] 1 WLR 314, at 320.

firms legal acceptance of bank money as a form of money that can replace cash. That, in turn, requires a tacit consensus about the creation of credit – probably also out of nothing – through loan making by commercial banks whereby that credit then operates as a medium of transfer, exchange and payment. A certain insufficient appreciation of the money creation process by lawyers may support this consensus or acceptance of this banking custom.

In Germany, a lack of comprehensive understanding of the commercial banks' money creation mechanism could play an even more important role.[237] A naïve reading of § 3(1)(3) of the German Banking Act 1998 (*Kreditwesengesetz* 1998, KWG), a provision that had a predecessor in § 3(3) of the German Banking Act 1961, could suggest that the creation of money by commercial banks is actually prohibited. The provision says that the conduct of lending business or deposit business is prohibited if, by agreement or in accordance with normal business practice, it is impossible or made seriously difficult to dispose of the credit amount or of the deposits by way of withdrawal in cash.[238] The reason usually given for this prohibition is to prevent misuse of bank money or cashless payment because banks could otherwise provide credit without having liquidity (cash) available as backing assets, and could disproportionately strongly influence or increase the quantity of circulating money and therefore disturb the financial stability of a national economy.[239] Furthermore, if deposits could not be readily withdrawn in cash, a deposit guarantee would be doubtful and a bank could obtain unlimited capacity to grant loans.

At first glance this provision is directed exactly at the creation of bank money through credit. Normally cash withdrawal should be possible: the credited (lent) amount could in principle be withdrawn in cash by the borrower himself and subsequently by the creditor-recipient of the loan money for payment for the sale which the seller will have deposited in her account. However, commentators interpret the prohibition of § 3(1)(3) as applicable only if cash withdrawal is completely excluded, either by agreement, or factually made difficult, for example because of disproportionately high withdrawal fees, which means that the exclusion of cash withdrawals in individual cases is arguably not covered.[240] According to a German court decision, if a bank does not generally exclude or inhibit cash withdrawals of its loans or deposits, it does not fall under § 3, even where

237 For the following passage, see the more detailed discussion in Rahmatian (2018a: 231–235).

238 Section 3 (1) (3) Kreditwesengesetz 1998: '*Verboten sind . . . der Betrieb des Kreditgeschäftes oder des Einlagengeschäftes, wenn es durch Vereinbarung oder geschäftliche Gepflogenheit ausgeschlossen oder erheblich erschwert ist, über den Kreditbetrag oder die Einlagen durch Barabhebung zu verfügen*'.

239 The relevant statement in the preparatory material for the draft Banking Act 1961 is quoted in Schäfer, § 3 n 20 in Boos et al. (2016: 226), and at length in Bundesanstalt für Finanzdienstleistungsaufsicht (BaFin), *Merkblatt verbotene Geschäfte* (15 Nov 2012), pt. 4. See www.bafin.de/SharedDocs/Veroeffentlichungen/DE/Merkblatt/mb_121112_tatbestand_verbotene_geschaefte.html (visited 10 July 2018).

240 Schäfer, § 3 n 23 in Boos et al. (2016: 227); Schwennicke, § 3 n 17 in Schwennicke and Auerbach (2009: 219).

the bank excludes frequently cash withdrawals from loan deposits in individual cases.[241] The courts also said that if cash payout of a loan is not available, but only crediting to an account opened for the borrower instead from which giro transfers can be made, this is not a violation of § 3.[242] The reason given was that 'this practice corresponds to an ever-increasing need for cash-less transfer of money' and the bank does not evade the monetary policy measures of the German central bank in this way.[243] The question arises, however, whether the practical possibility of a cash withdrawal is perhaps the most crucial part of the loan agreement (given that technically only cash is legal tender), and whether the prohibition of § 3 is not exactly geared towards preventing banks from inflating their credit capacity by avoiding to honour their cash obligations in a great majority of individual cases of loan deposits. By creating bank money through credit, commercial banks also increase immensely the quantity of money circulating in the economy. The cash withdrawal of that bank money (credit) may not be formally prevented altogether, but significantly hindered through normal business practice,[244] which is precisely what the prohibition of § 3(1)(3) envisages. However, the creation of bank money through credit by commercial banks happens in Germany in the same way as anywhere else.[245]

If this prohibition of § 3(1)(3) BWG 1998 were operative in reality or considered applicable to bank loans that create bank money (that is the norm), then such loans would theoretically be void, and the borrower would be under no obligation to repay the loan. The problem is exacerbated by the fact that the loan provisions in the German civil code (BGB)[246] still seem to assume commodity money or physical cash for their operation and do not appear to recognise a loan sum in form of bank money or credit as being properly paid out in law.[247]

For Germany it is more difficult than for the UK to determine an established banking practice of bank money creation through credit, because there is technically the prohibition of § 3 which must be considered as relevant in principle. Section 3 is not properly appreciated and ineffective in Germany, and there is only very superficial discussion about the exact applicability of this provision. A lack of knowledge and clear understanding among lawyers of the concepts of money and money creation may also contribute to the generally held presumption of a legally recognised custom of bank money creation in Germany.

241 OLG Stuttgart, 7 December 1971, *Versicherungsrecht (VersR)* (1972), 380–387, at 381.

242 OLG Frankfurt am Main, 29 March 1972, *Wertpapier-Mitteilungen (WM)* (1972), 1196–1198, at 1197.

243 Ibid.

244 In the original provision of § 3(1)(3): '*geschäftliche Gepflogenheit*'.

245 See e.g. the outline discussion of money creation (*Geldschöpfung*) in Deutsche Bundesbank (2017: 75–82).

246 Section 488 BGB.

247 A detailed discussion of this problem in Rahmatian (2018a: 233–235), and in Chapter 5, sec. 2.

Vague as it is, the privilege of the commercial banks to be able to create new bank money is apparently recognised by the law. In England,[248] a common law country, this is perhaps through convention and long-standing banking practise, recognised indirectly by the common law, because court decisions presuppose this mechanism, otherwise they would not make sense. In Germany, a civil law country, this recognition is apparently also the presumption of a custom, without much reflection and consideration, although a statutory provision can be interpreted as actually standing against it. One may assume that similar situations can be found in most other countries.

In a broadcast of BBC *Question Time* during the election campaign for the UK general elections in 2017, former Prime Minister Theresa May famously told a nurse who did not have a pay rise for eight years: 'There isn't a magic money tree'.[249] There is no magic money tree for nurses and other non-banks, but for banks there is, only its legal basis is obscure.

7. New technologies: digital currencies, electronic forms of money[250]

(a) Electronic money

In the discussion of cash as a form of money, some issues in relation to electronic money and digital currencies have already been raised.[251] The following section will not deal with the new technology as the basis of digital currency, but with the far less new legal concepts behind it. Today, bank money transfers (giro transfers) happen electronically only, and cheques do not pass physically through the clearing cycle but are 'truncated', and now the data are transferred electronically (electronic presentation of cheques).[252] Central bank reserves are electronic records,[253] as are all commercial bank accounts. Bank money is no longer 'fountain pen money'[254] but computer data money. The difference between classical forms of money (cash and bank money) using electronic methods of recording, storage and transfer, and, on the other hand, electronic money proper and digital currency lies in the respective origin, that is, what is the authority of the source the money in question comes from – a question of the second case of money (*casus genitivus*).[255] The origin of conventional cash and bank money has been

248 There is no indication that the situation could be any different in Scotland.

249 Lizzie Dearden, 'Theresa May prompts anger after telling nurse who hasn't had pay rise for eight years: "There's no magic money tree"', *The Independent*, Saturday, 3 June 2017.

250 This section follows largely Rahmatian (2019: 115–121).

251 See Chapter 1, sec. 3(b).

252 For discussion regarding the UK, see Booysen (2018: 292–295): payment is not processed as cheque clearing, but as a debit funds transfer.

253 Bank of England (2014b: 11).

254 Tobin (1963: 1).

255 For this terminology, see Chapter 4, sec. 2.

dealt with. Electronic money is regulated in the EU Directive 2009/110/EC, which defines electronic money in Art 2 (2) as

> electronically, including magnetically, stored monetary value as represented by a claim on the issuer which is issued on receipt of funds for the purpose of making payment transactions . . . and which is accepted by a natural or legal person other than the electronic money issuer.

Money issuers include banks,[256] authorised post office giro institutions, and the European Central Bank and national central banks when not acting in their capacity as monetary authority.[257] The electronic money issuer must be authorised,[258] has to meet minimum capital and 'own funds' requirements, is required to safeguard funds received in exchange for issued electronic money, must issue and redeem electronic money at par value, and is prohibited from paying interest on the electronic money held.[259] In its nature this electronic money is a form of bank money, not legal tender and not cash in its physical form. Even if issued by central banks, it is probably still bank money because the central banks are supposed to act as a normal commercial bank and not 'in their capacity as monetary authority or other public authorities'.[260]

The difference between traditional bank money which was at one time written down in the books of the bank ('fountain pen money') and electronic money which never was, is determined by the origin and authority of the issuer or creator of that money. Electronic money may allow a bigger circle of (still authorised and regulated) issuers beside the usual commercial banks creating traditional bank money, but the quantity of electronic money issued may be subject to restrictions[261] different to those for traditional bank money where the creation is only – rather notionally – limited by the fractional reserve system. A central bank that issues its own electronic money effectively launches a digital currency beside cash or legal tender currency and competes as commercial bank with the other commercial banks and other authorised issuers. This digital currency can be a cryptocurrency, but that is a technological, not legal, categorisation.

The Bank of England defines cryptocurrencies as private currencies: 'Cryptocurrencies combine new payments systems with new currencies that are not

256 Directive 2009/110/EC, Art. 1(1)(a): 'credit institutions as defined in point 1 of Article 4 of Directive 2006/48/EC'. According to this provision 'credit institution' is: (a) an undertaking whose business is to receive deposits or other repayable funds from the public and to grant credits for its own account; or (b) an (authorised) electronic money institution, the authorisation being granted under Title II of the Directive 2009/110/EC).

257 Directive 2009/110/EC, Art. 1(1)(c) and (d).

258 Directive 2009/110/EC, Art. 10.

259 Directive 2009/110/EC, Arts. 4, 5, 7, 11, 12.

260 Directive 2009/110/EC, Art. 1(1)(d).

261 Directive 2009/110/EC, Art. 5.

issued by a central bank',[262] and gives Bitcoin and Ethereum as examples.[263] This definition is not compelling because a central bank can, and presumably would, also use cryptocurrency technology for its own digital currency, and central bank reserves are also 'electronic money'. However, since the terminology is really a question of labelling, one can make the distinction between regulated digital currencies (electronic money) which are issued by central banks, commercial banks and other electronic money issuers, all of which are authorised, and cryptocurrencies which are privately created and not necessarily authorised or regulated. The terminology is not stringent in any particular direction. The Bank of England has recently dropped plans to launch its own digital currency to rival private cryptocurrencies because of fears that the issuing of digital currencies by central banks could lead to instabilities of the global financial system,[264] a concern that was echoed by the Bank for International Settlement (BIS).[265]

A digital currency issued by an ordinary commercial bank is similar to the old commercial banks' practice to issue their own banknotes, a practice which continued well into the nineteenth century. Digital currency is cash and currency, but not legal tender. But that is not a novelty either: traditional bank money essentially also operates as currency today, and although it is not technically legal tender, there is very little difference in effect. Both traditional bank money and electronic money undermine the old State theory of money[266] with its arguably already outdated idea that money ('cash') must be issued by a state authority, either by the state itself (coins) or its central bank (banknotes). Electronic money and digital currencies are therefore not really new phenomena from a legal-conceptual perspective.

It can become complicated to distinguish the pedigree of different versions of electronic money if a central bank does decide to issue digital currency: what is traditional cash and what is electronic cash? As long as traditional cash is a *res* reified by banknotes (paper money), such a distinction is possible in principle. However, 'cashless payment', that is, electronic (commercial) bank money transfer, looks the same as a central bank money transfer of this new electronic money/digital currency, and any concept of legal tender becomes doubtful. The origin and creation of these versions of electronically recorded, stored and transferred money are nevertheless fundamentally different: the central bank money creation on the one hand and the commercial bank money creation on the other have been discussed before,[267] as well as the problems that are attached to the commercial bank money creation system. There could also be the option of issuing

262 See Bank of England, 'Digital Currencies', available at: www.bankofengland.co.uk/research/digital-currencies (visited 12 July 2018).

263 See below under (b) for these private digital currencies.

264 David Thorpe, 'Bank halts crypto-currency plans over stability fears', *FT Adviser*, 4 Jan. 2018.

265 Claire Jones, Hannah Murphy, 'Central bank cryptocurrencies pose stability risk, says BIS', *Financial Times*, 12 March 2018. See also Chapter 1, sec. 3 under the discussion of cash.

266 Proctor (2012: 50–51).

267 See above under secs. 2 and 3.

electronic money not through creation of a debt: the fundamental distinguishing factor between central and commercial bank money and forms of electronic money would then be whether the *res* comes into existence as a debt – like with cash and commercial bank money – or not. In case of a difference, parallel systems of electronic currency (electronic bank money and e-money) could hardly be maintained separately in banking practice. However, the EU Directive on electronic money seems to envisage electronic money based on debt anyway.[268]

This difficulty of distinguishing also affects the discussion about the abolition of cash: in principle, the abolition of paper notes does not necessarily mean that cash will be abolished, as long as the electronic money replaces the paper money but the origin and method of money creation remain the same: the issue of electronic money stays with the central bank on the same terms as with old paper money. However, it will be hard to ascertain the conversion of electronic central bank money ('cash') into commercial bank money when a customer pays her electronic cash into her bank account, for example. The underlying idea of the abolition of cash is, however, not so much the progress towards digitisation but the complete replacement of central bank money by commercial bank money, so that the creation of money is entirely in the hands of commercial banks, that is, private enterprises. That obviously raises serious economic and political concerns.[269] But it would be a move with results probably not too different from the effect of private digital currencies or cryptocurrencies.

(b) Private digital currencies: cryptocurrencies – Bitcoin

'Cryptocurrencies', the best known being Bitcoin, are defined here as private digital currencies or 'virtual currencies'[270] that are not – or in principle are not – originating from a central or commercial bank or another authorised issuer of electronic money. As said before, this definition is arbitrary but may be expedient. Sweden, for example, is currently looking into a 'cryptocurrency', but that also appears to be a form of e-money, and the Swedish Riksbank has recently warned

268 Directive 2009/110/EC, Art. 2(2): '"electronic money" means electronically . . . stored monetary value as represented *by a claim on the issuer* which is issued on receipt of funds *for the purpose of making payment transactions*' (emphasis added). That seems to mirror the *Foley v. Hill* rule of customer's deposits in a bank account and the transferability of the customer's *res*-claim or credit for the purpose of payment, so that rule does not indicate a conceptual difference.

269 E.g. Chris Giles, 'Scrap cash altogether, says Bank of England's chief economist', *Financial Times*, 18 September 2015; Patrick Jenkins, 'We don't take cash: is this the future of money?', *Financial Times*, 10 May 2018.

270 Definition of virtual currencies now by EU Directive (EU) 2015/849, Art. 2(1) point (18) added by EU Directive 2018/843 of 30 May 2018, Art. 1(2)(d): '"virtual currencies" means a digital representation of value that is not issued or guaranteed by a central bank or a public authority, is not necessarily attached to a legally established currency and does not possess a legal status of currency or money, but is accepted by natural or legal persons as a means of exchange and which can be transferred, stored and traded electronically'.

against false reports that it sells 'e-kronas'.[271] From the viewpoint of dematerialised property, it is irrelevant whether the *res* is a debt, reified in form of paper or coin or not, or a token, physical or virtual, that acts as a medium of exchange, such as a 'Bitcoin'. As with electronic money or digital currency issued by banks, the most important distinguishing factor with cryptocurrencies is whether the *res* comes into existence as a debt – like with cash and commercial bank money – or not. If not, then it also matters whether this virtual monetary unit is expected to be converted readily into conventional cash or bank money, in which case one may ask whether there is a need to interpose this unit as an additional means of exchange if one finally resorts to conventional debt-based money anyway. The following discusses Bitcoin as the most important example of a private digital currency or cryptocurrency.

Bitcoin operates on the basis of blockchain technology. Blockchain ensures the digital transfer of information with a mathematical algorithm, a hash function, that takes an input and transforms it into an output (hash). The algorithm used is cryptographic, so that the input data can hardly be recreated from the algorithmically transformed value. Blockchain consists of a chain of transactional records that network participants or 'miners' enrich by solving difficult mathematical-computational problems. Miners then compete anonymously on the network to solve the mathematical problem and in this way add the next block to the blockchain. The block reward for this endeavour are 'newly minted coins' (newly created digital tokens), which are sent to the miner's public address. The more miners exist, the more complicated the computational problems become to mine a new block. For the transfer of information, for example payment, blockchain technology ensures the elimination of double payment.[272] Each agent is assigned a private key (kept secret) and a public key (shared with all other agents). A transaction is initiated when the future owner of the 'coins' sends his/her key to the original owner. The 'coins' are transferred by the digital signature of a hash. Public keys are cryptographically generated addresses stored in the blockchain. Each coin is associated with an address, and a transaction is a transfer from one address to another. If the miner wants to use/spend these 'coins', he/she has to sign with the corresponding private key. Transactions do not disclose the actors' identity but remain traceable as such.[273] The potential use of blockchain technology is not restricted to cryptocurrencies but can extend to the safe signing and transfer of digital contracts and documents of all sorts, like conveyancing documents or negotiable instruments.[274]

271 See Swedish Central Bank (Riksbank), available at: www.riksbank.se/en-gb/financial-stability/payments/e-krona/ (visited 19 July 2018).

272 Usually Bitcoin explanations talk about the 'double-spending' problem, a legally imprecise term, because what we are interested in here is 'payment' in a technical sense.

273 Pilkington (2016: 226, 228).

274 For example with the use of Ethereum, a blockchain-based platform for digital contracts, see Pilkington (2016: 240).

Blockchain is a distributed ledger technology – 'ledger' because any change of information appears as a new entry in the ledger, a new 'block', so that all changes of information are recorded and not replaced and can therefore be traced. When a party makes a transaction to another, a number of Bitcoins are transferred, and the parties' public addresses and the transaction time are recorded on a public ledger. This distributed, as opposed to a centralised, method, makes the apparent appeal of Bitcoin.[275] The most important feature is that it is a peer-to-peer system of electronic cash creation and transmission: transactions occur among users directly without the involvement of a financial intermediary, that is, a bank.[276] This decentralised public ledger system can become a competitor to traditional payment agencies, and since the transfer system is effected by millions of anonymous users, any regulation is difficult. That is the original idea of Bitcoin: digitally sending something of actual value directly between the parties to the transaction, without any human intermediary,[277] with greatest reliance on the accuracy of the encrypted data, but without any possible interference by a regulating body which could seize upon an intermediary, such as a bank, and, equally important, without an intermediary bank imposing costs and fees. Bitcoin also competes with the fiat currency issued by the central banks.[278]

This brief explanation of Bitcoin should be sufficient for present purposes. It has been commented that available descriptions of Blockchain and Bitcoin 'are marked by an apparent widespread absence of sufficiently authoritative description. It appears that most descriptions of the two are liberally sprinkled with metaphor, ostensibly in order to more carefully explain it to a business readership'.[279] This reflects the author's own observations at respective conferences and elsewhere: when the merits of Bitcoin or otherwise will be discussed now, one should never forget that Bitcoin is just another financial business product that wants to be sold, like mortgages or credit derivatives and the underlying specialist software. Its apparent libertarianism and anarchistic freedom are only advertising strategies that pretend an alternative. But it seeks to present itself as a social movement.[280]

The system of Bitcoin is based on scarcity,[281] that is, the 'mining' of 'coins' is limited by the algorithm to just under 21 million Bitcoins. In this regard it is not

275 Lilienthal and Ahmad (2018: 50).

276 Lu (2018: 178). In the words of the purported inventor of Bitcoin, Satoshi Nakamoto, *Bitcoin: A Peer-to-Peer Electronic Cash System* (2008): 'What is needed is an electronic payment system based on cryptographic proof instead of trust, allowing any two willing parties to transact directly with each other without the need for a trusted third party. Transactions that are computationally impractical to reverse would protect sellers from fraud, and routine escrow mechanisms could easily be implemented to protect buyers', available at: https://bitcoin.org/bitcoin.pdf (visited 15 July 2018).

277 Lilienthal and Ahmad (2018: 50).

278 Raskin and Yermack (2018: 474, 476).

279 Lilienthal and Ahmad (2018: 49).

280 Dodd (2018: 39–40).

281 Dodd (2018: 42).

dissimilar to commodity money or commodity-backed money based on precious metals. The difference is that technological advances can make the mining of gold and silver quicker and more efficient, while the Bitcoin system makes mining more complex with every new Bitcoin created. The intensive use of energy for mining by computers is already dangerously high, and given the challenging situation of the world climate any extensive further mining for more widespread use of Bitcoin would be out of question just because of that.[282] This scarcity – literally a virtual scarcity – was a principal reason behind the speculative bubble of Bitcoin until late 2017; the bubble burst just before Christmas: on 16 July 2017 the price of Bitcoin was US$1,938.94; on 15 November 2017 it was $7,279.00; on 15 July 2018 it was $6,349.04; and the peak came at $19,343.04 on 16 December 2017. This is market behaviour comparable to the historical Dutch tulip speculation of 1637, and equally perilous. Not surprisingly, Bitcoin has already been termed a 'scam'.[283] A member of the executive board of the European Central Bank described Bitcoin as 'the evil spawn of the financial crisis' and as 'a combination of a bubble, a Ponzi scheme and an environmental disaster'.[284]

The scarcity inbuilt in the Bitcoin system invites hoarding and speculation, and if Bitcoin is a currency, then this is a particularly extreme example of the non-neutrality of money (which mainstream economics however denies). It is certainly not an invariant unit of account or *numéraire* but a commodity for speculation purposes, whereby the original purpose of the commodity becomes irrelevant in the speculation. Bitcoin is not a generally accepted means of payment either, so it is not a medium of exchange as normal money would be. And Bitcoin is not a store of value because that cannot be achieved with these massive changes in value due to the speculative movements of a small number of issuers and of investors in the high-tech sector. Thus Bitcoin is not a currency as normally understood. If anything, Bitcoin gives a chance to obtain currency of an increased amount of value at a later point in time. A major reason for the Bitcoin boom has been that with Bitcoin, businesses in China could circumvent the official banking channels for transferring money abroad, which are severely restricted and closely monitored by the Chinese government. So transferors convert currency into Bitcoin and then reconvert Bitcoins into the currency of the destination to avoid government regulation. Leaving aside the further concern of Bitcoin as a vehicle for money laundering and other criminal activities,[285] this shows that Bitcoin, though technically a separate *res*, still operates with reference to a real currency only for the foreseeable future: in this regard, there is no difference to property or gold as an object of speculation, transfer and/or money laundering. The nature of Bitcoin has also

282 Lu (2018: 178–179).

283 Bill Harris (founding CEO of PayPal), 'Bitcoin is the greatest scam in history', *recode*, 24 April 2018, available at: www.recode.net/2018/4/24/17275202/bitcoin-scam-cryptocurrency-mining-pump-dump-fraud-ico-value (visited 15 July 2018).

284 Claire Jones, 'ECB official dubs bitcoin 'evil spawn of the financial crisis', *Financial Times*, 15 November 2018.

285 Lu (2018: 178, 180).

been likened to a bill of lading or another registrable security or documentary intangible.[286] This may be so, but a bill of lading refers to property with an intrinsic value, goods and physical property, while Bitcoin ultimately refers to currency as the most fungible property. So its interposition is superfluous, given that real currency can achieve at least the same as Bitcoin, especially payment. Since for its actual purpose, payment, Bitcoin must ultimately rely on existing currency, this suggests that the real role of Bitcoin at the moment is to enable speculation and the circumvention of fiscal regulations in particular.

The distinguishing and seemingly attractive feature of Bitcoin, to cut out the middleman in the money transfer, the bank, or to become independent from state-issued fiat money,[287] is no longer that appealing after a closer look. The Bitcoin idea suggests decentralised 'money' and therefore independence from banks and denationalisation of money or cash that is supposed to become free from central banks as issuers. The argument for a denationalisation of money is not a new one; a prominent representative of this argument was F. A. Hayek. In his view, a free trade in money would ensure that monetary and financial agencies were forced to issue a kind of money that is not substantially less reliable and useful than that of their competitors, because the public would otherwise switch to the more reliable alternative currency. Since discharge of debts does not have to happen with legal tender, and legal tender is a mystical and dispensable concept anyway, there is no need that the state issues the money. Hayek argues that private money can perfectly well operate as a payment method: it is sufficient if the law enables the judge to decide in what sort of money a particular debt can be discharged. Far better than government monopoly, competition would control and safeguard the value of a currency. The situation for such private money, Hayek says, is similar to that of existing bank money: here depositors also trust their banks that they will always be able to exchange demand deposits for cash, even if they know that a bank can never meet all cash payment obligations at the same time. Money which preserves its purchasing power without significant variability would remain in continuous demand.[288] M. Friedman and A. J. Schwartz seconded Hayek and added that government intervention was at least as often a source of instability and inefficiency as the reverse, and that the establishment of a central banking system (the US Federal Reserve System) did more harm than good; monetary and banking arrangements should rather be left to the market.[289]

As with all ideas of *laissez-faire* liberalism, this one also presupposes all market participants being on a level playing field which has never existed at the beginning and which becomes increasingly skewed with further progress. If one assumes that Bitcoin is already a fully functioning currency, this and other private (digital) currencies would have the following effects. As all currencies, these 'free' currencies would be the object of speculation, so every market participant would have

286 Lilienthal and Ahmad (2018: 55).
287 On this narrative, see e.g. Dodd (2018: 39).
288 Hayek (1990: 23, 37–38, 48–49, 52).
289 Friedman and Schwartz (1986: 40, 59).

to decide which currency should be used for the discharge of debts: effectively, all businesses and all individuals would have to be their own informed private trader and follow closely the currency market to avoid severe exchange losses. That would also apply to the pensioner, the specialist in medieval history, the French teacher, the garden designer and the doctor because we all pay with currency: we all would have to acquire the relevant business skills to cope with keeping our purchase power afloat. (These skills come perhaps at the expense of our existing expertise – the day has only 24 hours, or we would have to retain a currency manager with a disastrous increase of transaction costs for this new currency.) There would also be an unprecedented rise in carry trade which may contribute to the destabilisation of currencies,[290] and this trade would not only happen between different national currencies as it is now, but between parallel global private currencies, and further perilous speculation would ensue. The 'free market' would necessarily lead to monopolies and oligopolies soon, so that a few remaining players would dominate the Bitcoin and cryptocurrency market in respect of mining, hoarding and payment facilities. The history of the internet in the 1990s is a role model for such a development: the supposedly democratic-anarchistic internet has become an internet of Facebook, Google and Amazon. The entities which control cryptocurrencies can be the existing or new transnational internet giants, but also banks themselves who either directly, or through subsidiaries, become the hidden dominant powers in the cryptocurrency market. That can assist them in circumventing banking regulation applicable to them.

Once a domination of the 'free' market of cryptocurrencies is established, large multinational entities can then exercise economic pressure against other businesses and individual employees as to which currencies have to be accepted as payment of business debts or of salaries. One can be sure that the currency issuers/controllers will not lose out, so that they may stipulate that specific currencies are not (always) accepted as full discharge of debt. That would be possible because there is not supposed to be a fiat money system anyway. Every payment in a certain currency is therefore really *in lieu of* payment, and the accepted concrete payment will be the one with a currency which gives the creditor the best purchasing power according to the market at a given moment. Currency market manipulations, and more extensive ones than the recent LIBOR (London Interbank Offered Rate) manipulations,[291] will be likely. While the present banking system controls people and business through debt as a result of the bank money creation, a free digital currency system would additionally allow creditors to control when and with which currency the debt can be discharged at all. Since Bitcoin prides itself of providing a secure encryption to prevent fraud and of being open to an indefinite number of users in a peer-to-peer network, an effective banking regulation is practically impossible. While the transactions can be traced,

290 Brunnermeier et al. (2008: 313, 341–342).

291 Douglas Keenan, 'My thwarted attempt to tell of the Libor shenanigans', *Financial Times*, 26 July 2012; Philip Stafford, 'Global regulators warn banks must abandon reliance on Libor', *Financial Times*, 12 July 2018.

the identity of the multitude of users cannot, and there is no established entity (like a bank) which could be the addressee of regulatory measures. For a regulator and the law, this is asymmetric warfare. That may appeal to some internet gurus, but large corporations can and will do the same as private techno-freaks, like the established fashion industry that also sells cool insurgency-style outfits: you can do anything, as long as you retain paying consumers, and consumers in relation to different systems of payment at that.

For these reasons, liberalisation of currencies in form of Bitcoin and other private digital currencies should be rejected;[292] even an open prohibition should be a debatable option.[293] Bitcoin was never 'free', libertarian or 'anarchistic', this is only a sales pitch of the companies that sell the technology for cryptocurrencies. Bitcoin also has a tinge of the clandestine and secretive with its complex energy-intensive computer operations and the opacity of its private actors, which does not make it an appealing alternative currency in a democratic society. Myths seem to stand at the cradle of systems of money: the mysterious inventor of Bitcoin[294] reminds of the mystical Hermes Trismegistus (who we will encounter later) as the purported author of foundational alchemistic texts.[295] Reams of pages of mathematics, economics and techno-speak cannot do away with the fact that the functioning of money ultimately rests on myth, creed and irrationality, and on a modicum of shiftiness.

8. Conclusion

In this chapter it has been shown why money is a debt.[296] This becomes apparent from an examination of the way in which money is supplied, or more accurately, created. There are three different theories of money supply, but the only one which is in accordance with banking law is the credit creation theory that explains money supply as an *ex nihilo* creation of money through a special accounting record of a bank. This is particularly the case of bank money. Over 95% of all circulating money is bank money created by commercial banks through granting loans (credit) without recourse to customers' deposits that the banks hold. Banks grant credit by indebting themselves, and the borrower pays his debts with the debts of the bank. It has also been discussed why banks can create money through lending while non-banks are unable to do the same, and what the legal basis for that privilege of the banks could be; the examples given are the laws of the UK and of Germany. The creation of cash by central banks is the second way

292 A similar problem could arise with non-digital private currencies or complementary currencies. However, in reality these are so far very locally restricted and often expressly reject the liberal market model, for example the 'Chiemgauer', see Chapter 5, sec. 5.

293 On the crackdown on Bitcoin exchanges by the Chinese authorities, see Lu (2018: 181).

294 L.S., 'Who is Satoshi Nakamoto?', *The Economist*, 2 November 2015.

295 See Chapter 4.

296 At least among critical economists that does no longer seem to be doubted. See e.g. Haribey et al. (2018: 17, 85).

of money creation and in the eyes of the general public the more important, if not the only, form, although in reality less than 5% of all money is cash.

The creation of money through a debt and as a debt conceptualises money as a debt in law. It is a janiform debt, being created as a loan debt against the borrower and at the same time being a circulating debt operating as money (medium of exchange). In its form as a circulating debt, it is a claim against a bank where the amount of money appears in credit in an account with the bank as a book debt (bank money). Since it is a (loan) debt, it (almost without exception) attracts interest that rises, broadly, exponentially. That debt, plus interest, is enforceable in law, and it is that enforceability which makes this circulating debt operative as money because the reliance on potential enforcement makes it generally accepted as payment. Thus money is entirely a creature of law. The chapter finishes with an outline of the way in which digital currencies, such as Bitcoin, could fit into, or upset, the present system of money.

Many economists, but by no means all, reject the credit creation theory of money. Keynes, for example, considered this concept as a 'new-fangled' erroneous view,[297] while Schumpeter recognised it. Despite the frequent criticism voiced against economists in this book, it is necessary to emphasise that there were always great economists who clearly understood the system of money creation and its economic consequences, for example Walter Eucken (1891–1950), the father of ordoliberalism. The brevity of his discussion is particularly impressive:[298]

> How can monetary instability be explained? – Mostly because banks became 'mints'. Since the 18th century it increasingly happened that money originated through acts of granting credit by banks, and disappeared with the repayment of loans to the banks – that applies to the banknotes and bank money of central banks as well as to the bank money of commercial banks. These are the two most important forms of money in the present age. Fluctuations in the quantity of bank loans also leads to a change of the quantity of money. Expansion of credit means increase of the quantity of money; restraint in granting credit – while earlier loans are repaid – reduction of the quantity of money. Every day money comes into existence with the grant of credit by banks, and every day money disappears with the repayment of credit.

Chapter 3 will demonstrate that a major reason for most economists' lack of understanding of money is their idea of a static concept of the market and of the role of money in it. In such a theoretical static market equilibrium, money can then be cancelled out as a neutral *numéraire*. In fact, money is not a neutral unit but a quasi-alchemic agent in the exchange. Chapter 4 will discuss that only a dynamic concept of money can explain the function of money in the market properly.

297 Keynes (1964: 83).

298 Eucken (1959: 163) (own translation from the German). See also Lautenbach (1952: 45) for the accounting procedure involved.

3 Money as a static concept: money in economics

1. The (non)recognition of money by economists in microeconomics

Chapter 1 has included a discussion of some definitions of money by economists.[1] From that it has become clear that the *legal* concept of money needs a legal definition first, which was the main subject of Chapter 1. Chapter 2 has explained how money is created within the legal framework that makes the legal concept of money. Chapter 2 has also shown that economists often have an incorrect idea about the money creation/money supply process. That contributes to unsatisfactory economic definitions of money. This chapter will show why economists rarely attempt to develop a satisfactory conception of money. A major reason is the role economists assign to money in the prevalent static microeconomic market model.

(a) *Sale as a form of barter and the absence of money in microeconomics*

It is slightly astonishing that there does not seem to be a real conceptualisation of money in microeconomics.[2] The modern economic market analysis of supply (s) and demand (d) uses the equilibrium model of quantity and price which intersect at a point at which a notional market is cleared (that is, the equilibrium price at which the equilibrium quantity is demanded and supplied, not more and not less).[3] At that point, '*chaque acheteur ou vendeur trouve exactement sa contre-partie chez un vendeur ou acheteur. Il y a équilibre du marché*' (Walras).[4] As already explained briefly in the first chapter, this model does not refer to money at all. In the equation for the market's equilibrium ($s = d$, or $q = p$, with

1 Chapter 1, sec. 3(b).
2 E.g. Ingham (2004: 22).
3 One can find a discussion of the supply-demand model in all economics textbooks, e.g. Mankiw (2012: 67–78). An early discussion of the market equilibrium by Smith, *Wealth of Nations*, book 1, chapter 7 (2000: 64–65).
4 Walras, *Éléments*, § 47 (1926: 52). See also ibid., § 60 at p. 64.

q = quantity, p = price), money is effectively cancelled out and does not feature. This is consequent, because money is postulated as a neutral means of exchange to facilitate barter but, in economic theory, not to replace barter by sale.[5] The fact that sale is a barter in the economists' reductionist conceptualisation of sales transactions conceals the fact that money does not constitute a real commodity itself but represents an expectation in relation to real commodities in the future; nevertheless, for economists money is already a complete representation of that (possible) future real commodity. In this way money is seen as effectively a 'real commodity'[6] itself, while at the same time it serves as an empty conceptual vessel of no intrinsic value that can be filled with randomly exchangeable real commodities. For example, I sell a ballpoint pen for £5, eventually to buy a loaf of bread. The banknote I receive denotes an expectation in relation to a real commodity in the future, in my case a loaf of bread. Economists regard this sale as equivalent to a real barter (pen against bread directly), while at the same time consider money as an entirely neutral vehicle that represents any other kind of future commodity (because I can also buy chocolate with it). This paradox is an essential part of the microeconomic market model and rarely discussed. It is also characteristic that the time factor (one does not get the bread immediately in exchange) and the risk element (one may get less or nothing for one's banknote, which one cannot eat and which is worthless by itself) are blanked out totally by microeconomics.

(b) Just price and market price

(i) The price in sale and 'barter'

The discipline of economics disguises the legally extremely important difference between barter and sale in its market model.[7] However, it is the law which makes transactions of this kind possible, because it enforces and safeguards such transactions. Without these legal transactions, there would be no market.[8] For a lawyer this blurring of barter and sale is astonishing, not only because of the required distinction between these types of contract in statutory rules and case law, for example terms which protect the purchaser in a sale but not in a barter,[9] but also because the question of the satisfactory price, established for 'barter' (to use the

5 Similar criticism as here by Heinsohn and Steiger (2013: 21–23), and in more scientific depth Binswanger (2013: 2–3, 16–19), more detail in the German edition of Binswanger (2009: 24–26, 40 et seq.). Adam Smith tended to distinguish between 'treaty, barter and purchase', see Smith, *Wealth of Nations*, book 1, chapter 2 (2000: 15–16).

6 On this term, see Chapter 4, sec. 3(c): real commodities have an intrinsic or contemplative value, while imaginary commodities (such as money) define their value through their exchange value only.

7 Economists generally do not seem to be aware of that. Streissler (1984: 2) is an exception.

8 See also Commons (1924: 241), with particular reference to money and legal tender.

9 E.g. in the UK: Sale of Goods Act 1979, s. 2(1) (definition of a sale of goods contract), *Dawson v. Dutfield* [1936] 2 All ER 232 (England), *Sneddon v. Durant*, 1982 SLT (Sh. Ct.) 39 (Scotland).

economists' transaction concept of sale equalling barter), is answered potentially differently by economists and by lawyers.

For the economist, the best price is the price that balances quantity as supplied and quantity as demanded, the equilibrium price, as a result of the supposedly autonomous market forces, that is, free competition. For the lawyer, the acceptable – that is, lawful – price is the 'just' price, and that is not necessarily the market price, so there is an element of perhaps paternalistic intervention in the theoretically free forces of market competition.[10] For example, in a Scottish court case decided in 1976 it was held that a 'reasonable price' (a term used in a rule of the UK Sale of Goods Act)[11] means something different from the market price or market value, and the court can reach a determination as to what was a reasonable price. The court also observed that a 'reasonable price' must be fair and just to both parties.[12] Intervention may not only happen by a deciding judge but can be ordered by the statute directly (we leave aside issues of defects in the contract formation, such as error or mistake, fraud and deceit, which permit the aggrieved party to rescind the contract). In some jurisdictions the old *ius commune* remedy of *laesio enormis* is still part of the law in force.[13] The *laesio enormis* addresses the point of gross disproportion between value and price: if the value of the goods is less than one-half of the price paid for it, the buyer can rescind the contract, without any further conditions. Other jurisdictions do not have this rule and so avoid being too interventionist.[14] The question arises how one arrives at the 'real', 'just', 'common' price or 'fair market value'.[15] The economic supply-demand model of the equilibrium price is here not of much assistance because it is quite possible that an equilibrium price emerges which is no fair reflection of the 'value', especially if there are only few sales on that market and/or an assessment of the value is particularly opaque (antiquities, real estate).

10 It may be necessary to point out that the 'just price' has nothing to do with the 'natural price' of the Classical School of economics. On that see Smith, *Wealth of Nations*, book 1, chapter 7 (2000: 62–63), and Marshall, *Principles*, V, 3, § 6 (2013: 289). The 'natural price' is the price of the long-term market equilibrium the Classical School is interested in, while the market price is the actual price at which the commodity is commonly sold in specific transactions which are by nature short term, so that the market price can be above or below the natural price. Both the classical natural price and the neo-classical (or also classical) market price could be just or unjust. However, the *long-term* natural price was likely to be considered as just in principle by the classical economists, such as Adam Smith.

11 According to Sale of Goods Act 1979, s. 8 (2), where the contract of sale does not determine the price the buyer must pay a reasonable price. What is a reasonable price is a question of fact dependent on the circumstances of each particular case.

12 *Glynwed Distribution Ltd. v S. Koronka & Co.*, 1977 S.C. 1, at pp. 7–8, 11.

13 E.g. § 934 Austrian ABGB, Art. 2589 Louisiana Civil Code (restricted to corporeal immoveables), Art. 1674 French Code Civil (restricted to immoveable property, and the quota is 7/12).

14 E.g. Germany. The argument not to include the *laesio enormis* in the German BGB was that the certainty of commercial transactions would suffer. However, the usury provision of § 138 (2) BGB refers to a 'conspicuous disproportion of the performance given in return' which includes cases of *laesio enormis*.

15 The last term is used by Art. 2589 of the Louisiana Civil Code.

Economists would probably agree that nobody can determine with certainty what a 'fair' or 'just' price really is. Free-market economists obviously viewed any (ultimately ideological) intervention in the development of prices with great suspicion, for example Hayek in the *Road to Serfdom*:[16]

> Most people find it difficult to admit that we do not possess moral standards which would enable us to settle these questions [of common good or social welfare] – if not perfectly, at least to greater general satisfaction than is done by the competitive system. Have we not all some idea of what is a 'just price' or a 'fair wage'? . . . What standards we have are derived from the competitive regime we have known, and would necessarily disappear soon after the disappearance of competition. . . . What the 'just price' of a particular commodity . . . is, might conceivably be determined objectively if the quantities needed were independently fixed. . . . We need say no more about the likelihood of men in a free society submitting to such control – or about their remaining free if they submitted. . . . [S]ocialists everywhere were the first to recognise that the task they had set themselves required the general acceptance of a common *Weltanschauung*, of a definite set of values. It was in these efforts to produce a mass movement supported by such a single world view, that the socialists first created most of the instruments of indoctrination of which Nazis and Fascists have made such effective use.

These passages show how much Hayek's text, published for the first time in 1944, has to be seen in a historical context and cannot be dissociated from a certain intellectual climate, although mainstream economics usually adopts a universal, ahistorical view. Hayek's proposed alternative against a '*Weltanschauung*' or worldview provided by socialism or fascism is the liberal idea of the free market to protect a free society of free individuals against totalitarianism of the left or the right. This can be explained from the historical circumstances. But it is also a *Weltanschauung*, and this market-fundamentalist (or 'neo-liberal')[17] *Weltanschauung* was even considered as compatible with entirely unfree societies, such as the dictatorship in Chile in the 1970s and 1980s. At least that was seen as a lesser evil for an unspecified interim period of time.[18]

The ordoliberalism of the Freiburg School after the Second World War was suspicious of the idea that prices alone would be able to regulate the market

16 Hayek, *Road to Serfdom* (2001: 114–117).

17 This is the usual term today to denote the market-fundamentalist position of economic *laissez-faire* liberalism, and it still carries with it a pejorative polemic overtone, as did the term 'capitalism' originally, too, see Jessua (2010: 3–4). The term 'neo-liberalism' is and was never an exact one, see immediately below.

18 That was the view of Friedman, *Free Markets and the Generals* (1982: 59). However, Friedman qualified his position considerably (ibid.): 'I have long argued that economic freedom is a necessary but not sufficient condition for political freedom. I have become persuaded that this generalisation, while true, is misleading unless accompanied by the proposition that political freedom in turn is a necessary condition for the long-term maintenance of economic freedom'.

satisfactorily. This ordoliberal school, which helped to develop the 'social market economy' of the post-war period on the European continent, can claim to be as much part of the 'neo-liberals' as the Austrian School (Hayek) or the *laissez-faire* economists; in fact the term 'neo-liberalism' originally sought to distinguish the ordoliberal economic order from classical *laissez-faire* liberalism.[19] But the Freiburg School and the Austrian School parted company soon after 1945.[20] Therefore the term 'market-fundamentalism' is used in this book instead of the vague label 'neo-liberalism'. That may not have a less derogatory flavour, but it has more precision: the market-fundamentalist view – based on neo-classical economics and being apparently the prevalent one in economics now – emphasises the fundamental and foundational importance of the market and its operations according to quasi-natural laws in all social relations well beyond the traditional spheres of commerce and economics. Hence 'law' in relation to contracts and prices is, or must be, a function of the operations of the market and cannot be their framer or designer. In contrast, Walter Eucken (1891–1950), one of the fathers of ordoliberalism, stressed that any system of market regulation, also the *laissez-faire* idea of (selective) non-regulation,[21] has so far failed and different methods used concurrently do not interact or complement each other. For example, market regulation that is left to the 'free' change of prices does not take account of the fact that prices can be misleading because they do not necessarily reflect the forces of supply and demand of the market but can be the result of instabilities of the monetary system, the workings of monopolies or oligopolies and so on. So economic policy should not be subservient to the potentially deceptive development of market prices.[22] This applies all the more to legal considerations: a 'just price' in law can regard the market price only as an indicator but not as decisive direction.

(ii) Historical-philosophical and religious ideas of the 'just price'

The question of the just price has an old theological and philosophical pedigree. In the sixteenth century the Salamanca School in Spain prepared the debate of economic thinking which would be influential well into the eighteenth century, when the discipline of modern economics started. For Luís Saravia de la Calle, the just price arises from the abundance or scarcity of goods, merchants and money and not from costs, labour and risk.[23] According to Francisco García, the just price corresponds to the value which itself depends on a (subjective) utility of the thing in question, but scarcity of goods, buyers/sellers and money play a

19 A more detailed and sophisticated discussion of the origin and use of the term 'neo-liberalism' is not possible here, see instead e.g. Willgerodh (2006: 61, 65–67, 71).

20 Goldschmidt and Hesse (2013: 123).

21 This apparent contradiction expresses the fact that *laissez-faire* markets are also, and invariably, enforced by the state, see Polanyi (2001: 145).

22 Eucken (1959: 107, 113–114).

23 Luís Saravia de la Calle, in Grice-Hutchinson (1952: 82).

role.[24] Martín de Azpilcueta also equates just price with what the thing at issue is worth.[25] Leonardus Lessius distinguishes between the legal price imposed by the state (the prince) which is fixed, and the common price[26] which allows some flexibility as it appears as the lowest (pious), the middle, and the highest (rigorous) price. The common price is the result of the common estimation of knowledgeable people, and with reference to Roman law, Lessius says that 'it is obvious that this price is just'.[27] Luis de Molina observes that if a price is the current price in the public market, that 'greatly contributes to considering it just'.[28] Both Molina and Lessius already point towards the modern market price as the appropriate yardstick.[29]

Adam Smith's distinction between the natural price and the actual price (market price), which is either above, below or the same as the natural price,[30] reflects some of the discussions of the Salamanca School. However, he no longer focuses on the 'just price' but the price as exchange value which, in his view, is itself determined by the quantity of labour from which the commodity in question results.[31]

Today, the just price has been replaced by the economists' equilibrium price to all intents and purposes, so that the intrinsic or contemplative value of real commodities has been superseded by the exchange value of imaginary commodities, which is a precondition for commodification and monetisation.[32] The potential, and very limited, intervention in the market by the law through its usury provisions and the *laesio enormis* can be seen as a remnant of the idea of the just price.[33]

(c) *The orthodox economic model of the market forces of supply and demand*

The further discussion will show that the free market is no guarantee for fair prices at all, also because of the system of money involved, and yet, the impact of money is explained away and masked in the economic model of commodity

24 Francisco García, in Grice-Hutchinson (1952: 104–105).
25 Azpilcueta, *On Exchange*, secs. 1–4, 14 (2014: 33).
26 See also Domingo de Soto with reference to Aristotle, in Grice-Hutchinson (1952: 85).
27 Lessius, *De iustitia et iure*, book 2, ch 21, question 2 (2016: 16–17).
28 Molina, *De iustitia et iure*, Argument 404 (2015: 84).
29 A discussion of definitions of 'price' with a historical overview e.g. in Fetter (1912: 784, 798).
30 Smith, *Wealth of Nations*, book 1, chapter 7 (2000: 63).
31 Smith, *Wealth of Nations*, book 1, chapter 5 (2000: 33).
32 For these terms, see Chapters 1 and 4.
33 Discussion of the *laesio enormis* by Lessius, *De iustitia et iure*, book 2, ch 21, question 4 (2016: 25–26) who sees this remedy as an application of the just price principle, but that does not end there: conscience dictates a duty of restitution of any amount above or below the just price.

exchange. In microeconomics, money is a *numéraire*[34] or unit of account that does not influence the transaction and its price as such, so it can be omitted. Money has only a nominal value, and, as Say asserted,[35] money is only an agent of the transfer of value.[36] Money equals price. The value of a commodity is only the exchange value[37] (and the need to exchange to obtain value makes the thing a commodity).[38] Exchange means here barter-exchange. Since the exchange value replaces any intrinsic value, there is a tendency to regard everything, whether commodities or money proper, as 'monetised'. Indeed, both the concept of dematerialised property[39] and the fact that 'barter' can even be the exchange of different versions of money (different currencies) and not only of money against commodity, lend themselves to a general idea of 'monetisation'. A passage in Say indicates already such an interpretation:[40]

> [C]haque fois que vous faites une emplette, vous comparez la valeur de toutes les choses que vous achetez. Mais il n'ensuite pas que des écus soient des valeurs d'une autre nature que toutes les autres; chaque marchandise a son usage; l'usage des écus peut différer de l'usage des vêtements; mais comme richesses, ils ne diffèrent qu'autant que leur valeur diffère.

The specific use value or intrinsic value of the commodity is eclipsed by the exchange value, so that from an economists' perspective the commodity does not differ much from money,[41] the medium of exchange *par excellence*. The value lies in the exchange and, as will be shown, in the action and *process* of exchange.[42]

In this highly abstract model of commercial transactions, it does not matter that the usual causality is displayed reversely in the supply and demand curve, something that would be quite problematic in the sciences, for example in physics. The x-axis represents supply or quantity (q) while the *dependent* y-axis indicates price (p). In reality it is typically the other way round: the quantity is dependent on, that is, determined by, the price. If a higher price can be obtained because there is a higher demand, a higher quantity is likely to be supplied and

34 Walras, *Monnaie* (1886: 12, 15).

35 Say, *Cours à l'Athénée, Première Séance* (1996: 101): 'J'ai voulu enfin écarter de vos esprits cet importune préjugé que la richesse, la fortune, un capital, n'étaient que des sacs d'argent'.

36 See also Dillard (1988: 302, 305).

37 The exchange value represents the 'social wealth', as opposed to the 'natural wealth' of natural products without an exchange between human beings, see Say, *Cours à l'Athénée, Première Séance* (1996: 98).

38 Walras, *Éléments*, § 41 (1926: 44).

39 See Chapter 1.

40 Say, *Cours à l'Athénée, Première Séance* (1996: 101): 'Each time you make a purchase, you compare the value of all things you buy. But it does not follow that the thalers have a value of another nature than all the others; every commodity has its use; the use of the thalers can differ from the use of clothes; but as to wealth, nothing but the value differs' (own translation).

41 Compare discussion by Walras, *Monnaie* (1886: 12–13).

42 See Chapter 4.

a new equilibrium develops.[43] In this way, money need not appear in microeconomic discussion at all.[44]

(d) *Outline of some flaws of the orthodox economic model of supply and demand*

After the discussion of the model for the explanation of supply/demand development, one should mention briefly that this model is nevertheless itself problematic, even if one does not consider the disregard of money in the supply and demand curves as problematic. If, for example, pears are now sold for a price of 10% less, orthodox theory would postulate that the demand for pears goes up because people's income has more purchasing power. This is plausible, and this may happen indeed in many cases. But it is also possible that many consumers are more reasonable and realise that pears go off quickly, and rather than buying more pears, even for the same price, than they can eat before the pears decay, they buy apples instead because they can be kept for longer. This phenomenon is of course well-known to economists as the substitution effect,[45] but they seem to realise less often that with this model predictions upon which business decisions may be based cannot be made. One cannot foretell whether consumers will (a) buy more pears and how many, (b) substitute pears with apples and to what extent, (c) or save their additional money, or some of it, and deposit it with their bank. For the pear and apple farmers, an *ex post* analysis of what *has happened* is rather uninteresting and gives no indication or guidance for the outcome of a future similar scenario. In addition, the model has no way of differentiating between specific properties of the commodities (apples generally decay later than pears). It is also irrelevant whether the pears bought are eaten or decay and are thrown away (because too many are bought for consumption), because only the exchange value attributed to the goods is relevant, contrary to the idea of a more ecological intrinsic value and of an efficient use of resources.[46] These observations ought to be self-evident but play no part in mainstream economics.

43 This example is one of a shift in demand. If there is a shift in supply, the equilibrium price may go down and the equilibrium quantity goes up, or the price increases and the quantity decreases to reach the equilibrium: in either case the quantity depends on the price. See examples of shifts in demand and shifts in supply by Mankiw (2012: 79–81), Bofinger (2011: 65–71).

44 As a (macroeconomic) contrast, see Keynes, *General Theory*, chapter 21 (1964: 296–297) for a discussion of the relationship between (effective) demand and the quantity of money.

45 Mankiw (2012: 450–451).

46 The situation is even more extreme with food speculations. In this case the exchange, distribution and consumption of foodstuff, important as it would be to a great number of people, is not even intended with the market transaction. The food is only an increasingly virtual reference point for a supposed value or object of speculation, thus a form of dematerialisation exercised in fact, not only postulated as a legal concept. The real wheat or rice stored in a warehouse may stay and rot there, it is not the relevant subject matter of the transaction. See also Chapter 4, sec. 3.

Matters become even more problematic if this schematic model is applied to other scenarios after adding another level of abstraction. One often hears the argument that wages and salaries need to be cut to reduce unemployment and to benefit the economy.[47] This appears plausible because if one conceptualises one's labour force as a commodity like pears and uses the usual supply-demand model,[48] one may conclude that a lower price for work by 10% increases the demand for workers with entrepreneurs who have obtained more purchasing power as a result of the reduction of labour costs. So the employment rate goes up.

The difficulties with this argument are twofold. First, entrepreneurs (like consumers buying apples instead of pears) may also decide to save the money[49] or use it for speculative investments, not for creating jobs or for innovation and new technologies.[50] Indeed they will often do so, because the risk of a speculative financial investment, partly financed on the basis of money creation through credit,[51] is now frequently regarded as lower (and the return as higher) than the entrepreneurial risk of investing in workforce, machinery and innovation. For shareholders, it is irrelevant *how* a company makes a profit, and more and more manufacturing or retail enterprises obtain their highest profits not by selling their goods/services but through speculation, and some also have their own banks as subsidiaries.

Second, the argument ignores the fact that cheaper pears and cheaper human workers are not the same, or in the words of Walter Eucken, one of the fathers of ordoliberalism in Germany: '*Arbeit ist keine Ware*' ('Labour is not a commodity').[52] Humans buy goods; pears do not. If wages are cut, this leads to less purchase power (a negative income effect) and fewer purchases of pears. A reduction in wages does not have a direct tendency to increase employment.[53] Following the reduction of purchases, pear farmers must dismiss workers to survive as businesses or close down completely: a greater number of unemployed leads to a greater loss of general purchase power which causes fewer purchases of goods – a disastrous spiral downwards for the general economy. This example shows that the political call for the reduction in wages is rather a political strategy that invokes seemingly value-free and autonomous laws of economics to support businesses to undertake apparently safer speculations instead of taking the greater entrepreneurial risk of investment in labour and machinery. The latter form of investment is often riskier in the short term because products or

47 Discussion of this argument with criticism from a Keynesian perspective by Dillard (1970: 208).

48 It was Alfred Marshall already who cautioned against this complete equalisation of commodities market and labour market, see Marshall, *Principles*, V, 2, § 3 (2013: 279–280).

49 For example in Germany, where enterprises hardly reinvest their large profits for various (presumed) reasons, see Catherine Hoffmann, 'Deutschland spart sich sein Wachstum kaputt', *Süddeutsche Zeitung*, 12 June 2017.

50 For the United States see e.g. Robin Harding, 'Corporate investment: A mysterious divergence', *Financial Times*, 24 July 2013.

51 See e.g. Binswanger (2013: 118–119), and Chapter 2.

52 Eucken (1959: 185).

53 The surrounding factors are more complex, see Keynes, *General Theory*, chapters 1, 19 and 20 (1964: 11–13, 260–261, 266–267, 286–288).

providing services as a result of these investments are much more exposed to open market competition. Speculative investments in shares and other instruments do not require (at least for a long time) consumers of 'real' commodities, especially tangible expendable goods, at all. But if entrepreneurs were legally forced to use savings from wage cuts for investments in the manufacturing and services economy, that would generally be regarded as an unacceptable interference of the state with the free market and incompatible with a free society, as Hayek stresses in the quote given above.

Finally, one cannot resist emphasising that the concept of an equilibrium of supply and demand at the equilibrium price is more a religious tenet than a scientifically verifiable natural law. The lofty ideal this concept may represent can sound thus, for instance:

> It is often said that political freedom is meaningless without economic freedom. This is true enough, but . . . it must be the freedom of our economic activity which, with the right of choice, inevitably also carries the risk and the responsibility of that right.[54]

This political idea then translates into a kind of scientific axiom in economics textbooks, such as: 'The actions of buyers and sellers naturally move markets toward the equilibrium of supply and demand'.[55] In this context, Adam's Smith's 'invisible hand' metaphor is often also invoked,[56] though without a proper understanding of the intellectual background, both in relation to the discussion of the *Wealth of Nations* where it appears[57] and within moral philosophy of the Scottish Enlightenment in general; in particular, it was not intended to be a metaphor of the market price mechanism.[58]

But if we want to be inveterate empirical scientists, then we really have to embark on a proper experiment. Let us go to the next branch of a food store chain and ask for a lower (or perhaps higher)[59] price of a packet of one kilogram of rice which we want to purchase. We will not be able to influence the price; either we buy for the set price by the seller or we will go hungry, and that is it. A hundred remonstrating customers will not change the price. A whole community may do so, but that requires some concerted action, and that is exactly what market fundamentalism

54 Hayek, *Road to Serfdom* (2001: 104).

55 Mankiw (2012: 77).

56 E.g. Mankiw (2012: 12), Bofinger (2011: 4, 15). A paraphrase of the 'invisible hand' idea by Hayek (2013: 276).

57 Smith, *Wealth of Nations*, book 4, chapter 2 (2000: 485). Smith uses this metaphor only once in the *Wealth of Nations*, in the discussion about restraints on imports from foreign countries, as a criticism of such restraints, against mercantilism and for free trade (on this point see immediately below), ibid. at 485: 'To give the monopoly of the home-market to the produce of domestic industry, in any particular art or manufacture, is in some measure to direct private people in what manner they ought to employ their capitals, and must, in almost all cases, be either a useless or a hurtful regulation'.

58 Rahmatian (2017: 126–130).

59 For example, if the price is to be increased to reflect a 'fair trade' concern.

discourages to ensure an atomised society of freely competing human actors. Furthermore, concerted action in relation to a number of products may drive the seller into insolvency, which interrupts supply, but that does not necessarily influence the price. If it does, prices may go up: this can be the case if other suppliers step in and sell the products at a significantly higher price only, either because the products have become scarcer (since the sources of availability have become fewer), or because suppliers obtain larger profits through other sources, such as rent and speculation (also food speculation), so that it is irrelevant to them that they sell far fewer units of products at this high price. The 'market's equilibrium' is then artificially high[60] and the market is not 'efficient' at all. Such scenarios are typical. The supposed dominance of the buyers in the demand-oriented neo-classical market model historically really had wholesalers as buyers in mind, not, as it is commonly now, the individual consumer who is informed (or otherwise) of commodities through advertising.[61] Another artificially high price is frequently generated in the housing market, for example, to enable banks to create (bank) money through lending for the payment of the overestimated purchase prices.[62]

The free interplay of forces of supply and demand is in reality a rare occurrence which requires, among other things, equal power and no information asymmetry on the part of all parties involved. The existence of a large advertising industry proves how artificial any assumptions about the absence of asymmetric information are, otherwise advertising to the fully informed consumer would be redundant.[63] Advertising is rather designed to create information asymmetry and disinformation of consumers to influence demand.[64] The Nestor of public relations, Edward Bernays, was clear about that when he said in 1928:[65]

> But instead of a mind, universal literacy has given [the common man] rubber stamps . . . inked with advertising slogans, with editorials, with published

60 The question is, 'high' – compared to what. The orthodox doctrine regards every outcome as the result of the forces of the efficient market and sanctions every price level as representing the market's equilibrium, so every price is 'correct'. This reflects the demand-based short-term orientation of the Neo-Classical School. We are reminded of Hayek's comment that economic models are not designed 'to arrive at a numerical calculation of prices', see the discussion and quote immediately below under (e). In contrast, Adam Smith postulated a 'natural price' (commodity sold for what it is worth/what it costs to bring it to the market), and ideally the market price (the actual price at which the commodity is commonly sold) should be the same as the natural price, see Smith, *Wealth of Nations*, book 1, chapter 7 (2000: 62–65). The idea of the 'natural price' reflects the supply-oriented, long-term based approach of the Classical School which focused on a long-term market equilibrium.

61 This convincing argument has been made by Kaldor (1950–51: 17). See also Marshall, *Principles*, V, 3, § 3 (2013: 283).

62 See Chapter 2, sec. 3(d).

63 Needless to say that standard textbooks of economics typically devote book sections on the problem of asymmetric information, e.g. Mankiw (2012: 468), though without suggestions to rework the orthodox supply-demand model.

64 Kaldor (1950–51: 8): 'It is only by making the demand for a commodity . . . different from what it would have been without advertising, that advertising activity can have any consequential influence'.

65 Bernays (2005: 48, 52, 77).

> scientific data, with the trivialities of the tabloids and the platitudes of history, but quite innocent of original thought. Each man's rubber stamps are the duplicates of millions of others, so that when those millions are exposed to the same stimuli, all receive identical imprints. . . .
>
> Modern propaganda is a consistent, enduring effort to create or shape events to influence the relations of the public to an enterprise, idea or group. . . .
>
> What are the true reasons the purchaser is planning to spend his money on a new car instead of on a new piano? . . . He buys a car, because it is at the moment the group custom to buy cars. The modern propagandist [wanting to sell pianos] therefore sets to work to create circumstances which will modify that custom.

Advertising, as one form of 'propaganda' in Bernays's terminology, creates (artificial) demand, and that demand determines the price level. Advertising seeks not to offer to the buyer but makes the buyer demand from the seller or manufacturer. That demand is effectively orchestrated and controlled by the supply.[66]

In the twenty-first century this is probably a rather trivial finding, except for economists who still hang on to a theoretical equilibrium of supply and demand as the origin of the market price. In fact, prices are largely arranged through advertising for demand; they are set and offered, and then accepted or rejected, thus the commercial relationship develops in legal-contractual categories, not according to postulations by neo-classical microeconomics. These prices are also set somewhat arbitrarily according to the seller's internal costing of variable plausibility. Often they may serve the protection of cartels and quasi-monopolist interests of sectors of the manufacturing or service industry by being kept artificially high against the professed free-market model, something Adam Smith was already aware of.[67] Despite all of that, the efficient markets hypothesis (that is, the equilibrium of supply and demand sets the market price) still reigns supreme, though usually presented with some remarks that satisfy the image of scholarly critical distance without challenging the principal concept.[68]

Prices are not intended to reflect an intrinsic value of the product, otherwise, for example, the common offer in retail of 'take two for the price of one' could not be explained. In fact, any form of haggling starts with a set price by one party which may lead to a compromise between an individual seller and an individual buyer. That cannot be described as a *generally* existent 'market equilibrium'

66 Bernays (2005: 79).

67 See the discussion in the *Wealth of Nations* in the context of a refutation of mercantilism, e.g., book 1, chapter 7 (2000: 68–70) (monopolies granted to trade and manufacturing industries), book 4, chapter 8 (2000: 717) (monopolies for the benefit of merchants and manufacturers who are the principal architects of these), book 5, chapter 1, part 3 (2000: 791) (regulated and joint stock companies). Obviously, Smith is hostile to monopolies and cartels of any kind, save for the furthering of knowledge, science and engineering (he accepts, within limits, temporary monopolies of patents and copyright), see Smith, *Wealth of Nations*, book 5, chapter 1, part 3 (2000: 814).

68 See e.g. Mankiw (2012: 585), for an example, here in relation to the stock market.

but as an *individual* contract between two people which may or may not be (fairly) representative. Apparently it is, however, necessary for the preservation of political power relationships to maintain the scientifically backed illusion that the prices arise indeed from a free interplay of forces of supply and demand as a result of our freedom of our economic activity and right of choice. Therefore this economic doctrine fulfils the same purpose as religion, that is, social control. A further debate about the price mechanism can be left to economists because here we discuss money as a legal concept – what economists do not normally do.

(e) *The limited informative value of economic models; the irrelevance of much economic modelling for lawyers*

The foregoing few remarks demonstrate that the highly schematic Marshallian supply-demand model has a very limited scope and cannot be expected to provide comprehensive information about market developments and predictions of patterns in relation to market behaviour. Those who invoke economics for their political and ideological aims rather tend to forget that. However, economists themselves (at least the excellent ones) are generally aware of the limitations that economic models entail. Hayek explains the restricted effectiveness of economic models with reference to Walras and Pareto:[69]

> [E]conomic theory is confined to describing kinds of patterns which will appear if certain general conditions are satisfied; but can rarely, if ever derive from this knowledge any predictions of specific performance. This is seen most clearly if we consider those systems of simultaneous equations which since Léon Walras have been widely used to represent the general relations between the prices and the quantities of all commodities produced and sold. They are so framed that *if* we were able to fill in all the blanks, i.e. *if* we knew all the parameters of these equations, we could calculate the prices and quantities of all the commodities. But, as at least the founders of this theory clearly understood, its purpose is not 'to arrive at a numerical calculation of prices', because it would be 'absurd' to assume that we can ascertain all the data.

The absence of money in the supply-demand model makes the explanatory value of this model even more questionable. As already discussed, money is believed to be a concrete measure of value (or *numéraire*/unit of account) for stating prices, and then it is omitted from the supply-demand model out of which the equilibrium price is to be distilled. In fact, the supposed neutrality of money has nothing to do with the question of an equilibrium between supply and demand.[70] Despite all that, some mathematising of that model to arrive at supposedly scientific

69 Hayek (1964: 62). See also the discussion by Streissler (2012: 75–77).
70 Stützel (2011: 192).

precision has been introduced, only that the variables can never be filled with absolute numerical terms in reality. Not only do all real economic transactions operate with concrete figures; the mathematical equations which seek to define the relations of supply and demand and so try to emulate a precision as in natural laws of physics, are in fact also based on arbitrary assumptions. The mathematical formulae and derivations serve as a fully functioning typewriter under the hands of an illiterate person.

The debate between the mathematician-economist Walras and the mathematician-scientist Poincaré illustrates this problem well. Walras claimed that the exchange value of commodities[71] is uncontestably a mathematical fact; and pure economics, which has this fact as its subject matter, is a mathematical science. Pure economics, as Walras terms it, proceeds in the same way as physics, expressed in mathematics, especially for mechanics and celestial mechanics in astronomy. Walras then seeks to demonstrate his thesis (*'il me semble facile de faire voir aux mathématiciens'*) with mathematical derivations that represent the exchange of commodities. The premise for these derivations is the scarcity (*rareté*) and demand satisfaction (*besoin satisfait*) of goods, although mathematicians maintain that satisfaction cannot be measured.[72] Poincaré refuted this approach briefly and elegantly, which is worth quoting at length because it is still an accurate description of the shortcomings of the prevalent mathematised economics of today:[73]

> La satisfaction peut-elle se mesurer? Je puis dire que telle satisfaction est plus grande que telle autre, puisque je préfère l'une à l'autre. Mais je ne puis dire que telle satisfaction est deux fois ou trois fois plus grande que telle autre. Cela n'a aucun sens par soi-même et ne pourrait en acquérir un que par une convention arbitraire.
>
> La satisfaction est donc une grandeur, mais non une grandeur mesurable. Maintenant, une grandeur non-mesurable sera-t-elle par cela seul exclue de

71 Explanation in Walras, *Éléments*, § 41 (1926: 44–45).

72 Walras (1909: 314–316).

73 Poincaré in Walras (1909: 326): 'The satisfaction can be measured? I can say that some satisfaction is greater than another, since I prefer one to the other. But I cannot say that a satisfaction is twice or three times greater than another. This does not make any sense by itself and can only obtain a meaning by arbitrary convention. Satisfaction is therefore a quantity, but not a measurable one. Now would an immeasurable quantity be excluded from mathematical speculation just because of that? Not at all. Temperature for example (at least until the advent of thermodynamics which provided a meaning to the term of absolute temperature) was an immeasurable quantity. It was in an arbitrary way that one defined and measured it, through the expansion of mercury. . . . In your premisses appear a certain number of arbitrary functions; but once these premisses are stated, you have the right to draw conclusions from these by way of calculation. If these arbitrary functions still appear in these conclusions, these conclusions are not wrong, but they are devoid of any interest because they are subordinated to the arbitrary conventions made at the outset'. (Own translation. I am grateful to Professor Giuseppe Longo, CNRS, Collège de France & Ecole Normale Supérieure, Paris, for informing me of this source.)

> toute spéculation mathématique? Nullement. La température par exemple (au moins jusqu'à l'avènement de la thermodynamique qui a donné un sens au mot de température absolue) était une grandeur non-mesurable. C'est arbitrairement qu'on la définissait et la mesurait par la dilatation du mercure. . . .
>
> Dans vos prémisses vont donc figurer un certain nombre de fonctions arbitraires; mais une fois ces prémisses posées, vous avez le droit d'en tirer des conséquences par le calcul; si, dans ces conséquences, les fonctions arbitraires figurent encore, ces conséquences ne seront pas fausses, mais elles seront dénuées de tout intérêt parce qu'elles seront subordonnées aux conventions arbitraires faites au début.

One must conclude that a separate microeconomic conceptualisation of 'money' does not exist, since it is superfluous in the prevailing market model, no matter how mathematised it may appear to be a truly 'scientific model'. And yet, in reality money is involved in every microeconomic transaction.

In macroeconomics, however, money plays an important role. The problem is, however, that money in macroeconomics is regarded as a separate occurrence in relation to the economy as a whole (in form of income, expenditure etc.), and not as an interacting phenomenon in specific (that is microeconomic) sales transactions of individual households,[74] which is what money is first and foremost about. Since macroeconomic analysis must be based on an aggregate of a vast number of individual sales or 'barters', it is hard to imagine on what the role of money in macroeconomic analysis can be grounded, if money is eliminated from the aggregate of microeconomic data as a basis for macroeconomic examination. But this problem is for economists to solve; some of them argue indeed that monetary theory (macroeconomics; quantity theory of money) and value theory (microeconomics; market equilibrium) are in fact incompatible.[75]

The lawyer need not be concerned about that, because he/she has to consider the individual, that is, 'microeconomic', transaction. Here it becomes apparent that the lawyer's focus is a different one: for a lawyer the national economy consists of a large number of individual transactions which are either lawful or unlawful, for example because they ultimately violate ideas of 'justice' (to use this term in an unsophisticated sense here). Not only may a just price not be the same as an equilibrium price, as we have seen, also the aggregate of transactions as a separate entity as such is irrelevant. This is because justice is primarily individual, directed at a specific contract and only then, from the individual decision as a starting point, it may refer to a more general policy decision. For the economist, however, more precisely, the macroeconomist, the question of efficiency of markets also has a general, non-individual, national or international dimension.[76] The

74 See the usual textbooks on macroeconomics, e.g. Mankiw (2013: 11, 16–17).

75 See the critique by Binswanger (2009: 26–39).

76 This is, however, something which law-and-economics representatives tend to forget, see Rahmatian (2013: 225–226).

law remains decisive for economists as well because it is the law which enables the individual economic transactions:[77] without contract and property law and without public law regulations there would be no markets in a modern society.[78] So economists cannot dismiss this different conceptualisation as an irrelevant approach from another discipline.

(f) The incorrect equation: money = price

Money does not equal 'price' at all, if one understands by 'price' the equilibrium price or any price diverging from the reference parameter of the equilibrium price. A proper supply and demand model would have to be three-dimensional if it wanted to take into account that money is an interim commodity which is interposed between the seller's real commodity (for example, a ballpoint pen), and the real commodity the seller later obtains as a buyer (a loaf of bread). This commodity 'money' is not neutral, but comes at a cost, as any commodity. The provision of money involves the cost of holding money, in cash, or in a current account, for example, and, particularly, interest.[79] One can see that money is a separate commodity with a cost element, especially interest, if one studies the modern money supply or money creation mechanism, as was discussed in Chapter 2. Since in the modern monetary system money is a debt which almost invariably attracts interest, this aspect is extremely important particularly in microeconomic analysis because the interest that money entails influences the development of prices significantly, independently from the market equilibrium conception of the microeconomic barter model. A loan, thus bank money, with interest requires the seller of goods to increase the price to cover capital and interest of the loan he is bound to repay. Since all money is debt with interest, someone must always be debtor and therefore prices become increased to cover the loan and interest, whereby the interest is the price of credit (or debt).[80] How economists develop a model to encapsulate this relation between *quantity* of real goods, *money* as a commodity in its own right, and *price* in a true sales transaction (not just in a conceptual reduction to barter that eliminates money) must be left to them. Perhaps the *x*-axis (or *z*-axis) would be the quantity, the *y*-axis the cost/benefit of the money

77 Rahmatian (2013: 195).

78 Obviously there can be black markets in criminal societies with supply and demand trends where the enforcement of debts happens by shooting the debtors, but we assume an organised system of a modern state here.

79 In macroeconomics the (opportunity) cost for holding money is of course generally discussed, see e.g. Mankiw (2013: 112), but that is partly directed at another issue. The opportunity cost perspective considers the difference between holding cash (no interest) or an account balance on a current account (nowadays practically no interest) and using it to buy shares or bonds (which attract interest): in that case the opportunity cost of holding money is the nominal interest rate. That disregards the fact that money as such, being a debt of someone else (with legal, thus socio-economic, consequences), whether bank money or cash, *itself* attracts interest and is not solely a means to buy another commodity which attracts interest (e.g. bonds).

80 Binswanger (2013: 43–44), Binswanger (2009: 125, 129).

used for payment, and the *z*-axis (or *x*-axis) the price that is (or may be) dependent both on the quantity of the commodity (or conversely) and on the cost and benefit of the money involved. That constellation might be modelled as a kind of economic version of the three-body problem, as it is known from physics.

The next problem, addressed further in Chapter 4, is the fact that the economists' microeconomic model is static. One can, although in an oversimplifying way, maintain this static model more easily if the market is analysed two-dimensionally as quantity and price only, with the elimination of money. Once the model is three-dimensional, the dynamic nature of the exchange/sale event inevitably forces itself on the model. Money and interest fluctuate over a given time, and there is always a time given, the sale is not an abstract point, but a concrete process. Perhaps the only way in which such a movement can be expressed mathematically is by way of calculus.[81] A fixed point of transaction with a possible fixed price for the commodity of money as the medium of the exchange or transaction can only be determined for past transactions and with hindsight, and only if one has the opportunity to collect the necessary raw data to draw exact conclusions.

2. The suppression of money in classical economics and from neo-classical market equilibrium concepts

(a) *The classical school of economics: polemic suppression of the relevance of money for capital formation*

It is generally presumed that the elimination of money from the microeconomic market model is significantly owed to the polemic of Adam Smith and the classical school of economics against mercantilism.[82] Mercantilists stressed the need for a surplus of exports over imports of a country. That also furthered the objective to increase the supply of precious metals and of money (which was commodity money then, gold and silver) in the country as a pre-condition for a prospering economy.[83] Stressing the latter point, Adam Smith made the exaggerated claim that mercantilism sees the wealth of a country only in its hoarding of money, gold and silver:[84]

> [T]he law for the encouragement of coinage derives its origin from those vulgar prejudices which have been introduced by the mercantile system. . . . Nothing could be more agreeable to the spirit of that system than a sort of

81 A popular mathematical discussion by Devlin (2000: 100–118).

82 Dillard (1988: 301), Commons (1924: 240–241), Binswanger (2009: 162), Binswanger (2013: 58–60).

83 Barber (1977: 18). Schumpeter cautioned against the blanket term 'mercantilism' for this position, see Schumpeter (1954: 343). For the classical (biased) analysis, see Smith, *Wealth of Nations*, book 4, chapter 8 (2000: 694).

84 Smith, *Wealth of Nations*, book 4, chapter 6 (2000: 597–598). See also ibid., book 4 chapter 1 (2000: 456–457).

> bounty upon the production of money, the very thing which, it supposes, constitutes the wealth of every nation.

In contrast to mercantilism, the classical school refused to accept the importance of money for the formation of capital (real and financial) and the wealth of a nation. That was a result of Adam Smith's and the classical school's position to advocate free trade to increase wealth against mercantilist monopolisation and trade restrictions. As Smith said:[85]

> Consumption is the sole end and purpose of all production; and the interest of the producer ought to be attended to, only so far as it may be necessary for promoting that of the consumer . . . but in the mercantile system, the interest of the consumer is almost constantly sacrificed to that of the producer; and it seems to consider production, and not consumption, as the ultimate end and object of all industry and commerce.

And:[86]

> We trust with perfect security that the freedom of trade, without any attention of government, will always supply us with the wine which we have occasion for: and we may trust with equal security that it will always supply us with all the gold and silver which we can afford to purchase or to employ, either in circulating our commodities, or in other uses.

The argument for free trade and against import taxes or against export bounties[87] necessarily questions the need for the import of gold, silver and (commodity) money. If, as Adam Smith does,[88] one denies that the import of money is of any benefit for the increase of a country's wealth, because an increase in the quantity of money shall only lead to nominal increases of prices without any real effects on the economy, one attacks directly the most central objective of mercantilism. From the English, and later British, perspective of the seventeenth and eighteenth centuries, mercantilist protectionism wanted to prevent the import of goods from, say, Spain and Portugal to force them into a trade deficit towards England or France. That would prompt Spain and Portugal to pay for their debts to England and France in gold and silver, so that gold and silver, and with these the quantity of money, would be increased in England and France to create wealth.[89]

85 Smith, *Wealth of Nations*, book 4, chapter 8 (2000: 715).

86 Smith, *Wealth of Nations*, book 4, chapter 1 (2000: 462–463).

87 Smith, *Wealth of Nations*, book 4, chapter 5 (2000: 540, 552–553).

88 Smith, *Wealth of Nations*, book 1, chapter 11, part 3 (2000: 202–203), book 2, chapter 3 (2000: 370–371), book 4, chapter 1 (2000: 465–471).

89 See discussion of this aspect in Smith, *Wealth of Nations*, book 4, chapter 1 (2000: 459–465), book 4, chapter 5 (2000: 547–549), book 4, chapter 6 (2000: 587–591). See also Binswanger (2009: 164–165), Binswanger (2013: 59–60).

However, the classical school regarded these mercantilist policies as meaningless. It rather sought to deny the relevance of the quantity of money for the economy of a country. This classical quantity theory of money was postulated particularly by David Hume:[90]

> It seems a maxim almost self-evident, that the prices of every thing depend on the proportion between commodities and money, and that any considerable alteration on either of these has the same effect, either of heightening or lowering the price. Increase the commodities, they become cheaper, increase the money, they rise in their value. . . . a diminution of the former, and that of the latter, have contrary tendencies.

And:[91]

> The rate of interest . . . is not derived from the quantity of the precious metals. Money having chiefly a fictitious value, the greater or less plenty of it is of no consequence, if we consider a nation within itself; and the quantity of specie, when once fixed, though ever so large, has no other effect, than to oblige every one to tell out a greater number of those shining bits of metal, for clothes, furniture or equipage, without increasing any one convenience of life.

Adam Smith followed Hume:[92]

> Money is neither a material to work upon, nor a tool to work with; and though the wages of a workman are commonly paid to him in money, his real revenue, like that of all other men, consists, not in the money, but in the money's worth; not in the metal pieces, but in what can be got for them.

The real value was labour, money was only a nominal value:[93]

> But when . . . you raise the nominal or money-price of corn, you do not raise its real value. . . . The nature of things has stamped upon corn a real value which cannot be altered by merely altering its money price. No bounty upon exportation, no monopoly of the home market, can raise that value.

90 Hume, *Of Money* (2003: 121–122). The old spelling has been modernised.

91 Hume, *Of Interest* (2003: 127).

92 Smith, *Wealth of Nations*, book 2, chapter 2 (2000: 321). For paper money, see ibid., book 2, chapter 2 (2000: 353).

93 Smith, *Wealth of Nations*, book 4, chapter 5 (2000: 551–552). This passage has been used here as it is a neat summary. The labour theory of value is discussed more extensively in Smith, *Wealth of Nations*, book 1, chapter 5 (2000: 33): 'Labour . . . is the real measure of the exchangeable value of all commodities', ibid., chapter 6 (2000: 56–57), book 2, chapter 3 (2000: 360–380) and passim. That theory is followed by Ricardo, *Principles*, chapter 1, section 1 (2004: 5–7), chapter 7 (2004: 88–89) and the classical school.

> The freest competition cannot lower it. Through the world in general that value is equal to the quantity of labour which it can maintain, and in every particular place it is equal to the quantity of labour which it can maintain in the way, whether liberal, moderate, or scanty, in which labour is commonly maintained in that place.

Smith did not invent the labour theory of value, or, more precisely, cost-of-production *and* labour theory of value, for it was later Karl Marx in particular who put forward a 'pure' labour theory of value.[94] There were earlier statements in this vein, for instance this anonymous passage from around 1740 (quoted in part by Marx in *Capital*)[95] that sets out a simple labour theory of value:[96]

> The true and real value of the necessaries of life, is in proportion to that part which they contribute to the subsistence of mankind; and the value of them when they are exchanged the one for the other, is regulated by the quantity of labour necessarily required, and commonly taken in producing them; and the value or price of them when they are bought and sold, and compared to a common medium [money],[97] will be governed by the quantity of labour employed, and the greater or less plenty of the medium or common measure.

That passage still has a mercantilist perspective; money is not neutral or nominal. Rather, the quantity of money, together with the quantity of labour, determines the 'value or price' of goods. However, as the classical school focuses on labour almost entirely as the measure of value, 'money' as such has no effect on value and capital and can be eliminated from economic theory.[98] But, in striking contradiction, the classical school never doubted that all means of production are to be paid for in money and that businessmen make money. The position of the classical school overlooks the fact that part of the money introduced as payment for the trade deficit reaches first the credit and capital market (something John Locke rightly assumed),[99] which leads to a higher supply of money and a reduction of the interest rate before it becomes available on the general market for the

94 Marx, *Kapital I*, chapter 1 (1975: 20–23).
95 Marx, *Kapital I*, chapter 1 (1975: 21, note 9).
96 Anon., *Some Thoughts on the Interest of Money in General* (1738: 36–37).
97 For that explanatory insertion, see Anon., *Some Thoughts on the Interest of Money in General* (1738: 29): 'Money may be considered in two respects; either as the common measure of things bought and sold, or as producing a certain income by use'.
98 Compare the following passage in Smith, *Wealth of Nations*, book 2, chapter 2 (2000: 317): 'Money, . . . the great wheel of circulation, the great instrument of commerce, like all other instruments of trade, though it makes a part and a very valuable part of the capital, *makes no part of the revenue of the society to which it belongs*; and though the metal pieces of which it is composed, in the course of their annual circulation, distribute to every man the revenue which properly belongs to him, *they make themselves no part of that revenue*' (emphasis added).
99 Locke, *Some considerations of the consequences of the lowering of interest and raising the value of money* (1991: 225–226, 267–268).

purchase of commodities. Only at this later stage the prices for commodities may fall. Before that time, money is also available for speculation of any kind and may lead to speculative bubbles. It is interesting to note that Hume, whom Smith generally follows but ignores on this specific point, had an awareness of non-neutral money: Hume said that in the interval between an increase in the supply of money and the following rise in prices, employment and output will increase significantly.[100] Contrary to the classical school, capital is money, as is profit and interest, and therefore capital is subjected to the monetary risk of realisation: the risk of obtaining commodities in return for money at a later stage.[101]

Say and Ricardo followed Smith.[102] As said earlier, for Say money is only an agent of the transfer of value.[103] Ricardo stressed the neutrality of money, for example in this passage: 'Productions are always bought by productions, or by services; money is only the medium by which the exchange is effected'.[104]

(b) Neo-classical economic theory as the perfection of the classical school

The neo-classical school entrenched the idea from the neutrality of money further. This is not discussed here,[105] save for the contributions to the neo-classical market equilibrium conception by Walras and Marshall. Both have been mentioned already, Marshall briefly at the beginning of Chapter 1 and Walras at the beginning of this chapter, since the present neo-classical conception of supply and demand is so heavily indebted to them.

According to Walras's theory of the market equilibrium, with two commodities given, the proportion between the supply (O) and demand (D) for one commodity (b) is postulated as equal to the proportion between the demand and supply for the other commodity (a): $O(b)/D(b) = D(a)/O(a) = a$. Hence the demand and the supply of commodity (a) are equal, as well as of commodity (b). If we assume that $a = 1$, $D(a) = O(a)$, $O(b) = D(b)$, the quantities of commodities (a) and (b) demanded and supplied, respectively, for the respective prices $p(a) = 1/\mu$ and $p(b) = \mu$[106] are equal, then there is an equilibrium of the market. Each seller and each buyer finds his buyer and seller, respectively. For the equilibrium price of $1/\mu$ and μ, respectively, the quantity $D(a) = O(a)$ of commodity (a) is exchanged for the quantity $O(b) = D(b)$ of commodity (b),

100 Hume, *Of Money* (2003: 118–119), Dillard (1988: 303). Similar, but brief, observation by Ricardo, xxi (2004: 198).

101 Binswanger (2009: 162–165) for this passage.

102 Dillard (1988: 304–307). See Ricardo's Introduction to his *Principles* (2004: 2).

103 Say, *Catéchisme d'économie politique*, XII (1996: 353). See also Dillard (1988: 305).

104 Ricardo, *Principles*, chapter 21 (2004: 194). Some interesting qualifications in relation to the invariable nature (in value) of money, see ibid., I, vii (2004: 30).

105 For further discussion, see e. g. Dillard (1988: 311–314).

106 Walras defines earlier: $1/\mu$ is the quotient of the proportions of prices of commodities (a) and (b), so if (b) costs twice as much as (a), that is $2(a) = (b)$, this equals the proportion of 2 or 1/2, respectively, see Walras, *Éléments*, § 44 (1926: 49).

in which case the market is cleared.[107] In relation to a number or aggregate of commodities exchanged Walras conceived his famous mathematical theory of the general equilibrium.[108] This general (not just partial) equilibrium analysis, a long mathematically expressed comment to Adam Smith's overworked 'invisible hand' metaphor, is a wonderful example of 'pure economics', or, put less charitably, of economic theory detached from the reality of commerce. The presupposition for this theory is, characteristically: '*Plusieurs marchandises étant données, dont l'échange se fait avec intervention de numéraire*'.[109] Again, we have money as the neutral *numéraire*, the unit of account, as the starting point for the analysis of a plurality of sales ('barters').

Walras is said to represent general equilibrium theory, while Marshall is generally associated with partial equilibrium theory. This division is not uncontroversial, and it is not clear either whether Walras and Marshall held opposing views, as Milton Friedman has however claimed. The prevailing opinion, probably ultimately following John Hicks, is that Walras and Marshall complement each other. This debate is a matter for economists and not of interest here.[110]

Marshall concentrates on the investigation of the equilibrium of normal demand and normal supply in general, without taking account of special cases. Thus the forces of demand and supply are assumed to have free play: there is no close relationship between dealers/suppliers, and there is free competition, so that sellers compete freely with sellers, and buyers with buyers.[111] All parties involved benefit from efficiency in information in relation to finished goods, factors of production, hire of labour and borrowing of capital.[112] In this assumption of the market there is the demand price, a price at which each particular amount of the commodity can find purchasers in a certain period of time, whereby the unit of time chosen is short by comparison to the market under consideration. The supply price is the price that has to be paid in order to obtain an adequate supply of the efforts that are required for making the commodity.[113] If the amount produced is such that the demand price is greater than the supply price, the sellers receive more than is sufficient to make them offering their commodities on the market, so an active force emerges that tends to increase the amount brought forward for sale. Conversely, if the amount produced is such that the demand price is less than the supply price, sellers obtain less than is sufficient to bring the goods to the market on the same scale, so there is an active force that tends to reduce the amount brought forward for sale:[114]

> When the demand price is equal to the supply price, the amount produced has the tendency either to be increased or to be diminished; it is in equilibrium.

107 Walras, *Éléments*, §§ 46–47 (1926: 51–52).
108 Walras, *Éléments*, §§ 104, 111, 117 (1926: 109, 115, 122), and especially § 130 (1926: 133).
109 Ibid., at § 130 (1926: 133).
110 See De Vroey (2009: 321, 329), for further discussion.
111 See Mankiw (2012: 280), for the perfect competitive market.
112 Marshall, *Principles*, V, 3, § 4 (2013: 284).
113 Marshall, *Principles*, V, 3, §§ 2, 4 (2013: 282–283, 285).
114 Marshall, *Principles*, V, 3, § 6 (2013: 287) (emphasis original).

> When demand and supply are in equilibrium, the amount of the commodity which is being produced in a unit of time may be called the *equilibrium-amount*, and the price at which it is being sold may be called the *equilibrium-price*.
>
> Such an equilibrium is *stable*; that is, the price, if displaced a little from it, will tend to return, as a pendulum oscillates about its lowest point; and it will be found to be a characteristic of stable equilibria that in them the demand price is greater than the supply price for amounts just less than the equilibrium amount, and *vice versa*.

This is the standard supply-demand model that can be found in every economics textbook today: a model that is said to explain essentially every type of market (commodity and financial markets alike)[115] and that is graphically represented by the combination of supply and demand curves as the characteristic 'Marshallian cross' (scissors diagram).[116] While Walras's equilibrium is an adjustment of price by elimination of excess supply and demand, Marshall's equilibrium is an adjustment of quantities by elimination of differences between supply price and demand price.[117] In either case, money does not feature as a separate entity; it is absorbed in the other parameters, as has been observed several times already. When Marshall discusses the interest of capital and money markets, he emphasises the underlying assumption about the qualities of money:[118]

> [W]e are supposing [as a rule] . . . that all values are expressed in terms of money of fixed purchasing power just as astronomers have taught us to determine the beginning or the ending of the day with reference not to the actual sun but to a *mean sun* which is supposed to move uniformly through the heavens.

And yet, according to Marshall, money is needed to bring about a stable equilibrium, because only a medium of exchange that is in constant demand as a purchasing medium is able to stabilise the market and enable a real equilibrium, while in a true barter situation (commodity A against commodity B) the 'steadying influences which hold together a market in which values are set in money are absent', and only accidental equilibria arising out of the circumstances of specific transactions emerge.[119] Thus money is sufficiently neutral, first, to stabilise the supply-demand relation of the market and, second, to be conceptually eliminated from the market equilibrium model. But then it is ushered in again as a ferment that enables exactly that postulated market equilibrium. In fact, money is not

115 E.g. Mankiw (2013: 66–69).
116 E.g. Mankiw (2012: 77), Bofinger (2011: 66–76), Streissler (1984: 31). The so-called Marshallian cross as a schematic diagram of the market supply-demand relation was not invented by Marshall but had predecessors, especially Cournot and Jenkin, see Humphrey (1992: 3, 19–21).
117 Humphrey (1992: 3).
118 Marshall, *Principles*, VI, 6, § 7 (2013: 493).
119 Marshall, *Principles*, Appendix F (2013: 653).

only a commodity that is a purchasing medium and a unit of account, which would be no commodity in the ordinary sense according to the orthodox view. Money is rather a kind of 'proper' commodity (or, as we have seen, a form of dematerialised property[120] with consequences which we will discuss again later).[121] Furthermore, it may produce certain effects not too dissimilar to those Marshall discussed in relation to the conventional barter of apples against pears, that is, it may cause an accidental equilibrium or a distortion of the 'real' equilibrium.

3. The current neo-classical concept of money: modern quantity theory of money

Milton Friedman's method of 'positive economics' seeks to be 'an "objective" science, in precisely the same sense as any of the physical sciences', in which the model assumptions are supposed to be unimportant, only the methodological correctness of the conclusions is relevant.[122] As Friedman said:[123]

> One confusion that has been particularly rife and has done much damage is confusion about the role of 'assumptions' in economic analysis. A meaningful scientific hypothesis or theory typically asserts that certain forces are, and other forces are not, important in understanding a particular class of phenomena. It is frequently convenient to present such a hypothesis by stating that the phenomena it is desired to predict behave in the world of observation as if they occurred in a hypothetical and highly simplified world containing only the forces that the hypothesis asserts to be important. In general, there is more than one way to formulate such a description – more than one set of 'assumptions' in terms of which the theory can be presented. The choice among such alternative assumptions is made on the grounds of the resulting economy, clarity, and precision in presenting the hypothesis. . . . Such a theory cannot be tested by comparing its 'assumptions' directly with 'reality'. Indeed, there is no meaningful way in which this can be done. Complete 'realism' is clearly unattainable, and the question whether a theory is realistic 'enough' can be settled only by seeing whether it yields predictions that are good enough for the purpose in hand or that are better than predictions from alternative theories. Yet the belief that a theory can be tested by the realism of its assumptions independently of the accuracy of its predictions is widespread and the source of much of the perennial criticism of economic theory as unrealistic. Such criticism is largely irrelevant, and, in consequence, most attempts to reform economic theory that it has stimulated have been unsuccessful.

120 See Chapter 1.
121 See Chapters 4 and 5.
122 Friedman (2009: 4 (quote), 7, 14–15, 30–34).
123 Friedman (2009: 41–42).

Here one finds the apotheosis of the Walrasian idea of '*l'économique pure*'. This is despite Friedman's trenchant, but not necessarily convincing, criticism of Walras. Particularly in Chicago many economists, among them Friedman, associated Walras with collectivism, socialism and politically naïve welfare economics, and set him against Marshall, whom they regarded highly. This distorted image was one disadvantage for the recognition of Walras, together with the fact that Walras's works were not translated from the French for a long time.[124] Nevertheless, the idea of a mathematised, highly abstracted *économique pure* seems to have been carried out to its logical conclusion in Friedman's (modern) quantity theory of money. Its starting point is the classical quantity theory of money.

The classical quantity theory of money has its roots in the early modern period, with Jean Bodin,[125] John Locke[126] and especially David Hume,[127] and was revisited by Irving Fisher and others in the twentieth century. It explains inflation as a result of a relation between the circulating quantity of money and the transaction of goods as priced. The formula given is the following quantity equation: $M \times V = P \times T$, with M being the quantity of money and V the transactions velocity of money, which measures the rate at which money circulates in the economy, for example, how often a banknote changes hands within a defined time period. P is the price of a typical transaction and T is the sum total of the transactions in a given time period. Thus the price level can be expressed as $P = M \times V/T$, or a simple money demand function as $M = P \times Y/V$, whereby the number of transactions T is normally replaced by Y, the total output of the economy which is easier to measure. V, the transaction velocity, cannot be determined independently but only by way of solving the quantity equation ($V = P \times T/M$) with the statistically ascertainable data M, P and T. The quantity equation is an identity, that is, the definitions of the four variables render it true.[128] V is small when people hold much money for each unit of income (£, €, $ etc.), because money changes hands infrequently. When people want to hold a little money only, so it changes hands frequently, then V is large.[129] From the quantity equation and the additional presupposition that the transactions velocity of money is constant (fixed), it follows that the money supply M set by the central bank determines the nominal value of the output $P \times Y$. The inflation rate can be derived from the quantity equation because the inflation rate is the percentage rate in the price level. So a change in % of M + change in % of V = change in % of P + change in % of Y (since $MV = PY$).

124 De Vroey (2009: 323, 334–335).

125 This is the prevalent narrative. However, Schumpeter (1954: 313) questions whether Bodin's discussion really comprises the considerations of the actual quantity theory of money. Furthermore, it is debatable whether M. Jehan Cherruyt de Malestroit, to whom Bodin responded, is much more a predecessor of the quantity theory of money than Bodin in his answer, see Tortajada (1987: 869, 873–874).

126 Locke, *Some considerations of the consequences of the lowering of interest and raising the value of money* (1991: 264–266). Vickers (1960: 53–58).

127 See above under sec. 2.

128 Thus more precisely: $M \times V \equiv P \times T$.

129 Mankiw (2013: 101–103), Bofinger (2011: 429–430).

That means (according this theory) a growth in money supply determines the rate of inflation. Therefore a central bank, which controls the money supply, has ultimate control over the rate of inflation. If a central bank increases the money supply quickly, the price level will rise quickly: a quantity of money that rises quickly is not balanced by a quantity of goods which remains about the same during that short period of time.[130]

It is for economists to debate whether these findings are accurate or need adjustment and correction. There are, however, several concerning aspects. The classical quantity theory cannot explain the phenomenon of a very limited inflation despite an extreme rise of the quantity of money in Europe and the United States as a response to the financial crisis from 2008 onwards.[131] It is also a questionable assumption that a central bank can control entirely or predominantly the money supply today, as we have seen in the discussion of the modern money creation system.[132] The orthodox quantity theory of money and the traditional idea of the regulatory powers of central banks seem to focus too much on central bank money and mostly disregard the fact that over 95% of all money is (commercial) bank money or credit created through loans. Furthermore, the assumption of constant velocity of money is problematic (which Friedman addressed), and the velocity of different types of money (cash or bank money) is likely to be different (something Fisher took into account). As a non-economist, one may also doubt the usefulness of the purely numerical parameter of the transactions velocity (V) if one seeks to examine the way in which money influences the price of (an aggregate of) individual transactions.

From the point of view of a *legal* theory of money, the quantity theory of money is of almost no relevance. It cannot explain the legal qualities of money and its economic effects. But that has not been its purpose in the first place: the quantity theory seeks to demonstrate the relationship between quantity of money and price level and inflation – whether it is able to do that is left to economists to discuss.

The reason why the classical quantity theory of money has been considered here is because it is the basis of Friedman's monetarism. Friedman's theory as such is not particularly relevant to a legal theory of money either. However, it will be discussed now because the principal definitions of wealth in Friedman's monetarism, and on the other hand the legal concepts of money and dematerialised property advanced here, have certain similarities, although my own conclusions are entirely different from Friedman's.

Friedman restates (and in effect qualifies) the classical quantity theory of money: the quantity theory is a theory of the demand for money, not of output,

130 Mankiw (2013: 104) with the omission of some of the mathematical derivations.

131 Mankiw (2013: 93–94). The principal reason is that the newly created money has not (yet) left the banking system and is part of the reserves of the banks. The question whether it is ever supposed to do so, and if so, what the effects are, highlights one of the major points of criticism of the present monetary system, see Chapter 4, sec. 4.

132 See Chapter 2.

or money income, or price level. It has the unusual characteristic of combining the supply of capital and the demand for capital. As with any other goods, the demand for money depends on (a) the total wealth to be held in various forms (equivalent of the budget restraint), (b) the price of and return on this and other forms of wealth, and (c) the tastes and preferences of the wealth-owning 'units' (i.e. customers as physical and legal persons).[133] Wealth is 'to be expressed in terms of monetary units at the prices of the point of time in question'. The five different forms in which wealth can be held are:

> (i) money (*M*), interpreted as claims or commodity units that are generally accepted in payment of debts at a fixed nominal value; (ii) bonds (*B*) [claims to payments at points in time] that are fixed in nominal units; (iii) equities (*E*) [claims to dividends declared on shares of companies]; (iv) physical non-human goods (*G*); and (v) human capital (*H*).[134]

Physical goods (*G*) are similar to equities, except that the annual stream of income they yield is in kind rather than in money; that return depends on the behaviour of prices. In addition, the appreciation/depreciation in money value also yields a nominal return. Human capital (*H*) is most problematic in that in modern non-slave societies one cannot define well in market prices the terms of substitution of human capital for other forms of capital. Non-human capital can be substituted by human capital when an individual enters into a contract to render personal services for a specified period in return for a definitely specified number of periodic payments, whereby the number of payments does not depend on the individual's physical capability of rendering the services. 'But, in the main, shifts between human capital and other forms [of capital] must take place through direct investment and disinvestment in the human agent, and we may as well treat this as if it were the only way'.[135]

This series of definitions is quite important for a theory of dematerialised property, with money as a principal example. The abstract nature of these definitions also conceals the practical consequences of this idea of 'monetarism', here not only understood as the emphasis on the macroeconomic effects of money supply.[136] It becomes apparent that the basis for Friedman's version of the quantity theory of money is a complete *monetisation* of all goods and services, either in the form of money in the narrow sense, money in the wider sense (bonds and shares), physical goods and human labour force ('human capital'). So conceptually everything is money, only with a different liquidity factor. As already discussed in the explanation of the idea of dematerialised property,[137] the term

133 Friedman, *Quantity Theory*, pts. 1, 3 (1956: 4).
134 Friedman, *Quantity Theory*, pt. 5 (1956: 5).
135 Friedman, *Quantity Theory*, pt. 5 (1956: 7–8).
136 'Monetarism' usually denotes for economists the focus on the macroeconomic effects of money supply, see e.g. Mankiw (2013: 530).
137 Chapter 1, sec. 2(a)(iv).

propertisation emphasises the transformation of factual objects of any kind into a legal *res*; *commodification* stresses the interchangeable, fungible and standardising nature which the transformation into a *res* brings about; and this process can also be called *monetisation*, since these standardised (notional) commodities or *res* can come close to, or can indeed operate as, forms of money, at least for conceptual and modelling purposes. Or, as Friedman says, '[t]here is no hard-and-fast line between "money" and other assets'.[138]

The problem is that legal or economic concepts do not remain in the conceptual or modelling stage but enter social reality. Friedman mentions that it is difficult to 'commodify' or 'monetise' human labour force as 'human capital'.[139] However, modern human resource management and managerialism work hard to achieve exactly this goal. The numerical calculation of the substitution of non-human capital by human capital can be done much better with 'zero-hours' contracts.[140] These have the additional advantage that they promote a complete atomisation of society and a destruction of any solidarity in the work force, and give no employment protection. Here, as well as in other precarious work relationships, the human being is reduced to its labour force that is rather accurately expressed in market prices. These, in turn, provide sufficiently clearly the desired terms of substitution of human capital for other forms of capital. In that way the modern non-slave society and slavery start converging, of course not in technical law but in the changed social function of the legal concept behind the possibly unchanged formal legal rule (positive law).[141] This aspect of alienation is an essential part of the conception of all-encompassing monetisation which the modern money system entails.[142] Where labour force cannot be sufficiently reduced conceptually to substitutable capital, shifts between human capital and other forms of capital 'must take place through direct investment and disinvestment in the human agent', as Friedman says – or, in plain speech, mostly through people's employment and redundancies at short notice, without employment protection, in order not to distort the (money) market forces.

The amount of money that business enterprises earn when they hold money depends on the cost of the productive services and their substitutes. For each dollar of money held, the cost depends on how the corresponding capital is raised, for example, by raising additional capital as bonds or equities, by substituting cash for real capital goods, and so on. Essentially these alternatives are the same as the ways in which wealth-owners can change the forms of holding their non-human wealth (i.e. *M, B, E, G*).

138 Friedman, *Quantity Theory*, pt. 23 (1956: 19).

139 Becker (1992: 85) who publicised the term 'human capital' widely, said that in the past 'many people were criticising this term and the underlying analysis because they believed it treated people like slaves or machines', but now it is readily accepted in all the social sciences and in the media. People can get used to all sorts of crudeness quickly.

140 These are on-call contracts with pay to the employee only when work arises.

141 Renner (1949: 75–77, 252–254, 257).

142 See Chapter 4, sec. 5.

Friedman has several points of criticism in relation to the classical quantity theory. The classical theory emphasises that in transactions there is a 'mechanical link' between money payments per unit time and the average stock of money required to effect that. On the contrary:[143]

> [T]he average amount of money held per dollar of transactions is itself to be regarded as a resultant of an economic equilibrating process, not as a physical datum. If, for whatever reason, it becomes more expensive to hold money, then it is worth devoting resources to effecting money transactions in less expensive ways or to reducing the volume of transactions per dollar of final output. In consequence, our ultimate demand function for money in its most general form does not contain as a variable the volume of transactions or of transactions per dollar of final output; it contains rather those more basic technical and cost conditions that affect the costs of conserving money, be it by changing the average amount of money held per dollar of transaction per unit time or by changing the number of dollars of transactions per dollar of final output.

The same principle applies to the payment conditions which affect the velocity of money circulation. They are not mechanically determined data (such as payment of workers by the day, week, month etc.), but are also the result of an economic equilibrating process.[144] Thus the demand of money is the result of the same economic equilibrating process of the market forces as on the commodity market. The money market follows the classical market equilibrium model of the commodity market. Conversely, every commodity market can also be interpreted as a form of money market; the laws of the market are essentially the same in either case. This idea of monetisation is an important basis for a legal theory of money, and of its critique of economic monetarism.

Furthermore, according to Friedman, the demand for money is not stable, as the old quantity theory of money however claims, and the velocity of money circulation is not numerically constant over time.[145] Nevertheless, there is a clear relation between substantial changes over short periods in the stock of money and in prices: 'the one is invariably linked with the other and is in the same direction; this uniformity is, I suspect, of the same order as many of the uniformities that form the basis of the physical sciences'.[146] The quantity theory of money shows that the growth in the quantity of money is the primary determinant of the inflation rate.[147] Thus the central results of the new quantity theory of money according to Friedman do not differ substantially from the classical quantity

143 Friedman, *Quantity Theory*, pt. 11 (1956: 12–13).
144 Friedman, *Quantity Theory*, pt. 11 (1956: 13).
145 Friedman, *Quantity Theory*, pt. 18(i) (1956: 16).
146 Friedman, *Quantity Theory*, pt. 25 (1956: 21).
147 Mankiw (2013: 105).

theory. Inflation theory is a matter for economists and will not be commented upon here.[148]

The focus on demand does not lead Friedman to talk much about money supply and the role of the banks in it which is the lawyer's primary concern. He does, however, acknowledge that banks create money ('"banks" or producers of money' – this follows the credit creation theory, something generally not expressed so directly in Friedman's time).[149] He also gives the example of enterprises assigning debts to banks in what lawyers would call 'factoring', as an alternative in corporate finance instead of selling shares: '[the enterprise] can sell its claims to banks, getting "money" in exchange . . . the bank coins specific liabilities into generally acceptable liabilities'. But this phenomenon does not change the analysis of the quantity theory of money.[150]

The last passage hints at the role of banks as money creators and the concept of bank money which has been discussed already.[151] One can summarise Friedman's interpretation of the quantity theory of money as follows, no doubt with all the distortions that the lawyer's prism entails: Emphasis of the money market and general market analysis is on demand, not on supply, hence the money supply mechanism and the role of banks do not feature as a point of discussion (or criticism), and, in any case, the analysis is not affected by this aspect. The old quantity theory of money is not abandoned, only adjusted: the price level is dependent on the money supply; growth in the quantity of money primarily determines the inflation rate. The demand for money is not stable and the velocity of money circulation is not numerically constant over time. The money market and the commodity markets act essentially in the same way: the demand of money is the result of the same economic equilibrating process of the market forces as the demand on the commodity market. There is no clear line between 'money' and other assets, and so all of them can be conceptualised as exchangeable and fungible abstract '*res*'. Ultimately, the markets for bonds (*B*), equities (*E*), physical goods (*G*) and human labour force (*H*) are the same as the market for money (*M*) with standardised and priced assets as their subject matter, thus *B, E, G* and *H* are instances of *M* and all are forms of holding *wealth*.

148 There is a heterodox alternative view to the monetarists, but with a certain tradition behind it: inflation can be, but need not necessarily be, the result of a rise of wages (purchase power theory of wages), put forward particularly in Germany in the interwar period by Fritz Tarnow, a social democrat and trade unionist, see Tarnow (1928: 58–66). A possible inflationary effect of a rise of wages can be reduced or even eliminated through increased investment as a result of increased consumption (based on higher wages) and regulatory measures. A different explanation of the effect of wage rises on commodity prices already by Ricardo, *Principles*, chapter 5 (2004: 60).

149 For example, the Bank of England addressed the fact that commercial banks create money through accounting entries for the first time directly in an article as late as in 2014, see e.g. discussion by Werner (2014a: 71), and Chapter 2.

150 Friedman, *Quantity Theory*, pt. 15 (1956: 14–15).

151 See Chapter 2 and the definitions in Chapter 1.

Overall, Friedman also adheres to the belief that economic laws, once established, are comparable to the unchangeable natural laws of physics, a mechanistic-deterministic model of the world of the seventeenth and eighteenth centuries which seems to have been retained, in this purity at least, in the discipline of economics alone today:[152] here it is the supposed uniformity of the relationship between substantial changes in the quantity of money and in the level of prices that 'is, I suspect, of the same order as many of the uniformities that form the basis of the physical sciences'.[153] With the emergence of quantum physics, physicists would consider the idea of strict predictability of natural phenomena much more cautiously.[154]

Economics as a social, not natural, science, has even far more factors of uncertainty built into its conceptual frameworks, since it relies on empirically ascertained statistical data that form the basis of its economic laws, and this measuring is more critical than (normally) in physics. Friedman argues that inflation is a monetary phenomenon, but the basis of his finding is an empirical study he made in relation to changes of the quantity of money in the United States since the 1870s. To ascertain a causal link between quantity of money and inflation rate, one needs to have established the data of the inflation rates of the time period studied.[155]

There are further problems. The method of the calculation of the consumer price index to measure the inflation rate is well known: one fixes a basket of products and services, supposedly to be typical to the average consumer, and determines the prices for these. Then one computes the basket's cost, and after that one determines a base year and computes the index: the result is the consumer price index. The percentage change in the price index from the preceding year is the inflation rate.[156] It is obvious that one can influence the inflation rate figure (especially bringing it down) by substituting certain goods in the basket which have risen in price more sharply by goods which have risen less in price in the year in question. One can justify this replacement by changed consumer behaviour, so that the new basket claims to reflect the current average consumer choices more accurately. So if one replaces (within limits of credibility) foodstuff, produced in Europe, that has become more expensive, by imported computers and other products of digital technology in East Asia that have fallen in price because of cheap labour costs in these countries (and also because of a lack of employment protection and safety protection measures), then one can bring down the inflation rate noticeably. Such corrections may partly account for the fact that after the introduction of the euro in 2002, the generally perceived sharp increase in prices for some products, for example food[157] (incompatible with the teachings of

152 Discussion of that phenomenon in Rahmatian (2017: 126, 131).

153 Friedman, *Quantity Theory*, pt. 25 (1956: 21).

154 Heisenberg (1994: 42–50).

155 On Friedman's study, see e.g. Mankiw (2013: 105).

156 Mankiw (2012: 514–516).

157 For example, the sale of vegetables for 1 euro could have been about 1 German DM just before the introduction of the euro, effectively an increase by about 100%. This is an

the quantity theory of money), did not mirror in the published inflation rates at that period, and economic research maintains that the inflation rate as a result of the introduction of the euro has not been significantly higher overall.[158] An inflation rate that appears low is politically most attractive to all political parties which want to get (re)elected. That is an underlying problem of all empirical data which form the basis of economic 'laws', such as Friedman's interpretation of the quantity theory of money. And that example leaves aside the enormous difficulty of the reliability of data material from the nineteenth century which Friedman used.

Only for the purpose of comprehensiveness a few words shall be said about the differences of Friedman's theory to Keynes.[159] In one persuasive interpretation, Friedman's approach does not depart much from Keynes's. Friedman's idea of the demand for money is principally in relation to the demand for an asset, since the income variable in the demand function is mostly a surrogate for wealth, not a measure of the 'work' to be done by money. Hence Friedman is primarily interested in the optimal relationship between the stock of money and the stocks of other assets, while the (classical) quantity theorists were mostly interested in the relationship between the stock of money and the flow of spending on goods and services. Friedman's criteria are also the ingredients of the Keynesian monetary theory of portfolio choice.[160] Friedman's conceptual framework for his analysis of the demand for money is that of the Keynesian theory of liquidity preference (with the caveat that this demand is, and remains, relatively inelastic). So Friedman's insistence on his theory as being a reformulation of the quantity theory of money is actually misleading.[161]

The reason why Keynes's *General Theory* has not been considered much in this context is that the principal object of Keynes's work, the question what determines the volume of employment at a given time,[162] is outside the scope of this study.

4. The relevant elements of the monetarist approach in economics for a legal theory of money, and for a critique

It has already been said that Friedman's modified quantity theory of money as such is not particularly relevant for a legal theory of money. However, his theory rests on certain monetarist conceptualisations of property, including money, and these are important for the present legal theory of money, as will

---

extreme example. Often there was 'rounding-up': so a price was calculated as, say, 1.80 euros as the equivalent of the old currency, and was then rounded up a few months later to 2 euros. This has led to a perceived inflation by the public, see e.g. Jens Meyer, 'Doch ein Teuro?', *Frankfurter Allgemeine Zeitung*, 22 January 2002.

158 Sturm et al. (2009: 17, 50, 166).

159 Friedman himself makes a short comment in this regard, see Friedman, *Quantity Theory*, pt. 18 (1956: 17).

160 Compare Keynes, *General Theory*, ch. 15 (1964: 195) et seq.

161 Patinkin (1969: 60–61), Patinkin (1972: 886, 900–901).

162 Keynes, *General Theory*, chs. 3, 18 (1964: 25–32, 245–249), Dillard (1970: 3).

be explained in Chapter 4 in the discussion of the externalisation element in the alienation cycle.[163]

The significant aspects of Friedman's analysis can be repeated as follows: wealth, most broadly understood, includes all sources of 'income' or consumable services, one such source being the productive capacity of human beings, so that is one form in which wealth can be held.[164] Whether there is a hidden labour theory of value in this definition is for economists to ascertain. It is certainly a commodification of (theoretically all) human actions as services, being a form of wealth. Labour is obviously a commodity, as one would expect from Friedman's market-fundamentalist or 'neo-liberal' outlook, quite in contrast to Walter Eucken's position that could historically correctly be termed 'neo-liberal' or ordoliberal: labour is not a commodity, and there are differences between the commodity market and the labour market.[165]

Wealth, according to Friedman,[166] can be held as money in a narrow sense, and as money in a wider sense – being fungible but with less liquidity: bonds and equities. Besides, there is wealth in form of 'physical non-human goods', as Friedman puts it (non-human in contrast to human labour force or capital), although it is mysterious why such goods necessarily have to be physical, which seems to exclude, for example, intellectual property, for no good reason. Finally, there is wealth in the form of human capital, as already mentioned. Friedman stresses that all these forms of wealth yield income. For example, money may yield a return in form of money as interest on demand deposits, equities yield income (again in money) through the claims to stated pro-rata shares of the returns of enterprises which equities constitute.[167] Physical goods yield income in kind rather than in money. An ultimately monetary yield also applies to human capital, although it is in reality difficult to define in form of market prices the substitution of human capital for other forms of capital.[168]

One can now transform and restate this model in the light of the concepts of dematerialised property. In essence, things, whether land or chattels, and undoubtedly also intangible forms of property, that is, together all instances of legal *res*, can be expressed as monetary value in the form of the income they yield or could yield (the difference is a concern for the economist and the accountant, not the lawyer), either through periodic rent income or through their exchange value in a one-off sale. The same applies to human capital in principle, only that the valorisation is more difficult in practice. All forms of property, including human capital, are therefore money *in spe* ('expectation money') or versions of actual money, depending only on the respective current level of liquidity. All objects of the physical world, and all objects created by the law (particularly

163 Chapter 4, sec. 4(a).
164 Friedman, *Quantity Theory*, pt. 4 (1956: 4).
165 Eucken (1959: 185).
166 Friedman, *Quantity Theory*, pt. 5 (1956: 5).
167 Friedman, *Quantity Theory*, pt. 5 (1956: 5–6).
168 Friedman, *Quantity Theory*, pt. 5 (1956: 7–8).

intellectual property) are *res*, that is, the normative propertisation through property law. All *res* are ultimately forms of money, these assets being distinguished only by their fungibility and exchangeability which determines their liquidity, that is the monetisation as a result of the conceptualisation of any *res* as money in principle. Friedman therefore does not see a clear boundary between money and other assets, and it may rather be expedient to distinguish between different forms of 'money' only.[169] Human capital is also a *res*, or a form of money *in spe* (at least) with a potential or actual yield of income. That is, historically, the ultimate consequence of Locke's labour theory of property: 'every Man has a *Property* in his own *Person*. This no Body has any Right to but himself. The *Labour* of his Body, and the *Work* of his Hands . . . are properly his'.[170] This is Locke's strange idea that the relationship to oneself is proprietary, one of self-*ownership*. From this notion it follows that if the allocation of the labour-property (or labour-*res*) is not to oneself but to a third person, then we have fully established slavery. It is therefore no surprise that Chicago School representatives of the law-and-economics movement under Friedman's influence discuss the possibility of slavery liberally as an economic option and free from any moral concerns when they conceptualise property rights as 'externalities' from a law-and-economics perspective.[171]

The value of the *res* is realised by way of (a) the exchange (sale) or (b) the periodic income the *res* yields. The difference is notionally not very important. For example, if a flat is sold, its value is expressed in the exchange of the flat against the money paid, that is, the flat is monetised or the flat-*res* is turned into a more liquid asset: money. If the flat is rented out, the service (grant of the use of the flat) is exchanged against the rent in form of money, thus the service is monetised. In both cases the contemplative value or value of the actual use of the flat is irrelevant. Human capital or labour power as service-*res* are equally valorised through the exchange.[172] This realisation or expression of value through the transfer or exchange that money brings about is the essence of the idea of the externalisation cycle.[173] As a next step, one can assume that every *res* is potential money already and can therefore be regarded as money in essence.[174] This notion has a legal predecessor in the old idea of the trust for sale (now abolished) in English land law:[175] a trust for sale was a trust which directed the trustees to sell the property, invest the proceeds and hold the gained funds of sale on trust – that trust declared by the settlor. The trust for sale therefore considered the trust

169 Friedman, *Quantity Theory*, pt. 23 (1956: 19).
170 Locke, *Second Treatise*, § 27 (2013: 287–288) (original emphasis).
171 Demsetz (1967: 349).
172 An early analysis of this kind by Simmel (2011: 101).
173 Discussed in Chapter 4, sec. 4(a).
174 The intellectual historian will detect here an alchemistic notion: as the noble metal is contained in the base metal already and has to be brought out by the alchemist's craft and the application of the philosopher's stone, the absolute fungibility and monetary nature has to be brought out of the *res* by the money as the medium of exchange, see Chapter 4, sec. 3(c).
175 See Law of Property Act 1925 (England and Wales), s. 23 (in the originally enacted version, repealed 1997 by the Trusts of Land and Appointment of Trustees Act 1996, s. 25(2) Sch. 4).

property as potential money. This was an application of the doctrine of conversion (of property into money): there is the presumption of the law of equity that equity considers to have been done which ought to have been done under the trust, so that land held under a trust of sale was considered as a conversion into money *in spe* and so treated as money in equity. However, the trustees had the power to postpone the sale.[176] In this way, the trustees could choose if and when the trust property was to be liquidated. Put differently, the trustees could treat the trust property as property for use and concentrate on an intrinsic value, or as property for exchange/sale and therefore focus on the exchange value. In the latter case they would effectively consider the trust property as a form of money, to be realised later and transformed into a more liquid form of *res*, that is, actual money. By applying this concept from land law more generally, all *res* can be modelled as ultimately a form of money. The practical application of this model can however have horrendous social consequences.[177]

5. Some critical points by 'heterodox' economists; the spurious historical basis of the 'barter' narrative for the introduction of money

The all-encompassing market with its notional equilibrium between supply and demand and its apparently immutable rules that were, historically at least, shaped in the spirit of natural laws in physics and astronomy[178] is currently the predominant conception of the market in economics and hardly questioned. As explained earlier, it equates sale and barter in economic terms and therefore blanks out from the exchange model the existence of money, so that money and its significant role in the exchange and price fixing process can be ignored. This approach is not only the result of a scientific position but also a political decision.[179] Economists have noticed that, and for the sake of completeness, an outline of a few dissenting voices will be given, without venturing into discussing comprehensive critiques of economics or the capitalist system.[180] However, apart from the fact that a proper examination of these heterodox positions would deserve a separate book, there is the cruel truth that heterodox economists in the area of the system of money are rare (they exist in France and to some extent in the United States, but apparently almost not in Germany, for example), and even where they can be found, they have no significant influence on states' economic policy or the economics curricula at universities, so even in a rather comprehensive study they could theoretically be disregarded. Furthermore, criticism of the monetary and financial system does not necessarily come from economists but from other disciplines, such as,

176 Harpum et al. (Megarry and Wade) (2008: 393–394, 401, 404).
177 Discussed in Chapter 4, sec. 5.
178 Rahmatian (2017: 126–136).
179 See particularly Chapter 5, secs. 1 and 2.
180 One of the high-quality critiques in this regard by Polanyi (2001: 59–70), Polanyi (2014: 47–51). Unfortunately, such excellent analyses are rare.

very occasionally, law and economic history, but more often from political science and sociology,[181] and from anthropology.

The foundational narrative of the present market model is that exchange and barter (or sale) were at the inception of markets and money. Adam Smith is usually cited for this orthodox theory of economic development from the supposed primitive stage of the barter economy to the more advanced money economy,[182] but that narrative can already be found with representatives of the Salamanca School, such as Lessius.[183] Anthropologists have shown that the economists' historical account cannot be corroborated with anthropological evidence. Available ethnography suggests that a pure barter economy never existed, let alone that money emerged from it.[184] At the onset of transactions were rather gifts, or, if there was barter, it was quite often not a simultaneous but a delayed exchange, effectively a grant of credit. That required mutual trust, so delayed barter would happen in face-to-face communities, where the exchange partner would have knowledge of the other and can assess his trustworthiness. Money would only become relevant if there was lack of information about the reliability and credit standing of the trading partner who may have been distant and there was not sufficient trust for a delayed barter. The delayed delivery would be substituted by a generally recognised payment medium: money. But money was not introduced to do away with the unwieldiness of barter transactions, as orthodox economic theory suggests.[185] Delayed barter was effectively a loan that could then slip into a gift if the transfer had not been conceived as a gift outright and required trust; money and immediate barter without delay did not.[186] Money exchange existed alongside barter, and money was mainly symbolising credit rather than a means of facilitating exchange.[187] This research confirms Polanyi's view that it was not a 'natural propensity' to barter on local markets which started barter and money, but long-distance trade which created markets that, in turn, initiated barter and the need of money, contrary to orthodox economists' doctrine.[188] All that shows that money did not emerge naturally as a facilitator of exchange of commodities, and it is not neutral either, being a debt with legal and economic consequences.

Economists (of the heterodox kind) are familiar with this flaw of the orthodox market model. For the theme of the present book most relevant is probably the work by Hans Christoph Binswanger, then professor of economics at the University St. Gallen in Switzerland, who presents alternative market models that include money and discusses the historical reasons for the conceptual elimination of money from the market model in classical economics. He also stresses

181 E.g. Arnoldi (2009: 11–13, 67–70).

182 Smith, *Wealth of Nations*, book 1, chapters 1 and 4 (2000: 14, 25–26).

183 Lessius, *De iustitia et iure*, book 2, ch 21, question 1 (2016: 6). Lessius also says that money itself cannot be a commodity or be sold as a commodity, thereby stressing the supposed neutrality of money as a mere medium of exchange.

184 Humphrey (1985: 48).

185 Humphrey (1985: 49–51, 63).

186 Humphrey (1985: 67), Graeber (2011: 30–33).

187 Humphrey (1985: 50), Graeber (2011: 39, 45–46, 52).

188 Polanyi (2001: 61–62).

the development of markets from the 'provision economy' to the 'profit-oriented acquisition economy'.[189] It was Aristotle who already had a good understanding of that problem when he distinguished two types of wealth-getting. One is household management, which is necessary and honourable; the other is retail trade or exchange, which is unnatural because it is a mode by which men gain from one another, and when money is involved, it leads to hateful usury: money is to be used in exchange, not to increase at interest.[190] Walras's idea of the market actually follows Aristotle's household management and provision economy concept, so that money need not play a separate role: all gains and losses even out in an equilibrium of exchanges or barters since all economic actors level out only excess and scarcity according to their subsistence requirements. Therefore money is for Walras merely a *numéraire*, a unit of account, not a payment device. However, the real economy does not correspond to this model at all. Not provision and subsistence but production for the market is the principal aim; the economy is directed at growth and results in ecological problems from the overexploitation of natural resources. Growing production for the market (and increasing profit) is, in turn, dependent on the availability of money, whereby the quantity of money can grow permanently and without real limitations.[191] The question in the modern economy is not mere exchange to balance inequalities in subsistence between different households, as symbolised in a market equilibrium, but economic growth and the gain of wealth which is ultimately created, and represented, by money. Therefore money plays a central role in the market, also from a microeconomic perspective, despite its absence in the microeconomic market model.

Other economists have also emphasised that orthodox economics with its idea of the neutrality of money presents a market model that is artificial and detached from the real economy. These include André Orléan,[192] Jacques Sapir,[193] Gunnar Heinsohn and Otto Steiger,[194] Bruno Théret[195] (also with an interesting discussion of the splitting of the debt into an economic and a political-social element in the context of the political economy),[196] Michel Aglietta[197] and others.[198] However, a number of economists analysing the financial and euro-crisis

189 Binswanger (2009: 56–70, 162–165, 377–387), and above under sec. 2. Reference is made to the German edition because the English edition does not contain all sections.

190 Aristotle, *Politics* [1258a–b].

191 Binswanger (2009: 381–383, 386–387).

192 Orléan (2011: 163–170).

193 Sapir (2003: 217–227).

194 Heinsohn and Steiger (2009: 39–52). Reference is made to the German edition which discusses this aspect in more detail.

195 Théret (2011: 10), para. 36.

196 Théret (1998: 254–258). This piece goes well beyond the usual economists' discourse and takes an interdisciplinary approach, arguably the most suitable one for a discussion of money.

197 E.g. Aglietta and Brand (2013: 66–72, 175–179), discussing the European banking and euro crisis with reference to the workings of the monetary system and the nature of money as a form of debt (and social contract) and not detached from them, as however do so many other economists.

198 E.g. Harribey et al. (2018: 44–46).

after 2009 tend to blame politicians and lawyers for the unsatisfactory solutions of the problem,[199] but do not seem to look critically at the monetary system itself which, one may assume, contributes structurally considerably to the crisis. One may be allowed to argue that lawyers are needed first to understand the monetary system. Since money at its inception, particularly the concept of debt under classical private law, is a legal construct (with all its economic, social and political ramifications), a legal understanding of money would perhaps benefit economists so significantly that their theories might overlap more with reality.[200] Admittedly, most lawyers only have a foggy idea about the legal concept of money and assist little.

The idea of the market equilibrium, rather removed from commercial reality and not allowing space for money within it, has historically the idea of a balance provided by the laws of nature at its root, when it developed during the onset of classical economics in the second half of the eighteenth century. For the Physiocrats, the political economy was an example of a universality of causalities organised naturally, but generally not in an abstract geometrical, Cartesian fashion that could ideally be expressed mathematically, although the Physiocrats' idea of the economy nevertheless owed a lot to Descartes. Quesnay's analysis of value contained a mechanistic equilibrium model and a more biologist model of reproduction at the same time. Under certain conditions, there would be a compensatory effect or balance between expenses and revenue which create an economic equilibrium as an expression of natural laws. This idea was considered as a variant of the cosmological and physiological systems, like that of the blood's circulation as first described by William Harvey. Quesnay, a physician himself, could easily make the connection.[201] Adam Smith's 'invisible hand' metaphor, though in the different context of foreign trade relations,[202] also derives from this spirit of a balanced, cosmological, physical and ultimately moral order, and Smith was, as is well known, strongly influenced by Quesnay. Smith would probably have dedicated to him the *Wealth of Nations* (1776) had Quesnay not died in 1774 already.[203]

In the late nineteenth century, a distinctly biologist, anthropological and evolutionary explanation was added to the notion of the mechanical equilibrium of the markets. Alfred Marshall, one of the founders of neoclassical economics and

199 E.g. Flassbeck (2013: 36–37, 53).

200 Otherwise not altogether accurate speculations about the system of money and banking might continue, for example in the context of the euro-crisis by Sinn and Wollmershäuser (2011: 11): 'When a bank customer effects a transfer from one commercial bank to another, it is fundamentally central bank money that flows between the commercial banks. If a Greek purchaser of a good transfers money from his checking account to the checking account of a vendor at another Greek commercial bank, money is debited from the central-bank account of his bank and credited to the central-bank account of the vendor's bank'. That presupposes (wrongly) that commercial banks only hold central bank money, especially cash.

201 Markovits (1986: 166–168, 171–173).

202 Smith, *Wealth of Nations*, book 4, chapter 2 (2000: 484–485).

203 Ross (2010: 296).

very influential on Keynes and Friedman alike, said in his *Principles of Economics* (1920):[204]

> A business firm grows and attains great strength, and afterwards perhaps stagnates and decays; and at the turning point there is a balancing or equilibrium of the forces of life and decay . . . we shall need ever more and more to think of economic forces as resembling those which make a young man grow in strength, till he reaches his prime; after which he gradually becomes stiff and inactive, till at last he sinks to make room for other and more vigorous life. But to prepare the way for this advanced study we want first to look at a simpler balancing of forces which corresponds rather to the mechanical equilibrium of a stone hanging by an elastic string, or of a number of balls resting against one another in a basin.
>
> We have now to examine the general relations of demand and supply; especially those which are connected with that adjustment of price, by which they are maintained in 'equilibrium'.

Marshall underpins his approach with a stadial conjectural history of human society and history[205] which is very much reminiscent of the Scottish Enlightenment.[206] Both Marshall's and the eighteenth-century versions of this conjectural history are often unsound speculations in the light of modern scientific research, but this shows that no other discipline has been influenced to the present day by the Scottish Enlightenment and its anthropology, sociology and moral philosophy as fundamentally as economics.

6. Conclusion: the disregard of time, and consequently money, in the static market conception of microeconomics

Alfred Marshall was himself open to a critique of the microeconomic market model that he helped to establish. He was very aware of the limitations of such abstractions and the neglect of the element of time, though apparently not with regard to the effects of money:[207]

> [M]arkets vary with regard to the period of time which is allowed to the forces of demand and supply to bring themselves into equilibrium with one

204 Marshall, *Principles*, V, 1, § 1 (2013: 269).

205 Marshall, *Principles*, III, 2, §§ 1–2, and Appendix A, §§ 1–11 (2013: 73–74, 602–616). Appendix A is a beautiful example of a speculative philosophical history of the eighteenth and early nineteenth centuries in the spirit of Montesquieu, Turgot, Condorcet, Kames, Ferguson, Smith, Herder and Hegel, only that it was written about 100–150 years later, when economic and social history existed already as modern disciplines.

206 On the stadial conjectural history of the Scottish Enlightenment, and particularly on one of its founders, Lord Kames, see Rahmatian (2015: 142–150, 192–198) with further references.

207 Marshall, *Principles*, V, 1, § 6 (2013: 274).

> another, as well as with regard to the area over which they extend. And this element of Time requires more careful attention just now than does that of Space. For the nature of the equilibrium itself, and that of the causes by which it is determined, depend on the length of the period over which the market is taken to extend.

And:[208]

> The element of time is a chief cause of . . . difficulties in economic investigations which make it necessary for man with his limited powers to go step by step; breaking up a complex question, studying one bit at a time, and at last combining his partial solutions into a more or less complete solution of the whole riddle. In breaking it up, he segregates those disturbing causes, whose wanderings happen to be inconvenient, for the time in a pound called *Cæteris Paribus.*

In the present orthodox model of the market, time does not appear at all.[209] A major reason why this is possible is that money, as one of these constantly inconvenient wanderings, is eliminated from the exchange process in the supply-demand model; a sale is being reduced conceptually to a barter. At the same time barter is considered as a crude device in early commerce to be replaced by the sale with the introduction of money in the progress of human society, and yet exactly that money as a symbol of progress in commercial transactions is edited out from the present concept of the market model. The result is a static, timeless market model, where supply and demand prices are interlocked in a notional market equilibrium,[210] a frozen point in time that may never have existed in reality. Were money let back into this otherwise unsubstantial mathematical equation, it would soon become apparent that money does not only influence the price but actually makes it, and it does so by enabling a transformative exchange of the commodity sold against an exchange value or expectation value that money represents – philosophically effectively an alchemistic notion. Therefore the exchange which makes the price and exchange value is a completely time-bound phenomenon: it only exists through, and in, time. A conception that disregards time, as the static market model does, is as useful as a conceptualisation of music without time. For this reason, a *dynamic* market model is necessary. This will be discussed in Chapter 4.

In fact, one can speak of a dynamic concept of *money*, not only of a dynamic concept of the market, because – contrary to probably all, even heterodox, economists' opinions – money is the progenitor of the exchange which, in turn, creates the (theoretical) market; it is not just a medium of exchange, even if one concedes that it is non-neutral. The exchange is a *sale*, and its essential ingredient or agent is *money*, being a debt (at least under the present system of money),

208 Marshall, *Principles*, V, 5, § 2 (2013: 304).
209 Heterodox economists criticise that, for example, Sapir (2003: 177).
210 See again Marshall, *Principles*, V, 3, § 6 (2013: 287).

and that money-debt creates not only the exchange and thereby establishes the market, but, ultimately, it also conceptualises the commodity itself against which money is exchanged. These are all creations of legal theory (particularly property theory) and institutions of the *law* only. However, economists would not like to bow before the law and recognise its primogenital right, and so we have a fight between the disciplines for scientific or political power and influence. However, when it comes to money, the economists will have to give way to those who invented the discipline of economics in the first place: the political and legal philosophers, and the lawyers. The economists seem to know that, which is why they presuppose money in their economic models but do not seek to understand it.

Marshall rightly hinted at the problem time poses when incorporated in an economic model – not specifically in relation to money but with regard to fluctuations in the markets and so forth. The recognition of time in economics is a problem of science that cannot be removed by eliminating the problem from the model.[211] Only because it is difficult or currently impossible to explain certain occurrences scientifically, one cannot resort to a kind of theology to provide simple (and politically convenient) answers, like the postulation that the earth had to be in the centre of the universe because otherwise one could not explain certain celestial phenomena. Yet when we consider time in relation to money, we are not concerned about factual changes of market behaviour over time, but about the conceptual incorporation of time in the market model which an understanding of money as the exchange agent necessitates. Philosophically one could say, the sale or exchange involving money is a *temporal structure* (like music of which time is a constituent element), *not* a *structure in time* (like an architectural building that may decay over time).[212] It is, however, the latter which Marshall envisages.

There are rare examples of mainstream economists who are aware of the severe limitations of the timeless and static market model in relation to money specifically. The following statement, in the context of general equilibrium analysis of market clearing processes that include money, may serve as a transition to the next chapter:[213]

> [T]he role of money in exchange is not fully or well developed [in studies on market clearing processes to study the dynamic behaviour of the rate of interest]. Therefore, it must be admitted that, as far as the dynamic market clearing process is concerned, money is not successfully integrated in the general equilibrium analysis. The demand for money of the transaction motive, for example, should be based on the dynamics of exchange processes.

211 See also Marshall, *Principles*, Appendix D (2013: 644), where he cautions against unrestricted use of abstract reasoning and mathematical models in economics: 'If we shut our eyes to realities we may construct an edifice of pure crystal by imaginations, that will throw side lights on real problems; and might conceivably be of interest to beings who had no economic problems at all like our own' (at § 2).

212 For these terms, see Stambaugh (1964: 267).

213 Negishi (1965: 163).

4 A dynamic concept of money. The alienation cycle

1. The time-bound nature of money

The previous chapter indicated that the operation of money is contingent on time; it is a process. The workings of money can only be understood as a movement, not as a static structure. Time is a constituent element for money; without time, money could not operate. This is not a gloss on Benjamin Franklin's well-known remark, 'Time is Money' from 1748 (he also said, particularly relevant for the present discussion, 'Credit is Money'),[1] incidentally an indication that with industrialisation time has become a tool for social control and a currency: 'it is not passed but spent'.[2] Franklin's statement emphasises the usual view of money as being a part of a series of events – in this case: doing work and investing instead of sitting idle – during a timeline. In fact, money does not just occur in time, it is a phenomenon of time. The static coin or accounting entry (bank money) is not actually the money yet but the potential to operate as money. Thus it is not 'Time is Money' but 'Money is a Phenomenon of Time'. There is no money without time, as there is no music without time. However, economists and lawyers alike have great problems with such dynamic and fluid concepts.

This is not the place to embark on a philosophy of time.[3] It seems to be generally accepted, ultimately with reference to Aristotle,[4] that time involves change or there is no time without change.[5] There is certainly no change without time, but whether the reverse applies is less clear,[6] because not realising that time has elapsed does not mean that it really has not and there is no existence of time. Objects may appear in the present as permanent, independent of time (although the human perception of the object is necessarily time-bound).[7] This is important in relation to (legal and economic) concepts of the human mind which may be

1 Franklin, *Advice to a Young Tradesman* (1748), Franklin (1961: 306).
2 Thompson (1967: 61). Norbert Elias remarked that 'the setting of time, like the coining of money, became one of the monopolies of the state', Elias (1992: 53).
3 On the theory of time in the history of philosophy, see e.g. van Fraassen (1985: 11).
4 Aristotle, *Physics*, book 4 [218b].
5 McTaggart (1995: 25).
6 Shoemaker (1995: 64–66).
7 Husserl (2000: 77).

conceived or perceived as static, but are actually time-bound, so that their change is not realised, though in fact they are affected by the passage of time. Such a concept is money, a form of property – itself a static concept (the *res*, often reified as a physical object) and an entity within the framework of time. The economic market model of supply and demand is a similar static concept where time is not a constitutive factor.

This chapter will show that money is not a (theoretically) time-independent property object which serves as an economic medium of exchange for a transfer of value. Money is rather an agent or catalyst that enables a process of value creation through the exchange or transfer that it effects. The exchange that money brings about in a sale is dynamic, an intrinsically time-bound process, like music or dance in the arts. Before the operation of the transfers effected by money is considered,[8] there will be an outline of the framework of social and legal relations, a kind of social vector space, that money produces.[9] This will be followed by a discussion of the effect of money in the sales transaction: money operates as a transmuting agent that transforms the assets it apparently only facilitates to transfer as a means of exchange. This is a philosophical notion deriving from alchemy.[10] Esoteric as this may sound today, alchemy had a central importance in philosophy well into the seventeenth century. The alchemistic attempts at turning lead into gold, although seemingly important in the context of money, are, and always were, a side issue within alchemy; what matters for the present analysis are the philosophical concepts of alchemy. Therefore the reader will regrettably be disappointed that this text does not contain a recipe for *chrysopoeia*, the transmutation of base metals into gold. The philosopher's stone lies elsewhere.

2. The framework of relations that money designs: the four cases or aspects of money

Before we embark on an examination of a dynamic concept of money in contrast to the usual static one of economists and lawyers, it is worthwhile examining the abstract-conceptual space or framework in which the dynamic money relations unfold. Property rights are to be understood as social and legal relations between persons in respect of an object or objects,[11] and this relational concept of property rights also applies to money: as all property, money is based on social and legal relations.

These relations attached to money can be compared to spanning a vector space in mathematics. However, an analogy from grammar, or more precisely, from the morphology and the case or *casus* forms in Indo-European languages, is probably more instructive in the present context than mathematics to describe or symbolise this conceptual space of relations produced by money. In any case, neither

8 See below under secs. 4 and 5.

9 See below under sec. 2.

10 See below under sec. 3.

11 See Chapter 1.

the mathematical nor the linguistic analogy is entirely stringent because both are supposed to serve merely as similes for an abstract conceptual framework: this is not a material space as in physics or architecture but a legal-sociological space of legal and economic relations. Several space sociologies define space as a result of human relations in general and in respect of social goods in particular.[12] Language, the fabric of law, can serve here as a useful illustrative tool to arrange the various interlinked incidents of money and to organise its complex space.

Latin and other languages, as is well known, have 'cases' or *casus* for nouns and pronouns in particular. Their function is to express perspective and relations between the separate subjects and objects in reality and in its linguistic expression in the sentence. These cases bear names which shall reflect, though imperfectly, the (potential) perspective as articulated or conveyed.[13] The traditional nomination derives from Latin which the Roman grammarians (Varro, Quintilian) took over (also imperfectly) from ancient Greek.[14] The first case is the *casus nominativus* or standard case (*casus rectus*) which names or terms, and from which the other *casus* derive as special cases (*casus obliqui*): the second case or *casus genitivus* as the case of origin (*casus paternus, possessivus*), the third case or *casus dativus* as the case of giving (*casus dandi, commendativus*),[15] and the fourth case or *casus accusativus* as the case of accusation/blame or charge, but more properly the case of effectuation or operation, following the ancient Greek term (*aitiatikè*: '*causativus*') which the Romans translated inadequately.[16]

The different cases are articulated in the declensions, for instance in Latin, (1) arbor, (2) arbor*is*, (3) arbor*e*, (4) arbor*em*;[17] or in German, (1) der Baum, (2) des Baum*es*, (3) dem Baum(*e*),[18] (4) den Baum. Where these declensions have disappeared during the evolution of the language, the cases can be indicated by prepositions, for example in French, (1) l'arbre, (2) *de* l'arbre, (3) *à* l'arbre, (4) l'arbre;[19] or in English, (1) the tree, (2) *of* the tree, (3) *to* the tree, (4) the tree. The important point is that these linguistic devices denote and confer relations between the items and transform them into actors and objects,[20] as property rights do, expressed with the same linguistic devices: 'ce livre est à moi' (3rd case), or 'this book belongs to me' (3rd case) denotes an attribution of an object

12 Löw (2012: 73–82, 134–138, 177–178).

13 Köller (2004: 390–391).

14 Sandys (1915: 57).

15 See Quintilian, book I, 4, 26–27 (1969: 74–77) on the *casus dativus* and *ablativus*.

16 Köller (2004: 391), Sandys (1915: 57).

17 We are not concerned with the Latin 5th case, the *casus vocativus* and the 6th case, the *casus ablativus* here. The *casus ablativus* combines the simple *ablativus* (where from?) *ablativus instrumenti* (by what?), the *locativus* (where, when?). Other Indo-European languages have retained separate cases, for example Polish with its *instrumentalis* (5th case, *narzędnik*), *locativus* (6th case, *miejscownik*), *vocativus* (7th case, *wołacz*).

18 'Dem Baum*e*' for the third case becomes increasingly dated.

19 In French grammar the fourth case is referred to as '*complément d'objet direct*' and the third case as '*complément d'objet indirect*'.

20 The terms 'subject' and 'object' are deliberately not used so as to avoid confusion with the grammatical terms which do not coincide.

from a supposed or imaginary third person to me and indicates a proprietary relationship, most typically my ownership. If considered from the owner's perspective one would say: 'le livre de Luc' (2nd case), 'Luke's book (the book of Luke)' (2nd case, sometimes called Saxon genitive), to indicate possession or affiliation ('Jane's mother'). A change of relations or entitlements can be expressed thus: 'la mère donne le livre (4th case) à la fille (3rd case)', 'the mother gives the book (4th case) to the daughter (3rd case)'.[21] Here we have the linguistic depiction of an entitlement transfer, perhaps an ownership transfer, and also an image of property relations: the mother creates (or can create) a legal relation with her daughter (the actors) in respect of the property object 'book' (4th case) by transferring or giving – *casus dativus.* In this context we are not concerned with the actual underlying contractual relation in private law (sale, gift, loan/*commodatum*, or not an intended legal relation at all) and the property entitlements it relates to or confers (ownership, possession). The property object 'book' appears in the fourth case, denoting the static-passive 'oppositional' relationship ('*casus accusativus*') to the transaction or relationship which it is subjected to.[22] Put differently, the fourth case is a reference to the object which the transaction is directed at to effectuate something, potentially against other human actors ('*erga omnes*' in property law). The third case indicates a dynamic relationship, a transfer or change.

Obviously this interpretation must be regarded as entirely theoretical and schematic;[23] not even grammarians would apply that strictly to real languages because languages are not necessarily logically consistent.[24] For example, in German 'der Bruder hilft der Schwester' ('the brother is helping the sister') the 'dynamic' third case is used, while French uses the 'static' fourth case: 'le frère aide la sœur', a legacy from Latin ('*adiuvo te*').[25] However, relevant are

21 The order of these objects depends on the language; in German third and fourth case would normally change place in this example – 'Die Mutter gibt der Tochter (3rd case) das Buch (4th case)' – but that is not relevant here.

22 Therefore old property theorists also referred to the object of property or 'thing' as 'property *subject*' when they meant property object, for example Lord Kames in the eighteenth century, see Rahmatian (2015: 204, n. 73, 224–225) for further references.

23 The root of this argument in rhetoric is obvious, see Quintilian, book I, 4, 6–29 (1969: 64–79), and Kristeller (1990: 229) on the fundamental importance of rhetoric to the five *studia humanitatis* (grammar, rhetoric, poetry, history, moral philosophy) in the Renaissance period and later. A brief grammatical explanation in relation to property rights by Lord Kames (who also wrote sections on rhetoric within his *Elements of Criticism* (1762)), see Rahmatian (2015: 25) with references.

24 From what has been said above, the sentence 'He goes into the kitchen' and 'He is in the kitchen' would suggest the 'dynamic' third case in the first example and the 'static' fourth case in the second, but in German it is the other way round ('in *die* Küche' (4) and 'in *der* Küche' (3), respectively, and in Latin one would use in the first example the fourth case and in the second the sixth case (*ablativus* as *locativus*). So the grammatical use of the *casus* is not following a reliable pattern.

25 In case of the word 'follow' the French form is arguably more logical than the German one, according to what has been suggested above: 'il *la* suit' (4th case) ('he follows her') while in German the third case is used: 'Er folgt *ihr*'.

the different qualities of relations as expressed in different *casus* in language, not the practical realisations of the categories of casus in the specific languages. The notion of different *casus* expressing different qualities of (legal) relations can be used to represent the different relationships in a transaction involving money.

One can distinguish four aspects or cases of money, similar to grammatical cases. The *first case* is the case of naming (*casus nominativus*) and has been discussed in Chapter 1: it means simply that money is money because it is designated as such by law. That is true of *fiat money* or compulsory tender issued by the central bank as banknotes,[26] and it applies to bank money created by commercial banks through granting loans by way of accounting entries which are recognised as money, though not (yet) as compulsory tender. In principle that can also apply to private currencies, including electronic currencies. The quality of money arises out of the ability, conferred by law, to obtain (ultimately tangible) property by potentially enforcing the debt which money constitutes. Therefore the economists' common distinction between a 'state theory', 'institutional theory' and 'functional theory' of money[27] is futile.[28] If the law does not enforce a medium of exchange as creating or discharging a debt, it is not money. The reason for these redundant academic categorisations is mostly the fact that economists do not realise, or do not wish to realise, that the framework for their principal research object, the market, is normative and provided by the law: through contracts, property rights and so forth. Money is no exception.

The *second case* is the case of the origin (*casus genitivus*), that is, the requirement that the means of exchange derives from an accepted origin or source to be recognised as money. That has been discussed in Chapters 1 and 2. If the supposed money does not originate from a bank, it is not real money. It is the privilege of central banks and commercial banks to create money. 'Banknotes' from a Monopoly game, forged banknotes, and even an additional batch of banknotes which have not been forged but have not been authorised for release unlike the first lot (both having been manufactured by the same printer) are not money.[29] One's private drawing up of accounts and making a booking entry resembling that of banks when granting a loan does not make it bank money.[30] The privilege to create money is granted by the law, but the exact legal basis that provides this privilege is rather obscure for bank money created by commercial banks.[31]

The *third case* is the case of giving (*casus dativus*) or, in this context, particularly the case of *transfer* and transaction. While the first case identifies a given

26 Coins, issued by the Royal Mint (in the UK), are also fiat money, but lumped together with the banknotes because of their economic insignificance. See Chapter 1, sec. 3 and Chapter 2, sec. 2.

27 Proctor (2012: 9–25).

28 See Chapter 1, sec. 3.

29 *Banco de Portugal v. Waterloo & Sons* [1932] AC 452, HL, and discussion in Chapter 1, sec. 4.

30 Rahmatian (2014: 225, 229).

31 Rahmatian (2018a: 228–229), and Chapter 2, sec. 6.

res as money and the second case denotes the normatively approved origin for money, the third case indicates the operation of money as a medium of exchange and as an agent as well as ingredient of transfer within which money unfolds its 'powers of transmutation'.[32] Unlike in a proper barter, in a sale the money given in exchange for goods transforms the tangible property into an expectation to realise this hope in form of another tangible property at a later date, but it does not grant any entitlement to a specific item of property. The complex and multifaceted aspects of this transfer involving money will be examined in detail below.[33] Linguistically one cannot reproduce this multi-layered transaction as 'I (1st case) give the money (4th case) to you (3rd case)', because in the theoretical framework of legal relations used here money is 'active' subject, not 'passive' object. For good reasons money is not conceptualised as 'passive' property. Concerted human behaviour, enforced by law (ultimately again concerted human behaviour), makes money play an active, complex role.

The *fourth case* is traditionally called accusative (*casus accusativus*), but grammarians have regarded this name as something of a misnomer, and in the present context the original term *casus causativus* is as appropriate. The fourth case stands for several situations. There is the scenario of enforcement of the debt which money is and creates ('*accusativus*' properly, that is: arraign), but also the idea of direction: the third case deals with the transfer or 'cause', the fourth case with the effect of the transfer pertaining to it. Money is a debt to be discharged as a result of the loan which creates the money debt (borrower's monetary debt) in order to discharge another debt (e.g. purchase price arising from a sale) as the effect.[34] Furthermore, the *casus accusativus* signifies a notion of correlation between customer and bank that money creates: the banker becomes owner of the money paid into the customer's account in return for a debt to the customer to pay out the amount credited.[35] In the extreme case, the customer has to sue for repayment,[36] a proper *casus accusativus*, as it were. The situation of the *casus dativus* in form of a number of subsequent transfers seeks to defer the possibility of a *casus accusativus*, ideally eternally,[37] because if it occurs, there can be a risk of insolvency of the bank, particularly when a number of customers raise claims against the bank simultaneously for withdrawal of their deposits ('bank run').[38]

The condition of the third case is the most important one for the following discussion. First, the quasi-alchemistic transformation of assets by money in the

32 These 'powers of transmutation' are discussed below under sec. 3(c).
33 See below under secs. 3(c) and 4.
34 See Chapter 2 and below under sec. 4(b), and Chapter 5, sec. 2.
35 *Foley v. Hill* (1848) 2 HLC 28, and discussion in Chapters 1 and 2.
36 *Joachimson v. Swiss Bank Corporation* [1921] 3 KB 110.
37 Central bank money and legal tender is indeed an 'eternal debt' that is never repaid, see Rahmatian (2018a: 217) with further references and Chapter 2.
38 About the need to keep transferring incessantly to maintain the financial system, see below under sec. 4.

transaction will be discussed,[39] and then the cyclical nature of the transfer and its effects in the shape of externalisation[40] and alienation or estrangement.[41]

3. The quasi-alchemistic transformation of assets by money

(a) *The reference to 'alchemy' in the literature on money and banking*

A glance into the history of ideas and of science reveals that the qualities of money contain certain alchemistic notions, because the belief in money as deferred wealth resembles concepts in alchemy: money is a magical symbolising reifier of no intrinsic value with a perceived power of extracting genuine value by 'transmutation'.[42] Hence the German Central Bank (*Deutsche Bundesbank*) could say in one of its information brochures about the money creation process of the commercial banks: '*Der Geldschöpfungsprozess erscheint damit wie Zauberei*'[43] ('So the money creation process appears like magic'). The process of money creation has always been suspicious in the eyes of many, and although the system of money creation is no secret,[44] banks do understandably not promote wide knowledge of this quasi-alchemistic conception (it is *quasi*-alchemistic because a real alchemist seeks to transform existing matter, while the banks' money creation originates from nothing). For example, in the past the Bank of England has been very reticent in responding in plain language to a freedom of information request whether or not loans are given out of existing deposits.[45] The Bank of England is more forthcoming now about explaining the money creation process.[46] The Deutsche Bundesbank described the creation of bank money quite clearly already in its 2008 and 2009 information brochures on money for schools, but the later

39 See below under sec. 3.
40 See below under sec. 4.
41 See below under sec. 5.
42 Rahmatian (2014: 228).
43 These are the words of the Deutsche Bundesbank in its information brochure for schools, Deutsche Bundesbank (2008: 62).
44 See Chapter 2 for a discussion of the money creation process.
45 See the internet website www.whatdotheyknow.com with a letter by the Bank of England of 22 November 2010 in a response to a freedom of information request to the Bank of England (at www.whatdotheyknow.com/request/money_creation_2#incoming-149357, visited 5 June 2012, no longer live), in which the Bank of England states: 'The answer to your question is in the structure of the balance sheet of a financial institution that lends money: loans made by such financial institutions appear on the assets side of their balance sheet, and reserves are one part (alongside deposits and other funding) of the liabilities side of their balance sheet'. This is technically correct, but only a specialist will be able to understand it.
46 Bank of England (2014a: 15). See also a recent freedom of information request, answered in a letter by the Bank of England on 19 October 2017, available at: www.whatdotheyknow.com/request/433999/response/1056266/attach/2/Letter%20to%20Mr%20Carnihan.pdf?cookie_passthrough=1 (visited 5 December 2017), with a rather comprehensive answer.

2010 version of the brochure has been less explicit.[47] It appears, however, that from about 2012 the banks have become more cooperative in their explanations; whether that has been prompted by the banks' need to justify themselves before the general public after the financial crisis of 2008–9 and its aftermath can only be guessed. Perhaps the rescue of the banks by the states and the measures by the EU following the 2008–9 crisis have entrenched the banks so deeply in the political and economic system that the dissemination of more detailed knowledge about the money creation system is no longer a concern to the banks.

The money creation system confirms the dubious impression that money is created out of nothing (*ex nihilo*),[48] with all the connotations of divine and *ex nihilo* creation from religion and intellectual history,[49] and with a hint of the magic, occult and mystic with which alchemy was also associated. An orthodox economists' explanation will nevertheless point out that deposits with banks arise out of the acquisition of some asset or assets given as security, and every asset is a form of wealth, so that the bank does not actually create money 'out of nothing'. But even orthodox accounts of the money supply system cannot resist references to alchemy, such as that by Crowther in his *Outline of Money* (1940), still a standard text.[50] Bankers and representatives of the financial services also keep alluding loosely to alchemy and its magical secrets in their publications. An example is the recent book *The End of Alchemy* (2016) by the former governor of the Bank of England, Mervyn King, who speaks of the 'alchemy of money creation'[51] and uses the term 'alchemy' in several places in his work to denote something mysterious but also doubtful or dishonest. One is tempted to surmise that books like this seek to make money by describing the flaws of the existing monetary system without any fear that this system could ever change.[52] The use of the term 'alchemy' in this context is presumably also initiated by marketing considerations to make the title appear more appealing to potential readers,[53] especially where they have been prepared by popular fiction like *Harry Potter*.

An obvious association between money and alchemy is the alchemistic transmutation of base metals into gold which supposedly resembles the monetary system. But from the perspective of the history of ideas, this understanding of alchemy is

47 Compare Deutsche Bundesbank (2008: 59–62), Deutsche Bundesbank (2009: 89), and Deutsche Bundesbank (2010: 69–70).

48 See Chapter 2, sec. 3.

49 May (1994: 26, 73–74), and on *creatio ex nihilo* in relation to copyright, Rahmatian (2011a: 161–164). See also Köhler (2013: 910).

50 Crowther (1946: 47). See the further discussion of Crowther's account below under (c).

51 King (2016: 86). Other examples of loose use of alchemistic terminology, without going into much detail, in King (2016: 8, 104).

52 E.g. King (2016: 369): 'For many centuries, money and banking were financial alchemy, seen as a source of strength when in fact they were the weak link of a capitalist economy'. The alchemistic metaphor makes the (desired?) impossibility of reforming fundamentally the banking system appear more magical and mysterious.

53 Such marketing considerations even seem to apply to academic books on the history of alchemy and chemistry, see Principe (2013: 85): 'Would you have bought this book if its title were *The Secrets of Chemistry*?' (The book is called *The Secrets of Alchemy*).

so superficial that it is misleading and almost wrong. Alchemy is an ancient philosophical concept that is put into effect by using or 'perfecting' physical matter; turning lead into silver or gold was only one application of that concept[54] and – at least from the perspective of many alchemists – an apparent increase of individual wealth was not the main objective.[55] However, philosophical ideas of alchemy do linger on in the present system of money, though not in the way modern authors on banking and money suggest, and if they knew the proper context, they would probably find that perplexing. But for a good appreciation of the influence of alchemic notions on the concept of money it will now be necessary to present an outline of the ideas of alchemy.[56]

(b) An outline of the philosophical concepts of alchemy

Alchemy is primarily a philosophical concept that is concerned with the transformation of one form of matter into another. A principal source of alchemy is Greek natural philosophy, such as Aristotle's *On Generation and Corruption*[57] and particularly the fourth book of Aristotle's *Meteorologica*, a work that is now nearly forgotten because the natural philosophy in this work has in almost all instances been disproved by the modern sciences, but was influential well into the seventeenth century. Both in *On Generation and Corruption* and in the *Meteorologica* Aristotle discusses the change or transformation, whether or not reciprocal, of elements, for example:[58]

> [I]f we consider [the 'elements'] in general, that everyone is by nature such as to come-to-be out of every one: and when we come to consider them severally, it is not difficult to see the manner in which their transformation is effected. [. . .]
>
> No transformation . . . into any of the 'simple' bodies [that is: fire, air, water, earth][59] can result from the passing-away of one elementary quality in each of two 'elements' when they are taken in their consecutive order, because either *identical* or *contrary* qualities are left in the pair:[60] but no 'simple' body can be formed either out of identical, or out of contrary, qualities.

54 Koyré (1971: 109–110).

55 See e.g. Thomas Norton, *Ordinal of Alchemy* (1477), Norton (1975: 14).

56 A brief outline of the history of alchemy and chemistry directed at comparative lawyers and non-specialists also in Rahmatian (2018b: 233, 258).

57 Aristotle, *On Generation and Corruption* [314b–315a, 327a–332a].

58 Aristotle, *On Generation and Corruption* [331a–331b] (quote).

59 See Aristotle, *On Generation and Corruption* [330b].

60 There are four causal factors in the elements whose combinations yield four elements: two factors are active (the hot and cold) two passive (the moist and dry), and the elements contain a pair of prime contrarieties – fire (hot-dry), air (moist-hot), water (moist-cold), earth (dry-cold), see Aristotle, *Meteorologica* [378b], *On the Heavens* [303b–305a], *On Generation and Corruption* [328b–329b].

> Metals are the product of vaporous exhalation,[61] and are all fusible or ductile, for example, iron, gold, copper. These are all produced by the enclosure of the vaporous exhalation, particularly within stones, whose dryness compresses it together and solidifies it, just as dew or frost solidify when they have been separated – only metals are produced before separation has taken place. [. . .] [copper or gold are] the result of the solidification of the exhalation before it turns to water. So all metals are affected by fire and contain earth, for they contain dry exhalation. The only exception is gold, which is not affected by fire.[62]

Although not alchemistic texts as such, these passages indicate already the notion of metamorphosis or change and transformation of matter as the basis for alchemist transmutation, and the idea of physical treatment and processing of matter, such as metals, to effect such a change – these artisanal practices would become an essential part not only of alchemy but also of modern chemistry.[63]

Another important foundational text for alchemy was the writings in Greek presumably from the second and third centuries ad by (reportedly) Hermes Trismegistus ('the thrice great Hermes'), also identified mystically with the Greek god Hermes or the Egyptian sage or god Thoth, the messenger of the gods and interpreter of divine or secret and equivocal messages (hence 'hermeneutics' and the term 'hermetic art' for alchemy).[64] This *Corpus Hermeticum* by 'Hermes' was influential during the Middle Ages[65] and particularly important for Renaissance thinking (Giordano Bruno, Marsilio Ficino, Pico della Mirandola)[66] after the translation (in part) by the Renaissance philosopher Marsilio Ficino under the title *Pimander*.[67]

In relation to the cosmological part of alchemy, apart from the *Pimander*,[68] Aristotle's *On the Heavens* is especially important,[69] as well as the *Emerald Tablet*,

61 There are two forms of exhalation, dry and vaporous, which produce fossils [here: minerals and stones] and metals, respectively, Aristotle, *Meteorologica* [378a].

62 Aristotle, *Meteorologica* [378a].

63 Principe (2013: 85–86).

64 Also the expression 'hermetically sealed' for sealing a flask or crucible derives from that, see Principe (2013: 69, 123).

65 And already in Christian antiquity, see e.g. Yates (2002: 9–13) on St. Augustine's condemnation of Hermes Trismegistus.

66 Yates (2002: 66, 91, 130, 137, 210, 218), Taylor (1976: 156). On the reception of the *Corpus Hermeticum* in the sixteenth and seventeenth centuries as a (perceived) source of Ancient Egyptian theology and wisdom, see Assmann (2011: 123).

67 The *Pimander* (*Poemandres*) is the first of the fifteen treatises of the *Corpus Hermeticum*, fourteen of which Marsilio Ficino translated, see Yates (2002: 2–3, 13–14). Relevant to alchemy are, for example, treatises I.14–16, X.11–19, XI.2–17, see Chambers (1882: 7–9, 60–63, 68–74).

68 See e.g. treatises I.6–16, XI.2–8, Chambers (1882: 2–9, 68–71), with parallels to Plato's *Timaeus* and John 1,1.

69 Aristotle, *On the Heavens* [293a–298a]; on the more transformational/transmutational concepts in alchemy, see [304a–305b].

of which the author is supposedly also Hermes. The *Emerald Tablet* (*Tabula Smaragdina*) is, in its later Latin translations, perhaps the best known foundational text in alchemy. The original is a short text in Arabic, presumably from the eighth century and in substance perhaps of Greco-Egyptian origin, although no Greek original has survived if it ever existed.[70] The Arabs were not only important transmitters but also creators of alchemistic thought,[71] and the initially Arabic word 'alchemy' (*al-kīmiyā'*) is a reminder of that. The Greek origin of this word (*chemeia*) means the 'art of melting metals' – at least that is the most likely etymological explanation.[72] The cosmological, astrological, magical, cabbalistic, mystical, occult, artistic and scientific aspects of alchemy, as well as the (neo) platonic idea of the harmony of the world and the heavens' spheres which are central concepts in the *Emerald Tablet*, the *Pimander* and other alchemistic and pre-alchemistic writings,[73] will be left aside in the present discussion to concentrate on the continued relevance of alchemistic ideas to the concept of money. However, it must be stressed that this is a pragmatic and, from the viewpoint of an intellectual historian, very narrowly focused discussion of alchemy, a practical analytical approach not in line with holistic ideas of alchemy or the Renaissance. It must also be added that influential criticism and polemic against alchemy existed all along, particularly from the early Renaissance period.[74]

The essence of the idea of alchemy is set out lucidly in the *New Pearl of Great Price* (*Pretiosa Margarita Novella*) by Petrus Bonus of Ferrara, written around 1330.[75] This book has generally been regarded highly by alchemists themselves because of its philosophical clarity and methodological exposition compared to many arcane and deliberately obfuscating treatises on alchemy. Alchemy is not fraudulent magic but an art rooted in nature:[76]

> I stoutly maintain that the art of alchemy is clear and true, and founded upon nature; that its products are as truly silver and gold as the precious metals which are produced in the bowels of the earth.

It is a speculative as well as an empirical art (or science):[77]

> If you wish to know that pepper is hot and that vinegar is cooling, . . . that arsenic whitens brass, . . . you will, in every one of those cases, have to verify the assertion by experience. It is the same in geometry, astronomy, music,

70 Principe (2013: 30–32), Taylor (1976: 77–78). Translation of the *Emerald Tablet* also in Holmyard (1968: 97–98).

71 Holmyard (1968: 60–104) on Islamic alchemy; Principe (2013: 28, 33).

72 Principe (2013: 23–24, 29), Holmyard (1968: 19).

73 For typical examples of visualisation of alchemistic universalist cosmology in different epochs, see e.g. Roob (2016: 51, 58–59, 88, 168, 171, 204, 307).

74 Ogrinc (1980: 108–114).

75 Holmyard (1968: 141).

76 Petrus Bonus (1894: 103).

77 Petrus Bonus (1894: 86–87).

> perspective, and other sciences with a practical scope and aim. A like rule applies with double force to alchemy, which undertakes to transmute the base metals into gold and silver. Whatsoever has the power to transmute imperfect and incomplete metals into perfect and complete metals has the power to make gold and silver.

Alchemy only perfects nature. In particular, it perfects imperfect matter, such as turning base metals into noble metals, so that it does not create matter out of nothing:[78]

> The fact is that, in producing gold, the art of alchemy does not pretend to imitate the whole work of nature. It does not create metals, or even develop them out of the metallic first-substance; it only takes up the unfinished handiwork of nature (i.e., the imperfect metals), and completes it (transmutes metals into gold). It is not then necessary that nature's mode of operation . . . should be so very accurately known to the artist. For nature has only left a comparatively small thing for him to do – the completion of that which she has already begun. . . . Nature herself is set upon changing these metals into gold; the artist has only to remove the cause which hinders this change (i.e., the corrupting sulphur), and then he can depend upon nature for the rest. . . .
>
> In the generation of metals all common metals are potentially what gold is actually, they are imperfectly what gold is perfectly.

Matter and its transformation are understood in an Aristotelian way:[79]

> It is thus very well possible for our art to imitate nature in the generation of gold and silver. The whole process is admirably illustrated by Aristotle's remarks in regard to *atramenta* [black liquids] in the fourth chapter of his *Meteorology*.

The transmutation is achieved with the aid of the 'philosopher's stone' which the alchemist seeks to produce:[80]

> Our magistery is speculative in so far as it teaches us the nature and relations of metals; it is practical in so far as it teaches us how to utilise this knowledge for the production of the philosopher's stone, and the transmutation of common metals into gold and silver.

The philosopher's stone is primarily an idealised philosophical concept in alchemy. But because of the characteristic practical side of alchemy – which indicates already

78 Petrus Bonus (1894: 152–153, 173).
79 Petrus Bonus (1894: 216–217).
80 Petrus Bonus (1894: 186).

the early onset of the modern empirical natural sciences – the philosopher's stone must also be a kind of physical matter, since transmutation should also really happen in the physical world. However, the alchemistic sources are always particularly obscure when they have to characterise the philosopher's stone or even give a recipe for its production. Usually mercury and sulphur[81] (together with a certain treatment of the metals,[82] such as grinding, heating, melting, distillation, condensation) are the principal agents for the transmutation and play the role of the philosopher's stone, but neither were these necessarily the only appropriate substances (or 'elements' in modern chemistry), nor did the alchemists always refer to these in a modern chemical sense, hence often the term 'philosophical mercury/sulphur' was used. Mercury and, in combination, sulphur, were often the most attractive ingredients for the philosopher's stone because of their reactiveness, and the liquidity of mercury makes this metal stand out from all others. But the name of the substance (often deliberately disguised in ancient and occult texts) rather denoted one class of substance or one mixture, and commonly not the modern chemical equivalent. The substances 'mercury' and 'sulphur' also represent an Aristotelian pairing of complementary principles (liquid-solid, wet-dry etc.) which are reactive toward each other.[83] The 'philosopher's stone' was also referred to as 'elixir' or 'tincture'.[84] We will come back to this idea of the mystical agent or catalyst.

This 'elixir' or 'tincture' can also be understood in a medical sense, particularly since John of Rupecissa[85] and Paracelsus (Theophrastus von Hohenheim, 1493/1494–1541). Paracelsus[86] was of the opinion that in the same way as the philosopher's stone perfects the imperfect metals by transmutation, it will perfect a sick or old human body by curing it or removing its infirmities through transmutation. That prolonged the person's life, and the elixir became a mystical elixir for (eternal) life.[87]

81 Ganzenmüller (1938: 139). Mercury is of course Hermes, the mystical father of alchemy, and the alchemists also made the connection between the seven recognised metals and the planets in their cosmology: gold corresponded to the sun, silver to the moon, copper (Venus), iron (Mars), mercury or quicksilver (Mercury), lead (Saturn), tin (Jupiter), see Holmyard (1968: 153) with the common alchemical/astronomical-astrological symbols.

82 This 'treatment' usually had a religious connotation with the alchemists, and was often referred to as the 'tormenting of the metals' in a 'crucible' (flask), as Jesus was crucified on the cross, see Principe (2013: 69).

83 Principe (2013: 36, 118–119, 122–123), Moran (2005: 26–31), Reidy (1975: lxii–lxiii), Holmyard (1968: 15–16).

84 See *Mundus Subterraneus* (1678) by the seventeenth-century polymath Athanasius Kircher, Book 11, Section 2, chapter 1, 'De Lapide Philosophorum' (About the philosopher's stone) (1678: 268) for an explanation of the philosopher's stone.

85 John of Rupecissa (14th cent.), *De consideratione quintae essentiae omnium rerum* (On the consideration of the fifth essence of all things), see Principe (2013: 69).

86 Paracelsus did not invent this idea, but his methodological use of 'tinctures' or medicines made him the father of medicinal chemistry.

87 Paracelsus (1978: 554–557), Koyré (1971: 113), Moran (2005: 24).

Paracelsus was not interested in *chrysopoeia*, the transmutation of base metals into gold,[88] but other alchemists were, and especially their princes who sought to fill their depleted treasuries with newly transmuted gold. After around 1300 the scarcity of precious metals made rulers resort to the art of alchemists to increase their financial resources.[89] In England, the chronic shortage of (commodity) money from the early 1600s onwards and during the Civil War revived alchemist ideas of transmutation and of socio-economic progress in Francis Bacon's spirit.[90] Two methods were applied to address the scarcity of money: the attempt at proper transmutation of a base metal, mainly lead, into gold, and the development of replacing commodity money in gold and silver coins by money in form of credit. This 'credit' was effectively an application of the concept of the philosopher's stone, and such 'credit money' could be backed by assets other than precious metals as security, particularly land.[91] When the Bank of England was founded in 1694, the creation of Bank of England money – which would later become central bank money and even later legal tender – was also based on the idea of credit money:[92] hence all money today, central bank money as well as commercial bank money, is credit, or a debt (from the debtor's perspective). The establishment of the Bank of England met the need to finance the Nine Years' War with France under Louis XIV between 1688 and 1697.[93]

The lack of gold and metal money was also a reason why the English alchemists John Dee and his dubious assistant Edward Kelley came to the court of Emperor Rudolf II in Prague in 1584.[94] Since gold cannot be created through the transmutation of base metals,[95] alchemists who had to show publicly a successful transformation into gold were necessarily forced to deceive. Therefore alchemy always had a tinge of dishonesty (as bankers and moneylenders had), and alchemistic practices were sometimes prohibited by law,[96] also to curb the practice of

88 Koyré (1971: 110).

89 Moran (2005: 31).

90 Wennerlind (2011: 44–47). I am grateful to Professor Bruno Théret, Université Paris Dauphine, for informing me of this text.

91 Wennerlind (2011: 61, 67, 73).

92 Bank of England Act 1694, s. 19 (still in force) and s. 18 (repealed, on the authorisation to take subscriptions for £1,200,000, subsequently to be lent to the English government, paid out in notes or sealed bills, rather than coin). Richards (1929: 145–147), Clapham (1944: 17–18, 20).

93 Kenyon (1978: 280, 284–285), Wennerlind (2011: 5, 108–109).

94 Dee was in Central Europe between 1583 and 1589, Rampling (2012: 498, 500); Holmyard (1968: 207).

95 Gold can be created by way of changing the atomic structure of the original element, such as bismuth, with a particle accelerator, and that has been done already in 1980, but it is wholly uneconomic. See Morrisson (2007: 135).

96 Principe (2013: 61–62, 84–85, 170). A papal decretal of 1317 prohibited making gold, and in 1404 in England Henry IV had a statute passed against gold making, but soon, under Henry VI, gold making by alchemists could be licensed if the transmuted gold was sold to the Royal Mint. Ironically, one of the persons who effectuated the abolition of this law in 1689 was Robert Boyle.

doubling gold and therefore of debasing the value of gold coins.[97] In the eighteenth century alchemy became wholly discredited as a fraudulent art, while in the seventeenth century even founders of the scientific revolution, like Robert Boyle and Isaac Newton, still believed in the possibility of transmutation.[98]

The Church's opinion about alchemy was variable. Christian alchemists could find obvious analogies to their faith,[99] and saw alchemy and the philosopher's stone as a gift of God.[100] As Petrus Bonus said:[101]

> Our art is partly natural and partly supernatural, or divine. . . . the soul and spirit [are] permanently fixed at the end of the sublimation . . . through the addition of the hidden stone, which is not sensuously apprehended, but only known intellectually, by revelation or inspiration. . . . The hidden stone may be called the gift of God,[102] and if it does not mingle with our stone, the work of alchemy is marred. . . . In this way alchemy is supernatural and divine, and in this stone consists the whole difficulty of the art.

Christian alchemists also regarded God as the highest and ultimate alchemist.[103] The processes of the exterior world and physical nature are repeated and symbolised by those of the soul, and man and nature or the world and God are two in one.[104] The philosopher's stone is the Christ of nature, and Christ is the philosopher's stone of the spirit. Mercury (Hermes), the intermediary between the sun (gold) and the moon (silver), is Christ, the mediator between God and the world and the spiritual mercury of the universe. The symbols of alchemy also symbolise the spiritual and religious world, because the processes of transmutation (that is, inorganic transformation and organic evolution) are the same in the physical and the spiritual or invisible world.[105]

97 Moran (2005: 30–31). Doubling gold was the practice of mixing gold with other metals (particularly silver, copper) to increase the amount without altering much of its colour and weight.

98 Principe (2013: 86–87, 89, 116–118, 168–169).

99 Principe (2013: 198–200) with the example of the alchemist and hermetic philosopher Heinrich Khunrath (around 1560–1605), the author of *Amphitheatrum Sapientiae Aeternae* (1595). See also Ganzenmüller (1938: 219). On spiritual and religious alchemy in seventeenth-century England, see Schuler (1980: 293).

100 See e.g. Thomas Norton, *Ordinal of Alchemy* (1477), Norton (1975: 10): 'Mastrie ful mervelous & Archymastrie/Is the tyncture of holye Alchemye/A wonderful science, secrete philosophie/A singular grace & gyfte of almyghtie/which neuir was fownde bi labour of man/But it bi teching or reuelacion bigan'.

101 Petrus Bonus (1894: 123–124).

102 This is a standard statement: all knowledge was regarded as a gift of God, see Principe (2013: 194).

103 Matton (2009: 708).

104 This idea also had a root in hermetic thought deriving from Hermes Trismegistus and the idea of the nameless god and its possible equation of that nameless god with the Hebrew tetragrammaton JHWH, already discussed by Nicolaus Cusanus (Nicolae de Cusa), *De docta ignorantia*, see Assmann (2011: 180–181).

105 Koyré (1971: 114) with particular reference to the Paracelsians.

The transubstantiation of the Catholic Church is also an (allegorical) alchemistic notion.[106] According to the dogma of transubstantiation of the fourth Lateran Council of 1215, Christ's 'body and blood are truly contained in the sacrament of the altar under the forms of bread and wine having been changed in substance, by God's power into his body and blood'.[107] The Protestants repudiated this dogma.[108] This perfection of bread and wine as the body and blood of Christ is an idea of alchemistic transmutation, initiated by the alchemist-priest.[109] Ironically, Hermes (Mercury), the intermediary between heaven and man and, according to some, the divine force behind the philosopher's stone, was also the patron deity of luck and financial profit, of commerce,[110] as well as of the travellers, tricksters and thieves.[111]

For the Church, the perception of (Christian) alchemy potentially involved in profit, magic and trickery looked perhaps a bit too close to orthodox acts of worship. In 1317, a decretal by Pope John XXII prohibited making gold, because alchemists normally do not succeed in producing gold and therefore are tempted to make counterfeits of coins to defraud honest people.[112] One could also arrive at the conclusion which the Heidelberg professor of medicine Thomas Erastus reached in 1572, that alchemists arrogate for themselves the position of God as the creator. The origin of substantial forms is considered as from God, and the insertion of such a form into matter is nothing but a creation which is reserved to God. Hence in this view alchemists (especially the Paracelsians with their description of the homunculus)[113] assume the power of God and compete with nature.[114] Alchemy was also considered as not being able to match the 'real sciences', particularly theology which enabled the reading and understanding of the holy scriptures and the prophets, while alchemy could rather be used for

106 Ogrinc (1980: 126), Matton (2009: 720–725).

107 Fourth Lateran Council 1215, const. 1. MacCulloch (2009: 405).

108 MacCulloch (2009: 565, 611). It is possible, but uncertain, that the word 'hocus-pocus' might have come from the words of the liturgy of transubstantiation, being a corrupted '*Hoc est enim corpus meum*'. This was the explanation by John Tillotson (1630–1694, then Archbishop of Canterbury), Tillotson (1684: 34): 'And in all probability those common *jugling* words of *hocus pocus* are nothing else but a corruption of *hoc est corpus*, by way of ridiculous imitation of the Priests of the Church of *Rome* in their *trick* of *Transubstantiation*' (original emphasis).

109 Musso (2017: 293).

110 The Latin name of the god Hermes, Mercurius, derives from *merx*, trade.

111 Grant and Hazel (2002: 173).

112 Principe (2013: 61), Moran (2005: 32–33), Ogrinc (1980: 114–117), Migliorino (1981: 15). (I am grateful to Maria Sole Testuzza, Università di Catania, Department of Law, for informing me of Migliorino's text and for providing me with a copy.) From the decree: 'Alchemies are hereby prohibited and those who practise them or procure their being done are punished. They must forfeit to the public treasury for the benefit of the poor as much genuine gold and silver as they have manufactured of the false or adulterate metal. . . . they shall be considered criminals. If they are clerics, they shall be deprived of any benefices that they hold and be declared incapable of holding others'.

113 Newman (1999: 326, 332–333, 337).

114 Newman (2006: 47, 63–64).

idolatry. However, if alchemy were reduced purely to a form of metallurgy and stripped of the religious, occult and symbolical aspects and of the philosophical speculations that were linked with transmutation, alchemy could be regarded as useful to society and saved from indiscriminate public censure and prohibition by the Church.[115]

(c) Ideas of alchemy in the modern system of money

When Lloyd Blankfein, the then chief executive of the investment bank Goldman Sachs, said in 2009 that he as a banker was 'doing God's Work',[116] he presumably wanted to provoke, but from the perspective of intellectual history he was not too far from the truth.

A fundamental idea of alchemy was that the alchemist does not create new substances but assists in completing the course of nature: the 'new' substance is already contained in the original (base) substance, and through the transmutation, initiated by the alchemist, nature is only perfected. The big difference between alchemy and the modern natural sciences, like chemistry, is that the alchemists started from speculative philosophical (also normative and religious) concepts which they sought to make existent in a physical world through experiments and with their activities to create the 'great work' of transmutation. The alchemists tried to perfect processes of nature as they understood them through speculative reasoning, while modern natural scientists seek to discover general natural laws of matter through experiment and then – in a converse process – describe these ascertained natural laws in academic texts that always remain open to falsification; they are – unlike Aristotle's texts embedded in religious tenets and interpretations by Christianity or Islam – not dogmatic and absolute.[117] What alchemists and chemists share are the practical techniques, such as weighing, pulverisation, filtration, evaporation, crystallisation, distillation and sublimation.[118]

One begins to realise that the present system of money creation contains several ideas from alchemy. In a typical sales contract a commodity and its consideration (*quid pro quo*) in the form of money get exchanged. Economists who regard the sale as only another example of the barter[119] necessarily overlook a trivial, but important aspect: with a *barter* as understood in law, the person giving the commodity *obtains* a true consideration of real intrinsic value, another commodity (one cow against three sheep). With a *gift*, the giver does *not expect*

115 Migliorino (1981: 21–22, 41) on this argument by the lawyer Oldrado da Ponte (around 1270–1348), member of the Papal Court (Rota) and influential on the Roman curia.

116 See John Carney, *Business Insider*, 9 Nov. 2009: www.businessinsider.com/lloyd-blankfein-says-he-is-doing-gods-work-2009-11?IR=T (visited on 10 December 2017).

117 Taylor (1976: 145–146).

118 See the founder of modern chemistry, Lavoisier, Part III, 'Description of the Instruments and Operations of Chemistry' (1965: 291, 295, 357, 363, 365, 375, 379, 384, 388). A predecessor in this regard was to some extent Paracelsus (1988: 133–138), and, with a more modern scientific approach, Andreas Libavius, see Newman (2006: 66).

119 See discussion in Chapters 1 and 3.

a consideration and does not get one. In the case of a *sale*, the seller *does expect* a consideration of real value, but unlike with a barter, the seller obtains merely an *expectation* to real value (the money) which may or may not be realised later in form of a proper consideration of value. This is not only a psychologically different scenario from the barter but also conceptually and economically distinctive. One could summarise the differences between gift, sale and barter briefly as follows: a gift expects no consideration of intrinsic value forthcoming, a sale fears no consideration of intrinsic value forthcoming, but a barter *has* a consideration of intrinsic value forthcoming. We will see soon that money in the contract of sale operates economically as a kind of 'philosopher's stone', as a mystical agent.

Economists presume that in a functioning economy money can be exchanged for commodities without any difficulty, which is indeed typically the case. Therefore, they say, if complete liquidity of money is ensured, money is nil as such and can be edited out from the transaction as a separate unit with specific qualities and effects (except as being a price measuring unit or *numéraire* or unit of account):[120] it is a pure medium of exchange, but does not influence the transaction otherwise.[121] This conflicts with the other function of money as being a store of value,[122] since something that is nought as such without any separate qualities cannot be a store of value either because it cannot refer to or represent objects of property which have intrinsic or/and market value. But if money is supposed to be removed from the sale as conceptually irrelevant, then there is indeed no theoretical difference between barter and sale, and any idea of an occult 'philosopher's stone' as mystical catalyst or agent is also removed to preserve a modern, seemingly scientific environment for economics.

However, money is not conceptually irrelevant, but creates the sale as a specific transaction and separates it from the barter through its particular qualities. These qualities – being an object of dematerialised property itself, a debt, and a debt that typically attracts a claim to interest beside the principal sum[123] – do have an effect on a transaction where money is interposed between the exchange of two commodities. In fact, money is not just a medium of exchange, but *a means to prepare* the exchange, or more precisely, to *delay the exchange* by granting the recipient of the money an expectation to realise value at a later date at his own option, and that expectation induces him to part with his commodity.[124] Put simply, nobody would hand over a loaf of bread against some bills of old printed paper if he does not have the reasonable expectation that he can exchange that paper *later* against a bag of apples or something else at his own option. For a meaningful exchange can eventually only be an exchange of a commodity of real value against another commodity of real value, thus ultimately against tangible property: one cannot eat a banknote or another debt, or a patent. All such

120 Mankiw (2012: 621).
121 See discussion in Chapters 1 and 3.
122 Mankiw (2012: 621).
123 See discussion in Chapter 2.
124 See also Chapter 1, sec. 4.

'titles' – including rights in the strict sense, such as rights of a creditor arising from a contract – must eventually lead to physical property objects, or 'real commodity', even if, as in the sale, 'imaginary commodities' (or 'anticipated commodities') in form of money are meanwhile interposed.[125] The cyclical nature of this flow of real and imaginary or expected commodities will be discussed below.[126] The difference between real and imaginary commodities is that *real commodities* have an *intrinsic* or *contemplative value* (if the market chooses to recognise this), while *imaginary commodities* define their value through their *exchange value*[127] only, that is, their transfer confers their value on them. This is the *casus dativus* of the money relations explained before.[128] Money, itself an imaginary commodity, creates these imaginary commodities by being interposed as a *medium of exchange delay*, not simply as a neutral facilitating medium of exchange under the orthodox definition. This will also be explained further below.[129]

Money in the sales contract operates as a kind of 'philosopher's stone'; that is the principal legacy of alchemistic concepts. As discussed earlier, the philosopher's stone was a conceptual/philosophical as well as a practical agent – to trigger a reaction, as a modern chemist would say, or to elicit the superior substance already contained within the base matter, as an alchemist would interpret this process. In the words of the late medieval alchemist Petrus Bonus: 'The perfection of philosophical quicksilver is the purification of its agent . . . from all corrupting influences by means of our Art [i.e. alchemy]'.[130] This 'Art' imitates and perfects or purifies nature[131] (or, put differently, 'God's Work') both in the generation of the philosophical stone itself and in the perfection of metals.[132] The quicksilver (usually together with sulphur) is 'philosophical' because it was not strictly necessary to use mercury as the agent;[133] it could also be antimony, vitriol (iron and copper

125 In case of payment for services, the service is not a 'real commodity' as such, but an activity that is supposed to lead finally to a real commodity, such as food, clothing, housing (in the widest sense). The service is an interpolation on the way to the real commodity.

126 See below under sec. 4.

127 See e.g. Walras, *Éléments*, § 41 (1926: 44).

128 See above under sec. 2.

129 See below under sec. 4.

130 Petrus Bonus (1894: 194).

131 Compare Athanasius Kircher, *Mundus Subterraneus* (1678), Book 11, Section 2, chapter 1, 'De Lapide Philosophorum' (1678: 268): '*Lapis Philosophorum* definitur ab Alchymicis . . . quae non modò corpus humanum validum in suo vigore conservat, laesumque pristinae sanitati restituit, sed etiam metalla imperfect depurando, decoquendo, et nativum colorem ministrando ad summum finem, quem Natura intendit, brevi temporis spatio in purum *aurum*, *argentum* que transmutat in infinitum multiplicabile'. ('The Philosopher's Stone is defined by the alchemists as what not only preserves the powers of the human body in its full vigour and restores it from injury to its former health, but what also transmutes, in infinite and multipliable quantity, imperfect metals in a short time span to pure gold and silver though depuration, melting (boiling) and supplying its original colour to the highest end which Nature intended'.)

132 Petrus Bonus (1894: 194–195).

133 During the fourteenth century, some alchemistic theories claimed that mercury alone is the ingredient of the philosopher's stone, because mercury supposedly contains sulphur, see Ganzenmüller (1938: 142).

sulphate), salts[134] or, particularly with the Paracelsians, organic matter.[135] Hence the name of 'philosophical' mercury and sulphur, or '*rebis*' ('two-thing'), as these two mutually reactive substances were often called.[136] The idea of the 'philosophical' (conceptual) transformation through an agent is relevant in relation to the transaction involving money, whereby initial and transformed 'substances' (which are not necessarily real substances) are as much concepts as the 'transmuting' agent.

In a sale, the money as agent transforms or 'transmutes' the real commodity[137] that is sold into an imaginary commodity or anticipated commodity: at a later stage the anticipated commodity is likely to be turned into another real one. Similar to alchemistic thinking is the idea that any real commodity has an intrinsic value later expressed through purification as anticipated commodity (money), and the exchange creates the purifying transformation and later retransformation proper. Different from alchemy is the idea that an *exchange* is necessary to bring about this transmutation. If one is unable to exchange a real commodity against money, then there would be no intrinsic imaginary commodity in the real commodity – the gold would not be contained in the base metal, as it were – and the base commodity could not be purified and perfected to an actual value, that is, to the realisable expectation to retransform into another real commodity at a later date. In simple terms, if one cannot sell the commodity, it is worthless.

This inherent rule in economics can have disastrous consequences. The obvious example is natural resources: water counts little in Scotland where it is available in abundance because it rains a lot. But that rule also applies to 'human resources': people who look after elderly and infirm relatives at home provide work that is worthless; only if they offer their services successfully on the labour market does their work obtain value. The 'barter' or sale in economics considers intrinsic value only as the (potential) transmutation to money (imaginary commodity), the probable realisation of the *casus dativus*. The contemplative value of water or of looking after an elderly relative is not transmutable and therefore irrelevant, although their existence may be essential to life or to the functioning of society. The impossibility to monetise – that is, to transmute from the base substance of the initial real commodity to a supposedly purified version as the option to obtain new real commodities – renders the initial real commodity valueless.

Bankers provide money as the transmuting agent. Similar to alchemistic concepts the *rebis* (mercury-sulphur), money, is prepared or made by the 'alchemist' banker; different from alchemy is that the *rebis* is here really made *out of nothing*, as the money creation process demonstrates.[138] So that is not a perfection

134 Important for Paracelsus, see Paracelsus (1988: 101–102).

135 Newman (1999: 326–328).

136 Principe (2013: 122).

137 'Real commodity' is to be understood in the sense of (1) a tangible object of property, but also immoveable property (in English law: 'real property'), and (2) an intangible/incorporeal object of property, such as gas or electricity, but also legal concepts, such as intellectual property rights. All these property objects have a use value specific to their individual properties or qualities.

138 See the discussion in Chapter 2.

of nature with a catalyst that brings out what is already innate in the existing base materials. It is rather a perfection of nature, if at all, which is accomplished by using an agent that is created out of nothing. For a medieval or Renaissance alchemist, such an *ex nihilo* creation could only be the work of God.[139] Today it can apparently also be the work of a banker if we follow Lloyd Blankfein. Furthermore, the *ex nihilo* creation entails that money creation can theoretically be limitless, without reference to a real commodity: the final abolition of the gold standard in the 1930s removed gold as the classical reference point for money.[140] However, it is noteworthy that when the increasing and abundant amount of money could no longer be linked with a corresponding amount of gold available, there was a rising interest in alchemistic thought and alchemical projects in the 1920s which sought to apply a blend of notions of old alchemy and of modern radiochemistry and nuclear physics to synthesise gold, since classical material transmutation had proved impossible.[141]

The idea of a theoretically unfettered *ex nihilo* creation of the transmuting agent 'money' by the banker also has a tinge of moral dishonesty and deception. In 1593, Luis de Molina, a central figure of the Salamanca School, considered bankers as trustees of their depositors: if bankers are unable to return the full deposit in due time because of their business activities, they 'mortally sin', for 'they sin against justice and against the pact they have with the depositors'.[142] In the seventeenth and early eighteenth centuries the modern practice of money creation was indeed fraud in law;[143] today it is perfectly lawful.[144] Nevertheless, the god Hermes or Mercury seems to have remained the patron deity of the alchemists, of profit and money, of the merchants and of the thieves.

Such a proximity, real or perceived, may be considered as uncomfortable. As mentioned above, Crowther uses the analogy with alchemy when he discusses money creation in his well-known *Outline of Money*, but he does so with great caution:[145]

> Nearly every loan made by a bank is secured upon some form of valuable security. Even if it is granted without security, the earning capacity of the

139 We have seen above that even the traditional alchemistic practices have been criticised as arrogating for themselves the powers of God, see the discussion on Thomas Erastus by Newman (2006: 63–64).

140 Morgan (1965: 165–169).

141 Morrisson (2007: 135–138, 142–145).

142 Molina, *De iustitia et iure*, Argument 408 (2015: 111, 113).

143 For example the first issuing of banknotes without sufficient backing by gold and silver by the Swedish Imperial Bank (Sveriges Riksbank) under Johan Palmstruch in the 1660s, see Heckscher (1932: 11), or John Law's issuing of banknotes via the Banque générale (later Banque royale) in France around 1720, see Dessert (1984: 420–425), Schumpeter (1954: 321); on Law's Lockean position on money supply, see Vickers (1960: 122–124). The situation is, however, not entirely comparable because the socio-economic and political conditions were very different from today.

144 Köhler (2013: 913). On the curious situation in German law, see briefly Chapter 2, sec. 6, and in detail, Rahmatian (2018a: 230–235).

145 Crowther (1946: 47).

> borrower is a form of wealth. Thus the bank does not 'create' money out of thin air; it transmutes other forms of wealth into money. Even the medieval alchemists never hoped to make gold out of nothing; their highest hope was to transform lead into gold. The banker's power is not even so great as this, for he cannot change a worthless substance into a valuable one. But he can turn immobile wealth into the mobile (or 'liquid') form of wealth known as money. He takes the immobile wealth as his asset and gives his IOU (which is money) in exchange. This is the very essence of the banker's business.

The defects of this interpretation lie in the fact that (a) the analogy with alchemy is misleading and (b) the claimed correlation between asset and money (to which the asset is converted) is imprecise and variable.

As to (a), there is no direct alchemical transmutation from an object of physical property or real commodity to another one which is purified and refined and supposedly more valuable. This 'transmutation', as it is called here, is only a diffuse transformation from one form of 'wealth', otherwise not further defined, to 'money' which is, in Crowther's interpretation, only another form of 'wealth'. What this transformation indeed does is that it converts a less fungible asset into a more fungible or liquid one, but what this account leaves out is the crucial point that money is not the result of the transmutation but the transmuting agent that *delays* a proper exchange between real commodities as would be the case in an actual barter. Crowther's explanation bears the traces of the concept of money as the neutral and void medium of exchange that is nevertheless supposed to be a store of value.

Furthermore, Crowther's account tries to circumvent the problem of the *ex nihilo* creation of money by referring to forms of valuable security, but one cannot escape from the actual problem. A valuable security does not transmute the asset (being another form of wealth) into money either but brings about the transfer of an *already existing* asset as a result of an *already existing* claim directed at the payment of money, whereby claim and security asset have existed separately from the outset and are initially unrelated. Thus the money (strictly speaking, the claim to money) is not the transmutation of the asset or real commodity as security to another real commodity. Here we do not have an alchemistic transmutation from lead to gold, if we keep the alchemistic metaphor, but rather an entitlement to the transfer of the *existing* gold owned by someone else by virtue of the existing lead which the bank owns: but where does the lead owned by the bank come from? Does the bank then replace the lead by the gold and pretend it has performed a transmutation, something reminiscent of those alchemists who were charlatans and fraudsters?[146]

Trying to resort to security rights for arguing that the bank lends existing wealth helps as little as the vague reference to 'the earning capacity of the borrower' if there is no secured loan. The earning capacity of the borrower is as much

146 See Holmyard (1968: 206–208, 231–236) with regard to the notorious alchemists and charlatans Edward Kelley or Edward Talbot (1555–1597) and Michael Sendivogius (1566–1646).

an expectation to wealth (or to real commodities) as money itself, only that the creation of money from nowhere additionally creates a debt which has to be serviced with the earning capacity of the borrower, and that necessitates a shift of wealth from the borrower to the bank, not a transmutation from one form of wealth to another more liquid one. This is certainly true with regard to the interest, but also with regard to the capital sum of the loan. If the loan is secured, the security constitutes a conditional entitlement of the bank, either to the physical asset or real commodity if the condition is fulfilled (default on loan payment), or often the physical asset is transformed into money for the bank (sale of the asset, auction etc. as a realisation of the security). With regard to an unsecured loan the judicial enforcement of the debt also leads ultimately to the transfer of a real commodity. In either process the bank has a stronger position than the customer.[147] The entitlement to specific physical assets is created through loans (and interest) with the device of bank money, thus merely through accounting entries on paper and on computers,[148] not through a direct transmutation of one less fungible form of wealth (asset) to another more fungible one (money): and that is an '*ex nihilo*' creation.

As to (b), it is impossible to discern a fixed attribution that Crowther suggests: here asset – there money as the asset's transformation, both corresponding to a specific owner (or a person 'entitled' in a wider sense). In reality money is a very general reference to an asset, a means to acquire some asset, not even an entitlement *strictu sensu*,[149] which will be realised in the future (imaginary commodity), as has been explained before. Crowther's approach also presupposes a conceptual fungibility and replaceability of any asset, and that hints at the idea that, put in alchemistical terms, a real commodity *should* be transmuted into an anticipated/imaginary commodity to be perfected: assets ought to be monetised to obtain value.[150] We remember that idea from Friedman's monetarism in positive economics.[151] Alchemistic metaphors can reveal even when their 'magic' may befog first.

Sometimes writers and poets can have a better understanding than specialists. In Germany, Johann Wolfgang von Goethe (1749–1832) had a good comprehension of this 'magical' or quasi-alchemistic money creation process, even at a time when the issuing of paper money was new. In Act I of the second part of his play *Faust*, Goethe demonstrates theatrically this endeavour, and his studies on alchemy in his youth may have inspired him to refer to alchemy to portray the problem.[152] Faust made a bet[153] with the devil Mephistopheles: if

147 See Chapter 5 for the discussion on the 'weak creditor' and the 'strong debtor'.

148 See discussion in Chapter 2.

149 This is simply demonstrated by the fact that offering money does not mean that the owner *has to* sell his asset for it, he can refuse (the rare cases of possible duties of utility companies etc. to contract in some circumstances are left aside). Thus money does not carry an entitlement to an asset at all.

150 See discussion below under sec. 4.

151 See Chapter 3, sec. 3. and sec. 4, and below under sec. 4.

152 Goethe, *Dichtung und Wahrheit*, Part 2, book 2 (1982b: 341–344).

153 In Goethe's *Faust* – unlike in the folk tale and in Christopher Marlowe's *Dr Faustus* (Act II, scene 1) – it is not a pact, but a bet with the devil. See Faust I, 'Studierzimmer', lines 1696–1698, Goethe (1982: 57).

there is a moment which is so beautiful for him that he wants it to last forever, he will lose the bet.[154] The devil loses the bet when he wants to seduce Faust by endowing him with eternal youth and love,[155] but he wins the bet when he provides Faust with the power of making gold and money and the establishment of economic activity.[156] Goethe's *Faust* recreates in the money making process the alchemist notion of gold as being already contained in a base metal (e.g. lead) and extractable from it by transmutation. In the alchemist process of money making, gold in the earth, and perhaps already extracted from it and turned into coins, is transformed into paper money, and in this way a worthless substance (paper) is transformed into a valuable one (money referring to gold coins of intrinsic value). This transformation process happens through words and behaviour implementing these words. In *Faust II*, Faust and the devil suggest to the emperor the scheme of creating money in the form of paper money.[157] Not only is paper money much more convenient to handle,[158] it also suggests that the gold in the ground (which need not be extracted, so that the labour to do this can be saved) and existing treasuries of gold will back the paper money.[159] The emperor guarantees its value with his signature.[160] As Mephistopheles says:[161]

Ein solch Papier, an Gold und Perlen Statt,	(These notes, when used in lieu of gold and pearls,
Ist so bequem, man weiß doch, was man hat;	are handy, too; you know right off how much you own
Man braucht nicht erst zu markten, noch zu tauschen,	and can, without first bargaining or haggling,
Kann sich nach Lust in Lieb' und Wein berauschen.	enjoy the full delights of love and wine.
Will man Metall, ein Wechsler ist bereit,	If metal's wanted, there are money-changers,
Und fehlt es da, so gräbt man eine Zeit.	And if it's short, you go and dig a while.)

154 Faust I, 'Studierzimmer', lines 1699–1700, Goethe (1982a: 57), Faust II, Act 5, lines 11581–11582, Goethe (1982a: 348). There is also the underlying idea that making a moment lasting forever means stopping the time – which is impossible – and stopping time means death.

155 Especially the final scene, Faust I, 'Kerker', lines 4605–4612, Goethe (1982a: 145). Mephistopheles wanted to get Faust to seduce Gretchen without him falling in love with her, although Mephistopheles is not (entirely) successful.

156 Faust II, Act 5, lines 11553–11586, Goethe (1982a: 348). See Binswanger (1985: 18), for this interpretation. Faust's last monologue before his death is, however, open to several interpretations. At least the devil wins the bet with Faust, but he loses the bet he made (or tried to make) before with God in heaven, see Faust I, 'Prolog im Himmel', lines 312–329, Faust II, Act 5, lines 11817–11831, 11934–11941, Goethe (1982a: 18, 355–356, 359).

157 Faust II, Act 1, lines 6054–6170, Goethe (1982a: 186–190).

158 Mephistopheles in Faust II, Act 1, lines 6105–6110, Goethe (1982a: 188).

159 Chancellor in Faust II, Act 1, lines 6057–6062, Goethe (1982a: 187).

160 Treasurer in Faust II, Act 1, lines 6066–6072, Goethe (1982a: 187).

161 Mephistopheles in Faust II, Act 1, lines 6119–6124, Goethe (1982a: 188). Translation by Stuart Atkins (translation slightly changed by the author).

It is the court's fool who questions the value of paper money and decides to rely on landownership instead,[162] which prompts Mephistopheles to comment approvingly: 'Who would still doubt our fool's wit'.[163]

What Faust really wants is power and ownership by using up natural resources, not by their sustaining use.[164] The 'great work' of alchemy that makes the monetary system function is only achieved by way of a combination of 'magic' forces: imagination, technological progress, faith, human passions such as avarice and greed, and the state authority as a backer of paper with no intrinsic value that turns the paper into money – the illustration of the *casus genitivus* of money relations.[165] The 'philosopher's stone' is capital or money itself as a catalyst of the transmutation process: money, also paper money, circulates by way of loans granted, but these loans are only granted if interest will be paid or a profit will be made.[166] So seemingly valueless natural resources will be transformed into valuable property – quite in the spirit of Locke's labour theory of property.[167] The reductionist traditional economic models understand economic growth only as a result of human labour, capital and technical developments, but they ignore the 'alchemistic' process of the transformation of nature into raw material, and of raw material into money.[168] Goethe's view of the process is more holistic.

This detour via the concepts of alchemy and alchemy in literature, when applied to money, has highlighted the following aspects: a sales contract involves a transformation or 'transmutation' from the genuine, real value of a commodity to an expectation value, that is, an imaginary value brought about by money as agent or 'philosopher's stone'. The imaginary value is represented either through a physical object of virtually no intrinsic value, such as a banknote, or through an accounting entry in the books of a bank. This imaginary expectation value that money represents must eventually find its way back into the world of tangible commodities or other objects of property which one can eat, wear or live in – to summarise the most important ones. This final further exchange completes the alienation cycle. Let us look first at the externalisation cycle as the primary component of the alienation cycle.

4. The alienation cycle I: the externalisation or transfer cycle

This section starts with a warning, because many people quietly and happily accept certain dark corners of the monetary system but they are very sensitive to any open description of the consequences. It seems to affect adversely their

162 Fool, in Faust II, Act 1, line 6171, Goethe (1982a: 190).
163 Mephistopheles, in Faust II, Act 1, line 6172, Goethe (1982a: 190).
164 Binswanger (1985: 34–35).
165 See above under sec. 2.
166 Binswanger (1985: 46–48).
167 Locke, *Second Treatise*, §§ 27–30 (2013: 287–289).
168 Binswanger (1985: 49).

aesthetic ideas of their world. Perhaps fittingly in this context one may refer to David Ricardo, and in response to him, Karl Marx, for a riposte. First Ricardo:[169]

> Diminish the cost of production of hats, and their price will ultimately fall to their new natural price, although the demand should be doubled, tripled or quadrupled. Diminish the cost of subsistence of men, by diminishing the natural price of the food and clothing by which life is sustained, and wages will ultimately fall, notwithstanding that the demand for labourers may very greatly increase.

To whom Marx replies:[170]

> Doubtless, Ricardo's language is as cynical as can be. To put the cost of manufacture of hats and the cost of maintenance of men on the same plane is to turn men into hats. But do not make an outcry at the cynicism of it. The cynicism lies in the subject and not in the words which express the subject.

(a) *Externalisation or transfer through money: the model of the transfer cycle*

Let us begin with the cynicism Marx refers to and recapitulate neutrally the concepts of propertisation, commodification and monetisation.[171] Objects of any kind, irrespective of whether these are tangible (like goods), intangible (like gas) or legal-conceptual (pure intangibles, such as a debt or copyright) enter the world of private law through transformation into a *res*: this is the process of *propertisation*. The transformation into a *res* brings about a standardisation, as it is no longer an apple, a car, a house, but all are a *res*, and (ideally) a fungible, easily interchangeable property or commodity, preferably with high liquidity: this is what the term *commodification* emphasises when it is used to describe this transformation process. If the ability to facile exchange is the desired and most favoured faculty of the commodity, then it approaches the quality of money, and one can conceptualise any commodity as soon-to-be-money. Or, by applying a more alchemistic notion, every commodity, corporeal or incorporeal, contains already the higher form of money in itself. This conceptualisation can be termed *monetisation*, and it characterises Milton Friedman's approach:[172] 'There is no hard-and-fast line between "money" and other assets'.[173] Thus all assets, whether

169 Ricardo, *Principles*, chapter 30 (2004: 260).
170 Marx, *Das Elend der Philosophie*, sec. (a) (1932: 538). Translation used from *Marx-Engels: Collected Works* (1976), vol. 6, with slight alterations by the author.
171 Chapter 1, sec. 2(a)(iv), Chapter 3, secs. 3 and 4.
172 See Chapter 3, sec. 4.
173 Friedman, *Quantity Theory*, pt. 23 (1956: 19).

actual tangible or intangible, or potential, such as the human labour force, are soon-to-be-money, or effectively forms of money for conceptual purposes.

This conceptualisation can turn everything into *res* or commodities of which their principal purpose is the exchange or sale to realise the innate monetary potential. Two aspects follow from that idea: first, only if something is propertised and turned conceptually into a *res*, it 'exists' and its existence is recognised by the law. Second, if the *res* is exchanged, the potential monetisation becomes actual and the existence of the *res* as a commodity becomes relevant for the market and the economist. As a result of this approach, the *contemplative value* of the *res* which the lawyer would be able to recognise is erased by the *exchange value* of the *res*, which is the primary or only value the economist would consider as relevant. Hence, for example, the purchase of a house is not directed at the enjoyment of living in it (contemplative value, value of use), but at the possible profit it yields in a subsequent sale (exchange value) because house prices may have risen in the meantime. The house is therefore considered as money in waiting, and money in the exchange acts as a catalyst or 'philosopher's stone' to bring out its outright liquidity that effectively equates it with money proper. The intrinsic value does not matter, so that if something has no exchange value it is economically worthless. Furthermore, everything, not only goods but also services, that is, human labour, must be subjected to the concept of a market in order to gain the exchange value innate in all these *res*.

Therefore one cannot escape the market to effectuate the necessary exchange and to obtain the intrinsic exchange value by monetising any commoditised entity. Perhaps somehow reminiscent of Francis Bacon's idea of the idols of the market,[174] but actually concentrating on something else, one can distinguish between five markets that encompass human life: (1) the market of necessaries (food, clothing), (2) the housing and property market, (3) the labour market, (4) the marriage and procreation market,[175] and (5) the marketplace of ideas. The market of necessaries is inescapable, because we all need food and clothing, and the housing and labour markets are normally also inevitable, unless one has the rare chance to be born in a house one owns and never sells and has enough assets to live on without the need to go to work. The marriage market one can enter by choice (leaving aside the usual social pressures), whereby this perspective focuses on marriage as the pooling of families' property for the raising of children as future property holders. From the viewpoint of law and economics marriage is merely a power and property relationship, sometimes sweetened by love and affection. The 'marketplace of ideas' is theoretically also dispensable but has become central to the modern service economy and is an excellent example for the study of the commodification process: any kind of, what one can call broadly, 'intellectual production' (a term borrowed from Hegel) is propertised and standardised as a *res* through the legal framework of intellectual property rights, par-

174 Bacon, *Advancement of Learning*, book 5, chapter 4 (1886: 207, 210).
175 See Becker (1973: 814, 818–820), as an almost beautiful example of repelling market fundamentalism.

ticularly copyright as the most polymorphic right. As a result, people no longer believe in ideas but trade in them as commodities ('copyrights'), and those who produce intellectual creations are mere 'content providers' (a marvellous term to denote commodification), whereby only the provided exchange value counts, not the contemplative value of the content. That development has also contributed to the disappearance of the public intellectual.[176]

With this idea of the comprehensive market in its varieties one has squeezed all goods, services and human relations into an all-encompassing corset of The Market. That market fundamentalism is worse than God who may comfort us by giving the illusion of listening to our prayers, while the market is supposedly only an inorganic machine in which cold natural laws unfold mathematically. Francis Bacon might be more apposite than it seemed at the beginning when he says about the idols of the market:[177]

> Terms of art also, which prevail only among the skilful, may seem to remedy the mischief, and definitions premised to arts in the prudent mathematical manner, to correct the wrong acceptation of words; yet all this is insufficient to prevent the seducing incantation of names in numerous respects, their doing violence to the understanding.

From a humanist perspective, the reconceptualisation of the whole human life as a 'market' is an idol, a mathematised reductionist definition that avoids deeper social understanding, and a seducing incantation of the name 'exchange value' as the only relevant value – but this is the essence of the currently prevailing market fundamentalism or 'neo-liberalism'.

It may have been noticed that in the previous passages the definition of *res* has been extended quietly to human labour, while normally *res* refers to 'things' as conceptualised by the law. Absent outright slavery, the human being is not a commodity itself, but the products of human labour are, whether these are material (goods) or incorporeal (service industry, partly expressed as intellectual property rights). It suggests itself to take the shortcut to reduce the human being to a property maker, to let the human as human drop out of the model and to focus only on the product of his labour and its propertisation/commodification. To speak with Marx, one turns men into hats – the cynicism lies in the subject matter, not in its description. However, that is exactly what Friedman proposes: human capital is wealth that can be monetised,[178] and it is therefore potential money, only with a lower liquidity factor that can be improved by removing all possible labour law regulations and restrictions on hiring and dismissing employees. Accordingly, the human being is reduced to the exchange value of his or her productions and has no value beyond that, nor has any of his or her productions if they can only show a contemplative value, but no exchange value. Thus, for

176 Rahmatian (2011a: 81, 254, 264, 278).
177 Bacon, *Advancement of Learning*, book 5, chapter 4 (1886: 210).
178 Friedman, *Quantity Theory*, pt. 5 (1956: 7–8).

example, the work of raising children or of looking after an elderly neighbour without obtaining a salary for either is *per se* economically worthless.

How is the exchange value realised? Here money plays its central role, very much in contrast to the orthodox economists' proposition of the neutrality and irrelevance of money in the (microeconomic) market.[179] It becomes clear that in this monetarist approach, *res* of any kind obtain their value through the exchange itself. There is not a transfer of value in form of the exchange – the sale or 'barter' – but the value manifests itself in the exchange as such. The transfer *itself* constitutes the value, not the result of the transfer after the completion of the sale. Contrary to the orthodox static market model with a market equilibrium point, the proper approach is a *dynamic* one: the process of the transfer itself creates the value, it is not transient, an otherwise unimportant passage that leads to the generation of value, but the time-bound process of the transfer *is* the generation of value. Therefore one can formulate the following *first rule* (*monetisation rule*):

> The exchange (sale) creates the value, it does not realise an existing value. The value of a *res* (tangible goods, intangible property) consists and materialises in the transfer itself, not as a result of a preceding transfer (sale or 'barter'). The very event of the exchange confers on the *res* a value expressed in the price. All *res* not (yet) exchanged are dormant or potential value, and it is the constant need to exchange that confirms them as being considered as less liquid, and less desirable, forms of, ultimately, money – with money proper being the ideal, the most liquid and fungible *res* that subsists just in the very exchange itself. Only in the temporary process of the exchange the potential value of the *res* becomes an actual value. Where such an exchange cannot be realised, the *res* has no (exchange) value; a possible contemplative value is disregarded. Particularly where the product or *res* is the result of the human being bringing out from his personality a concept or idea (especially an intellectual creation),[180] then the expressing of that personal will in the creation of that product (put differently, the exercise of a service) and the subsequent transfer can also be termed externalisation or alienation (in the sense of transfer).[181]

According to this rule, all *res* (goods and services or human labour) are potential money or 'expectation money' (and money as a debt is obviously a *res* itself).[182]

179 See Chapter 3, sec. 1.

180 The typical cases are inventions and artistic works in a broad sense which are covered by patent and copyright laws, see Rahmatian (2011a: 216, 225–226, 234).

181 These definitions of 'externalisation' (*Entäußerung*) and 'transfer' or 'alienation' (*Veräußerung*) are inspired by Hegel, *Philosophie des Rechts*, particularly §§ 65–68 (1986: 140–146) and will be discussed below under sec. 5, where the second meaning of 'alienation' (*Entfremdung*, estrangement) will be added.

182 A certain indication of this idea can already be found in Commons (1924: 157–159, 246–247).

The transfer cycle is not, as Marx memorably set out in his model for the circulation process of commodities, Commodity-Money-Commodity (*Ware-Geld-Ware, W-G-W*),[183] but Money-Commodity-Money (*Geld-Ware-Geld, G-W-G*),[184] thus actual money (and real unrestrictedly fungible value) gets – ideally only for a short time – transformed into a commodity less than money and then retransformed into money proper; the quicker the better. One may find this postulation grotesque, because the exchange value of foodstuff in particular must ultimately be irrelevant: one need not exchange it all the time but has to eat it (use value or contemplative value) to avoid starving. However, what is discussed here is not a sensible theory but a description of the present economic and monetary system. One can see why little time has been spent on a discussion about the nature of the 'value' (value being the value of labour, of utility and so forth),[185] because finally only the imaginary exchange value matters: there is value if, and to the extent to which, money and the other *res* are exchanged, numerically expressed in money as the unit of account.

Since the exchange creates the value and does not just transfer it, there is pressure for effecting as many exchanges as possible in as little time as possible. The most obvious example is the high frequency trade of shares and other securities on the financial markets, whereby any intrinsic value, for example the share price as a reflection of the economic condition and reputation of the company, is irrelevant or may not even exist. The value lies in the exchange itself. At present, the number of transactions is increasingly limited by the natural laws of physics only, such as the speed of light, which restrict the speed of transmission in computers and cables. The speed of transactions is, however, not constrained by any commercial considerations: what changes could happen in a company within a fraction of a second? But its shares may well change hands several times during this extremely short period of time, and each time perhaps with a different share

183 Marx, *Kapital*, book 1, sec. 1, chapter 3 (1975: 81).

184 Or one considers every *res*, including money, as capital from the outset, not only (according to Marx) as being transformed to capital, then Marx's circulation of money formula G-W-G could be used, see Marx, *Kapital*, book 1, sec. 1, chapter 4 (1975: 119, 121, 127), although it nevertheless symbolises partly another idea. In addition, the expression of the surplus value G-W-G' (M-C-M') (in that context as interest-bearing capital), which Marx aims at, is disregarded here. However, in connection with the 'general formula of capital' (G-W-G'), Marx does remark (ibid., 127): 'While in the simple circulation [C-M-C] the value of commodities obtains in relation to their use values the independent form of money at most, [in the circulation of capital, M-C-M] that same value now suddenly presents itself as an independent substance with its own motion and process, in which money and commodities are both mere forms'. Put differently, in the ordinary exchange C-M-C retains its use value alongside a separate expression of its value specified in money, while in the capital circulation M-C-M commodity and money proper are just different forms of money, or *res* with different liquidity. This hints at the idea put forward here, only that, unlike with Marx, all commodities are 'money' (and are 'capital' subject to the circulation formula M-C-M) from the outset because the use value is irrelevant.

185 See Chapter 3, sec. 2 for a discussion from a historical perspective (Classical School of economics).

price. Hence one can state a *second rule* (*exchange multiplication and financialisation rule*):

> Since the exchange itself creates the value (that is, the exchange value as the only relevant value), there is a push for as many exchanges as possible in as little time as possible. With *res* that are conceived as being close to money in relation to their liquidity factor, such as shares and other securities, or with money itself as the commodity to be transferred, such as foreign currencies, these exchanges are implanted in the very nature of the instruments: such instruments subsist in the exchange itself; any contemplative value is inexistent or negligible (Scrooge McDuck–type owners excepted).[186] As a result of the development towards a commercially and socially increasingly accepted propensity to monetisation of all commodities (after having all objects and services commodified through propertisation to a *res* by the law), this principle of high exchange velocity in the financial economy gets gradually adopted in the 'real economy'.[187] In the 'real economy' the use value or contemplative value of the commodities matters and may normally even prevail over the exchange value. In the financial economy the exchange value eclipses or erases any contemplative value entirely. With monetisation, the exchange of commodities, which would normally have significant use value, becomes the predominant goal, either in form of speculative transfers (e.g. food speculation) or/and through an ever shorter lifespan of manufactured goods with no commercially viable possibility to repair (obsolescence)[188] to reduce the contemplative value and force the customer to a new purchase, that is, exchange, soon (e.g. cars, household goods, computers). Thus not only is there a drive for an ever increasing number of exchanges in an ever shorter time period, there is also a drive for real commodities with an intrinsic use value to be treated as financial *res* and to be subjected to an ever increasing velocity of exchanges to augment their liquidity to move them closer to the ideal of money-to-be that eclipses their actual use value.

186 The purpose of a banknote is not to look at it (use or contemplation), but to spend it (exchange).

187 The reason why the term 'real economy' appears in inverted commas is because the financial economy is also a 'real' economy, but the term 'real economy' is a convenient and often used shorthand to denote that part of the economy that concerns particularly physical property, tangible commodities, chattels, goods, and not financial products akin to money or actual money.

188 This obsolescence can be achieved by using insufficiently durable materials or manufacturing, or, more recently, by applying technological protection measures, for example, software which renders the product inoperable if changed by using unauthorised repair parts, or by using defective software as a weak link which turns the computer-controlled mechanical parts inoperable, a typical problem with modern cars, for example. See e.g. the studies from a consumer protection perspective by Schridde et al. (2013: 15–20), and from an economist's view, Bulow (1986: 742, 746).

Speculation, for example food speculation, is often an attempted interference in the exchange value or liquidity through price influence whereby the intrinsic use value of the commodity in question is disregarded because the commodity is only treated as money-to-be. Since the constitutive factor of the genuine exchange value of the *res* in the *financial* economy and the adopted exchange value of the *res* in the '*real* economy' is only the exchange itself, the catalyst or agent for this exchange, money, has central importance to effect this exchange. Money is not a neutral facilitator but the central agent or 'philosopher's stone' without which the exchange and its inherent transmutation does not happen. As discussed,[189] money defines itself exclusively through its exchange value and can be termed an imaginary commodity because it has no intrinsic value or use or contemplative value at all which a real commodity (e.g. goods) would have. Money also operates as transmuting agent that brings the 'noble metal' (absolute liquidity, like money itself) out of the 'base metal' that a real commodity constitutes (limited or no liquidity, but contemplative value). One can express these matters in a *third rule* (*transmutation or liquidification rule*):

> Money as the catalyst or agent transmutes the commodity that is the subject matter of the sale into money-to-be, a *res* with lesser liquidity but, if saleable and fungible, something getting close to actual money, and at the same time money conveys the idea that this money-to-be can be exchanged into money proper. Parallel to that, money operates as exchange delay in that it gives the seller and recipient of the money an expectation to realise use value (intrinsic value or contemplative value) at a later date at his own option by buying a real commodity, e.g. food. This is the scenario of the *casus dativus* explained earlier.[190] Money is therefore janiform again: not only is it (1) a debt created through the credit that banks grant to the borrower and (2) at the same time circulating credit which is transferred and acts as money,[191] it is also transmuting agent in that it (1) liquidifies real commodities into exchange commodities (or quasi money-*res*) and at the same time (2) operates as anticipated commodity or imaginary commodity because it creates an expectation, though not a legal entitlement, to a real commodity in the future.

In this double Janus-faced nature of money lies a paradox. One the one hand, money delays the exchange of two real commodities of which their contemplative or use value matters, since a sale and not a true barter takes place; on the other hand, money pushes the monetisation of real commodities towards money-to-be and higher money-like liquidity where the contemplative/use value does exactly not matter but is replaced by the mere exchange value. This paradox could perhaps explain quite a few incongruities of the present economic system

189 See above under sec. 3(c).
190 See above under sec. 2.
191 See Chapter 2, sec. 4.

if economists were prepared to cast aside some of the prevalent orthodoxies. A hint at the (unacknowledged) self-contradictory approach of orthodox economics is the postulation that money is a 'store of value' and, in connection, the economists' conceptualisation of 'safe assets' (short-term safe instruments, such as cash, treasury bills, bonds) after the banking crisis in 2009.[192] If safe assets are supposed to have money-like attributes, then money cannot be considered as a neutral *numéraire* at the same time, but must be a non-neutral *res* with effects.

Furthermore, since money is an agent and a commodity itself with its own exchange value – its price being determined particularly by the cost of credit creation which brings the money into existence – it influences heavily the price of the real commodities exchanged and is not at all neutral. The present use of the term 'cost' may be idiosyncratic for the economist. In this context, the cost of credit creation, that is, money creation, includes the loan interest and is borne not by the bank as creator but by the customer as borrower. Another element of this cost is the driving up of prices, for example in real property, by banks' generous grants of created money, that is, credit sums, to borrowers and property buyers which allows these to pay for overpriced real estate with larger amounts of created, and borrowed, money.[193] Real estate is a particularly good example, but the phenomenon can exist with any asset or commodity.

Important are the exchange and the ability of money to effect the exchange. It becomes apparent that matters of the quantity of money in an economy and velocity of circulation of money which excite economists are in fact only of minor and indirect relevance. As long as money retains the creed that it can operate as a transmuting and liquidifying agent of real commodities (and of course imaginary commodities akin to money, such as securities), it does not really matter what the exact quantity of money in the economy is. As Savigny already observed in the nineteenth century,[194] circulation of too much money in the economy may undermine the creed in the money as transmuting agent (similar to the creed of the alchemists in the philosopher's stone), so there is an indirect influence of the quantity of money on the operation of money, but the conceptual direction taken here is different from the quantity theories of the economists. This can be summarised in a *fourth rule* (*exchange operation rule*):

> The quantity of money in the economy is only of limited importance as such. What matters is if and to what extent money can be *believed* to effect exchanges and the transmutations these exchanges entail. Since money operates through the exchange only, the belief in the ability to effect the exchange creates the effectiveness of the money and so proves the creed as accurate. Money which does not flow is not money proper or 'dead', because money is only money in the moment of, and through, its operation as exchange-procuring agent.

192 E.g. Carlson et al. (2016: 309).
193 See Chapter 2, sec. 3(d).
194 See Chapter 1, sec. 6.

This also explains why quantitative easing (increase of money supply by central banks' expanded purchase of private sector business assets and longer-term bonds from the market) that has been implemented immensely in the wake of the banking crisis from 2010 onwards,[195] has so far not led to high inflation, although according to orthodox quantity theories of money the massive increase of money in the economy should have caused that.[196] However, the money created for the purpose of quantitative easing has largely never left the financial markets and the banking sector and, where it does not constitute reserves, it is used for internal exchanges of expectation values within the banking system only, either in form of money in the narrow sense or in form of financial products.[197] Only when this newly inserted money leaves the banking sector to a significant extent and enters the 'real economy', the problem arises that the money cannot be correlated sufficiently with commodities of the 'real economy' of intrinsic or contemplative/use value, such as consumer items or real estate.[198] In this case inflation emerges because the expectation value the money carries can only be less and less realised with an exchange into commodities in the 'real economy'. In such a situation there is too much money around that could correspond, in form of an exchange (sale), with non-money-*res* where their contemplative value prevails over their exchange value. Thus the exchange value of the money-*res*, increasingly unable to materialise the expectation value through effecting the exchange as transmuting agent, goes down: one has to pay more and more money to obtain the same non-money commodity and to gain its intrinsic use value.

It is quite possible that the vast amounts of money created by quantitative easing will never leave significantly the banking sector, presumably also with the argument that an inflation needs to be avoided. After all, money consists only of computer data and an indefinite amount can be kept inside the system for an unlimited period of time. However, the measure of quantitative easing has helped making the banks the masters of the economic system, despite the fact that they were only supposed to be saved from failure: through purchases of enterprises, real estate and commodities the banks can decide how much money they want to release into the economy and how they want to influence the prices. The insertion of money into the economy beyond a certain, hardly

195 Krugman and Wells (2015: 905, 941).

196 Krugman and Wells (2015: 920–925), Mankiw (2012: 648–652).

197 Hence the criticism by Krugman and Wells (2015: 941) that quantitative easing did not do much to boost the economy. However, the increased funds of money in the banks can hardly be used for investments in the 'real economy' where they potentially cause high inflation, so the money rests largely within the banking sector for speculation in the financial economy.

198 The recent rise of property prices in parts of the UK (London and South East) is, however, caused significantly by quantitative easing (there were other factors: the devaluation of the pound after the 'Brexit' referendum, fall of real earnings) because money made available through quantitative easing which leaves the banking sector is often invested particularly in real estate. See Thomas Hale, 'The Bank of England has a strange idea of what QE achieved', *Financial Times (Someone is wrong on the internet series)*, 3 August 2018.

definable, level will erode the general public's creed in the ability of money to effect exchange operations. Yet, the quicker the exchanges occur, the more one can delay inflation or ineffectiveness of money as exchange operating agent ('medium of exchange' – it becomes clear that the 'store of value' function of money is hardly relevant). As long as there is the creed of the market participants in the ability of the money to effect the exchange, the market can theoretically sustain any given quantity of money: this can generate the spiralling of the amount and velocity of exchanges to ensure that the exchange value remains effective, particularly by means of financial products and money itself which subsist only in the very exchange itself and allow a theoretically infinite delay in the (potentially precarious) realisation of the expectation value that relates to commodities of use value predominately. The fewer realisations of the expectation value are actually effected, the better, and the banks can decide more and more how many realisations are to happen when.

Even if the quantity of money circulating in the real economy rises and its exchange value reduces, the banks will by then own, after exchanges/sales, *res* of contemplative or use value (such as commodities, real estate, enterprises) which can be exploited (rented etc.), so the emergence of an inflation and depreciation of money is less relevant to them. If the reduction of the exchange value of money has to be compensated because of the inflation, banks are still free to create money in the usual way by granting credit to offset that effect, at least in part. The analysis of quantitative easing leads to the discussion of the practical workings of the transfer cycle.

(b) The transfer cycle in practice

Quantitative easing only emphasises the features of the transfer or externalisation cycle in general. Money can only operate as money if it is a transmuting agent that extracts higher liquidity from *res* (as money-to-be) by conferring exchange value through the actual exchange (see second and third rules above), and if there is an enduring belief in the market that money will continue to be able to exercise these exchange operations, largely irrespective of the actual – also increasing – quantity of money circulating in the economy (see fourth rule above). The chain of exchanges or transfers is therefore as follows:

The shortest version of the transfer cycle is simple. It starts with the exchange of commodity into money, thus the transformation of the commodity as money to be (a less liquid form of *res*) into money (the more liquid *res*), whereby the intrinsic contemplative or use value is also transmuted (by the money) into exchange value that carries the expectation value of a later retransformation of the more liquid *res* 'money' into the less liquid *res* 'another commodity'. This is the barter delay that money effectuates: not commodity *C1* against commodity *C2* directly, but commodity *C1* against money *m* (that carries the barter delay and expectation value) and later money *m* against commodity *C2*. The realisation of the expectation value as actual intrinsic use value of a commodity *C2* is the closing of the cycle *C1-m-C2*. The value intrinsic to *C1* leaves the real commodity and is transferred to, and transformed into, an imaginary commodity[199] with exchange value only (money) and is later retransformed to *C2* where the value re-enters the world of real commodities. Since *C1* and *C2* are increasingly considered as money-to-be, or 'expectation money' (application of first rule above), the circulation of commodities is in fact rather a circulation of broad and narrow forms of money, thus a cycle of Less Liquid Money–Money–Less Liquid Money, rather than Commodity-Money-Commodity. In any event, the process is cyclical; therefore one can speak of a *transfer cycle*. One can also speak of an *externalisation cycle*, following Hegel's terminology in his *Philosophy of Right*. According to Hegel, the human will, which can express itself in the ownership over a thing (through external signs, like possession or use), can also withdraw from that thing in a transfer (alienation) and allow the transferee instead to express his will in relation to the thing. Thus here the original owner externalises (*Entäußerung*) his ownership through the transfer or divestment (*Veräußerung*); the thing in question is external in nature, hence externalisation.[200] This conception is particularly relevant in relation to 'intellectual production', intellectual and artistic works, where the will is externalised through the creation of the work that can then be objectified and turned into intellectual property as a result of this externalisation.[201] This terminology is, however, more relevant for the idea of estrangement (*Entfremdung*) in the estrangement cycle as the second component of the alienation cycle.[202]

The re-entering and retransformation from an imaginary commodity to a real commodity that completes the transfer cycle is important. Only at this point it becomes apparent if a certain *res* indeed operates as money. As said, money is credit or legally enforceable debt,[203] and it is this operation of the law which enables money to effect the retransformation of an imaginary commodity into a real commodity and thereby complete the transfer cycle. Only because money is an enforceable debt backed by law can it carry expectation value. Therefore a retransformation of the fictitious exchange value of an imaginary commodity into an actual use value and into a real commodity can occur. The enforceability of the debt that money constitutes by virtue of the law makes a *res* acceptable as money and function as money (*casus accusativus* of money).[204] Here it becomes particularly apparent that money is primarily a legal concept, not just an economic or sociological phenomenon. Without this legal and factual enforceability, a *res* would not be accepted as money because there is no belief in the ability of the *res* to complete the transfer cycle: a transformation of real commodity into an imaginary commodity may happen, but a retransformation back to a real com-

199 See also above under sec. 3(c).
200 Hegel, *Philosophy of Right*, §§ 59, 61, 65, 73 (1986: 128, 130, 140–141, 156).
201 Hegel, *Philosophy of Right*, § 68 (1986: 145), and more detailed discussion of Hegel's conception with regard to copyright by Rahmatian (2011a: 216).
202 See below under sec. 5.
203 See Chapter 2, secs. 1, 2, 4.
204 See Chapter 2, sec. 4 and Chapter 5, sec. 2.

modity not: people would not accept banknotes, for example, but rather resort to true, not delayed, barters, as it indeed happens in times of economic and monetary crises.[205]

The simple transfer cycle *C1-m-C2* is obviously not the only and usually not even the most common version. Often the cycle would have to be described as *C1-m1-m2-m3 . . . mx-C2*, whereby *m1 . . . mx* are not necessarily money in the narrow sense, but 'broad money', securities and other forms of *res* of high liquidity and fungibility, such as shares, derivatives and other financial products, also in securitisation structures (e.g. special purpose vehicles or SPV, in securitisation transactions),[206] which are all characterised by their exchange value as the predominant or only form of value. That means money and/or various other forms of liquid *res m1, m2 . . . mx* akin to money will ultimately have to be transmuted back into real commodities *C2*, such as food, clothes and housing. In many cases, however, *m1 . . . mx* are interposed, not to *effect* a retransformation from *m* to *C2* quickly for the completion of the transfer cycle, but rather to *delay* such a retransformation, potentially for an unlimited period of time. The exchanges from, say, *m1* to *m2* may in fact be from money (*m1*) to shares (*m2*) or other securities, whereby the exchange itself creates exchange value (see first and second rules above). A retransformation of existing value (real commodity use value) from, initially, *C1* to, finally, *C2* is less important or even undesirable (and should be delayed by an ideally infinite number of interim exchanges from *m1* to *m2* to . . . *mx*), because such a transformation to *C2* could unmask the interim exchange values *m1 . . . mx* as eventually valueless.

For example, the sub-prime mortgage market before the financial crisis in 2008 was based on the idea that an ultimately unrealisable value (mostly due to under-collaterisation of mortgage loan debts) became packaged in investment products that appeared to have exchange value because of their specific design as financial products,[207] approved by rating agencies.[208] Their value was confined to their exchange only, that is, to the *m1 . . . mx* phase of the transfer cycle (an application of the second rule above); an entering into the stage of retransformation from *mx* to *C2* would, and eventually did, reveal that the exchange value could frequently not transmute into a contemplative/use value of a real commodity, even in case of judicial debt enforcement ('foreclosures'). This example also shows that the transition from *mx* to *C2* in the transfer cycle need not be effected by a sale or other contractual agreement, but can also occur in form of a judicial enforcement of a debt (typically arising from a sales or loan contract) by

205 E.g. Streissler (1984: 320). It is clear that money, even if undoubtedly legally enforceable debt, may still not be accepted to complete the transfer cycle, for example in situations of high inflation: legal enforceability is a necessary but not sufficient condition for a *res* being able to operate as money.

206 E.g. Hudson (2013: 1173, 1298, 1303).

207 In this case assets (mortgage)-backed securities collateralised debt obligations (ABS CDOs), see e.g. Hudson (2013: 1304).

208 United States: Financial Crisis Inquiry Commission (2011: 104, 109, 117–118, 127–129); Hudson (2013: 1313, 1315).

seizing assets of the debtor in case of non-payment.[209] Other examples are high frequency trade, already discussed in the context of the second rule, or short selling. Short selling is usually the borrowing of company shares from an existing shareholder and then selling these borrowed shares at the current market price against payment, with the expectation that the share price will go down, so that the short seller can then buy equivalent shares back at this lower price, replace the borrowed shares by delivering them to the lender, and obtain the difference as a profit.[210] This activity rests entirely on the exchange value that is realised through the exchange, but there is potentially an empty real commodity value (as the German term *Leerverkauf*, 'empty sale', expresses well). A transformation from *mx* to *C2* could lead to high speculative losses, particularly if the shorted shares have gone up in the interim.

In all these situations, real value is obtained by extending the chain of *m1-m2-m3 . . . mx*, and then, as a trader, abstracting from the chain and transmuting from, say, the stage of *m2* to some other commodity *CX*, but *before mx* in the chain will be transmuted to *C2* which may prove impossible by then. In the case of such an impossibility, *m2* is revealed as intrinsically worthless and cannot bring about an abstracted transformation *m2* to *CX* anymore either (and a transformation from *m2* or a later *mx* to *C2* in the chain fails anyway). In other words, the trader at the stage of *m2* will seek to exchange *m2* against money, and may buy real estate (contemplative value) with it before the subsequent transactions can no longer lead to a retransformation from *mx* to *C2*, that is, from pure exchange value to predominantly contemplative value of a real commodity for the completion of the transfer cycle. For when the creed or trust in the retransformation of liquid *res* (including money) stops, an interim transaction at stage *m2* to *CX* is obviously no longer possible either. To sustain this creed, ever more and ever quicker exchanges from *m1* to *m2*, to *m3* to . . . *mx* must occur, like a twister, to give the impression of real value which seemingly manifests itself in the exchange value, because an exchange can be effected. These exchanges must preferably remain untested, so no transmutation from *mx* to *C2* shall ideally ever take place that would attempt the extraction of contemplative value, otherwise the speculative bubble will burst at some point, with the usual crash of the market.

5. The alienation cycle II: the estrangement cycle

Alienations can lead to alienation, or more specifically, transfer is susceptible to estrangement. Thus the alienation cycle has a second component, and that is the estrangement cycle, since the externalisation or transfer has fundamental social and psychological consequences for the actors in the transfer and on the market generally. The externalisation or transfer cycle determines the value of a *res*

209 More on that point under Chapter 5, sec. 2.
210 E.g. Angel and McCabe (2009: 240).

through exchanges whereby the exchange value obscures or displaces completely the contemplative/use value of the *res*, if any. The estrangement cycle determines the value of the human beings involved in the exchanges on the market and the economic value of their social relations in general.

Alienation as a philosophical and sociological concept may have fallen out of favour somewhat in academic discourse today, compared to the 1960s and 1970s. However, in a time of omnipresent market fundamentalism, and in connection, temporary and precarious work, it unsurprisingly seems to be a recurring theme.[211] The theory of alienation is associated mostly with Marx, building upon Hegel, which Marx set out in his *Economic and Philosophical Manuscripts* of 1844. These were published completely only in 1932.[212] Marx's alienation theory will be used in the following as a point of departure. The Marxian alienation theory is hardly Marxist; in fact, orthodox Marxist narrative plays down the *1844 Manuscripts* as early works with no significant relevance for whichever interpretation of the later Marx, particularly *Capital*,[213] or it ignores them altogether.[214] This is not only because the totalitarian-bureaucratic communist regimes of the twentieth century were excellent practical examples for alienation, but also because Marxists usually reject the idea of Marx having an ethical theory[215] – and the alienation theory is that – which they would regard as a bourgeois distortion. In contrast, the Frankfurt School rightly emphasises Marx's alienation theory[216] and has popularised it particularly through Erich Fromm[217] and Herbert Marcuse.[218] It must be left to a future research project to work out the parallels between communist bureaucratic and 'neo-liberal' economic systems, and because both are based on the glorification and a religious-dogmatic interpretation of the economy,[219] alienation theory would provide very good insights. Obviously, that does not give much support to a closer examination of the concept of alienation from either the political Left or the political Right. For the Right it is too 'Marxist', for the Marxist versions of the Left it is not 'Marxist' enough, and indeed Marx was not (and never claimed to be) a founder of a novel religion but followed considerably Hegel and Rousseau as the predecessors of the idea of alienation.[220] There were also several intermediary thinkers from the classical and Romantic period in Germany, especially Schiller and Fichte.[221] However, there is no need for a history of

211 Henning (2015: 10–13, 19).
212 Schacht (1971: 65).
213 Henning (2015: 22).
214 The question of alienation is often not mentioned at all even in the discussion of the most related Marxian concept of commodity fetishism, see, for example, Albritton (2012: 66). On the fetishism of commodities, see Marx, *Kapital*, Part 1, sec. 1, 1, 4 (1975: 50), Ollman (1976: 195).
215 See Ollman (1976: 44–47) about such interpretations.
216 Schacht (1971: 115), Henning (2015: 157–167).
217 Fromm (2002: 117).
218 Marcuse (1972: 57–60, 68).
219 The only author I am aware of who hinted at this similarity is Klein (2007: 60–61).
220 Schacht (1971: 10, 35–56), Henning (2015: 35, 78).
221 Schacht (1971: 13–17), Henning (2015: 62–77).

alienation theories and their reception; these exist already,[222] whereby one should better shun arid and rigid aberrations of 'Marxist' writings on particularly Marx's alienation conception.

As already said, Marx's alienation theory provides the starting point. Here a very brief outline suffices, not only because this theory is well known and extensively discussed in academic literature,[223] but also because the present discussion of alienation departs from Marx's alienation theory in several aspects or develops it further. Marx initially follows Hegel[224] when he says that commodities produced by man are products and objectifications of labour.[225] The worker creates products through his work, but his work estranges him from the commodities he produces and also estranges him from nature and the outside world he perceives with his senses. He becomes a servant to his work and its products and is reduced to merely a physical being not much more than an animal; the work estranges him from the products of his work and from himself as a human being. Human life is limited to mere subsistence. The very production process is also a process of alienation. This estrangement comprises self-alienation which separates man from himself, and also from fellow human beings as his own species. Man is dominated by the products which he creates with his labour. Private property is the result of such alienated or externalised labour and a manifestation of man's relationship to nature, to himself and to other human beings, especially his employer and factory owner. The worker's existence is degraded to physical subsistence only. The alienation through the labourer's production of commodities destroys the social relations to other human beings.[226] More from the consumer's perspective, as it were, Marx regards the commodity, the product of alienated labour, as a fetish: the societal faculties of man's own work are mirrored back through the natural qualities of the commodities man has produced. The commodity itself is a lifeless thing, but in man's mind it contains the (proprietary) social relationships on which the production of the commodity is based.[227] All aspects of the illusion of the commodity fetish are conveyed further in the fetish of money, because money represents all possible commodities. Every commodity is essentially money and objectified expression of human labour.[228]

222 See e.g. Schacht (1971: 8, 13–29, 153), Henning (2015: 134, 170), Ollman (1976: 250).

223 E.g. Schacht (1971: 71–114), McLellan (1972: 213–232), Henning (2015: 109–128), Ollman (1976: 131–201).

224 Hegel, *Philosophy of Right*, § 67 (1986: 144), and § 80 (employment contract, with reference to Kant's *Metaphysics of Morals*) (1986: 167); Hegel, *Phenomenology*, B., IV., A. (2012: 153–154), Schacht (1971: 76–77).

225 Marx, *1844 Manuscripts* (2004: 79).

226 Marx, *1844 Manuscripts* (2004: 80–87).

227 Marx, *Kapital*, Part 1, sec. 1, 1, 4 (1975: 51–52). Although Marx's discussion of the commodity fetish seems to be a direct extrapolation of his writings on alienation, most commentators (also Marxist ones) do not appear to appreciate that.

228 Marx, *Kapital*, Part 1, sec. 1, 2 (1975: 70). One can see a proximity to the third rule above on money-to-be. When Marx also says, 'These objects [of value], gold and silver, just as they come out of the bowels of the earth, are at the same time the direct incarnation of all

In the modern Western business world, where manufacturing has been shifted to Asia in particular and replaced by a service industry, the estrangement of man from the commodity he produces and from himself through the process of production has become a less significant concern. Since every commodity is considered as lesser money or money-to-be aspiring to the liquidity status of money itself,[229] any commodity fetish has turned into a deferred money fetish. Alienation occurs not only in the classical Marxian sense that the worker is alienated from the work and the commodity he produces, because it is sold (and his labour with it), but rather because nobody obtains any relationship to physical things over which he can exercise his will and express himself through them, because everything only has an exchange value and is supposed to be an anonymous highly fungible monetised asset, a substitute of money with no contemplative value. The use of a commodity or even a commodity fetish requires at least the enjoyment of a contemplative value of a *res*, and exactly that contemplative value becomes increasingly suppressed by the exchange value even for *res* that are commodities produced for use, such as food, furniture and cars. Only the accelerated production and sale matter, not the use. Consumer goods like cars, furniture and fashion clothes have an ever-shorter lifespan so as to trigger replacement purchases (the payment of which also needs to cover the cost of money creation, especially interest), and the disastrous consequences of this forced economic growth for the world's resources and environment are well-known.[230] If a physical commodity is regarded as a mere liquid asset, a relationship to a thing (whether natural or pathological-fetishist) cannot even arise properly.

According to the 'classical' idea of alienation, a man may have exerted his commodity fetishism with the purchase of a sports car,[231] where he may have become alienated from himself through the product as a false substitute of his personality, and this condition has indeed been criticised in the 1950s and 1960s.[232] However, today, the market-conformist man will relish even more in the fact that the car can be sold for a good price to enable him buying another one instead, than in driving his car fast and having it for ostentation and for impressing his male and female mates. Or he may combine his transaction with an environmental agenda (since capitalism swallows everything) and purchase a battery-powered electric vehicle, in which case he experiences a form of alienation from nature that Marx already postulated,[233] but he is made to feel good about it. The Bitcoin speculation frenzy,[234] whereby the actors convince themselves that they are part of a global social movement by trading in a seemingly anarchistic-subversive

human labour. Hence the magic of money' (ibid.), then he refers (whether consciously or not) to Goethe's *Faust II*, discussed above under sec. 3(c), which Marx certainly knew well.

229 See the third rule above under sec. 4(a).

230 Binswanger (2013: 71–73, 116–120, 156).

231 On the car as an object of psychosexual narcissistic projection, see e.g. the amusing discussion by Baudrillard (2014: 97).

232 Fromm (2002: 133, 138, 144–145).

233 Marx, *1844 Manuscripts* (2004: 83).

234 See Chapter 2, sec. 7, and Rahmatian (2019: 119) with further references.

alternative currency against the evil multinationals and banks, is a similar example of a second-tier alienation beyond the classical, almost old-fashioned alienation through the production of physical commodities.

Alienation happens not only because every *res* is a *res* of (ideally) exclusively exchange value – ultimately a consequent application of Milton Friedman's idea of monetisation where assets and money are theoretically hardly distinguishable[235] – but also because the exchange value can only be realised by way of exchanges, the more and the quicker, the better. This materialises in the actual estrangement cycle.

The *estrangement cycle* can be characterised thus: exchanges, often unnecessary ones, are interposed between human relations to effect the realisation of exchange values through such exchanges. The typical situation is the imposition of a service against payment, whereby the service 'returns', but in fact emulates or pretends, the human relation (either to oneself or to other humans) that has been interrupted or removed by that service. This happens particularly in two ways.

(1) Something that you can do and experience yourself is taken from you and then returned against payment, perhaps repackaged, to allow you a commercially exploited and controlled experience. The personal, perhaps creative, activity is looked after or taken over by a separate person or entity and sold back as commodified activity, either as product or as service:[236] the activity can be propertised as a *res*, for example in form of intellectual property and appurtenant licences, trade secrets, business reputation, but also as airport slots (airline takeoff and landing rights)[237] or as the European Union cap-and-trade Emissions Trading Scheme of the greenhouse gas carbon dioxide.[238] In any event, it is exchanged, whereupon it obtains value. Propertisation is a prerequisite for transfer-alienation, but does not automatically involve estrangement. Only when an experience which you can have yourself is taken from you and returned against payment of money under the pretext of that being your own experience, then there is estrangement. The personal activity and psychological experience is alienated from you through that interpolated transfer and retransfer. The process is cyclical, because it returns to the initial person.

There are manifold examples. The obvious ones are the fetishes attached to consumer items, such as: only a certain perfume makes the consumer irresistible or certain sports gear makes him or her invincible, or a computer game which makes interaction with other players superfluous because the player plays against a computer or against other anonymous players mediated by a computer. The consumer's personality dissolves into the commodities and services which are sold to him and represent or define him. For example, only with this or that smartphone one can apparently be a successful businessman. The multifaceted and highly

235 See above under sec. 4(a), and under Chapter 3, sec. 4.

236 This returned product is then the apparent expression of customers' standardised and levelled desire, compare Adorno (2003: 178–179).

237 Olbrich et al. (2009: 898–899, 916).

238 See e.g. Lederer (2008: 4).

personal ability to act as a successful businessman is reduced to a consumer item that is sold back to the purchaser and replaces his individual experience of life and his personal achievements. Other examples are the award of university degrees against the payment of tuition fees as their commercial validation, or scholarly articles delivered to academic publishers for free and returned as printed journals against a high fee to be paid by university libraries to obtain acknowledgement as valid academic publications. A less obvious example is the recent rising interest of adults in reading (classical) children's books,[239] which can indicate the making up for a consumed but unlived childhood (that is apparently returned by the book sold), or the need for an illusion of a childlike world in denial of the unappealing real world of adults. The purchased book is the commodity that achieves this illusion;[240] without this exchange against money the illusion is discouraged or deceptively impossible. One could analyse the whole economy for various appearances of an estrangement cycle.

(2) The second typical version of the estrangement cycle is that a relationship between humans is transformed into a commodity and sold back to the humans concerned as their relationship. It is not necessary that these humans involved pay for this; it may also be somebody else. A standard case are 'Facebook friends' and other social media connections. People emulate real friendships by assigning the relationship to a commercial entity and obtain an imitated relationship back through the services of that company, perhaps with the successful illusion that they have real friendships. Money does not necessarily change hands between the users and the social media company, but it does elsewhere through advertising, based on the personal data the users invariably provide the social media company with.[241] Any real personal relationship is destroyed by the commodifying substitute; herein obviously lies the alienation. In fact, (2) is a subset of (1), because (2) is effectively the situation that a coordinated activity (which creates the relation) of two or more people is taken from them and then returned against money. In such cases it is imperative that the atomisation of human beings that a market-fundamentalist society inevitably brings about by conceptualising everyone as a fierce competitor is masked by the illusion of exchanged products and services that sell back commodified human relations which emulate and replace the lost real ones.

This atomisation of society into unrelated individuals[242] through competition also affects the real market and market prices. To avoid addressing this problem, orthodox economics postulates artificially for its supply and demand model that

239 Donna Ferguson, 'Why Harry Potter and Paddington Bear are essential reading . . . for grown-ups', *The Guardian*, 20 April 2019.

240 The alienation does not lie in reading a book as a child or an adult, but in the illusion of a childhood purchased through the book. In effect, the book as a work of literature is reduced here to a commodity and does not serve (as would be with a real child reader) as a source of imagination and expression of an active inner life. Compare the interesting comment by Walter Benjamin, *Bücher und Lektüre des Kindes*, Benjamin (2002: 186).

241 Schroeder (2018: 131–133, 139–146).

242 That includes groups that are not interacting teams but aligned persons in their (social media) echo chamber looking at their leaders for guidance.

there be 'perfect competition' where neither individual consumers nor individual producers can influence the price at which the commodity is bought or sold.[243] That is complemented with efficiency criteria for the exchange/barter according to Pareto: nobody can become better off without making somebody else worse off, an argument that is frequently used to discourage political decisions (and legal rules) from interfering in the market mechanics.[244] The reality differs from this hypothesised fairness model. Usually sales are completed with the feeling that we have gained disproportionately more than the other party, like we have cheated or tricked the other party or have made a very good bargain. Advertising frequently gives the same impression: every sale is made to be a clearance sale, a special offer, an unusual price reduction. It does not mean that any cheating really took place, but subjectively one wants to have the sentiment that one has the edge over the other. In a competitive society (though devoid of 'perfect competition') one would expect that, because we do not trade with the other in trust, but against the other in suspiciousness. Hence the market price embodies the subjective feeling of having gained more than the other party to the transaction. The price is not an objective equilibrium price, a sale of a commodity or service for a just and fair market price, but it is rather a *price of subjective taking advantage or of cheating*. This is a 'fair deception paradox', because subjectively the equilibrium price is not the result of objective and fair rules of the market, though presented by economists as such, but of a subjective impression of taking advantage successfully. This subjective impression may well be an illusion, but the boundaries between perceived taking advantage and real cheating can obviously become blurred in practical situations. Everyone may have to cheat a little in order not to be crushed by the forces of the market.[245] This phenomenon can be seen as an example of alienation, that of man being estranged from his fellow men,[246] because the necessary trust relationship between members of a society is destroyed. A monetary society is exactly not about trust[247] but about self-sufficiency.[248]

It becomes apparent that any human relation which cannot be commodified through an emulating *res* and is therefore capable of being exchanged is effectively worthless in such a human society because it lacks exchange value. That also applies to human beings themselves, because their *res* for exchange is labour or services that may be externalised in commodities or propertised in form of intellectual property rights.[249] If human activities cannot crystallise in any form of *res*

243 Krugman and Wells (2015: 358).

244 Bofinger (2011: 195).

245 The Volkswagen diesel car emissions test scandal of 2015 is a prominent example of this attitude. In that case there was real cheating, not only a subjective impression of taking advantage, see e.g. Gwyn Topham and Graeme Waerden, 'VW faces deluge of UK legal claims over emissions tests', *The Guardian*, 24 Sept. 2015.

246 Marx, *1844 Manuscripts* (2004: 85).

247 Humphrey (1985: 57, 67).

248 Vohs et al. (2006: 1155–1156).

249 See, with regard to copyright, Rahmatian (2011: 226–237).

capable of exchange value, the human being, reduced to such a *res*, is effectively worthless. Speaking with Ricardo and Marx, men are reduced to saleable hats. (One may remember the warning at the beginning of section 4 above.) This is the logical consequence of Friedman's monetisation conception and now largely the reality in the present economy and society. What matters is not what the human being is, but what the human being yields. The result of that condition resembles more and more the distinction between life worthy and unworthy of life by the Nazis, only that today race is largely, though not entirely, substituted by efficiency.

The observation that human relations, when reduced to monetary relations, lead to alienation is not new. In 1900, Georg Simmel remarked that money renders human relationships impersonal: one is independent of every specific member of society (because our interest on either of them is expressed in objective money terms), but it is rather a *non-dependence* or isolation and loneliness, not actual *independence* imbued with the positive attribute of freedom. Dependence does not exist in relation to individual persons but rather with regard to objective services carried out by any interchangeable person with whom one is connected by a money relationship. Purchases with money involve a valuation of objects more in relation to quantity (of the money spent) than quality (of the thing). At the same time, money allows a greater distance between person and possession, since money enables technical management remotely, like land leased or shares in a company invested.[250]

Money creates an independence from individual humans, but not from commercial society as such. It perforates and disintegrates a human being's nucleus of social relations in a community, the 'social atom' (Moreno),[251] because it replaces highly personal networks that support and define the individual by exchange relationships with interchangeable actors. The wider psychological networks may persist on a utilitarian basis, but the nuclear relations gradually desiccate. Everybody can observe that with employees in banks, financial services, insurance companies, accountancy and law firms and generally in management, a development assisted by ever-increasing working hours. Furthermore, those who succeed best in a market-fundamentalist economy based on competitive money relationships are sociopaths[252] and narcissists, so not surprisingly, scholarly research has recently focused increasingly on narcissism.[253] Narcissism is certainly an advantage when aiming for a career in corporate leadership.[254] The current emphasis on individualism, even if only suggested by purchasable commodities and services

250 Simmel (2011: 322, 324, 334–335, 359–360).

251 Moreno (1987: 26).

252 Including, interestingly, economists, see the study by Frank (1993: 159), according to which economists tended to be more socially uncooperative, less honest and more prone to free-ride. There are several similar studies. What a 'sociopath' is, however always remains a question of definition.

253 Germain (2018: 3) and on the clinical measures of narcissistic personality disorder, ibid. (2018: 12).

254 Germain (2018: 43).

that mask the isolation, also fosters narcissistic personality traits. Here we witness the emergence of a paradox: a drive for ever more freedom and individualism, but at the same time only for a partial and instrumental freedom to consume or, more generally, to exchange. Freedom is reduced to a celebration of the narcissistic *amour-propre* of the individual who insofar falls in line with the crowd anyway.[255] Again, this is an instance of the estrangement cycle where individual experience is taken and returned as a packaged commodity against money: it is alienation from freedom by pretending freedom with an imposed exchange and consumption.

The alienation process which the transformation of individual personal bonds into exchange relationships through money produces, is further supported by abstract institutional frameworks, for example companies with their artificial legal personality. That will be discussed in the following Chapter 5, insofar as the institution of companies is relevant for banks and the operation of the monetary system. For the moment, one may finish with a statement by Theodor W. Adorno, who said in a televised discussion in 1965 about alienation:[256]

> All I want is for the world to be established in such a way that humans are not its superfluous appendages, but . . . that things are there for the sake of humans and not humans for the sake of the things that they have even made themselves. And that they have made them themselves, that the institutions ultimately refer back to the people, that gives me, in any case, very little comfort.

That fact that our commodities and our institutions refer back to us provides us with the illusion that a purely commercial transaction between atomised competitive units of persons is the result of personal social and emotional relationships. We obtain the impression of unrestrained freedom while still being in a personal social network without recognising the underlying business transactions that undermine real human and social relations. However, a wider realisation of one's alienation may lead to a general behavioural change, for example, that monetisation becomes secondary and the intrinsic value more important than the exchange value in a new economic system. This would entail a departure from the second (financialisation) rule above. It would also show that in economics and sociology there are no immutable quasi-laws of nature, contrary to some economists' opinions.[257] The four rules formulated earlier[258] are no exception.

255 Hall et al. (2008: 168–169).

256 'Ich will ja gar nichts anderes, als dass die Welt so eingerichtet wird, dass die Menschen nicht ihre überflüssigen Anhängsel sind, sondern . . . dass die Dinge um der Menschen willen da sind und nicht die Menschen um der Dinge willen, die sie noch dazu selbst gemacht haben. Und dass sie sie selbst gemacht haben, dass die Institutionen schließlich auf die Menschen zurückweisen, das ist für mich jedenfalls ein sehr geringer Trost'. See Adorno in Grenz (1975: 249), own translation.

257 Generally, Rahmatian (2017: 126–137). On Milton Friedman's theory of positive economics as a pertinent example, see Friedman (2009: 4, 7–9).

258 See above under sec. 4(a).

5 The legal underpinnings for the functioning of money as money: the faith in money and the power of the banks

1. Money as a legally enforced creed

We saw in Chapter 4 in particular that the ability of money to operate as a transmuting agent in the exchange process is based on a belief that money will effect the change from exchange value to contemplative value of (ultimately tangible) property (real commodities) for use and enjoyment. In this way, money carries an expectation value to be realised in the future and enables a delayed barter in form of at least two sales (transfer cycle). In addition, banks have the privilege to create (within limits difficult to ascertain) *res* (circulating credit) that function as money because of the belief in this function by the market participants. It has also been mentioned[1] and will be discussed again[2] that banks maintain liquidity by sustaining the customers' belief, or concerted pretence of a belief, in the banks' liquidity which, if ever tested, would invariably reveal insolvency. Thus the monetary system operates on a creed or belief system. It may therefore be interesting to examine possible roots of this belief system.

What makes a seller part with a pound of cheese against the receipt of an intrinsically worthless piece of colourful paper is the seller's trust in the ultimate legal enforceability of the debt that this paper embodies.[3] Hence the debt resulting from the contract of sale (purchase price) can be extinguished with another enforceable debt, which is what money constitutes. In law this is indeed so, in reality not at all, because, apart from a few specialists, not even lawyers or economists are aware of the exact concept of money and its workings, let alone the general public.[4] Sociologically and historically this belief derives from elsewhere, and the legal enforcement only seems to support, rather than produce, this belief.

Adam Smith considered barter the result of a decision of rational human beings, and money a facilitator of that barter. There is a 'propensity to truck,

1 See Chapter 2, sec. 3(c).

2 See below under sec. 3.

3 See further below under sec. 2.

4 A good illustration is the misguided idea by the sociologist and economist Joseph Huber who advocates an alternative system of money (sovereign money), that money and credit are two different things. See discussion below under sec. 5.

barter, and exchange one thing for another', he said. However, he did not, as was otherwise characteristic for the moral philosophy of the Scottish Enlightenment,[5] derive this propensity from an innate moral sense ('original principles in human nature'), but from rational human thinking and acting.[6] The cultural history of mankind indicates a rather less rational, but more mythical and religious origin of money, and one not necessarily related to barter and trade initially. Coins may not have had their origin as being a device for exchange or trade, but rather served administrative needs and payment of officials and mercenaries. Coins could simplify payment of state salaries, taxes, tributes and fines. That would explain why hoards of coins found by archaeologists overwhelmingly contain local coins, which shows their local circulation.[7] Acceptance of coins by government officials would then procure their acceptance by merchants rather than the other way round.[8]

In ancient Greece, it appeared that the unit of barter was the ox, but it was not, according to several theories, barter and exchange which led to this development. It was rather the use of the 'ox-unit' in the context of state-religious institutions and the normative character that religion exercised. The archaic cities would seek to pacify their protective divinities by public and ritualised gift-offerings, in Ancient Greece oxen, whereby the state-religious authorities regulated carefully the types, quality and quantity of the oxen to be delivered as offerings. The result was effectively the creation of state-controlled and approved units of value by normative act of the state-religious authorities and temples. This 'ox-unit' then represented the yardstick for the repayment of debts to the deities: the temple authorities imposed, as apparent mediators, a debt relationship where man was his gods' debtor. It is not certain whether this relationship was regarded as a kind of sacred barter-exchange or, perhaps more plausibly, a reciprocal gift-exchange, that is, more likely gifts as gratitude for blessings obtained (or hoped for) rather than payments for blessings. In either case, giving objects was not considered an exchange of things for their own sake, detached from men and their interpersonal connections; such exchanges were exceedingly rare in Homeric times. The early form of economic exchange was gift and counter-gift, rather than barter or sale based on perceived equivalence of value.[9] Furthermore, participation at the communal sacrificial meal of the roasted bull as the offering to the gods acted as a redistribution or recompense for the goods or services the inhabitants provided

5 Rahmatian (2015: 47–49, 178).

6 Smith, *Wealth of Nations*, book 1, chapter 2 (2000: 14).

7 It depends, however, on the historical period. In late antiquity, for example, coins were obviously used for trade and payment of workers' wages. Cash payments by way of coin were still common in the late Roman urban economy of the decaying Roman empire, and migrant labourers as far as from Northern Europe would take the coins with them and hoard them (hence archaeological finds of hoards of Roman coins in South Scandinavia), but did not put them back into the Roman economy. See Fischer (2017: 317–318).

8 Grierson (1978: 4–5).

9 Hölscher (2014: 114–115).

to the temple-state.[10] Later coins came to represent an entitlement to a share in the sacrificial bull's meat, so that the coin denoted recompense and representation of entitlement to a share in the distribution of food, and not medium of exchange in commerce. Some corroboration for this plausible thesis are the many early coins with a bull's head on their surface. Thus a link between money and religion-state and law as normative authorisers and approvers of representing units appears to have existed from the outset.[11]

The assumption that money as a medium of exchange and standardised unit derived its powers from the law (and religion) first, and from commercial practice only later, is not a too speculative leap. The (ancient city-)states introduced an artificial system of economic exchange with the issuance of coins: long-term gift and counter-gift exchanges were gradually replaced by more short-term barter/sale-type exchanges. The state had a monopoly in issuing money and in fixing and controlling its value, and the state was also the first distributor of money.[12] This aspect reminds of the Chartalist theory of money which also sees money as originating from an act of law that establishes a debt-relationship between the individual and a state authority, in contrast to exchange-based explanations for the beginning of money that economists usually prefer.[13] The Chartalist theory of money is, however, too narrow for a description of the modern system of money.[14] Nevertheless, the law is the originator of money, not only today, but apparently also historically.

In the Middle Ages, money was imbued with Christian thinking and symbolism. Money as such was neither good nor bad, only its abuse was. Spending money for religious purposes was obviously encouraged.[15] Gregory the Great likened the false coin to the false prophets of the Antichrist. Anselm of Canterbury compared the penny to the monk: the pure metal of the coin signifies the monk's obedience, its accurate weight the steadfastness of monastic purpose, and the mintmark the monk's habit.[16] The Church was also directly involved in the creation of money. Coins were not only minted by secular rulers but also by bishoprics and abbeys, sometimes as representatives of royal or imperial power, sometimes in their own right enjoying privileges conferred on them (often together with market and toll rights). Profits from minting (seignorage) accrued to monasteries and bishoprics. However, many privilege holders did not actually make use of their minting rights.[17] Even where the Church itself was not involved in

10 On the early economic phase of the polis culture and the iron spits (*obeloi*) as pre-monetary means of pay, see Hölscher (2014: 114).
11 Semenova (2011: 381–384, 388, 392), with particular reference to the study by Bernhard Laum, *Heiliges Geld* (1924).
12 Hölscher (2014: 116–118).
13 Semenova (2011: 395).
14 See Chapter 1, sec. 3(b)(iv).
15 Naismith (2015: 26–27).
16 Dinkova-Bruun (2015: 79–80, 86).
17 Naismith (2015: 31–33).

the issuing of money, it gave its blessing to it and so underlined its legitimacy and confirmed its value.

The state and the rulers struggled, however, considerably in establishing and asserting the operative power of money. The English case of *Gilbert v. Brett* (1604), the so-called *Case of Mixt Monies*, illustrates this development. The case, which was handed down in the wake of Elizabeth I's debasement of the Irish currency in 1601, decided that a creditor who is owed a monetary debt has to bear the risk of changes between contract date and date of the payment due. The creditor can only sue for the nominal value of the debt at the time of the contract, irrespective of a subsequent change in the intrinsic value of the coinage because of changes of weight or fineness and, as a result, of purchasing power.[18] It was the sovereign's prerogative to determine the intrinsic fineness of coinage and to assign it a legal valuation in terms of money of account. The queen was entitled, if public necessity (such as the war in Ireland) demanded it, to debase the currency without seeking any authorisation from her subjects.[19] Thus with regard to coin, the nominal value was authoritatively established, irrespective of the coins' intrinsic material/metallic value. The case confirmed the sovereign authorship of money.[20]

This monetary nominalism – it is money of a determined value by a normative act – could theoretically easily be reconciled with paper money, since the intrinsic value of the medium of exchange did not matter, but there was a lot of psychological resistance for a long time. In the early years of the United States, John Witherspoon said in 1786 that money must not be a sign only but must have an intrinsic and commercial value and be a commodity itself.[21] Paper money (bills entitling the bearer to receive a certain sum specified in the bill) 'is not properly speaking money at all. It is barely a pledge or standard of value' and cannot be used well as medium of universal exchange. And further, 'to arm such bills with the authority of the state and make them a legal tender in all payments, is an absurdity so great that it is not easy to speak with propriety upon it'.[22] Witherspoon then also claimed, as an argument against paper money, that money had to have a standard of value, and if any prince or state debased the metal below standard, this would be 'utterly impossible to make it succeed'[23] – apparently in unawareness of the *Case of Mixt Monies*. In the German states in the first half of the nineteenth century, Savigny also struggled to regard paper money as proper money; paper money 'only represents real money'. For him, the operation of paper money was based on a belief in government, since a belief in the metal value of the money was no longer possible. What sustains this belief are a careful

18 Fox (2016: 224, 226–227).

19 Fox (2016: 227) with a discussion of the continental European civil law authorities referred to in this judgment and their selective use.

20 Desan (2014: 350).

21 Witherspoon, *Essay on Money as a Medium of Commerce* (1786: 24).

22 Witherspoon, *Essay on Money as a Medium of Commerce* (1786: 28–29).

23 Witherspoon, *Essay on Money as a Medium of Commerce* (1786: 29).

limitation of the quantity of paper money issued, a general acceptance of paper money as payment by the state authorities, and the unrestricted ability to change paper money to coins at a state institution (a central bank).[24] For Savigny, money, and particularly paper money, obtains its operation through a belief system reinforced by law and the actions of state authorities. In contrast, the Presbyterian minister Witherspoon might not have wanted to acknowledge this very worldly creed.

In the nineteenth century, Americans still found it difficult to accept paper money in the shape of the 'greenbacks'. For financing the American civil war, the government issued demand notes ('greenbacks') to pay the war debts, which were redeemable in 6% twenty-year bonds, but not in coin, and they were declared legal tender. In the case of *Hepburn v. Griswold*,[25] the US Supreme Court held that the making of notes or bills of credit as legal tender in payment of pre-existing debts was unconstitutional and outside the powers of Congress. This decision was overruled soon by *Knox v. Lee*,[26] which held that legal tender legislation was constitutional for both pre-existing and subsequent obligations, and which therefore established the legal backing of paper money.[27]

Most challenging was the legal recognition of bank money operating as money. Even today, the *statutory* legal basis for bank money as money is somewhat nebulous.[28] The legal recognition of bank money is, however, most explicitly a legal, normative invention, because the concept of bank money as being a debt in form of a transferable bank deposit (either a real one in case of a customer's deposit with a bank or an invented one in case of a bank's loan to the customer),[29] is invariably a legal creature. (Circulating) credit or debt originates normatively, by the law; like any property, debt does not exist in the natural world.[30] Presumably it was historically really the case of *Foley v. Hill*,[31] which for the first time unequivocally characterised the bank deposit as a loan, in that case a loan to the bank, which the banker could freely make use of, in contrast to the earlier forms of deposits with merchants and goldsmiths as mere depositaries of money. These earlier deposits were not (yet) fit to be considered as circulating credit. Before the seventeenth century, and particularly in the Middle Ages, a beneficiary other than the bailor could indeed sue in account and in debt a bailee of the money deposited by the bailor, but that quasi-contractual remedy did not mean transferability of the deposit-debt.[32] The transferability, which turns the deposit into circulating debt/credit and therefore into bank money, has been brought about normatively by later case law that reflected existing common banking practice.

24 Savigny, *Obligationenrecht I* (1851: 413). See also Chapter 1, sec. 6.
25 *Hepburn v. Griswold*, 75 U.S. 603 (1869).
26 *Knox v. Lee*, 79 U.S. 457 (1870).
27 Chung (2009: 131–133).
28 See Chapter 2, sec. 6.
29 See Chapter 2, sec. 3.
30 This argument goes back particularly to Jeremy Bentham, see Bentham (1891: 111–113).
31 *Foley v. Hill* (1848) 2 HLC 28.
32 Geva (2016: 362–363, 368, 383–384).

The common feature of all forms of money – coin, paper money and bank money – is that they are founded on a belief in the functioning of the money as money,[33] and if that creed is directed at the operative ability of money to transform lower liquidity *res* into higher liquidity *res* as 'alchemistic agent',[34] then precious metal as trigger for that belief is not necessary; in fact, no specific reification of the *res* is required.[35] This creed can be fed and strengthened by law and acts of state authorities, as Savigny already mentioned, and also by monetary policy decisions of central banks. All these activities are rituals, similar to the old alchemists' magical spells[36] that seek to transmute one substance into another that is already intrinsic in the original base substance. Here, instead of lead into gold, it is less liquid *res* of contemplative value transmuted into most liquid *res* of exchange value, and back, according to the alienation/transfer cycle.[37]

The belief-inducing or belief-enforcing magic spell or ritual is particularly visible in the case of financial products. In the US sub-prime mortgage crisis of 2008, the collateralised debt obligations (CDOs) had been turned into liquidified money-like *res* by a systematised structuring and pooling of financial assets, comprising riskier and less risky tranches of assets combined. The magic spell that enforced the belief in the transfer of value within these financial products was effected, less by legal regulation which was rather absent then, but by financial mathematics that gave a pseudo-scientific basis for a perceived prediction of risk and for risk management, and by the blessings of the credit rating agencies.[38] These agencies fulfilled a role similar to the temples in antiquity and the medieval Church for money issued by them or their ruler. Financial mathematics and the calculation of speculation, which started with Louis Bachelier in 1900,[39] confers on transactions, whether of money proper or of financial vehicles emulating money, the trust of intrinsic value to be transferred. Mathematical calculations,[40] for example of the performance of derivatives and similar financial products for speculation,[41] suggest mathematical predictability of the future (like the endeavours of the astronomer-priests in antiquity), and gives the perception of human control over the future, a power which would otherwise be reserved to God alone. But as one knows today that the worshippers create the god they worship

33 Chung (2009: 160).
34 See Chapter 4, sec. 4. A similar argument by Supiot (2015: 225).
35 See Chapter 1 on the concept of dematerialised property.
36 Mauss, *General Theory of Magic* (2001: 90–91).
37 See Chapter 4, sec. 4.
38 United States: Financial Crisis Inquiry Commission (2011: 118–122, 127–128, 131–132) for the factual basis of this interpretation. The Financial Crisis Inquiry Commission obviously did not couch its findings in these terms.
39 Bachelier (1900: 21–22): 'But it is possible to study mathematically the static state of the market at a given moment, that is to say, to establish the law of probability of price fluctuations that the market admits at that moment. Where the market in fact does not foresee such fluctuations, it considers them as more or less probable, and that probability can be evaluated mathematically' (translation from the French).
40 Together with accounting practices, see Supiot (2015: 226–227).
41 E.g. Ayache (2011: 471–472, 479, 483).

through the projection of their own attributes on their deity[42] and through acts and rituals of worship, so one also knows that bankers and the general public keep up the creed in the financial products and in money by pretending to believe in the intrinsic value of money, whether cash, bank money or electronic money. At least after the rising availability of information about the system of money in the wake of the financial crisis in 2008–9, it is unlikely that anyone who has shown any interest in the concept of money at all would genuinely believe that money represents a value – it only represents an expectation of a conversion into value in the future. However, in concerted pretence we maintain the belief in money to keep the system going.

Law itself, from which money originates, is actually not that different. We create the legal rule by complying with it in the belief of a duty to do so, and with this enforcement we make it existent. This argument has a distinct flavour of Scandinavian legal realism,[43] but that goes well beyond the scope of this book. The next section will look at the function of the law as the enforcer and enabler of money.

2. The genuine transfer of value through enforcement of money and debt

The term *fiat money* ('let there be/there shall be money') does invite a mythological or religious analogy with God's *fiat lux* at the beginning of the Creation,[44] and Thomas Hobbes remarked indeed that legal '*Pacts* and *Covenants* . . . resemble that *Fiat*, or *Let us make man*, pronounced by God in the Creation'.[45] Both *fiats* share the idea of a creation by way of words with normative effect ('shall'). In relation to human covenants, God's deeds are mirrored by man's covenants but, through these, God is also eliminated from the actions of humans as the images of God; human actions and laws originate in human nature and no longer in God's created nature.[46] So does the normative text that is money, but this institution is particularly in need of a belief preferably modelled upon the traditional religions to ensure its operability. The law provides the most essential backing for this pseudo-religious belief system.

The clear legal sources for cash and the more obscure ones (in the case of Germany even problematic ones) for bank money have already been discussed.[47] Here we look at the enforcement of the money debt which effects the transformation

42 Hence the age-old theological and philosophical problem where evil and sin (that is, human qualities) can come from if God is supposedly the originator of everything and at the same time infinitely benevolent and almighty, see e.g. the classical texts of the Enlightenment by Bayle, *Dictionnaire historique et critique*, 'Pauliciens', Bayle (2003: 204–208) and Hume, *Dialogues concerning Natural Religion*, Part 10, Hume (2008: 100–103).

43 E.g. Freeman (2008: 1039, 1057) with an extract from Karl Olivecrona, *Law as Fact* (1939).

44 Genesis 1:3.

45 Hobbes, *Leviathan*, 'The Introduction' (1985: 81–82) (original emphasis).

46 Musso (2017: 372–373).

47 See Chapter 2, sec. 6.

of *mx* into *C2* in the alienation/transfer cycle, thus the transformation of money as the most liquid *res* with merely exchange value back into a less liquid *res* with primarily contemplative or use value. The enforceability by law of the debt that money constitutes makes a *res* acceptable as money and function as money.[48] This is the most important aspect of the *casus accusativus* in the framework of relations of money (enforcement, effect of transfer): money is a loan-debt (borrower's money debt) in order to discharge another debt, for example a payment for delivery of goods under a contract of sale.[49] In this context, the janiform nature of money (the money-debt *res*) needs to be considered again.[50]

Money is a debt, created through a loan, theoretically in case of cash (banknotes) although in fact never repayable, and practically in case of bank money, the far most important form of money, and the loan that bank money constitutes is very much repayable. For cash or central bank–issued money, the enforcement of the loan debt is abstract; for bank money it is very real. The loan that bank money constitutes can operate in two ways, either as a loan to the bank as a customer's real deposit, or as a loan to the customer as a notional deposit created by the bank, that is, the new money. This appears as a lengthening of the bank's balance sheet, because while the customer-borrower's bank account is credited with the new money as deposit, the bank's loan account is debited.[51] This grounding of money on loan-debt is one face of the janiform nature of money. The other face is the quality of money as circulating credit. The deposit which is the (bank) money – that is, credit, either extant as provided by the customer-depositor or newly created by the bank by granting a loan to the customer – operates as money through giro transfer to a different account, for example to pay the purchase price under an otherwise unrelated contract of sale. The deposit also denotes a debt directed to convert (in theory) the amount into cash if requested.

The operation of bank money as circulating credit is guaranteed in law by the possibility of the enforcement of the debt that bank money embodies. Here we have a practical application of the belief system on which money relies.[52] For a good measure this creed works because (a) it misdirects the customers' belief in enforcement by making them think that cash is money backed by real assets, such as gold, and/or can always be redeemed by the central bank which will discharge the corresponding debt expressed on the banknote as promissory note; and (b) it does not raise awareness of the workings of bank money which is often not appreciated as money in the proper sense at all, so that the wish to ensure enforcement does not arise in the first place. However, for the knowledgeable businessman, the banker and the lawyer, it is the legal enforcement which makes the circulating credit operative money. Money is a belief in effectual exchange against genuine values because the exchange is enforced by law, ultimately in a judgment debt in

48 See Chapter 2, sec. 4 and Chapter 4, sec. 4(b).
49 See Chapter 4, sec. 2.
50 See Chapter 2, sec. 4.
51 Lautenbach (1952: 45), Bank of England (2014a: 14), and Chapter 2, sec. 3(a).
52 See above under sec. 1.

enforcement proceedings. Or, to use an analogy from Christian religion, spiritual belief in God is good, temporal enforcement of this belief by the inquisition is better.

Finally, a note for clarification: enforcement does not automatically mean obtaining value; it only conveys a generally reasonable belief in obtaining value. In the situation of a financial crash, one can still enforce, but the economic result will usually be nil. The ability to enforce and the reasonable belief in a commercially satisfactory outcome delays a financial crash, but does not prevent it.[53]

The legal enforcement of the transmutational forces of money to effect exchange appears in the same janiform way as money does itself:

(1) There is the circulating credit or bank money used for the payment of a money debt under a separate contract, such as a contract of sale: one has to pay £20,000 for the purchase of a new car, for example. The circulating credit or bank money, whether it derives from a customer's deposit or from a bank loan, discharges the monetary debt to pay for the car when paid into the seller's account by way of giro transfer. The possibility of withdrawing the money from the buyer's account in cash (in case of bank money created through a granted bank loan this may not be allowed by the terms of the loan), and paying that cash into the seller's account (reconversion into bank money) is rather theoretical in business reality today. However, it is this possibility of withdrawing money from the bank account of the customer as the bank's depositor and lender (or borrower in case of a loan), either by transfer to a different account or by conversion into cash, which realises and enforces the debt (that is: money) the bank has vis-à-vis its customer-depositor. In the situation of the giro transfer the circulating credit or bank money remains in existence; it is transferred from one account to another.[54] The creditor-seller can insist on the discharge of the monetary debt through transfer of the circulating credit by bringing action for breach of contract and subsequent enforcement of the judgment debt. The reason why the seller's claim against the buyer can be discharged by the circulating credit – and is therefore money – is because the seller-creditor, as the buyer-debtor, can withdraw this credit that has been transferred into his account and thereby the debt of the bank as depositee will be discharged. If the bank refuses to pay out, the customer can sue and obtain a judgment debt, however under the factual proviso of the bank being a 'strong debtor'.[55]

(2) The second version of enforcement is in relation to the loan that the circulating credit constitutes. The customer-borrower has to repay his loan, and the bank is here invariably a 'strong creditor'.[56] Once the customer has repaid

53 See Chapter 4, sec. 4(b).

54 See also Lautenbach (1952: 45). Whether this transfer of bank money from one account to another is a genuine *transfer* or assignment in law, or whether the giro 'transfer' in fact extinguishes (or reduces) the credit with the transferor and creates the equivalent credit with the transferee, depends on the legal system in question, see Chapter 1, sec. 3(b)(iii).

55 This idea is discussed below under sec. 3.

56 See below under sec. 3.

his loan, bank money is destroyed through discharge.[57] This is the necessary consequence of money being a debt: no debt (or no credit from the creditor's perspective), no money. It is, however, not specifically the circulating credit, such as the £20,000 paid for the purchase of the car in the example above, which gets destroyed through the loan repayment. The destruction affects the quantity of money in the economy as a whole. When a loan is granted for the purchase of a commodity, and the deposit through which the loan is given is transferred to the seller's account for this purchase, the loan-debt and the circulating debt are split apart, that is, the two Janus-faces of the money created by the loan are separated from one another and have a different fate from then on. The loan-debt stays with the bank customer and debtor, while the circulating debt moves to a third person and from then on operates as money. It does so as long as it is used for the exchange into commodities or other *res* less than money, according to the transfer cycle: it then effects the transition from *m* to *C2*, in fact often an interposed chain of exchanges of money and money-like fungible *res* (shares etc.) *m1*, *m2*, . . . *mx* and finally against a commodity *C2* which constitutes real/contemplative value.[58] This goes on until the circulating debt is used to discharge another loan-debt in which case the debt, and therefore the money, will be destroyed. The fact that the bank as the lender can enforce the repayment of the loan, if necessary by instituting enforcement proceedings in law against the borrower-debtor, makes this loan-debt circulating and capable of operating as money.

Legal enforcement means that the exchange value of the money transferred becomes (re)converted into real value, that is, contemplative or use value in form of a commodity. For the lawyer, this makes the 'money' to money, as has been stressed several times already. A judgment debt will often yield an amount of money again, and that can be exchanged subsequently for goods. However, this does not have to be like that: enforcement of a monetary loan debt secured by a mortgage can either lead to the realisation of the property through sale where the proceeds go to the creditor for covering the outstanding loan debt, or can entitle to foreclosure, if legal systems still provide this remedy, as in England in theory.[59] If there is foreclosure, the securing property itself goes to the creditor in satisfaction of the debt after a court order, but this remedy has practically no relevance today where almost always an order for judicial sale is sought.[60] In Germany, there still seems to be an old-fashioned metallist perception of money in the civil code. The loan provisions under § 488 BGB require the lender to make money available to the borrower, and that money, it appears, would have to be cash, not just a bank money deposit on a bank account (being a promise to deliver cash in due course), to discharge the lender's obligation under the loan contract. In effect that would mean that the loan agreements under usual German banking

57 Lautenbach (1952: 45), Bank of England (2014a: 16).

58 See Chapter 4, sec. 4.

59 English Law of Property Act 1925, ss. 88(2), 89(2), 91 (2). This concerns the legal mortgage, not the equitable mortgage. (Scotland has different property laws).

60 Harpum et al. (Megarry and Wade) (2008: 1098–1102, 1125).

practices would be unenforceable under German law, and so bank money could not operate as, and be, money.[61] Unawareness of the money supply system and pragmatism presumably prompts German lawyers and courts to interpret bank money as money, so that the obligations under the loan agreement are fulfilled and bank money can be circulating credit and money as everywhere else.

Money as a debt not only means that there is no money without an enforceable debt (because the debt has been discharged); it also means that in order to be creditor as a depositor who has saved money, there must be corresponding debtors, otherwise the depositor's savings cannot exist. Therefore the politically popular requirement for economic austerity does not really hold good: if the state stops indebting itself by taking loans for investments (for example for improving the infrastructure), the debts must be incurred by the businesses or private households, especially if there are savings to be serviced, because if there are no debts, there is no money in a debt-based monetary system (and, from an economic perspective, no loans and no investment). It is also possible to export the debts to countries abroad, which Germany has done for years within the EU (with large savings, i.e. credits with large corresponding debts abroad, and with an excessive export surplus)[62] and has so contributed to the euro-crisis (official German politics would deny that). Germany produces and exports cheap commodities and loan-debt (through German and French banks as creditors) to mostly southern EU countries. But because of the internal market these importing countries cannot impose protective tariffs for their local trade, and because of the monetary union they cannot devalue their currency to become more competitive. That leads to a spiralling indebtedness of these countries, but is supposed to provide the corresponding debts to the claims in form of savings and pensions of German people in particular. An increase in indebtedness of the German state as a corrective would currently be a breach of a sacred dogma of economic policy in Germany and the EU.[63] However, the principle remains: if there are debts, also circulating debts as bank money, there must be credit and conversely. Or to put it even more explicitly in terms of the mechanics of accounting:[64] as far as financial assets are concerned,[65] if someone has more, somebody else must have less, because only one balance sheet is entirely equalised with all debts and

61 A more detailed discussion of this problem in Rahmatian (2018a: 233–234).

62 The United States also criticised that. The US Treasury was concerned about Germany's current account surplus, which accounted for the bulk of the eurozone area's surplus. See e.g. Shawn Donnan, 'US adds China, Germany and Japan to new currency watchlist', *Financial Times*, 29 April 2016.

63 See e.g. the critical discussion of the non-mainstream German economist Flassbeck (2013: 20–21, 29–37).

64 See Stützel (2011: 43, 51, 211).

65 This is true without qualification for financial assets, but not necessarily for real, physical, assets. However, as described in this book (Chapter 4, sec. 4, second and third rules), there is the trend of regarding real assets as financial or liquid assets-to-be, money *in spe*. Due to this financialisation, real commodities are increasingly treated as financial assets, so that the zero balance rule would apply to these as well in economic and accounting terms.

credits together being zero,[66] and that is the all-encompassing balance sheet of the whole world trade on the planet, unless we start trading with Mars or Venus.

Since money, especially bank money in practical terms, is circulating credit created by and consisting of enforceable loan debts, the monetary system invariably embodies a silent expropriation system. The borrower and loan debtor has to repay the loan with interest. The individual debtor may do so, and this is indeed very often the case. But the whole economy can never do that – if all debtors were able to pay their loan debts, there would be no credit, no money, no investment and no economy. Thus some debtors will fail to repay their debts; often, especially if these are states, regional authorities, municipalities or larger enterprises, their debts are rolled over only to a new loan, obviously with a higher capital and increased interest sum. At some point, however, because of an economic crisis (exacerbated by economic austerity measures, for example), or when the banks choose to do so, the lenders may call in their loans which leads to insolvencies and sovereign debt crises, and states, banks and communities will have to be saved with taxpayer's money. Private enterprises and individuals may simply become insolvent. In such insolvency proceedings the property of the borrowers gets taken away from them and (usually) liquidised in a forced sale by the liquidator. The borrowers lose their assets. Banks, who have created their own assets (the loan credit) without touching their existing assets, since the money creation happens out of nothing,[67] can now seize real assets or their liquidised monetary value. If (especially in the role as a surety) countries get into financial difficulty, lenders can obtain assets from the public purse, usually in form of taxpayers' money. Individually a person or a business can work harder or obtain a windfall profit through a commercially very successful invention, a legacy or a lottery prize which enables them to pay off their loan, and states may invade other countries to obtain raw materials and (slave) labour for free (colonialism was largely based on that idea), but in the national and world economy overall, the debts can never be repaid by all, and these debts rise with the interest attached to them. Once the debtors default on their loans, their property will be taken from them to make up for the shortfall, a systemic expropriation by stealth. Pointedly one could say, the political Left expropriates noisily and temporarily through revolutions, and the political Right expropriates silently and permanently through the monetary system.

The monetary system reflects the old Christian indebtedness to God, a debt which man can never discharge. The modern capitalist system has, it seems, cleared the legal construct of the debt from religious and moral connotations of sin and guilt, but debts serve as a very good device for social control, as religion in the past. Those who are indebted will not rebel in their workplace to keep their job. They will study diligently and follow eagerly und uncreatively the mainstream to obtain work that allows them to pay off their loans, or they will make

66 Therefore the world economy as a whole cannot 'save money', because credit and debt cancel each other out worldwide.

67 See Chapter 2, sec. 3.

obliging art to be commercially successful. Whether student loans, credit card debts or mortgages, these ensure that people live in order to work and to die free from debt, perhaps. However, it is not quite true that debt has no longer censuring moral overtones in the modern economy. For example, the well-known economist Irving Fisher said in 1929 that the devaluation of debts by inflation (with the effect that the creditor loses and the debtor gains) 'is no violation of the letter of the law as to debts, but there is a defeat of its spirit and intent' and it is 'social injustice', because 'something is taken away from its rightful owner', similar to a burglary or robbery in moral terms.[68] This moral argument seems to explain the very commercial fear of inflation which institutional lenders and creditors, and the obliging EU, the European Central Bank and particularly Germany seem to have today. Moral disapproval may also be targeted at states as debtors who do not want to or cannot pay. This happens in the EU as well. In the debate of the European Parliament of 8 July 2015 during the Greek debt crisis, the leader of the European People's Party, Michael Weber, pointed out reproachfully to the then Prime Minister of Greece Alexis Tsipras (who was present) that a partial cancellation of Greek public debts would have to be paid by the people of poorer countries in Europe, not by financial institutions, and he accused Tsipras of showing lack of solidarity with other European countries.[69]

Whatever the political implications and skirmishes, the banks – not necessarily individual institutions, but the banking sector as a whole – will always win as creditors in the long run, maintained by the legal enforcement regime for debts. This confirms that the rich need not break the law, while the poor must not break the law. The position of the banks is guaranteed by the fact that banks are established, partly by the law itself, as 'strong creditors' and at the same time as 'strong debtors'. This will be explained now.

3. The idea of the 'strong debtor' and the 'weak creditor' and the relevance of the corporate structure of banks

In the following section an idea is discussed that is largely alien to orthodox private law and commercial law doctrine and is very little reflected in statutes or case law, not even in consumer protection regulation that is naturally biased in favour of one party: the idea of the 'strong debtor'. This means that someone may be debtor of a money debt but has a much stronger power than another debtor of the same type (or even the same amount) of debt; indeed, the power as a debtor may be much stronger than the power of his creditor ('weak creditor'), contrary to the usual liberal concept of the debtor-creditor relationship.

68 Fisher (1929: 60–61).

69 Debate of the European Parliament following Conclusions of the European Council (25–26 June 2015) and of the Euro Summit (7 July 2015) (2015/2719(RSP)) and the current situation in Greece, Wednesday, 8 July 2015 – Strasbourg, available at: www.europarl.europa.eu/doceo/document/CRE-8-2015-07-08-ITM-003_EN.html (visited 28 June 2019).

The liberal philosophical foundation of modern private law and contract law is not supposed to cater for such phenomena. Everyone must be equal before the law, therefore the law regards someone technically only as debtor, a status that arises out of an agreed contractual relationship. The law must not notice whether the party in question is white or black, male or female, Jewish or Christian, a national or a foreigner, a company or an individual and so on. It must therefore be irrelevant whether the debtor, for example, is rich or poor, and whether or not he has economic power that makes him a 'strong debtor'. In reality it matters enormously whether a person who has got a claim has the wherewithal or the necessary political powers to enforce his or her right. Conversely, an economically powerful person or legal entity may resist successfully the enforcement of (theoretically unassailable) rights against them. Having a right and enforcing it are two very different issues – this observation is apparently so trite that it is never mentioned in law schools or court rooms. However, in corporate and banking law, the condition of the 'strong debtor' is an unacknowledged systemic part of the fabric of the monetary system, not a mere accidental circumstance of an individual case.

Before we embark on a discussion of this phenomenon, a few words of caution are necessary. It would be wrong and dangerous to dismiss this liberal system of private and commercial law outright. I give an extreme example that contours the problem more sharply. In spring 1938, when Austria was made to join Nazi Germany, many landlords in my native city Vienna gave certain tenants notices to quit because these tenants were Jewish. Some tenants went to court, and while many judgments were passed in favour of the landlords, other decisions declared these notices to quit as inoperative and void under the Rent Act, because the fact that a tenant was Jewish was no recognised ground under the (liberal) private law for a landlord's notice to quit or for an eviction.[70] National Socialist legislation subsequently stepped in with a decree in May 1939 that removed any protection for Jews from eviction.[71] One has to remember this historical background when one reads F. A. Hayek's *Road to Serfdom*, published in 1944:[72]

> The Rule of Law was consciously evolved only during the liberal age and is one of its greatest achievements, not as a safeguard but as the legal embodiment of freedom. . . . It may well be that Hitler has obtained his unlimited powers in a strictly constitutional manner and that whatever he does is therefore legal in the juridical sense. But who would suggest for that reason that the Rule of Law still prevails in Germany?

Hayek saw the solution in free markets in which politics and the law interfere as little as possible.[73] Politics should refrain from any planning according to an ide-

70 Graf (2004: 28).
71 Graf (2004: 25).
72 Hayek (2001: 85).
73 Hayek (2013: 275, 287, 482–483).

ology.[74] Hayek's strong rejection of planning must also be understood as a sharp criticism against Karl Mannheim, who proposed a planned democratic society against *laissez-faire* liberalism.[75] We know today that Hayek's approach can lead to developments that are similar to those he wanted to prevent at all cost – a 'neo-liberal' far-right governance, and the recent political developments in Europe bear that out.

Yet, there is something Hayek rightly noticed about the role of the law, and he was one of the few economists who was aware of the importance of law for economics. If the law is at all capable of, and willing to, protect the freedom of individuals and therefore also of minorities, then the reliable area of law to accomplish that is rather private and commercial law, not constitutional law. In constitutional law, nationals, citizens or human beings as right holders can easily be redefined and their rights reduced or taken from them, all in a legalistically correct process, and this happens regularly today, even in democracies: only one obvious case is the example of the circumstances around Guantanamo Bay[76] in the United States.

But it is much more difficult to wreck the legal framework of a sales contract. Constitutional rights need not be invoked by the powerful, and often they cannot be invoked by the powerless when it comes to the test. Put pointedly, constitutional rights and human rights contained therein are to a considerable extent an ideal to aspire to, a (changing) superstructure over pre-existing law, including (persisting) private law.[77] Human rights in particular increasingly seem to play to self-righteous moral superiority and conceal hypocrisies in liberal political circles.[78] In contrast, private law and the law of sale cannot be posturing gestures but must *work*, otherwise there is a resource distribution crisis which affects everyone, also the powerful. To make the law of sale and generally the laws of contract and property work, seller and buyer or creditor and debtor must be equal, at least for this particular transaction to make the transaction happen at all. Therefore Jews and other minorities could perhaps not buy land or obtain citizenship or significant jobs or get to positions of power in society, but at least they were able to sell goods or to lend money and so made a profit that allowed them to eke out an existence on the margins of society. Private law gave them a position of limited freedom and equality, though only in the moment of being a seller, buyer, creditor or debtor. However, this is obviously not a generally valid principle. For

74 Hayek (2001: 117–118), and Chapter 3.

75 Mannheim (1943: 100–111).

76 E.g. Clover (2004: 355, 359, 383).

77 Hayek's irreverent comments about constitutional law, including his criticism that legal theorists are for the most part public lawyers who therefore overemphasise the organizational aspect of public law over individualistic private law, still have a certain relevance, see Hayek (2013: 126–128).

78 The discipline of human rights provides an ample source for self-appointed progressive members of the powerful to appear committed and to feel good about themselves. Some of these dedicated members may then opt for a military intervention in another country on human rights grounds, as has happened for example in the Iraq War in 2003.

example, black persons, after formal abolition of slavery, were usually compelled to sell their labour force and were consequently also deprived of this very reduced equality that private law would otherwise have had for them.[79] In times of political crisis constitutional law cannot even guarantee this short moment of freedom that private law grants by conferring on the actors the roles of equal parties to a contract (or consumers/competitors in a market, as a free-market economist would say). Thus any trenchant criticism of liberalism and even 'neo-liberalism', however apt it usually is, should bear in mind the historical reasons for the belief in markets and the liberal interpretation of private law contracts.

The powers of private law that safeguard small areas of freedom and equality within the law of contract operate nevertheless to a certain extent only – and one sees these practical limits quickly when one considers dealings with corporations. The legal construct of the company is well known but not as well appreciated. One can ascertain five criteria which characterise a company today, and these criteria are broadly the same worldwide: artificial legal personality distinct from its members, limited liability,[80] transferable shares, delegated management to directors and economic ownership of investors or shareholder primacy.[81] This corporate structure diminishes the equal standing of debtor and creditor considerably, contrary to the liberal conceptions of private law.

It took the law quite some time to grapple with the creation of the artificial legal personality of the company and with the consequences of this creature.[82] It was only in 1897, with the English landmark case *Salomon v. Salomon*,[83] that the courts drew the full conclusions as to what independent legal personality entails:[84] complete separation of the company and its members, particularly separation of the company's assets in the company's ownership from members'/shareholders' personal assets. While trivial for the corporate lawyer (and, if needed, issues of company formation, limited liability, requirements for shareholders acquiring shares, powers and duties of company directors, shareholders' rights and derivative claims can be found in every company law textbook), some emphasis on the nature of the company's separate legal personality and on the company's property *in the company's ownership* is necessary, because non-lawyers, including economists, keep fantasising about shareholders owning the company or its capital[85] and similar inaccuracies which nevertheless often form the basis of business analyses.

An illustrative explanation for the idea of legal personality can be found in a decision from 1915 where it was said that the 'artificial legal person called the

79 See e.g. Zinn (2005: 209).
80 Davies and Worthington (2012: 35, 39).
81 Turner (2018: 121), Ireland (2010: 837).
82 See Pickering (1968: 485–489) for an overview of English nineteenth-century court cases characterizing artificial legal personality.
83 *Salomon v. Salomon* [1897] AC 22, HL.
84 Discussion of this celebrated case e.g. in Davies and Worthington (2012: 35–37, 42).
85 See the critical discussion by Ireland (1999: 32–33, 49).

corporation has no physical existence' but 'exists only in contemplation of law', as it has 'neither body, parts, nor passions'.[86] William Hazlitt's harsh criticism of corporate bodies in 1821 seems to follow on from these observations:[87]

> Corporate bodies are more corrupt and profligate than individuals, because they have more power to do mischief, and are less amenable to disgrace or punishment. They feel neither shame, remorse, gratitude, nor goodwill.

Uneasiness about the company existed right from its inception, especially the question of delegated management to directors which the separate artificial personality of the company necessitates. None other than Adam Smith said in 1776 about the emerging joint stock company in foreign trade:[88]

> The trade of a joint stock company is always managed by a court of directors. This court, indeed, is frequently subject, in many respects, to the control of a general court of proprietors [shareholders]. But the greater part of those proprietors seldom pretend to understand anything of the business of the company; and when the spirit of faction happens not to prevail among them, give themselves no trouble about it, but receive contentedly such half yearly or yearly dividend as the directors think proper to make to them. This total exemption from trouble and from risk, beyond a limited sum, encourages many people to become adventurers in joint stock companies, who would, upon no account, hazard their fortunes in any private copartnery [partnership]. . . . The directors of such companies, however, being the managers rather of other people's money than of their own, it cannot well be expected, that they should watch over it with the same anxious vigilance with which the partners in a private copartnery frequently watch over their own. Like the stewards of a rich man, they are apt to consider attention to small matters as not for their master's honour, and very easily give themselves a dispensation from having it. Negligence and profusion, therefore, must always prevail, more or less, in the management of the affairs of such a company.

Adam Smith's assessment is still valid. These days fully-fledged limited liability, separate from the shareholders' and the company directors' personal liability, brings much more comfort for risky business decisions and inefficient internal company management than unlimited personal liability. A company, with 'no

86 *Continental Tyre and Rubber Co. (GB) Ltd. v. Daimler Co.* [1915] 1 KB 893, at 916 per Buckley LJ, Court of Appeal. The House of Lords subsequently approved this statement in [1916] 2 AC 307, at 344–345.

87 Hazlitt, *Table Talks*, essay 27 (1903: 359).

88 Smith, *Wealth of Nations*, book 5, chapter 1 (2000: 800). Smith also said that such joint stock companies, like the Royal African Company or the South Sea Company, could only survive on the market because they were granted a state monopoly ('exclusive privilege') which shielded them from competition.

physical existence' and no 'passions', can be sent into insolvency fairly easily with limited loss for the investors/shareholders and the directors (breaches of the law excepted). A company can also be run even where it is in theory potentially always in a state of insolvency, and when the potential becomes actual, the shareholders' and company managers' personal exposure is nevertheless limited: this is the case of banks.[89]

While in the UK the modern legal understanding of the company was settled by the end of the nineteenth century, in France the equivalent *Société Anonyme* appeared much earlier, in the *Code de Commerce* of 1807, with predecessors in the *Ancien Régime*. The *Société Anonyme* was recognised as a separate legal entity, but what mattered more was the limited liability. However, well into the second part of the nineteenth century, the idea of anonymous and limited liability contradicted the sense of creditworthiness and the business ethics of the time, and so the *Société Anonyme* was long rather seen as an exception.[90] In Germany, the General German Commercial Code of 1861 introduced company law provisions, following largely earlier Prussian corporations ordinances, which established companies as legal entities.[91]

In the UK, banks were initially excluded from limited liability until 1858. The Companies Act 1862 established the first modern company law legislation, and banks established under the Banking Copartnerships Act 1826 could reregister under the 1862 Act to benefit from limited shareholder liability. However, not many banks took that step then. Shareholders in banks and depositors believed that unlimited liability ensured a more stable banking system because it would reduce transferring risk and excessive risk taking. This attitude changed with the collapse of the City of Glasgow Bank in 1878 and the subsequent passing of the Companies Act 1879 which facilitated the banks' conversion to limited liability.[92]

Unlike in the nineteenth century, banks are today always companies limited by shares, or corporate groups of companies, whereby the shares are invariably held by institutional shareholders.[93] The banker-customer relationship,[94] or in reality, the connection between Bank plc and Customer (private individual, sole trader, partners of a partnership, company), may be described more comprehensively, beyond the focus on contract in the decision of *Foley v. Hill*.[95] The depositor-customer is creditor (not beneficiary) of the bank which is debtor (not trustee).

89 See Chapter 2, sec. 3(c) and below.
90 Rochat (2018: 246–248, 250).
91 Guinnane (2018: 183).
92 Turner (2018: 135–136).
93 There are legal definitions of 'bank', for example in the UK Banking Act 2009, s. 2 and s. 91, whereby a 'bank' means a UK institution which has permission under the UK Financial Services and Markets Act 2000 to carry on the regulated activity of accepting deposits (as defined). However, here we are concerned with the corporate vehicle of the bank, not the banking business.
94 The term 'banker' is still used, also in textbooks, for example, Ellinger et al. (2011: 119), but an individual person today is always an agent of the bank as a corporate body.
95 *Foley v. Hill* (1848) 2 HLC 28.

The depositor-creditor is, however, not a creditor of equal commercial standing as he would usually be vis-à-vis a debtor to whom he has given a personal loan, or vis-à-vis a shop that is supposed to deliver goods to him under a contract of sale. He is rather a 'weak creditor'[96] of the bank, because he is an unsecured creditor who can theoretically withdraw 'money' from his account, that is, convert bank money into cash, but practically only if not too many other customers do that at the same time (bank run), otherwise his claim is thwarted or (effectively) cancelled altogether.[97] Furthermore, he obtains cash, again a debt, this time of the central bank, and it is a debt of which he is forced to become creditor by becoming the bearer of the banknote (promissory note). However, as already discussed,[98] this debt can never be redeemed, as it is never repaid. Only the creed, bolstered by monetary policy decisions of the central bank, that this circulating debt embodied in the banknote will ultimately lead to a transformation into a commodity of real (contemplative) value, makes this debt function as money.[99] The customer can seek to escape his insecure position as a creditor of a commercial bank by refusing to open a bank account (in modern life virtually impossible), but he cannot prevent his role as a notional creditor with a central bank, because he cannot avoid cash.

At least central banks are closer to democratic parliamentary control via the government and its finance minister, despite their (normally) formal independence. In contrast, commercial banks are not subjected to any outside control in relation to company management and politics, no matter who outside the company may be postulated as 'stakeholder' (employees and other non-shareholders affected by the company's actions).[100] The shareholders' control in general meetings of the company is typically theoretical, particularly with institutional shareholders,[101] and many shareholders may hold non-voting shares anyway.[102] A cashless society based on bank money only (also private cryptocurrencies) would therefore be entirely withdrawn from any political control and supervision, especially because of the corporate structure of commercial banks.

The corporate structure of commercial banks makes banks 'strong debtors' and evidently also 'strong creditors'. The phenomenon of the 'strong creditor'

96 See also Chapter 2, sec. 6(a).

97 The claim is *thwarted* if cash can be obtained up to a certain maximum limit, beyond which there is only the availability of bank money; the claim is *effectively cancelled* if the customer is relegated to being an unsecured creditor of an insolvent bank; the claim is *formally cancelled* if an administrative decision by the banking authorities stops the paying out to customers from their bank accounts.

98 See Chapter 2, sec. 2.

99 Application of particularly the fourth rule in Chapter 4, sec. 4(a) above.

100 Deakin (2017: 57).

101 On the problem of the disengagement of institutional shareholders, and the 'stewardship code' as a countermeasure, see e.g. Reisberg (2015: 113).

102 It is noteworthy that in order to achieve more success with the public offering of shares, as early as 1928 the father of public relations, Edward Bernays, gave guidance as to how to counteract the undermining of public confidence in large corporations because of the shareholders' illusory voting power, see Bernays (2005: 95).

is easily explained. As discussed before,[103] banks as creditors of loans, which are invariably secured beyond a certain amount, always have the wherewithal and commercial power to enforce these loans in law if there is a default. Even where a debtor's insolvency may lead to a write-off of the outstanding debt, banks are unlikely to suffer financial difficulties with the usual private and business loans. Furthermore, banks are normally able to recall their loans early which usually provokes the borrowers' insolvency, and that allows banks to control significantly the market competitors of their own shareholders, of their group companies, and of the credit market generally. The corporate structure, especially the limited liability, allows banks to pursue less risk-averse lending than would be the case with unlimited and personal liability, a point Adam Smith already made. Furthermore, apart from raising capital through share issue as any company, banks can shore up their finances by creating new money if they find new borrowers as debtors, an option not available to a non-bank. Thus banks benefit in three ways from the present monetary system: first, they obtain the repayment of the capital of the loan they have granted without the loan sum coming from actual banks' funds.[104] Second, they obtain the interest on the loan. Third, they may obtain the secured property from the debtor (or money in lieu of the property in enforcement and insolvency proceedings), in case the debtor does not keep up repayments of the loan. All this obviously makes banks strong creditors.

The banks' position as a 'strong debtor' results predominantly from their corporate structure as well. A 'strong debtor' is a debtor who is commercially more powerful than the creditor, even in case of default. If a bank becomes insolvent, which means, the company-bank as independent legal person becomes insolvent and the shareholders become deferred creditors ranking at the bottom of the list of creditors of the insolvent company.[105] Thus commercially their claim under their shares can be written off. The company continues to exist as a separate legal person managed by the liquidator[106] in the company's name instead of the directors, until the company is wound up and dissolved.[107] Whether the company is trading or insolvent: once the share has been paid up, there is no shareholder liability at all because the company members are not liable for the company's debts (limited liability); even before the share is fully paid, the shareholder is technically a guarantor of the company for the outstanding amount (in case of a company limited by shares) and not directly liable to the company's creditors.[108] The shareholder's loss is restricted to the value of the share invested. If it is an

103 See above under sec. 2.

104 See Chapter 2, sec. 3.

105 In the UK: Insolvency Act 1986, s. 74(2)(f). Goode (2011: 253, 275).

106 In the UK: Insolvency Act 1986, s. 167. See also Banking Act 2009, s. 99 for bank liquidators.

107 Davies and Worthington (2012: 1284).

108 Davies and Worthington (2012: 39–40). In the case of the company's insolvency, see e.g. UK Insolvency Act 1986, s. 74(2)(d): if it is, as almost always, a company limited by shares, no contribution is required from any member exceeding the amount (if any) unpaid on the shares in respect of which he is liable as a member.

institutional shareholder, the 'personal' loss in form of the lost investment in the share is that of another company which may, in the worst case, suffer its own subsequent insolvency, again with the loss limited for that company's shareholders. A personal liability for the shareholders or directors does not arise at all (leaving aside rare instances of lifting the corporate veil),[109] and an economic loss that hits someone's personal property can be mediated and watered down immensely with chains of institutional shareholdings. Thus the only ones who are personally affected by a bank's failure are the customers-depositors as creditors of the bank, particularly individuals and customers who are not larger corporations.[110]

After the financial crisis in 2008–9, recently enacted special bank insolvency provisions[111] have alleviated the problem for depositors, and deposit guarantee schemes have been introduced. For example, the UK Banking Act 2009, s. 99, requires bank liquidators to work with the Financial Services Compensation Scheme (FSCS) as a statutory fund of last resort to ensure that eligible depositors have their accounts transferred to another financial institution, or receive payment from, or on behalf of, the FSCS.[112] Such statutory funds are also endowed with money created through loans in a functioning financial system and can give protection only in very locally confined crises; a bank's collapse quickly descends into a general systemic failure where neither a sound financial institution taking over deposits can be found nor a payment (capped anyway) out of the statutory emergency fund can be ensured. This is the reason why the separate rules for bank insolvencies have not been discussed here;[113] that special regime provides additional safeguards, but does not change anything in relation to the conceptual principles. As *borrowers*, customers obviously do not escape liability for their loan; this claim would be enforced by the liquidator on behalf of the bank.

The company directors or governors of the bank are not personally liable for the bank's debts either, this is the bank as a company and separate legal entity. There is of course the possibility that a company director becomes personally liable to the company or an outsider because he has committed a tort (negligence etc.) or a criminal offence.[114] An outsider may also establish vicarious liability of the company-bank for the tort committed by a director as its agent, whereupon the bank can then turn on the director for recovery,[115] though with very uncertain commercial success, especially in view of the size of a bank's business transactions. However, in practical terms it is very rare that a personal liability of a director can be established successfully. Making the wrong business decision that may cause the failure of the business does not automatically result in civil or

109 Davies and Worthington (2012: 214–223).

110 Traders using a corporate vehicle in form of a small limited company (including 'one-man companies') are economically hardly in a better situation as creditors of a failing bank than individuals.

111 At EU level the Bank Recovery and Resolution Directive 2014/59/EU.

112 The deposit limit covered under the FSCS is (as at 30 January 2017) £85,000.

113 For the UK, see Banking Act 2009, ss. 94 et seq.

114 Davies and Worthington (2012: 39, 191).

115 Davies and Worthington (2012: 196).

criminal liability; on the contrary, this would be an exceptional case. The same applies to directors of banks. These may be tempted to invoke *Foley v. Hill* as guidance for a standard of care in their management: 'The money [deposited] is . . . the money of the banker, to do with it as he pleases . . . he is not answerable to the principal [customer] if he puts it into jeopardy, if he engages in a hazardous speculation'.[116] It is clear that this statement no longer applies literally,[117] but, according to the present legislation, financial speculations as such, also those which later turn out to be risky or fatal, are not unlawful *per se*; and even where there has been illegal deception, this is hard to prove. Also, a disqualification of the company directors for unfitness to manage (dishonesty is not required) is very uncommon.[118] Here moral and legal condemnation can diverge widely. For example, the chief executive whose management decisions were considered to have contributed significantly to (effectively) the collapse of the Royal Bank of Scotland (RBS) in 2008[119] with the biggest annual loss in British corporate history,[120] did not seem to have faced criminal or civil liability,[121] and it is highly unlikely that he, or other directors, ever will.[122]

In addition, banks could be considered as potentially insolvent in the normal condition of operating, unlike a regular trading company of the 'real economy', such as a factory producing goods. This is particularly so if one queries the distinction between liquidity and solvency; a distinction that makes much less sense in case of a bank,[123] compared to a normal trading company. The non-monetary assets of a normal company can be the largest share, like buildings, stock, plant and machinery, and vans. The non-monetary assets of a bank (buildings, computers) are comparatively unimportant. As said before, the functioning of the banking system depends on the banks being solvent by giving the impression of liquidity. They keep honouring low-level debts and deposits without ever being put to the test: the customers' right to withdraw funds exists individually but not in aggregate. No banker could pay all his liabilities in cash on demand and, in that sense, is always insolvent.[124] It is therefore not an overstatement to say that banks

116 *Foley v. Hill* (1848) 2 HLC 28, at 36.

117 On the Corporate Governance Code and its application to banks, see e.g. Walker-Arnott (2015: 46, 55–58, 69), and the (weak) legislative reactions in the UK to the financial crisis regarding corporate governance of banks in the Financial Services and Markets Act 2000, s. 59ZA ('senior management functions'), introduced in 2013.

118 Lowry and Edmunds (2015: 92).

119 Financial Services Authority Board (2011: 34, 38–39, 221–235), Lowry and Edmunds (2015: 82–83).

120 Peter Thal Larsen, George Parker and Jane Croft, 'RBS taps UK Treasury for £25.5bn', *Financial Times*, 26 February 2009.

121 An action by shareholder investors for allegedly having been misled into buying shares in May 2017 (which was settled out of court) was directed against the bank, not the CEO, see Kirstin Ridley, Andrew MacAskill, 'RBS shareholders accept last-ditch settlement meaning Fred Goodwin spared court appearance', *The Independent*, 30 May 2017.

122 Lowry and Edmunds (2015: 83, 95).

123 See e.g. Goodhart (2002: 229, 231–232).

124 Crowther (1946: 45).

operate permanently in a form of insolvency. No banker would asseverate this fact; it would make bad press. However, it is difficult to expect from the executive board of a bank to distinguish between business decisions which lead to 'good' insolvencies, where the bank keeps trading as this is technically the permanent status of a bank, and 'bad' insolvencies, where the bank ends up being put to the test and invariably fails and is then typically rescued by the state anyway to avoid a systemic breakdown of the banking sector. Against such a background it is hard to establish a standard of care and to detect negligence, which would trigger the directors' civil liability. A directors' personal loss or liability for the bank's debts as a psychological corrective is ruled out because of the separate legal entity of the bank as a company.

The corporate structure of banks crystallises the age-old criticism of the separate legal personality of companies, which may have begun with Adam Smith if not earlier. With the possible exception of large institutional shareholders, ordinary shareholders have no factual control over the management of the company and its property, this is left to the directors. Ownership of company property lies technically with the company, but is invariably managed by its agents (directors), so there is a separation of ownership from control. The link between ownership and management is legally provided by the directors' duties owed to the company (not to individual shareholders).[125] It is a tenuous link that is difficult to substantiate, particularly in banking business, despite existing statutory definitions.[126] The separation of ownership from control results in a separation of management power from responsibility, because neither the shareholder-'owner' has responsibility as would be the case with a normal property owner,[127] nor the managing directors have responsibility that materialises in legal liability (provided they act within the usual standard of reasonable care, skill and diligence), as such liability always strikes the company as a separate legal entity. Shareholders are not owners of the company and have no direct interest in the company because the shares are separate property independent from the property of the company.[128] However, without obligations, responsibility or liability, shareholders enjoy income rights as dividends. Thus irresponsibility is built into the corporate legal form.[129] Calls for rethinking or restricting limited liability, after the 'calamitous decision in *Salomon v. Salomon & Co. Ltd.*' (Otto Kahn-Freund), have been, and probably remain, unsuccessful.[130]

Banks and their management can and do benefit widely from this corporate structure, and virtually always with impunity. Furthermore, unlike other companies, banks can additionally rely on their systemic importance for the economy.

125 Berle and Means (2003: 80–82, 113–114, 196–197, 250).
126 In the UK, Companies Act 2006, s. 174.
127 Berle and Means (2003: 249–251).
128 Ireland (1999: 41, 49).
129 Ireland (2010: 845).
130 Kahn-Freund (1944: 54–55), Ireland (2010: 848).

In the worst situation, when a bank becomes insolvent, or more precisely, when a bank actually collapses, rescue by the central bank and the state authorities is likely to happen to prevent a meltdown of the banking system.[131] So even the last sanction against a company – insolvency – is effectively eliminated, and the restructured bank can then carry on business, largely in the same way as before. With banks the real economic risks are assumed, not by the banks, their shareholders or their management, but by the depositors of the bank and its borrowers, by other participants of the financial system,[132] as well as by emergency lenders to the bank, such as states (via their central banks) in situations of bank rescues. Thus the bank is unquestionably a 'strong debtor': where a bank is debtor, this is a problem for its creditor, not the bank. The liberal idea of the law that all debtors and creditors are of the same standing has no sense for the different shades and qualities of the role of the debtor. The Treaty on Stability, Coordination and Governance (TSCG) and the European Stability Mechanism (ESM) of the European Union that seek to safeguard the financial system after the banking crisis in 2008–9 have only reinforced the banks' powerful position.

4. Strengthening the power of banks by the European Stability Mechanism (ESM)

The financial crisis of 2008–9 led to a government debt crisis (sovereign debt crisis) because some states in the euro area within the EU found it more and more difficult to refinance their existing maturing debts by borrowing new money from the financial markets. This was partly because states were compelled to bail out collapsing banks, partly because some states (Portugal, Ireland and Greece) became considered as high risk creditors on the credit market which increased considerably the cost of borrowing for them. With the rising of borrowing cost, states found it increasingly impossible to raise finance on private markets and were sliding towards state default. The 'bailouts' of (that is: loans to) the troubled states – Ireland,[133] Portugal and Greece – was initially achieved by financial assistance from the International Monetary Fund (IMF) and by two temporary measures within the EU, the European Financial Stability Mechanism (EFSM) and the much larger European Financial Stability Fund (EFSF). The grant of the

131 The rescuing states may even be ridiculed by the bankers of the failing banks, as happened, according to published recordings of telephone conversations, in the case of the collapsing Anglo-Irish Bank which was saved by the Irish state with largely German money, see 'Merkel hat für lästernde Banker nur Verachtung übrig', *Handelsblatt*, 28 June 2013.

132 Nesvetailova and Palan (2017: 277).

133 The UK quite keenly provided loans to Ireland in 2010 (see also UK Loans to Ireland Act 2010, ch. 41, s. 1(3): maximum loan payment to Ireland of £3,250 million until Dec. 2015), mainly because of its own banks' significant exposure to the Irish economy, see e.g. Scott Hamilton, '[Bank of England Governor Mervyn] King Says U.K.'s Exposure to Ireland is "By no means Trivial"', *Bloomberg News*, 16 November 2010.

loans was conditional upon the rigorous implementation of economic austerity measures.[134]

The legal structures of both the temporary EFSF and of the permanent ESM that succeeded the EFSF are unusual: they are not based on EU law, but on intergovernmental treaties between EU member states formally outside EU law. The EFSF and the ESM were created in the context of eight pieces of EU legislation on economic governance, including the Treaty on Stability, Coordination and Governance in the Economic and Monetary Union ('Fiscal Compact') of 2 March 2012.[135] The EFSF, designed to be a temporary measure until 2013 (it finally lasted until September 2012) was founded by an intergovernmental decision as a private company under Luxembourg law, whereby the shareholders of this company were all EU member states that were also eurozone members.[136] The ESM, which followed the EFSF, was constituted in September 2012 as an international organisation with its seat in Luxembourg, based on an intergovernmental treaty between 17 euro area member states to establish a permanent crisis mechanism to safeguard the financial stability of the eurozone.[137] Unlike the preceding EFSM and EFSF, the purpose of the ESM is to provide a permanent international financial facility under stipulated conditions to counteract financial difficulties that endanger the financial equilibrium in the eurozone and so to improve a country's financial stability and the whole eurozone.[138] Structurally the ESM imitates the IMF.[139]

Neither the EFSF nor the ESM has adopted legal forms within national constitutional laws and EU (constitutional) law where, as part of a democratic constitutional framework, organs of legislative control (a parliament) or judicial

134 Hinarejos (2015: 11–12, 24), Stein (2014: 25), Mitchell (2015: 257–271). This terse outline has only its relevance for the present topic in mind; it does not intend to be exhaustive in any way.

135 De Witte (2015: 437–438). On the Fiscal Compact, an intergovernmental treaty outside EU law between 25 EU States, see particularly Art. 3, which requires contracting parties to ensure a budgetary position of their governments that is balanced or in surplus. Given that money is a debt and therefore requiring debtors, this rule effectively means that if states are not to be in government debt, then somebody else has to be indebted (enterprises, private households, countries and economies abroad), otherwise there is no money (since repayment of debt destroys money).

136 Adam and Parras (2013: 849–850).

137 Armstrong (2013: 605–606), Schwarz (2014: 391), Adam and Parras (2013: 849–850).

138 The prevalent political idea (particularly instigated by Germany) has been that the euro is essential for the continued existence of the EU (arguably a questionable political position), see Peter Spiegel, 'If the euro falls, Europe falls', *Financial Times*, 15 May 2014.

139 Schwarz (2014: 391). See Art. 3 of the Treaty Establishing the European Stability Mechanism (ESM) (ESM Treaty): 'The purpose of the ESM shall be to mobilise funding and provide stability support under strict conditionality, appropriate to the financial assistance instrument chosen, to the benefit of ESM Members which are experiencing, or are threatened by, severe financing problems, if indispensable to safeguard the financial stability of the euro area as a whole and of its member states. For this purpose, the ESM shall be entitled to raise funds by issuing financial instruments or by entering into financial or other agreements or arrangements with ESM Members, financial institutions or other third parties'.

control (courts) could intervene in the operation of these financial mechanisms. The EFSF was formally a private limited liability company, and the ESM is an international organisation, both technically outside the EU and EU law. The ESM also follows the structure of a private company limited by shares,[140] with legal personality,[141] shares[142] with dividends payable in principle,[143] and a governance regime similar to that of companies.[144] The ESM as an 'international financial institution'[145] is not strictly speaking a bank (although it cooperates with the European Central Bank),[146] but it benefits from the corporate structure of banks[147] and engages in typical banking business (lending). Furthermore, unlike a normal company or bank, but rather in line with international organisations, the governors, directors and other staff members of the ESM enjoy complete immunity from legal proceedings with respect to acts performed by them in their official capacity; official papers and documents are also protected.[148] The Board of Governors decide on any dispute arising between an ESM member and the ESM,[149] and there is a final appeal to the CJEU for an ESM member against the governors' decision.[150] However, this regulatory framework is not exactly like diplomatic immunity for staff of embassies or international organisations, for diplomats do not enjoy immunity in their own sending state, and a receiving state can declare a diplomat as a *persona non grata* and then stop recognising immunity.[151] An ESM board member, however, only loses immunity if it is waived by the Board of Governors;[152] a real outside control or challenge by an EU member state or by organs of the EU is not provided. In fact, this is banking business, though perhaps more emergency loan central banking business (financial assistance), safeguarded against judicial control or other interference by democratic

140 ESM Treaty, Art. 8(5): 'The liability of each ESM Member shall be limited, in all circumstances, to its portion of the authorised capital stock at its issue price. No ESM Member shall be liable, by reason of its membership, for obligations of the ESM'.

141 ESM Treaty, Art. 32(2).

142 ESM Treaty, Art. 8(1) (Authorised capital stock: EUR 700,000 million, divided into seven million shares, having a nominal value of EUR 100,000 each, available for subscription). See also Art. 41 (payment of initial capital).

143 ESM Treaty, Art. 23.

144 ESM Treaty, Art. 4(1): 'Board of Governors and a Board of Directors, as well as a Managing Director and other dedicated staff as may be considered necessary'. See also Arts. 5–7.

145 ESM Treaty, Art. 1.

146 See ESM Treaty, Art. 11 on the contribution key for subscribing to ESM authorised capital stock.

147 See above under sec. 3.

148 ESM Treaty, Art. 35(1): 'In the interest of the ESM, the Chairperson of the Board of Governors, Governors, alternate Governors, Directors, alternate Directors, as well as the Managing Director and other staff members shall be immune from legal proceedings with respect to acts performed by them in their official capacity and shall enjoy inviolability in respect of their official papers and documents'.

149 ESM Treaty, Art. 37(2).

150 ESM Treaty, Art. 37(3). The procedure is Art. 273 of the TFEU, see ESM Treaty, recital 16.

151 Vienna Convention of Diplomatic Relations 1961, art. 9.

152 ESM Treaty, Art. 35(2)–(3).

and constitutionally legitimised institutions – whether of EU member states or the EU itself.[153] The structure of the ESM as a kind of private but quasi-sovereign joint stock company recalls Adam Smith's criticism of the Royal African Company and similar entities of his time which enjoyed an exclusive privilege by charter.[154] One can hardly resist the pointed remark that this structure could be the blueprint for the future of multinational corporations, especially commercial banks.

The constitutional method with which the ESM had been established has attracted much comment and criticism. That theme is outside the present discussion, so a few remarks must be sufficient. It appears that rules-based governance in the EU becomes gradually replaced by framework norms that are further developed and substantiated in a post-legislative phase in which the boundary between rule-formation and rule-implementation gets blurred. In addition, in the legislative packages responding to the financial crisis there is a diffusion of the structures and processes of policy co-ordination as a new form of governance.[155] It is also noteworthy that the ESM was established outside the legislative framework of the EU as a treaty under general international law. One reason was the European Council avoiding an open conflict with Art. 125 TFEU which prohibits the EU or its member states from becoming liable or assuming commitments of other member states ('no-bailout clause'). While the temporary ESFM was, and could probably be, based on Art. 122 TFEU (EU assistance to a member state permitted in situations of natural disasters and exceptional occurrences beyond its control), this was not available for the ESM as a permanent financial facility, but an EU Treaty change to Art. 125 was politically not realistic.[156] A Council Decision amended Art. 136 TFEU and provided some legal anchorage for the ESM in EU law.[157] However, the European Parliament[158] and the European Central Bank[159] expressed their preference for the financial stability mechanism being embodied *within* the EU legal system.

153 See e.g. Schwarz (2014: 402–404).

154 Smith, *Wealth of Nations*, book 5, chapter 1 (2000: 800–801), and see also above under sec. 3 for Adam Smith's criticism of the delegated management of such companies.

155 Armstrong (2013: 608–609).

156 Tomkin (2013: 171–172).

157 Subsection (3) was added to Art. 136 TFEU by way of European Council Decision of 25 March 2011 (2011/199/EU) that came into force on 1 May 2013, see Schwarz (2014: 405). It provided that 'the Member States whose currency is the euro may establish a stability mechanism to be activated if indispensable to safeguard the stability of the euro area as a whole'.

158 In particular pt. 7: 'the intention to establish the permanent stability mechanism outside the EU institutional framework poses a risk to the integrity of the Treaty-based system', see European Parliament Resolution of 23 March 2011 on the draft European Council decision amending Article 136 of the Treaty on the Functioning of the European Union with regard to a stability mechanism for member states whose currency is the euro (00033/2010 – C7-0014/2011 – 2010/0821(NLE)).

159 Opinion of the European Central Bank of 17 March 2011 on a draft European Council Decision amending Article 136 of the Treaty on the Functioning of the European

A challenge to the compatibility of the intergovernmental treaty for the ESM with the EU Treaties was brought before the ECJ in *Pringle v. Ireland*,[160] but was unsuccessful.[161] In particular, the court held that the no-bailout clause of Art. 125 TFEU did not prohibit financial assistance by the ESM because that financial assistance is subject to conditions 'provided that the conditions attached to such assistance are such as to prompt that Member State to implement a sound budgetary policy'.[162] Furthermore, the recipient member state remains liable for its own debts and commitments, and the ESM does not act as a guarantor of the member states' debts.[163] Therefore neither the ESM or EU nor other member states assume commitments of the recipient member state in breach of Art. 125 TFEU. The ECJ confirmed that the ESM is not subject to the EU Treaties, the Charter of Fundamental Rights or general principles of EU law.[164] Not surprisingly, critics of the legal framework of the ESM have pointed out that the funding mechanism of the ESM is subject to almost non-existent parliamentary oversight, both at the national and European levels,[165] that the circumvention of the EU Treaties challenges the EU's fundamental commitment to respect the rule of law, and that this circumvention also gives the impression that legal principles and provisions which are adopted by democratically elected representatives of the EU member states are in fact subordinated to political considerations.[166]

The powers of the ESM are far-reaching and can affect the economic and political situation of ordinary people immensely,[167] but there is no democratic corrective via a parliament or elected government – on the contrary, the organs of the ESM itself enjoy complete immunity. The example of Greece is a drastic case in point. In 2015, when Greece required financial assistance again in the context of a renegotiation of its bailout programme, the ESM provided such financial assistance through the Third Economic Adjustment Programme for Greece.[168] The circumstances of the negotiation and the treatment (some may say, humiliation) of Greece in the negotiation leading to the Greek government's request of 8 July 2015 to the ESM for stability support in the form of a loan can be gathered from the press.[169] In accordance with the amended Art. 136 (3) TFEU ('The granting of any required financial assistance under the

---

Union with regard to a stability mechanism for member states whose currency is the euro (CON/2011/24), especially pt. 8.

160 *Pringle v. Ireland*, Case C-370/12, 27 November 2012.

161 Tomkin (2013: 179–180), Adam and Parras (2013: 851).

162 *Pringle v. Ireland*, para. 137.

163 *Pringle v. Ireland*, para. 138.

164 *Pringle v. Ireland*, paras. 178–182.

165 Dawson and De Witte (2013: 833).

166 Tomkin (2013: 188).

167 See e.g. Schwarz (2014: 391–392, 397) with the example of Cyprus.

168 Council of the European Union: www.consilium.europa.eu/en/policies/greece-the-3rd-economic-adjustment-programme/ (visited 17 June 2019).

169 E.g. Neil Irwin, 'How Germany prevailed in the Greek bailout', *New York Times*, 29 July 2015; Katie Allen, 'Greece crisis timeline: the weekend that rocked the eurozone', *The Guardian*, 29 June 2015; Ambrose Evans-Pritchard, 'Greece is being treated like a hostile

mechanism will be made subject to strict conditionality'), Art. 3 ESM Treaty ('to mobilise funding and provide stability support under strict conditionality'), and the *dictum* in *Pringle*,[170] the ESM observed carefully the requirement of strict conditionality upon which the loan was to be granted. The conditions were, as usual, stipulated in the accompanying memorandum of understanding (MoU) which sets out the obligation of domestic economic and public administration reforms.[171] In the case of Greece, this MoU of 19 August 2015 between the ESM, represented by the European Commission, and Greece contains essentially a corset of special measures:[172]

> Pt. 1: This Memorandum of Understanding (MoU) has been prepared in response to a request of 8 July 2015 from the Hellenic Republic to the Chairperson of the Board of Governors of the European Stability Mechanism (ESM) for stability support in the form of a loan with an availability period of three years. In accordance with Article 13(3) of the ESM Treaty, it details the conditionality attached to the financial assistance facility covering the period 2015–18. . . . Success requires ownership of the reform agenda programme by the Greek authorities. The Government therefore stands ready to take any measures that may become appropriate for this purpose as circumstances change. The Government commits to consult and agree with the European Commission, the European Central Bank and the International Monetary Fund on all actions relevant for the achievement of the objectives of the Memorandum of Understanding before these are finalized and legally adopted.

One example of the numerous measures imposed in the MoU can be found in pt. 2.1 (Fiscal Policy):

> The Greek authorities commit to ensuring sustainable public finances and achieve sizeable and sustainable primary surpluses over the medium-term that will reduce the debt to output ratio steadily. The authorities will accordingly pursue a new fiscal path premised on a primary surplus targets of –1/4,

occupied state', *The Telegraph*, 13 July 2015; Wolfgang Münchau, 'Europas Rückfall', *Spiegel-Online*, 13 July 2015.

170 *Pringle v. Ireland*, para. 137: no breach of Art. 125 TFEU, provided that the conditions attached to financial assistance are such as to prompt that member state to implement a sound budgetary policy.

171 Armstrong (2013: 602).

172 Memorandum of Understanding between the European Commission acting on behalf of the European Stability Mechanism and the Hellenic Republic and the Bank of Greece, 19 August 2015, available at: https://ec.europa.eu/info/sites/info/files/01_mou_20150811_en.pdf (visited 16 June 2019), pp. 4, 6. See also ESM Press release, 19 August 2015, available at: www.esm.europa.eu/press-releases/esm-board-governors-approves-esm-programme-greece (visited 16 June 2019).

> 0.5, 1 3/4, and 3.5 percent of GDP in 2015, 2016, 2017 and 2018 and beyond, respectively. The trajectory of the fiscal targets is consistent with expected growth rates of the Greek economy as it recovers from its deepest recorded recession.

It becomes doubtful as to what extent the sovereignty of Greece as an independent country and, at the same time, as a member state of the EU has actually been preserved. This is an obvious example of the fact that whole states are now firmly in the grip of the banking and financial system, here via the supranational device of the ESM which has been created, but is hardly controlled, by the EU. While the EU probably had the opportunity to rearrange and reform the banking system after the financial crisis of 2008–9, it chose to put itself decisively under the control of the banks and empowered them further, although ironically, not the EU or its member states had to be rescued, but the banks. The raising of funds for financial assistance by the ESM also happens on the financial market, with the involvement of (private) banks,[173] ultimately for the rescue of banks or states defaulting because of the collapse of their banking sector. The next financial crisis is likely to be orchestrated and remedied by the banks, and the EU will be relegated to an executory role.

5. Alternative concepts of money

After having read through this book, the reader may have come to the conclusion that the present monetary system is fundamentally flawed, and so one expects alternative concepts of money which could improve the situation. There are indeed alternatives to the present system of money, but these would require a book on its own for a proper discussion, and there is practically no political will in governments and parliaments to change the system as it is.[174] This is also, perhaps regrettably, the general opinion of ordinary people: there is no widespread interest in, or no understanding for, the operation of the monetary system, and whether a specialised book like this one will change that significantly is doubtful. Even the problem of climate change, although scientifically more complex than the monetary and economic system, attracts more political interest, but there is almost no recognition of the connection between the current system of money

173 See also Recital 12 of the ESM Treaty: 'In accordance with IMF practice, in exceptional cases an adequate and proportionate form of private sector involvement shall be considered in cases where stability support is provided accompanied by conditionality in the form of a macro-economic adjustment programme'. An elastic interpretation of 'exceptional cases' may often be appropriate.

174 The debate in the (rather empty) UK Parliament on 20 November 2014 on money (Hansard, House of Commons, Debate: 'Money Creation and Society', HC 20 November 2014, Vol. 588, col. 434, see also video: www.youtube.com/watch?v=bXOkmD8Eozs, visited 11 June 2019) was an exception and did not go anywhere. The promoter of the debate, Steve Baker MP (Conservative), is now a Brexit hardliner busily trying to get the UK out of the EU.

and climate change which could increase an interest in theories of money instead of merely increase interest on money.[175] Thus in order to avoid indulging in lengthy utopian ponderings, any discussion about alternative concepts of money must be confined to a very brief sketch.

Alternative systems of money pursue different solutions to the problem that (a) money is a (circulating) debt or credit, (b) money as a debt attracts interest, (c) money has a store of value function which invites speculative hoarding, (d) money creation is private through commercial banks which makes public democratic accountability impossible, (e) there is hardly a practical limitation to the creation of money by commercial banks, and (f) there is no real value which is commensurate with or balanced against the amount of money created, because money is created through loans out of nothing. Most importantly, alternative concepts of money seek to convert money into a genuinely neutral medium of exchange, that which orthodox economics claims money already is. Two important forms of alternative money are 'demurrage-charged money' and 'plain money' ('sovereign money').

In the late nineteenth century, the German-Argentinian merchant Silvio Gesell (1862–1930) made a proposal for an alternative money system,[176] which had some relevance in central Europe in the early 1930s and also gained some favourable discussion in Keynes's *General Theory* (1936).[177] Modern regional currency projects are, to some extent, influenced by Gesell's concept of 'demurrage-charged money', also called 'stamped money' (*Freigeld*, 'free money', or *Schwundgeld*, 'depreciating money'), or 'money with assured circulation' (*umlaufgesichertes Geld*). The idea is that with such money, hoarding and speculation is prevented. There is an incentive to invest because there is pressure to circulate money as it depreciates; the amount of money circulating should correspond to the amount of commodities offered to eliminate speculation and to stabilise purchasing power. For Gesell money represents demand, the commodity represents supply; the purchase price has nothing to do with either: the value of money is rather defined by speculation and hoarding which seeks to withdraw money from circulation. Price is defined by supply and demand. Less money in circulation increases the price of money (and reduces the prices of commodities), and the

175 Unbelievably, there are now even plans for extraterrestrial mining of minerals and precious metals to maintain economic growth (i.e. ecologically non-sustainable growth) of about 3% per year (partly prompted by the monetary and financial system). See Ian Sample, 'Protect solar system from mining "gold rush", say scientists: Proposal calls for wilderness protection as startup space miners look to the stars', *The Guardian*, 12 May 2019.

As with interest on debts, this growth, for example of 3%, is supposed to grow exponentially, thus in ten years, as a rough guide, leaving aside particularly technological advances, the exploitation of resources must have grown by about 34%, because $100 \times (1 + 0.03)^{10} = 134.39$. If the earth cannot sustain this, then one apparently wants to exploit the moon and the asteroids instead.

176 Dillard (1942: 348).

177 Keynes, *General Theory* (1964: 353–358); Darity (1995: 27–28). Schumpeter, in turn, credited Keynes for having unearthed Gesell, see Schumpeter (1954: 1118), note 2.

bankers as the owners of the money can determine the price of money by deciding on the quantity of circulating money. Ironically, the state requires payment of the taxes with money, that is, property owned by private bankers.[178] When the farmer pays debts with the banker's money, then the use of that money is granted against interest which the farmer also pays indirectly by paying higher prices to the grocer who himself has borrowed money from the bank with interest.[179] In fact, money must be a communal means of payment and the bankers' money privilege must be abolished.[180] Gesell rejected (in 1892!) the gold-based currencies and favoured paper money instead to ensure better circulation;[181] he also rejected the idea that money is a commodity and a measure or representative of value, especially the value of labour.[182] Commodities decay and rust, money does not; the supply side is controlled by the fear for the decay of the commodity, while the demand side, that of money, is not.[183] Therefore, money should imitate commodities and their limited lifespan to counteract the powers of the holders of money.[184] Money should also 'rust' and decay, whereby the paper note should indicate, not a claim to an exchange into gold or silver, but rather a decreasing amount of (notional) units of commodities over time which can be bought with this paper note. These 'rusting banknotes' are really demurrage-charged money, which forces the circulation of money and is counterintuitive to hoarding.[185] Money should be compelled to circulate by means of a periodic tax which would offset the preference of wealth owners for hoarding money rather than spending it on commodities or other form of productive wealth. Gesell employs interest as a payment to prevent the hoarding of those who hold money.[186]

Gesell's writings, which show some influence of Proudhon,[187] are not free from a certain confusion and disarray, but contain some valuable ideas (leaving aside his anti-Semitism).[188] Keynes seems to have taken a similar view,[189]

178 Gesell (1892: 6, 9, 12–14, 40).

179 Gesell (1892: 46). This is an important insight because Gesell (possibly unknowingly) considers money as circulating credit or janiform debt that is created through an interest-bearing loan, see also Chapter 2.

180 Gesell (1892: 14).

181 Gesell (1892: 25–26).

182 Here Gesell makes the amusing comment about Marx, Gesell (1892: 36): 'Marx was not a merchant anyway, or if he was, he must have conducted his business in a very petty(minded) manner; I would not have given him a loan at any rate, because anybody who builds his business on such a theory today, becomes bankrupt in an instant'. Own translation.

183 Gesell (1892: 68–69).

184 Gesell (1911: 139).

185 Gesell (1892: 102–105). More detailed description of this 'reform money' in Gesell (1911: 135–149), here Gesell replaces the commodity units by notional money units.

186 Dillard (1942: 349).

187 E.g. Proudhon, *System of Economic Contradictions, or the Philosophy of Poverty*, chapter 10 (2011: 231–233), Gesell (1911: 138).

188 Gesell (1892: 86, 88, 94–96). In Gesell's examples, the speculating merchants and bankers are always Jews.

189 There is some academic discussion whether Keynes was much more indebted to Gesell than appears at first sight, see Darity (1995: 30–33, 38–39). This debate cannot be pursued here.

but criticises Gesell for not having realised that not only money has a liquidity-premium attached to it – money has just a greater liquidity-premium than any other commodity. If currency notes lose their liquidity premium by stamping in the case of demurrage-charged money,[190] then many other substitutes would emerge, such as bank money,[191] foreign money, precious metals and jewellery, as well as real estate.[192] Keynes's view must even be more accurate in the light of the position taken in this book – money and other commodities are only distinguished by their level of liquidity and obtain their value through exchange.[193]

There was one major project in history, in the small city of Wörgl in Tyrol, Austria, in 1932–33 that applied Gesell's alternative money concept. The city authorities of Wörgl issued stamped money or 'free money', as it was called, and, with this experiment, tried to counteract unemployment and lack of economic growth during the Great Depression. The paper notes issued lost 1% per month and 12% per year of their value (a stamp of 1% of the note's face value had to be bought and affixed on the note each month to retain the validity of the note). The notes were backed by cash deposited with local savings banks. The experiment stimulated the local economy and was a success; it also attracted great interest from abroad, notably from France and the United States, and many towns and communities in the region started to introduce their own stamped money system. As the Austrian National Bank (central bank) feared the undermining of its monopoly to issue money, it attained the prohibition of this alternative money as of September 1933.[194]

The other major alternative concept of money, and not confined to a local scheme,[195] is 'sovereign money' or 'plain money' (*Vollgeld*), as opposed to debt-based bank money.[196] A major representative of this approach is the German economic sociologist Joseph Huber (born 1948). His concept of sovereign money is essentially a Chartalist idea of money: the whole amount of (sovereign) money in an economy would be created and issued by an independent and impartial state body, typically a central bank, and only sovereign money would be circulating instead of a split between circulating and reserve money. The central bank would no longer be the bank of the banks, and would even become less a bank carrying out banking business, but would be the sole source of official money. In this function, the central bank would join the legislative, executive and judicial powers in the state as the fourth 'monetary power', being the sovereign money-issuing body: the principle of separation of powers would thus be guaran-

190 The demurrage would be charged with demurrage stamps affixed on the paper note.

191 However, today, with the computerised electronic system of bank money, such reduction of value over time could be implemented technically.

192 Keynes (1964: 357–358). Keynes also criticised Gesell's theory of the rate of interest.

193 Chapter 4, sec. 4, first and second rules.

194 Schwarz (2008: 46, 55, 67, 70–73), Blanc (1998: 475–476).

195 Gesell's demurrage-charged money would invariably be a purely local project, see Blanc (1998: 479–480).

196 See e.g. the information on plain money of the not-for-profit campaign organisation 'Positive Money' in London, https://positivemoney.org/ (visited on 20 June 2019).

teed.[197] Most importantly, commercial banks would lose their monetary privilege to create bank money, and money would no longer be created by way of credit, thus money would no longer be a debt. In this way, commercial banks would really operate as financial intermediaries, as some theories wrongly claim they do already now:[198] they would still lend (debiting from the customer's perspective) and deposit (crediting), but it would always be the transfer of existing funds, not created ones through credit/loan. Thus banks would remain private lenders; money, however, would turn into a public good. Money would no longer be credit, and providing enough money would not mean providing enough credit. Central banks would create the money, commercial banks would lend existing money, and in this way, central banks have genuine control over the quantity of money. Sovereign money would not be lent (is therefore debt-free and interest-free in nature) but be spent into circulation and would thus represent genuine seignorage, similar to historical coins issued under royal prerogative. Besides, there would be interest-bearing seignorage which would be sovereign money lent to banks – here there would be a normal debtor-creditor relationship, unlike with the issuance of sovereign money. Hence sovereign money should be regarded as government equity rather than as government debt.[199] Sovereign money is therefore not a 100% reserve banking system[200] but based on one integrated money supply. The introduction of sovereign money into the economy would happen over an appointed period of time (suggested are three to five years), whereby the bank money on customer current accounts with commercial banks would be converted into (sovereign) money, and the liabilities of the banks would be converted into a (real?) liability to the central bank. A repayment of a loan would not lead to a destruction of bank money (by way of redeeming the debt that money constitutes), but to a receipt of sovereign money that can be reused (as it is plain or 'full' money).[201]

The constitutional aspect is perhaps the most obvious problem of this reform proposal, among several others. If debt-money, which bank money on commercial banks' customer accounts constitutes, is converted into sovereign money, it is debatable whether the transformation of a debt-*res* (debt) to a non-debt-token-*res* (equity) could actually be a form of constitutionally unlawful expropriation. In any case, it would be an interesting task for constitutional lawyers to develop the argument whether these different types of *res* are equivalent. Another point, also related to constitutional law, is the actual position of the central bank in the framework of separation of powers in the state. It is unpersuasive to postulate the

197 Huber (2017: 144–145, 146–148, 151).
198 See Chapter 2, sec. 1.
199 Huber (2017: 154–155, 157–161, 166, 169).
200 As proposed particularly by Irving Fisher in 1936, see Fisher (1936: 406). The suggested solution is to keep a 100% cash reserve behind all demand deposits. The idea of nationalizing money supply but not nationalising banking and the lending of money to bankers is what the 100% money and the sovereign-money proposals share.
201 Huber (2017: 171–172, 179).

central bank as a separate 'monetary' state power, rather than to subject it to the executive power which is ultimately answerable to a parliament as the legislature. Otherwise it would assume a position of independence similar to the judiciary, and there is no reason to grant a central bank that role in a reformed monetary system.

The second major objection to Huber's proposal derives from private law and banking law. If Huber says that there is no natural imperative that money must be created as a credit and debt relationship and that '[t]his is just banking doctrine',[202] then there is another usual misapprehension of economists and sociologists about the concept of money. This is not just 'banking doctrine', but the law: the law decides whether there is money and determines its conceptualisation – currently as a debt, both for cash/central bank money and commercial bank money. It is theoretically possible to change the law and enact a system of sovereign money, but politically such an absolutely necessary Act of Parliament is a complete illusion. A lack of understanding for the division between the positive law (*de lege lata*) and future legal policy (*de lege ferenda*) appears in Huber's claim that there be a false identity of money and credit: if money is lent, he says, that indeed involves a debtor-creditor relationship, but payment upon sale, however, does not involve credit and debt but settles the transaction, and donating money is just a gift. Money and debt are two different things and therefore have two different words: we pay our debt with money. Granting a loan creates a debt, while transferring money discharges an obligation to pay, there is no 'credit'.[203] Either one considers this severe misunderstanding of the concept of money as the result of the wrong assumption that the proposed sovereign money is already the reality of the present monetary system (why then the proposal?), or there is no appreciation of the janiform nature of money that is created in form of a debt, both as a loan-debt to be repaid, and as a circulating debt to operate as money. When I pay for goods sold in a contract of sale, I discharge the debt from the sales contract with another debt (though not to the seller) in form of money.[204] In the transaction there are different types of debt involved, and while not every credit/debt is money, money is a form of credit, inexorably. If this is denied, then the usual view of much of orthodox economic doctrine is just reiterated, that money is only a neutral token and medium of exchange. Both the lack of understanding of the legal concept of money and the apparent endorsement of the understanding of money by orthodox economics undermine seriously the value of this proposal for monetary reform.

Regional and complementary currencies[205] sometimes show some influence of ideas deriving from depreciating money and sovereign money. The introduction of a sovereign money system (*Monnaie pleine/Vollgeld*) for Switzerland was put

202 Huber (2017: 167).
203 Huber (2017: 94–95).
204 See Chapter 2, sec. 4.
205 An overview of types of complementary currencies e.g. in *Komplementärwährungsgutachten Sparkasse Delitzsch-Eilenburg* (2004), sections 3, 4 and 5, available at: https://

to a referendum on 10 June 2018,[206] but was soundly rejected.[207] In Switzerland, there is perhaps the oldest still existing complementary currency, the 'WIR' ('*Wirtschaftsring*') since 1934,[208] founded as a cooperative bank (WIR-Bank), which initially took some of Gesell's ideas and established a system of book debts and credits. It is the world's largest and oldest exchange of all types of goods and services based solely on a private or 'club' form of money in a permanent mutual association of small businesses and household members. The prices are quoted in units of WIR-credit which are denominated in, but not exchangeable for, Swiss francs. On purchase of goods the seller obtains a credit with the buyer and the buyer a debt with the seller (today with the use of smartphones). The WIR-system is a form of extended multilateral trade credits on a permanent basis not redeemable in the national currency. Every WIR-credit matches an equal corresponding WIR-debit, so the system overall nets to zero.[209] In Upper Bavaria, in the Chiemgau region, there is the complementary currency of the 'Chiemgauer' since 2003.[210] It is a monetary system valid only within a smaller region and fosters money velocity against hoarding, so again an idea taken from Gesell. The 'Chiemgauer' is demurrage-charged money expressed in euros and exists as vouchers (notes) or in electronic form (debit card). The rules governing the 'Chiemgauer' are decided democratically within the community. Euros can be exchanged into 'Chiemgauer' (1 = 1 exchange) which are accepted in businesses in the region. An exchange back to euros is possible but attracts a 5% fee, which goes to charitable causes. All users of the 'Chiemgauer' must join a community benefit society (*Verein*).[211]

As already said, alternative systems of money are even more at the margins of academic research than the existing system of money, and their practical relevance is comparatively microscopic in size. Some texts on alternative monetary systems may have the irritating air of a religious doctrine of salvation, but that they share with the accepted religion, free market economics and its soteriology. Local alternative currencies for local communities may be appealing, particularly if one is an accepted part of the community. However, too much emphasis on locality can breed 'identitarian' in-group feelings which often postulate a hostile out-group, and regional complementary currencies might reinforce such identity building. The ensuing protectionism would not only be detrimental to the economy – a local complementary currency in a megacity is hard to imagine anyway – it would

---

monneta.org/komplementaerwaehrungsgutachten-sparkasse-delitzsch-eilenburg/ (visited 20 June 2019). This area would require extensive academic research.

206 See e.g. Romaric Godin, 'Comprendre le débat suisse sur l'émission de monnaie', *Mediapart*, 2 June 2018.

207 See e.g. SRF website for the results (75.7% against, 33.8% participation), www.srf.ch/news/schweiz/abstimmungen/abstimmungen/vollgeld-initiative/vorlaeufiges-schlussresultat-stimmvolk-erteilt-vollgeld-initiative-eine-klatsche (visited 20 June 2019).

208 See www.wir.ch/ (visited 20 June 2019).

209 Stodder (2009: 80–82).

210 See www.chiemgauer.info/startseite/ (visited 20 June 2019).

211 Gelleri (2009: 63–64, 69–71).

also hamper a liberal and humanist worldview in relation to fellow human beings internationally. Putting it maliciously, a neo-liberal monetary system may lead to one's starvation because of its inherent expropriation scheme in favour of the rich,[212] but at least it is irrelevant whether one belongs to a selected local community, or whether one is white, black, an Arab, Chinese, Mexican or a Jew.[213] If there is any salvation for mankind, then it must learn to live with the paradox of being indigenous and global at the same time, a conglomerate of personal local communities and generous citizens of the world who may also use regional currencies.

212 See above under sec. 2.
213 See above under sec. 3.

Conclusion

Money is a legal concept which lawyers have left to economists to deal with, at least as from the early 1900s. Therefore lawyers have rarely considered the nature and origin of money in law, and are almost exclusively concerned with issues of law on payment and money transfers, the bank-customer relationship and other matters of banking law. Economists usually take money for granted and reiterate, without reflection, the usual (sociological) definition of money as a medium of exchange, unit of account and store of value, criteria which indicate what money does, but not what money is, and where it comes from. Paradoxically, however, economists then omit money, the supposed medium of exchange, from the microeconomic market model and conceptualise incorrectly a sale involving money as a form of barter where money naturally does not feature.[1] This is consequent in a certain way, because money and money supply can only be explained as a legal creature, ultimately based on statutory and case law, where economists, being from a different discipline, need not contribute to.

Money is a practical example of the conception of dematerialised property in legal theory and property theory. The principal idea of this conception is that in order to turn 'things' in a very broad sense in the factual, material world into objects recognised by the normative world of the law, the law attaches an 'ought' to the 'thing': a property right or real right, most importantly, ownership. The right creates the thing for the purpose of the law: this thing, or *res*, is the 'property object', an abstract legal notion, which can, but conceptually does not have to be, represented by a physical object as social reifier. So the *res* or property object can be reified by a chattel or by a cheque; the *res* itself can be the legal notion of 'tangible property' (moveable or immoveable) or a legal concept itself, such as an intellectual property right or a debt, or, as here, money. The reification of cash is in form of banknotes and coins, the banknote being historically and conceptually still a promissory note (negotiable instrument). The reification of bank money is hardly extant; it merely consists of the numbers as account entries.[2]

Cash (the most important form of central bank money, besides the central bank reserves) and bank money (commercial bank money), as still almost the

1 Chapter 1, sec. 1, Chapter 3, sec. 1.
2 Chapter 1, sec. 2.

only versions of money in existence today, are a form of debt in law from the debtor's perspective or, from the creditor's perspective, a form of credit. This becomes apparent in the examination of the money creation process. Looking at bank money first (more than 95% of all circulating money in the economy is bank money), one realises – what neither orthodox nor critical economists or accountants normally do – that this type of money is the result of legal rules. It was particularly the English landmark case *Foley v. Hill*, decided by the House of Lords in 1848, which gave existing banking practise the legal backing and effectively made bank money functioning money. According to this decision, a customer depositing money, for example cash, in his bank account becomes the unsecured creditor of his bank, whereby the bank is not trustee of the customer in relation to the deposited money, and therefore does not keep the deposited money in a separate trust account. The relationship is just a contractual debtor – creditor-relationship, the customer being creditor of the bank which has to pay out the amount in credit on demand or under the specific stipulations of the account agreement. Bank money in the customer's account is therefore credit; any common distinction between money and credit which can be found widely in economic literature is inaccurate and against the law.[3]

When a customer obtains a loan from the bank, the bank 'pays' the loan sum into the customer's account, so that it appears in the customer's account as credit in favour of the customer, in the same way as if the customer had deposited the sum with the bank from his own funds. Thus the bank creates this credit or money by indebting itself, for it is invariably debtor in relation to the loan sum standing to the customer's credit in the account. Since the bank remains debtor in relation to the loan sum – because the loan money is not paid out to the customer-borrower in cash – it converts the loan sum debt deposit into a nominal and fictitious customer deposit, by re-classifying its liability: the loan payment debt (in cash) becomes a deposit debt to be paid out in principle. The bank can do that because it is a 'reservoir of money': it need not segregate customers' money because it is not the customers' trustee, but their contractual debtor. Only banks have the privilege of re-classifying their liabilities, unlike non-banks who have to segregate customers' money in separate trust accounts. As this re-classifying of liabilities shows, the loan money does not come from funds elsewhere in the bank, as would be the case with a non-bank lender granting a loan. The assets side of the bank is rather matched by the liabilities side of the bank, and this mere lengthening of the bank's balance sheet is the new money, created out of nothing through an accounting entry. It appears as credit in the customer-borrowers' account.[4]

Among economists the financial intermediation theory of money – loans are granted out of banks' deposits, the bank is only an intermediary – is widely accepted, but it contradicts actual banking practice, and it is also incompatible with current banking law. The fractional reserve theory of money (of each loan

3 Chapter 1, sec. 3, Chapter 2, sec. 1.
4 Chapter 2, sec. 3.

a certain percentage, usually less than 10%, has to be deposited with the central bank to ensure capital adequacy) is not a constitutive element of the money creation process, but rather a (mostly psychological) measure to maintain customers' confidence in the liquidity of the banks. Economics textbooks frequently claim that the central banks have the power to influence the money market by prescribing the fractional reserve percentage, but that is today not even claimed by at least one of the representative central banks, the Bank of England.[5] Thus the so-called credit creation theory of money, the third theory of money supply, is not actually a theory, but describes alone adequately the money creation process according to banking practice and according to the law.[6]

The reason why this new credit as a result of the grant of the loan is money, is because it is circulating credit. The loan money credited to the customer-borrower's account does not stay there but is used for payment and thus introduced into the economy. Money is therefore a janiform *res*:[7] it is (1) a *res* constituting a loan debt, with the borrower as debtor, and at the same time (2) the *res* is a credit or debt of a bank, originally with the borrower as creditor (since the loan sum has been paid into his account), but after the borrower's payment of the loan sum to a third party under an unrelated contract of sale, for example to the seller of a flat, the seller is creditor (because her account is credited as a result of the buyer's payment to her) and typically another bank is debtor, depending on which bank the seller has her bank account with. This credit has entered the economy and can be used for further payments: the credit has become circulating credit, that is, money. At the same time the borrower remains under the obligation to repay the loan, which destroys money,[8] because repayment means a discharge of the debt, that is, the debt that money constitutes is extinguished. Therefore the creation of money by commercial banks through credit (loans) is not entirely unrestricted, because loans granted also keep being repaid somewhere in the economy, and often old loans are repaid with new loans. However, the systemic boundaries for money creation (fractional reserve system, Basel Accord) have very limited practical relevance.

The quantity of bank money also rises because of the interest attached to the debt that money constitutes. Bank loans are in reality never interest-free. Since the capital is created through a bank loan, but the interest is not, repayment of the interest must be achieved with higher productivity, a greater exploitation of resources (also human labour), new loans with which old loans (or at least their interest sum) are repaid, and so on. This rolling over of increasing credit is a feature of the modern economy.[9]

5 Bank of England (2014a: 16).
6 Chapter 2, sec. 1.
7 Chapter 2, sec. 4.
8 However, it does not destroy the specific circulating credit created as loan sum and used for the purchase of the flat in the example above; when money is destroyed by way of loan repayment, this refers to the quantity of money in the whole economy.
9 Chapter 2, sec. 5.

Cash, in so far it is in form of banknotes, was historically also bank money, the debt-*res* of the banks (the credit-*res* of their customers) having been reified in form of an IOU, the banknote. In the nineteenth century the issue of banknotes has become confined to central banks (there are some exceptions). After the abolition of the gold standard this debt has become nugatory: the promise of a ten-pound note only extends to two five-pound notes in exchange, for example, not to the equivalent in gold. However, technically the banknote still embodies the central bank's debt to the respective holder; it is an eternal debt that will not be repaid by the bank. The law provides that only cash is legal tender, that is, cash (banknotes and coins) must be accepted by the creditor in full discharge of the debt owed to him (*fiat money*). In this way, money, although intrinsically worthless, can operate as a medium of exchange. Thus one debt, for example the purchase price arising from a contract of sale, is discharged through another debt, here money in form of cash. The concept of legal tender becomes increasingly obsolete because higher sums of payment are invariably accepted in form of bank money (the only practical form of payment), and more and more cash payment limits are in operation.[10]

The creation of cash is based on legal provisions (currency laws in the respective jurisdictions), and central banks are entrusted with the issue of cash (banknotes). The issue of the economically irrelevant coins lies either with central banks or with special bodies under the supervision of the respective ministry of finance.[11] There is also at least framework legislation in place that determines the maximum amount of banknotes to be issued, taking account of monetary policy decisions. In contrast, there are no specific statutory rules that provide for the creation of bank money: at best one can say that the creation of bank money through credit/loans is a customary law or at least commercial practice which the courts of law take for granted, otherwise certain decisions on banking law and money would not make sense. In Germany, however, such an interpretation is fraught with difficulties, because the creation of bank money could be considered as contravening a provision in the German Banking Act, but in practice this rule seems to be a dead letter. A sound statutory basis for the creation of bank money through credit does not seem to exist.[12]

Thus one can summarise: money, bank money as well as cash, and also electronic money where it is money at all (doubtful in case of certain cryptocurrencies at the moment),[13] is circulating credit, or put differently, a legally enforceable debt.[14] For this reason, the postulation of the orthodox microeconomic market model that money is merely a neutral unit of account and medium of exchange is untenable.[15] In fact, money is a *res*, property, that influences the price and any

10 Chapter 2, sec. 2.
11 Chapter 2, sec. 2.
12 Chapter 2, sec. 6.
13 Chapter 2, sec. 7.
14 Chapter 2, sec. 4, Chapter 5, sec. 2.
15 Chapter 3, secs. 1–2.

presumed market equilibrium. Money as a debt also attracts interest (practically relevant is only commercial bank money, not central bank money except, particularly, emergency loans of the central bank and the like). The way in which economists, taking account of the non-neutrality of money, need to reconceptualise the microeconomic market model must be left to them as experts of their discipline. However, the non-neutrality of money appears in the phenomenon of price making through lending, since for example prices on the property market can be driven up by the banks granting higher loans through credit out of nothing, or in the fact that prices rise because they have to cover sellers' increased debts because of the accruing interest which the loan as the source of the money attracts.[16]

The historical reason for the editing out of money from the relevant forces of the market is probably the polemic of the classical school of economics, particularly by David Hume and Adam Smith, against mercantilism. According to them, money (at that time commodity money, precious coins) has no value in itself, hence any hoarding of money and increase of the amount of money through an export surplus, as mercantilism claims (at least in Adam Smith's biased depiction), is meaningless. Real wealth is ensured and disseminated with free trade. From that idea follows Hume's classical quantity theory of money: if the quantity of money rises, so will the prices accordingly, and the proportion of value between money and commodity does not change. Thus in this view money is economically a neutral entity.[17] In the twentieth century, Milton Friedman has reformulated this classical quantity theory of money, and while the actual economic aspect of his theory is of little interest to the present legal theory of money, his presuppositions connect with the concept of dematerialised property and are therefore important here.[18]

Friedman presumes that there is essentially not a clear distinction between money and other assets, including human capital, that is, human labour force. In the terminology of dematerialised property, one can say, all assets are *res*, only with a different level of liquidity. One can call the legal transformation of everything into a *res* in law as 'propertisation', because only by turning whichever entity into property it becomes incorporated into the normative world of the law. This propertisation brings about a standardisation, the *res* being an easily interchangeable and fungible commodity, so that process can also be referred to as 'commodification'.[19] If the simple exchange of the commodity is the highest aim, it reaches a level of soon-to-be-money, money *in spe*, almost as liquid as the most fungible of all property, money. This interpretation of all *res* as potentially being money can be termed 'monetisation'. This conception is the first ingredient of the explanation of the role of money in the alienation cycle or transfer cycle.

The second element for the explanation of the function of money in the alienation cycle is a structural survey of the social relations that money operates in

16 Chapter 2, secs. 3, 5.
17 Chapter 3, sec. 2.
18 Chapter 3, secs. 3–4, Chapter 4, sec. 4.
19 Chapter 1, sec. 2, Chapter 4, sec. 4.

or creates. These aspects or cases of money can be conceptualised in parallel to the 'cases' in the grammar of languages, for example in Latin. The *first case* is the case of naming: money is money because it is named as such by law – this is particularly so with regard to fiat money or legal/compulsory tender issued by the central bank (banknotes and in the UK coins issued by the Royal Mint) but also with bank money created by commercial banks, where there is no explicit legal rule that terms it 'money'. Money is created as, and constitutes, a legally enforceable debt. The *second case* of money is the case of origin: the medium of exchange must derive from a legally devised or recognised origin or source to be money. Only if the medium of exchange is created by a source designated by law or recognised by law (the second category encompasses digital currencies of 'private' origin which can be used to discharge debts provided the law regards the debt as extinguished)[20] it is money, so it must typically originate from a central bank (cash) or a commercial bank (bank money), whether it is metal, paper, electronic. The *third case*, the case of giving or transfer and transaction, denotes that money in its role as medium of exchange transforms the property commodity into the seller's expectation to be able to retransform it later to another (as yet unspecified) property as buyer in a subsequent purchase from another seller, without conferring any legal entitlement to a specific item of property. The *fourth case* highlights the fact that the medium of exchange can operate as money in law because it constitutes a debt that is enforceable by law (*casus accusativus*, that is, 'arraign') but also because the money debt can discharge another debt (*causativus*). Furthermore, it denotes the essential debtor-creditor relationship between bank and customer/account holder which is the basis for bank money and the customer-creditor's enforceability of his claim vis-à-vis his bank.[21]

Particularly the third case of money (*casus dativus*) points towards the third ingredient of the alienation cycle: money is a transmuting agent that brings out the higher form of liquidity in every commodity or *res* through the exchange for which money is the medium. This notion essentially derives from the philosophical concept of alchemy. For the alchemists, well into the seventeenth century, the art of alchemy only perfects nature; it does not create new matter, but brings the perfect matter out of the imperfect one, such as gold out of lead, through the process of transmutation with the aid of the 'philosopher's stone' or 'tincture' or 'elixir'. However, the philosopher's stone or the transmutation are primarily philosophical concepts, not chemical processes (which would be impossible anyway).[22] Money also performs such a 'transmutation' in the exchange. It is not just a medium of exchange, but a means to delay the exchange by granting the recipient of the money an expectation to realise value in the future. In a sale, money as the agent 'transmutes' the real commodity, a tangible or intangible commodity with use value/contemplative value, into an imaginary commodity or anticipated commodity, whereby the imaginary commodity, represented by the

20 Chapter 2, sec. 7.
21 Chapter 4, sec. 2.
22 Chapter 4, sec. 3(b).

money with purely an exchange value, is to be retransformed into a real one at a later date. Money as the 'philosopher's stone' or agent brings out the exchange value already contained in commodities which have primarily a contemplative or use value. It raises their liquidity: assets (including human capital) must be monetised to obtain value, following Friedman. Every commodity is ultimately money-to-be, and can be exchanged, that is, sold, otherwise it is worthless in the present market system.[23]

With these three ingredients one can formulate the alienation cycle which consists of two components: the externalisation or transfer cycle and the estrangement cycle.

The externalisation cycle stresses that the concept of money must be a time-bound dynamic one, a *process* that the exchange, induced by money as the agent, constitutes, not a time-independent static one[24] where money, eventually obliterated from the microeconomic market model, brings about an immobile point between supply and demand as the equilibrium price. The exchange value of a commodity (or more generally: *res*) matters, and not the contemplative value, and it is the exchange value which money brings out in the transfer or exchange (sale), therefore it is the (dynamic) exchange process or transfer which constitutes the value: not existing values are transferred in a sale, mediated by money as a neutral medium of exchange, but the transfer itself constitutes the value through 'transmutation' of the money which brings out the higher level of liquidity in the commodity (*res*) transferred.

One can therefore formulate four rules which form the basis of the transfer cycle. (1) The exchange creates the value; only in the temporary process of the exchange the potential and contemplative value of a *res* becomes an actual value, and the higher liquidity makes the contemplate value of the *res* irrelevant. (2) Since the exchange itself creates the value, there is a drive for as many exchanges as possible in as little time as possible to approximate *res* closely to the most liquid form of *res* – money; the realisation of the value of *res* which have exclusively an exchange value from the outset (shares etc.) exists in their exchange/transfer only. *Res* with a contemplative value are increasingly absorbed by the financial market as financial assets *in spe* with a lesser liquidity; so that the 'real economy' becomes merely a special case of the financial economy. (3) Money as the catalyst or agent transmutes the commodity that is the object of the sale into money-to-be, and brings it closer to the most liquid *res*, money (liquidifying of the commodity), but it also operates as an exchange delay, since there is only an expectation to complete the barter in the future and to obtain another commodity. (4) The concrete quantity of money in an economy is only of limited relevance: what matters is if and to what extent money, irrespective of its actual quantity, can be believed to effect exchanges and the transmutations these exchanges entail.

23 Chapter 4, sec. 3(c).
24 Chapter 4, sec. 1.

The transfer cycle comprises a commodity *C1* (real commodity with contemplative or use value) being changed into money *m* (imaginary commodity with exchange value or expectation value) and *m* exchanged against another commodity *C2* in the future (barter delay, and conclusion of the transfer cycle). Usually, the transfer cycle is much longer, *C1-m1-m2 . . . mx-C2*, whereby *m1 . . . mx* need not always be money in the narrow sense, but other *res* with exchange value only, such as shares and financial products. Traders will often seek to delay a retransformation from *mx* to *C2* that completes the transfer cycle. They rather want to abstract from, say, the stage of *m2* some *res* to themselves in form of fees, commissions, bonuses, private purchases of property (given that every exchange from *m1* to *m2* to *m3* etc. will involve a price increase, that is, exchange value increase if the market is buoyant), because the whole quantity of money in the broad sense with purely an exchange value can never be tied to corresponding *C2*s with a contemplative value. Therefore the retransformation from *mx* to *C2* needs to be drawn out as long as possible before the bubble bursts when *mx* can no longer effect a transmutation into real, or contemplative, value in form of a *C2*.[25]

Alienation or transfer can also lead to estrangement. Alienation, as a further development from Marx's conception, is today, in the service industry of the Western world, rather the version of nobody obtaining any relationship to physical things with which he can seek to express himself (even where that is only a version of commodity fetishism), because exchange value trumps contemplative value these days. Products are no longer made for use, but for sale, with an ever shorter lifespan to compel replacement purchases to push economic growth without ecological sustainability and to service interest payments on loans across the whole economy. Value is only realised through exchange, and the more exchanges, the better for earning exchange value. The estrangement is usually also cyclical, like the transfer cycle, because exchanges and services against payment are frequently interposed in human relationships, commodify them and sell them back to the humans concerned, thereby emulating the real relationship with the commodity sold: a common example are the ubiquitous 'Facebook friends' who are perhaps even destructive of real friendships but emulate these through an interposed corporate seller. Generally, monetary and exchange relationships emerge because there is exactly not a human relationship of trust between the actors involved, but one of self-sufficiency and relentless competition. In this world of market fundamentalism, where every social relationship is dissolved into a market model, the narcissist and the sociopath are likely to succeed best.[26]

What makes money operate is ultimately a legally sustained creed with historical roots in religion.[27] Nowadays it is the law which enforces the janiform debt that money constitutes: the loan-debt, and the circulating debt or credit. The enforcement of the debt which the market participants can rely on makes the *res*

25 Chapter 4, sec. 4.
26 Chapter 4, sec. 5.
27 Chapter 5, sec. 1.

in question to functioning money. That is the fourth case or aspect of money (*casus accusativus*), as explained earlier. Only the guarantee of the ultimate legal enforcement of the debt which money constitutes (bank money in particular) ensures the transition from *mx* to *C2* and makes the debt circulating credit and therefore money. Put differently, because of the quality as a *legally enforceable* debt the *res* is circulating credit and money. Economists prefer the sociological money definition that everything that is accepted by the market as money operates as money. However, what is crucial is rather the fact that the debt which money constitutes (and/or which has brought money into existence) is enforceable in law. That ensures the market participants' acceptance of worthless tokens and numbers as account entries in the computer as money. It is not necessary that money must be issued by the state, as the State Theory or Chartalist Theory of money claims; it is only necessary that the debt that money constitutes can be enforced by the state authorities, especially the courts of law, finally through execution, such as a sale or auction of the debtor's assets, and insolvency proceedings, in which case genuine value will ultimately be exchanged or transferred.[28]

However, the banks as debtors (as depositees) and creditors (as lenders) have a special position not normally recognised in the generally accepted liberal conception of contract law: they are 'strong debtors' and 'strong creditors' by virtue of the corporate structure in which all banks today are organised. This is deepened by the banks' privilege to create bank money out of nothing: even the insolvency of a bank will not severely hit the framework of the banking system and its operations.[29] The introduction of the European Stability Mechanism (ESM) as a reform measure of the EU after the banking crisis of 2008–9 has reinforced the unassailable power of the banks: the ESM is a device detached from any democratic control by either the EU or its member states, and enjoys complete immunity.[30] In the light of this unsatisfactory situation, one may think of alternative concepts of money and the monetary system. These alternatives do exist, but they are not without significant flaws in their understanding of the current system and of the challenges for a transition to a new one.[31]

Will there be a change of the present monetary system by the political forces? Hardly. The conservative parties think, rightly or wrongly, that the monetary system helps maintaining the political power structures they stand for, and the political Left is too insignificant or too incompetent to effect a change that goes beyond tinkering around the edges. While the political Right has a certain tradition of destroying others, the political Left has a strong tradition of destroying itself. Either social-democratic parties have adopted the neo-liberal economic worldview (as in Germany) or they have sunk almost into oblivion because they were eclipsed by neo-liberal technocrats in new party formations (as in France), or they have embraced a romantic-atavistic idea of socialism that harks back to the

28 Chapter 5, sec. 2, Chapter 2, sec. 4.
29 Chapter 5, sec. 3.
30 Chapter 5, sec. 4.
31 Chapter 5, sec. 5.

1970s with little appreciation of the social changes of the present (as in Britain). It is therefore unlikely that politics will reform the monetary system.

Another problem is the fact that 'left-wing' economists operate with the same (often questionable) axioms in economics. Thus their criticism is not one of the system as such, but of an interpretation of certain effects in the system. The system itself is unselfconsciously considered as consisting of immutable natural laws which economists claim to have discovered, whether one calls these historical materialism or laws of the market. An example is the barely questioned need for economic growth. An old socialist text from Weimar Germany (1928) illustrates this:[32]

> The means of releasing mass consumption is the wage, which determines directly the purchasing power of two-thirds of the population. It is not that a greater fund of wages should be conjured up out of nowhere, but that there should only be a different distribution of the social product in favour of the wage. The *wage fraction* below the production costs and in the commodity prices must be increased, and this can be done by compressing the other cost factors.

The postulated need for economic growth (increase of mass consumption, particularly ecologically unsustainable consumption) and the glorification of work against wages, thus in exchange of money, are still cornerstones of left-wing economic thinking today, but are also pillars of the present monetary system, so that a fundamental critique from the political left is even conceptually, let alone politically, unlikely. On that basis, for example, any environmental reform concerning climate change is worthless and bound to remain gesture politics.

Self-proclaimed critics of the present society, whether academics or intellectuals, frequently immerse themselves in unintelligible concepts of social theory. They often also dismiss everything as unoriginal, outdated, too simplistic or naïve that could be understood without an intellectually degenerating study of their own scientific theory, and so they prevent that any practical action could ensue. This nips any critical reform in the bud, interestingly by those who proclaim to be the critical voices – perhaps the one lasting legacy of postmodernism, itself otherwise very much passé. What is left is some purely academic quibbling in social science departments about minor details that are closely to be observed by young 'critical' but career-focused academics who must arm themselves with a flood of irrelevant publications as a feature of the modern commodification of research.[33] The type of present discourse – for example as to the difference between 'left-wing' and 'right-wing' monetary economics and law – is mostly just a fight of different sects over the proper worshipping of their common god. The monetary

32 Tarnow (1928: 71) (own translation from the German, original emphasis).

33 On this specific point which is also a good illustration of commodification and alienation in general, see Rahmatian (2011a: 255).

system will probably not be shaken up soon, and both its proponents and apparent critics will help maintaining it. In peace or in war, in an age of sustainable economic development or of global warming, the monetary system benefits from all situations in its way, and that must be so in an economic system where man serves the economy, not conversely.

Bibliography

Adam, Stanislas and Parras, Francisco J. M. (2013), 'Case Comment: The European Stability Mechanism Through the Legal Meanderings of the Union's Constitutionalism: Comment on *Pringle*', 38(6) *European Law Review*, 848–865

Adorno, Theodor W. (2003), *Minima Moralia. Reflexionen aus dem beschädigten Leben*, Rolf Tiedemann (ed.) (Gesammelte Schriften, vol. 4), Frankfurt am Main: Suhrkamp

Aglietta, Michel and Brand, Thomas (2013), *Un New Deal pour L'Europe*, Paris: Odile Jacob

Ainsworth, Penne and Deines, Dan (2007), *Introduction to Accounting: An Integrated Approach*, New York: McGraw-Hill

Albritton, Robert (2012), 'Commodification and Commodity Fetishism', in: Ben Fine and Alfredo Saad-Filho (eds.), *The Elgar Companion to Marxist Economics*, Cheltenham: Edward Elgar, pp. 66–71

Angel, James J. and McCabe, Douglas M. (2009), 'The Business Ethics of Short Selling and Naked Short Selling', 85(Suppl. 1) *Journal of Business Ethics*, 239–249

Anon [sometimes attrib. to William Pulteney] (1738), *Some Thoughts on the Interest of Money in General, and Particularly in the Public Funds, etc.*, London: Printed for J. Roberts

Armstrong, Kenneth A. (2013), 'The New Governance of EU Fiscal Discipline', 38(5) *European Law Review*, 601–617

Arnoldi, Jakob (2009), *Alles Geld verdampft*, Frankfurt am Main: Suhrkamp

Arnon, Arie (2011), *Monetary Theory and Policy From Hume and Smith to Wicksell: Money, Credit, and the Economy*, Cambridge: Cambridge University Press

Assmann, Jan (2011), *Moses der Ägypter. Entzifferung einer Gedächtnisspur*, Frankfurt am Main: Fischer Taschenbuch Verlag

Ayache, Élie (2011), 'A New Philosophy of the Market', in: Alexander Lipton and Andrew Rennie (eds.), *The Oxford Handbook of Credit Derivatives*, Oxford: Oxford University Press, pp. 467–499

Azpilcueta, Martín de (Doctor Navarrus) (2014), *On Exchange: An Adjudicative Commentary*, Rodrigo Muñoz (ed.), Jeannine Emery (trans.), Grand Rapids: CLP Academic (extracts from *Comentario resolutorio de cambios*, 1st ed. 1556)

Bachelier, Louis (1900), 'Théorie de la spéculation', 17 *Annales scientifiques de l'É.N.S.*, 3e série, 21–86

Bacon, Francis (1886), *The Physical and Metaphysical Works of Lord Bacon, Including the Advancement of Learning and Novum Organum*, Joseph Devey (ed.), London: George Bell & Sons

Bagehot, Walter (1873), *Lombard Street: A Description of the Money Market*, E. Johnstone and Hartley Withers (eds.), London: Henry S. King and Co.

Bank of England (McLeay, Michael, Radia, Amar and Thomas, Ryland) (2014a), 'Money Creation in the Modern Economy', *Quarterly Bulletin Q1*, 14–27

Bank of England (McLeay, Michael, Radia, Amar and Thomas, Ryland) (2014b), 'Money in the Modern Economy: An Introduction', *Quarterly Bulletin Q1*, 4–13

Barber, William J. (1977), *A History of Economic Thought*, Harmondsworth: Penguin

Baudrillard, Jean (2014), *Le système des objets*, Paris: Gallimard

Bayle, Pierre (2003), *Historisches und kritisches Wörterbuch. Eine Auswahl*, Günter Gawlick und Lothar Kreimendahl (eds.), Hamburg: Felix Meiner Verlag (1st ed. 1696–97)

Becker, Gary S. (1973), 'A Theory of Marriage: Part I', 81(4) *Journal of Political Economy*, 813–846

Becker, Gary S. (1992), 'Human Capital and the Economy', 136(1) *Proceedings of the American Philosophical Society*, 85–92

Benjamin, Walter (2002), 'Bücher und Lektüre des Kindes', in: Detlev Schöttker (ed.), *Medienästhetische Schriften*, Frankfurt am Main: Suhrkamp, pp. 186–192

Bentham, Jeremy (1891), 'Principles of the Civil Code', in: *The Theory of Legislation*, 7th ed., R. Hildreth (trans.), London: Kegan Paul, Trench, Trübner (1st ed. 1840), pp. 88–236

Berle, Adolf A. and Means, Gardiner C. (2003), *The Modern Corporation and Private Property*, New Brunswick and London: Transaction Publishers (1st ed. 1932)

Bernays, Edward (2005), *Propaganda*, New York: Ig Publishing (1st ed. 1928)

Binswanger, Hans Ch. (1985), *Geld und Magie: Deutung und Kritik der modernen Wirtschaft anhand von Goethes Faust*, Stuttgart, Wien, and Bern: Weitbrecht Verlag

Binswanger, Hans Ch. (2009), *Die Wachstumsspirale. Geld, Energie und Imagination in der Dynamik des Marktprozesses*, 3rd ed., Marburg: Metropolis

Binswanger, Hans Ch. (2013), *The Growth Spiral: Money, Energy, and Imagination in the Dynamics of the Market Process*, Berlin and Heidelberg: Springer

Blackstone, William (1800), *Commentaries on the Laws of England: Book The First*, 13th ed., London: A. Strahan, T. Cadell

Blanc, Jérôme (1998), 'Free Money for Social Progress: Theory and Practice of Gesell's Accelerated Money', 57(4) *The American Journal for Economics and Sociology*, 469–483

Bofinger, Peter (2011), *Grundzüge der Volkswirtschaftslehre. Eine Einführung in die Wissenschaft von Märkten*, 3rd ed., München: Pearson Studium

Boos, Karl-Heinz, Fischer, Reinfrid, and Schulte-Mattler, Hermann (2016), *Kommentar zum Kreditwesengesetz*, 5th ed., München: C. H. Beck

Booysen, Sandra (2018), 'Cheques: To Be or Not to Be?', 4 *Journal of Business Law*, 283–299

Bridge, Michael (2015), *Personal Property Law*, 4th ed., Oxford: Oxford University Press

Brunnermeier, Markus K., Nagel, Stefan, and Pedersen, Lasse H. (2008), 'Carry Trades and Currency Crashes', 23(1) *NBER Macroeconomics Annual*, 313–348

Bulow, Jeremy (1986), 'An Economic Theory of Planned Obsolescence', 101(4) *Quarterly Journal of Economics*, 729–749

Bydlinski, Franz (1996), *System und Prinzipien des Privatrechts*, Wien and New York: Springer Verlag

Cannu, Paul Le and Dondero, Bruno (2009), *Droit des sociétés*, 3rd ed., Paris: Éditions Montchestien

Carlson, Mark et al. (2016), 'The Demand for Short-Term, Safe Assets and Financial Stability: Some Evidence and Implications for Central Bank Policies', *International Journal of Central Banking*, 307–333

Chambers, John D. (ed., trans.) (1882), *The Theological and Philosophical Works of Hermes Trismegistus, Christian Neoplatonist*, Edinburgh: T & T Clark

Chatfield, Michael (1977), *A History of Accounting Thought*, Revised ed., Huntington: Robert E. Krieger Publishing

Chung, John J. (2009), 'Money as Simulacrum: The Legal Nature and Reality of Money', 5 *Hastings Business Law Journal*, 109–167

Clapham, Sir John (1944), *The Bank of England: A History, Vol. 1: 1694–1797*, Cambridge: Cambridge University Press

Clover, Joshua S. (2004), 'Remember, We're the Good Guys: The Classification and Trial of the Guantanamo Bay Detainees', 45 *South Texas Law Review*, 351–393

Commons, John R. (1924), *Legal Foundations of Capitalism*, New York: Macmillan Co.

Cooter, Robert and Ulen, Thomas (1997), *Law and Economics*, 2nd ed., Reading, MA and Harlow: Addison-Wesley

Cranston, Ross (2002), *Principles of Banking Law*, 2nd ed., Oxford: Oxford University Press

Cranston, Ross et al. (2017), *Principles of Banking Law*, 3rd ed., Oxford: Oxford University Press

Crowther, Geoffrey (1946), *An Outline of Money*, London: Thomas Nelson and Sons

Darity, William (1995), 'Keynes' Political Philosophy: The Gesell Connection', 21(1) *Eastern Economic Journal*, 27–41

Davies, Paul L. and Worthington, Sarah (2012), *Gower & Davies Principles of Modern Company Law*, 9th ed., London: Sweet and Maxwell

Dawson, Mark and De Witte, Floris (2013), 'Constitutional Balance in the EU After the Euro-Crisis', 76(5) *Modern Law Review*, 817–844

Deakin, Simon (2017), 'The Corporation in Legal Studies', in: Grietje Baars and André Spicer (eds.), *The Corporation: A Critical, Multi-Disciplinary Handbook*, Cambridge: Cambridge University Press, pp. 47–63

Demsetz, Harold (1967), 'Toward a Theory of Property Rights', 57(2) *The American Economic Review*, 347–359

Desan, Christine (2014), *Making Money: Coin, Currency, and the Coming of Capitalism*, Oxford: Oxford University Press

Desan, Christine (2016), 'Money as a Legal Institution', in: David Fox and Wolfgang Ernst (eds.), *Money in the Western Legal Tradition: Middle Ages to Bretton Woods*, Oxford: Oxford University Press, pp. 18–40

Dessert, Daniel (1984), *Argent, pouvoir et société au Grand Siècle*, Paris: Fayard

Deutsche Bundesbank (2008), *Geld und Geldpolitik*, Frankfurt am Main: Deutsche Bundesbank, pp. 1–181

Deutsche Bundesbank (2009), *Geld und Geldpolitik*, Frankfurt am Main: Deutsche Bundesbank, pp. 1–247

Deutsche Bundesbank (2010), *Geld und Geldpolitik*, Frankfurt am Main: Deutsche Bundesbank, pp. 1–255

Deutsche Bundesbank (2017), *Geld und Geldpolitik*, Frankfurt am Main: Deutsche Bundesbank, pp. 1–271

Devlin, Keith (2000), *The Language of Mathematics: Making the Invisible Visible*, New York: W. H. Freeman and Company

De Vroey, Michel (2009), 'On the Right Side for the Wrong Reason: Friedman on the Marshall-Walras Divide', in: Uskali Mäki (ed.), *The Methodology of Positive Economics: Reflections on the Milton Friedman Legacy*, Cambridge: Cambridge University Press, pp. 321–346

De Witte, Bruno (2015), 'Euro Crisis Responses and the EU Legal Order: Increased Institutional Variation or Constitutional Mutation?', 11(3) *European Constitutional Law Review*, 434–457

Dillard, Dudley (1942), 'Silvio Gesell's Monetary Theory of Social Reform', 32(2) *The American Economic Review*, 348–352

Dillard, Dudley (1970), *The Economics of John Maynard Keynes: The Theory of a Monetary Economy*, London: Crosby Lockwood & Son

Dillard, Dudley (1988), 'The Barter Illusion in Classical and Neo-Classical Economics', 14(4) *Eastern Economics Journal*, 299–318

Dinkova-Bruun, Greti (2015), 'Nummus falsus: The Perception of Counterfeit Money in the Eleventh and Early Twelfth Century', in: Giles E. M. Gasper and Svein H. Gullbekk (eds.), *Money and the Church in Medieval Europe, 1000–1200*, Farnham, Surrey: Ashgate, pp. 77–91

Dodd, Nigel (2018), 'The Social Life of Bitcoin', 35(3) *Theory, Culture and Society*, 35–56

Elias, Norbert (1992), *Time: An Essay*, Edmund Jephcott (trans.), Oxford: Blackwell Publishers

Ellinger, Eliahu P., Lomnicka, Eva, and Hare, C.V.M. (2011), *Ellinger's Modern Banking Law*, 5th ed., Oxford: Oxford University Press

Eucken, Walter (1950), *Die Grundlagen der Nationalökonomie*, 6th ed., Berlin, Göttingen, and Heidelberg: Springer Verlag

Eucken, Walter (1959), *Grundsätze der Wirtschaftspolitik*, Hamburg: Rowohlt (Rowohlts Deutsche Enzyklopädie)

Federal Reserve Bank of Chicago (Dorothy M. Nichols, revised 1992 by Anne Marie L. Gonczy) (1994), *Modern Money Mechanics*, Chicago, IL (first version 1961)

Fetter, Frank A. (1912), 'The Definition of Price', 2(4) *The American Economic Review*, 783–813

Financial Services Authority Board (2011), *The Failure of the Royal Bank of Scotland*, London: Financial Services Authority

Fischer, Svante (2017), 'The Material Culture of 5th Century Returning Veterans', in: Charlotte Fabech and Ulf Näsman (eds.), *The Sösdala Horsemen – And the Equestrian Elite of Fifth Century Europe*, Aarhus: Jutland Archaeological Society/ Aarhus University Press, pp. 313–325

Fisher, Irving (1929), *The Money Illusion*, London: George Allen and Unwin

Fisher, Irving (1936), '100% Money and the Public Debt', *Economic Forum*, April–June, 406–420

Flassbeck, Heiner (2013), *Zehn Mythen der Krise*, 5th ed., Berlin: Suhrkamp

Fox, David (2016), 'The Case of Mixt Monies (1604)', in: David Fox and Wolfgang Ernst (eds.), *Money in the Western Legal Tradition: Middle Ages to Bretton Woods*, Oxford: Oxford University Press, pp. 224–244

Fraassen, Bas C. van (1985), *An Introduction to the Philosophy of Time and Space*, New York: Columbia University Press

Frank, Robert H. (1993), 'Does Studying Economics Inhibit Cooperation?', 7(2) *The Journal of Economic Perspectives*, 159–171

Franklin, Benjamin (1961), *The Papers of Benjamin Franklin, January 1, 1745, Through June 30, 1750*, vol. 3, Leonard Labaree et al. (eds.), New Haven: Yale University Press

Freeman, Michael D. A. (2008), *Lloyd's Introduction to Jurisprudence*, 8th ed., London: Sweet and Maxwell

Friedman, Milton (1956), 'The Quantity Theory of Money – A Restatement', in: Milton Friedman (ed.), *Studies in the Quantity Theory of Money*, Chicago: University of Chicago Press, pp. 3–21

Friedman, Milton (1982), 'Free Markets and the Generals', *Newsweek*, 25 January 1982, p. 59

Friedman, Milton (2009), 'The Methodology of Positive Economics', in: Uskali Mäki (ed.), *The Methodology of Positive Economics: Reflections on the Milton Friedman Legacy*, Cambridge: Cambridge University Press, pp. 3–43 (1st ed. 1953)

Friedman, Milton and Schwartz, Anna J. (1986), 'Has the Government any Role in Money?', 17 *Journal of Monetary Economics*, 37–62

Fromm, Erich (2002), *The Sane Society*, London and New York: Routledge

Fuller, Lon L. (1941), 'Consideration and Form', 41(5) *Columbia Law Review*, 799–824

Ganzenmüller, Wilhelm (1938), *Die Alchemie im Mittelalter*, Paderborn: Bonifacius-Druckerei

Gardner, Simon (2011), *An Introduction to the Law of Trusts*, 3rd ed., Oxford: Oxford University Press

Gelleri, Christian (2009), 'Chiemgauer Regiomoney: Theory and Practice of a Local Currency', 13 *International Journal of Community Currency Research*, 61–75

Germain, Marie-Line (2018), *Narcissism at Work: Personality Disorders of Corporate Leaders*, Cham: Springer International/Palgrave Macmillan

Gesell, Silvio (1892), *Die Verstaatlichung des Geldes: Zweite Fortsetzung zur Reformation im Münzwesen*, Buenos Aires: Silvio Gesell

Gesell, Silvio (1911), *Die Neue Lehre vom Geld und Zins*, Leipzig: Bernhard Hermann

Geva, Benjamin (2016), 'Bank Money: The Rise, Fall and Metamorphosis of the "Transferable Deposit"', in: David Fox and Wolfgang Ernst (eds.), *Money in the Western Legal Tradition: Middle Ages to Bretton Woods*, Oxford: Oxford University Press, pp. 359–385

Goethe, Johann Wolfgang von (1982a), *Werke. Hamburger Ausgabe in 14 Bänden. Band 3: 'Dramatische Dichtungen I'*, Erich Trunz (ed.), München: Deutscher Taschenbuch Verlag

Goethe, Johann Wolfgang von (1982b), *Werke. Hamburger Ausgabe in 14 Bänden. Band 9: 'Autobiographische Schriften I'*, Erich Trunz (ed.), München: Deutscher Taschenbuch Verlag

Goldschmidt, Levin (1868), *Handbuch des Handelsrechts, 1. Band, 2. Abteilung, enthaltend die Lehre von der Ware*, Erlangen: Ferdinand Enke

Goldschmidt, Nils and Hesse, Jan-Otmar (2013), 'Eucken, Hayek and the *Road to Serfdom*', in: Robert Leeson (ed.), *Hayek: A Collaborative Biography: Part I*, London: Palgrave Macmillan, pp. 123–146

Goode, Roy (2011), *Principles of Corporate Insolvency Law*, 4th ed., London: Sweet and Maxwell

Goodhart, Charles (2002), 'Myths About the Lender of Last Resort', in: Charles Goodhart and Gerhard Illing (eds.), *Financial Crises, Contagion, and the Lender of Last Resort: A Reader*, Oxford: Oxford University Press, pp. 227–245

Graeber, David (2011), *Debt: The First 5,000 Years*, Brooklyn: Melville House

Graf, Georg (2004), 'Der Entzug von Mietrechten', in: Georg Graf, Brigitte Bailer-Galanda, et al. (eds.), *'Arisierung' und Rückstellung von Wohnungen in Wien*, Wien and München: Oldenbourg Verlag, pp. 11–89 (Veröffentlichungen der Österreichischen Historikerkommission. Vermögensentzug während der NS-Zeit sowie Rückstellungen und Entschädigungen seit 1945 in Österreich, vol. 14)

Grant, Michael and Hazel, John (2002), *Who's Who in Classical Mythology*, London and New York: Routledge

Grenz, Friedemann (1975), *Adornos Philosophie in Grundbegriffen. Auflösung einiger Deutungsprobleme. Anhang: Th. W. Adorno, A. Gehlen: Ist die Soziologie eine Wissenschaft vom Menschen? Ein Streitgespräch*, 2nd ed., Frankfurt am Main: Suhrkamp

Grice-Hutchinson, Marjorie (1952), *The School of Salamanca: Readings in Spanish Monetary Theory 1544–1605*, Oxford: Clarendon Press

Grierson, Philip (1978), 'The Origins of Money', in: George Dalton (ed.), *Research in Economic Anthropology*, vol. 1, Greenwich: JAI Press, pp. 1–35

Grotius, Hugo (1916), *The Freedom of the Seas* (*Mare Liberum*), Ralph van Deman Magoffin (trans.), New York: Oxford University Press (1st ed. 1609)

Gruyaert, Dorothy and van Loock, Sander (2014), 'UK Supreme Court Decision on Lehman Brothers Client Money: Equity or Lottery?', 22(2) *European Review of Private Law*, 217–249

Guinnane, Timothy W. (2018), 'German Company Law 1794–1897', in: Harwell Wells (ed.), *Research Handbook on the History of Corporate and Company Law*, Cheltenham: Edward Elgar, pp. 170–204

Hale, John R. (1971), *Renaissance Europe 1480–1520*, London: Collins (The Fontana History of Europe)

Hall, Steve et al. (2008), *Criminal Identities and Consumer Culture: Crime, Exclusion and the New Culture of Narcissism*, Cullompton: Willan Publishing

Harpum, Charles, Bridge, Stuart, and Dixon, Martin (2008), *(Megarry and Wade) The Law of Real Property*, 7th ed., London: Sweet and Maxwell

Harribey, Jean-Marie, Jeffers, Esther, Marie, Jonathan, Plihon, Dominique, and Ponsot, Jean-François (2018), *La monnaie: Un enjeu politique (Les économistes atterrés)*, Paris: Éditions du Seuil

Hayek, Friedrich A. (1964), 'The Theory of Complex Phenomena', in: Michael Martin and Lee C. McIntyre (eds.), *Readings on the Philosophy of Social Science*, Cambridge, MA and London: The MIT Press, pp. 55–70

Hayek, Friedrich A. (1990), *Denationalisation of Money: The Argument Refined*, 3rd ed., London: The Institute of Economic Affairs

Hayek, Friedrich A. (2001), *The Road to Serfdom*, London and New York: Routledge (1st ed. 1944)

Hayek, Friedrich A. (2013), *Law, Legislation and Liberty: A New Statement of the Liberal Principles of Justice and Political Economy*, London and New York: Routledge

Hazlitt, William (1903), *Table-Talk: Essays on Men and Manners*, London: Grant Richards

Heckscher, Eli F. (1932), 'The Place of Sweden in Modern Economic History', 4(1) *The Economic History Review*, 1–22

Hegel, Georg Wilhelm Friedrich (1986), *Grundlinien der Philosophie des Rechts* (Werke 7), Frankfurt am Main: Suhrkamp

Hegel, Georg Wilhelm Friedrich (2012), *Phänomenologie des Geistes* (Werke 3), Frankfurt am Main: Suhrkamp

Heinsohn, Gunnar and Steiger, Otto (2009), *Eigentum, Zins und Geld. Ungelöste Rätsel der Wirtschaftswissenschaft*, 6th ed., Marburg: Metropolis Verlag

Heinsohn, Gunnar and Steiger, Otto (2013), *Ownership Economics: On the Foundations of Interest, Money, Markets, Business Cycles and Economic Development*, Frank Decker (ed.), London and New York: Routledge

Heisenberg, Werner (1994), *Quantentheorie und Philosophie. Vorlesungen und Aufsätze*, J. Busche (ed.), Stuttgart: Reclam

Henning, Christoph (2015), *Theorien der Entfremdung zur Einführung*, Hamburg: Junius Verlag

Hinarejos, Alicia (2015), *The Euro Area Crisis in Constitutional Perspective*, Oxford: Oxford University Press

Hobbes, Thomas (1985), *Leviathan*, Crawford B. Macpherson (ed.), London: Penguin (1st ed. 1651)

Holmyard, Eric J. (1968), *Alchemy*, Harmondsworth: Penguin

Hölscher, Tonio (2014), 'Money and Image: The Presence of the State on the Routes of Economy', in: Jürgen von Hagen and Michael Welker (eds.), *Money as God? The Monetisation of the Market and Its Impact on Religion, Politics, Law, and Ethics*, Cambridge: Cambridge University Press, pp. 111–136

Howells, Peter and Bain, Keith (2005), *The Economics of Money, Banking and Finance*, 3rd ed., Harlow: Pearson

Huber, Joseph (2017), *Sovereign Money: Beyond Reserve Banking*, Cham: Springer International Publishing-Palgrave Macmillan

Hudson, Alastair (2013), *The Law of Finance*, 2nd ed., London: Thomson/Sweet and Maxwell

Hueck, Götz and Christine Windbichler (2008), *Gesellschaftsrecht*, 21st ed., München: C. H. Beck

Hume, David (1984), *A Treatise of Human Nature*, Ernest C. Mossner (ed.), London: Penguin (1st ed. 1739–40)

Hume, David (2003), *Political Essays*, Knud Haakonssen (ed.), Cambridge: Cambridge University Press (Cambridge Texts in the History of Political Thought)

Hume, David (2008), *Principal Writings on Religion Including Dialogues Concerning Natural Religion and the Natural History of Religion*, J.C.A. Gaskin (ed.), Oxford: Oxford University Press (1st ed., 1779 and 1757)

Humphrey, Caroline (1985), 'Barter and Economic Disintegration', 20(1) *Man. New Series*, 48–72

Humphrey, Thomas M. (1992), 'Marshallian Cross Diagrams and Their Use Before Alfred Marshall: The Origins of Supply and Demand Geometry', *Federal Reserve Bank of Richmond, Economic Review*, 2–23

Husserl, Edmund (2000), *Vorlesungen zur Phänomenologie des inneren Zeitbewußtseins*, Martin Heidegger (ed.), 3rd ed., Tübingen: Max Niemeyer Verlag

Ingham, Geoffrey (2004), 'The Nature of Money', 5(2) *Economic Sociology: European Electronic Newsletter*, Max Planck Institute for the Study of Societies, 18–28

Innes, A. Mitchell (1914), 'The Credit Theory of Money', 31 *Banking Law Journal*, 151–168

Ireland, Paddy (1999), 'Law and the Myth of Shareholder Ownership', 62(1) *Modern Law Review*, 32–57

Ireland, Paddy (2010), 'Limited Liability, Shareholder Rights and the Problem of Corporate Irresponsibility', 34 *Cambridge Journal of Economics*, 837–856

Jarchow, Hans-Joachim (2010), *Grundriss der Geldtheorie*, 12th ed., Stuttgart: Lucius & Lucius

Kähler, Lorenz (2006), 'Zur Entmythisierung der Geldschuld', 206 *Archiv für die civilistische Praxis*, 805–842

Kahn-Freund, Otto (1944), 'Some Reflections on Company Law Reform', 7 *Modern Law Review*, 54–66

Kaldor, Nicholas (1950–51), 'The Economic Aspects of Advertising', 18 *The Review of Economic Studies*, 1–27

Kames, Lord Kames (Henry Home) (2007), *Sketches of the History of Man, Books I, II, III* (4 vols. in 3 books), James A. Harris (ed.), Indianapolis: Liberty Fund (1st ed. 1774)

Kant, Immanuel (1977), *Die Metaphysik der Sitten*, Wilhelm Weischedel (ed.), (Werkausgabe Band VIII), Frankfurt am Main: Suhrkamp Taschenbuch Verlag (2nd definitive, ed. 1798)

Kant, Immanuel (2017), 'Über den Gemeinspruch: Das mag in der Theorie richtig sein, taugt aber nicht für die Praxis', in: Wilhelm Weischedel (ed.), *Schriften zur Anthropologie, Geschichtsphilosophie, Politik und Pädagogik 1* (Werkausgabe Band XI), Frankfurt am Main: Suhrkamp Taschenbuch Verlag (1st ed. 1793), pp. 127–172

Kenyon, John Philipps (1978), *Stuart England*, Harmondsworth: Penguin

Kershaw, David (2012), *Company Law in Context: Text and Materials*, 2nd ed., Oxford: Oxford University Press

Keynes, John M. (1964), *The General Theory of Employment, Interest and Money*, London: Macmillan (1st ed. 1936)

Keynes, John M. (2013a), *A Treatise on Money: 1 the Pure Theory of Money*, Cambridge: Cambridge University Press (The Collected Writings of John Maynard Keynes, vol. V, The Royal Economic Society) (1st ed. 1930)

Keynes, John M. (2013b), *A Treatise on Money: 2 The Applied Theory of Money*, Cambridge: Cambridge University Press (The Collected Writings of John Maynard Keynes, vol. VI, The Royal Economic Society) (1st ed. 1930)

King, Mervyn (2016), *The End of Alchemy: Banking, and the Future of the Global Economy*, London: Little, Brown

Kircher, Athanasius (1678), *Mundus Subterraneus*, 3rd ed., Amsterdam: Apud Joannem Janssonium a Waesberge et Filios

Klein, Naomi (2007), *The Shock Doctrine: The Rise of Disaster Capitalism*, Toronto: Alfred A. Knopf

Knapp, Georg Friedrich (1924), *The State Theory of Money*, H. M. Lucas and J. Bonar (eds.), London: Macmillan

Köhler, Helmut (2003), *BGB Allgemeiner Teil*, 27th ed., München: C. H. Beck

Köhler, Michael (2013), 'Humes Dilemma – oder: Was ist Geld? "Geldschöpfung" der Banken als Vermögensrechtsverletzung', in: Georg Freund, Uwe Murmann, René Bloy, and Walter Perron (eds.), *Grundlagen und Dogmatik des gesamten Strafrechtssystems: Festschrift für Wolfgang Frisch zum 70. Geburtstag* (Schriften zum Strafrecht, vol. 244), Berlin: Duncker und Humblot, pp. 887–923

Köller, Wilhelm (2004), *Perspektivität und Sprache. Zur Struktur von Objektivierungsformen in Bildern, im Denken und in der Sprache*, Berlin and New York: Walter de Gruyter

Koyré, Alexandre (1971), *Mystiques, spirituels, alchimistes du XVIe siècle allemande*, Paris: Gallimard

Kristeller, Paul O. (1990), 'Rhetoric in Medieval and Renaissance Culture', in: Paul O. Kristeller (ed.), *Renaissance Thought and the Arts: Collected Essays*, Princeton: Princeton University Press, pp. 228–246

Krugman, Paul and Wells, Robin (2015), *Economics*, 4th ed., New York: Worth Publishers

Lautenbach, Wilhelm (1952), *Zins, Kredit und Produktion*, Wolfgang Stützel (ed.), Tübingen: J.C.B. Mohr (Paul Siebeck)

Lavoisier, Antoine-Laurent (1965), *Elements of Chemistry*, Robert Kerr (trans.), New York: Dover (facsimile reprint of the edition 1790)

Lederer, Nicole (2008), 'The European Emissions Trading Scheme and International Emissions Trading – A Comparative Analysis', 12 *New Zealand Journal of Environmental Law*, 1–37

Lepsius, Oliver (2002), 'Geld als Schutzgut der Eigentumsgarantie', 57(7) *Deutsche Juristenzeitung*, 313–321

Lessius, Leonardus (2016), *On Sale, Securities, and Insurance*, Wim Decock (ed.), Wim Decock and Nicholas de Sutter (trans.), Grand Rapids: CLP Academic (extracts from *De iustitia et iure*, 1st ed. 1605)

Lilienthal, Gary and Ahmad, Nehaluddin (2018), 'Bitcoin: Is It Really Coinage?', 24(3) *Computer and Telecommunications Law Review*, 49–56

Locke, John (1991), *Locke on Money*, Patrick H. Kelly (ed.), Vols. 1 and 2, Oxford: Clarendon Press

Locke, John (2013), *Two Treatises of Government*, 2nd ed., 24th printing, Peter Laslett (ed.), Cambridge: Cambridge University Press (1st ed. 1690)

Löw, Martina (2012), *Raumsoziologie*, Frankfurt am Main: Suhrkamp Verlag

Lowry, John and Edmunds, Rod (2015), 'Directors' Duties and Liabilities: Disqualifying "Unfit" Directors at Banks? Political Rhetoric and the Directors' Disqualification Regime', in: Iris H.-Y. Chiu (ed.), *The Law on Corporate Governance in Banks*, Cheltenham: Edward Elgar, pp. 75–98

Lu, Lerong (2018), 'Bitcoin: Speculative Bubble, Financial Risk and Regulatory Response', 33(3) *Butterworths Journal of International Banking and Financial Law*, 178–182

MacCulloch, Diarmaid (2009), *A History of Christianity: The First Three Thousand Years*, London: Allen Lane

Macleod, Henry Dunning (1883), *The Theory and Practice of Banking*, vol. 1, 4th ed., London: Longmans, Green, Reader and Dyer

Macleod, Henry Dunning (1886), *The Theory and Practice of Banking*, vol. 2, 4th ed., London: Longmans, Green, Reader and Dyer

Mandrella, Isabelle (2016), 'Gabriel Vázquez über das Naturrecht', in: Kirstin Bunge, Marko J. Fuchs et al. (eds.), *The Concept of Law (lex) in the Moral and Political Thought of the 'School of Salamanca'*, Leiden and Boston: Brill, pp. 129–149

Mankiw, N. Gregory (2012), *Principles of Economics*, 6th ed. (International Edition), Mason, O: South Western, London: Cengage Learning

Mankiw, N. Gregory (2013), *Macroeconomics*, 8th ed. (International Version), Houndmills and Basingstoke: Worth Publishers/Palgrave Macmillan

Mann, Frederick A. (1992), *The Legal Aspect of Money*, 5th ed., Oxford: Oxford University Press

Mannheim, Karl (1943), *Diagnosis of our Time: Wartime Essays of a Sociologist*, London: Kegan Paul, Trench, Trubner & Co

Marcuse, Herbert (1972), *One Dimensional Man*, London: Abacus/Sphere Books

Markovits, Francine (1986), *L'ordre des échanges*, Paris: Presses Universitaires de France

Marshall, Alfred (2013), *Principles of Economics*, 8th ed., Basingstoke: Palgrave Macmillan (1st ed. 1890) (Palgrave Classics in Economics)

Marx, Karl (1932), *Der Historische Materialismus: Die Frühschriften*, vol. 2, S. Landshut and J. P. Mayer (eds.), Leipzig: Alfred Kröner Verlag

Marx, Karl (1975), *Das Kapital. Band 1: Der Produktionsprozeß des Kapitals*, Karl Korsch (ed.), Frankfurt am Main: Ullstein Verlag

Marx, Karl (2004), 'Die entfremdete Arbeit' (in: ökonomisch-philosophische Manuskripte, 1844), in: Iring Fetscher (ed.), Karl Marx, Friedrich Engels, *Studienausgabe in 5 Bänden: Politische Ökonomie (Studienausgabe Band II)*, Berlin: Aufbau Taschenbuch Verlag, pp. 77–90

Matton, Sylvain (2009), *Philosophie et Alchimie à la Renaissance et à Âge classique: Scolastique et Alchimie* (XVIe–XVII siècles), Paris: S.É.H.A., Milan: Archè

Mauss, Marcel (2001), *A General Theory of Magic*, Robert Brain (trans.), London and New York: Routledge

May, Gerhard (1994), *Creatio Ex Nihilo: The Doctrine of 'Creation Out of Nothing' in Early Christian Thought*, A. S. Worrall (ed.), Edinburgh: T & T Clark

McKendrick, Ewan (2016), *Goode on Commercial Law*, 5th ed., London: Penguin

McLellan, David (1972), *Marx Before Marxism*, Harmondsworth: Penguin

McTaggart, John M. E. (1995), 'The Unreality of Time', in: Robin Le Poidevin and Murray MacBeath (ed.), *The Philosophy of Time*, Oxford: Oxford University Press, pp. 23–34

Medicus, Dieter (2003), *Schuldrecht I. Allgemeiner Teil*, 14th ed., München: C. H. Beck

Migliorino, Franceso (1981), 'Alchimia lecita e illecita nel Trecento: Oldrado da Ponte', 11 *Quaderni medievali*, 6–41

Mises, Ludwig von (1953), *The Theory of Money and Credit*, New Haven: Yale University Press

Mitchell, William (2015), *Eurozone Dystopia: Groupthink and Denial on a Grand Scale*, Cheltenham: Edward Elgar

Molina, Luis de (2015), *A Treatise on Money*, Rudolf Schuessler (ed.), Jeannine Emery (trans.), Grand Rapids: CLP Academic (extracts from *De iustitia et iure*, 1st ed. 1593)

Moran, Bruce T. (2005), *Distilling Knowledge: Alchemy, Chemistry and the Scientific Revolution*, Cambridge, MA: Harvard University Press

Moreno, Jacob Levi (1987), 'Sociometry', in: Jonathan Fox (ed.), *The Essential Moreno: Writings on Psychodrama, Group Method, and Spontaneity*, New York: Springer Publishing, pp. 20–31

Morgan, E. Victor (1965), *A History of Money*, Harmondsworth: Penguin

Morrisson, Mark (2007), *Modern Alchemy: Occultism and the Emergence of Atomic Theory*, Oxford: Oxford University Press

Müller, Adam Heinrich (2006), *Die Elemente der Staatskunst*, vol. 2, Hildesheim, Zürich, and New York: Georg Olms Verlag (facsimile reprint of the 1809 edition)

Murphy, Antoin E. (1997), *John Law: Economic Theorist and Policy-Maker*, Oxford: Clarendon Press

Musso, Pierre (2014), *L'imaginaire industriel*, Paris: Éditions Manucius

Musso, Pierre (2017), *La Religion industrielle*, Paris: Fayard/Institut d'études avancées de Nantes

Naismith, Rory (2015), 'Turpe lucrum? Wealth, Money and Coinage in the Millennial Church', in: Giles E. M. Gasper and Svein H. Gullbekk (eds.), *Money and the Church in Medieval Europe, 1000–1200*, Farnham and Surrey: Ashgate, pp. 17–37

Negishi, Takashi (1965), 'Market Clearing Processes in a Monetary Economy', in: Frank H. Hahn and Frank P. R. Brechling (eds.), *The Theory of Interest Rates*, London: Macmillan, pp. 152–163

Nesvetailova, Anastasia and Palan, Ronan (2017), 'Banks as Global Corporations: From Entities to "Ecological Habitats"', in: Grietje Baars and André Spicer (eds.), *The Corporation: A Critical, Multi-Disciplinary Handbook*, Cambridge: Cambridge University Press, pp. 268–279

Newman, William R. (1999), 'The Homunculus and His Forebears: Wonders of Art and Nature', in: Antony Grafton and Nancy Siraisi (eds.), *Natural Particulars: Nature and the Disciplines in Renaissance Europe*, Cambridge, MA and London: The MIT Press, pp. 321–345

Newman, William R. (2006), *Atoms and Alchemy: Chymistry and the Experimental Origins of the Scientific Revolution*, Chicago and London: The University of Chicago Press

Nicholas, Barry (1975), *An Introduction to Roman Law*, Oxford: Oxford University Press

Norton, Thomas (1975), *The Ordinal of Alchemy*, John Reidy (ed.), London: Oxford University Press

Ogrinc, Will H. L. (1980), 'Western Society and Alchemy From 1200 to 1500', 6(1) *Journal of Medieval History*, 103–132

Olbrich, Michael et al. (2009), 'The Valuation of Airport Slots', 74 *Journal of Air Law and Commerce*, 897–917

Olivecrona, Karl (1971), *Law as Fact*, London: Stevens & Sons

Ollman, Bertell (1976), *Alienation: Marx's Conception of Man in Capitalist Society*, 2nd ed., Cambridge: Cambridge University Press

Orléan, André (2011), *L'empire de la valeur. Refonder l'économie*, Paris: Éditions du Seuil

Pacioli (or Paciolo), Luca (1963), *Paciolo on Accounting*, R. Gene Brown and Kenneth S. Johnston (eds.), New York: McGraw-Hill

Paracelsus, Theophrastus (1988), 'Ueber die Natur der Dinge', in: Theophrastus Paracelsus (ed.), *Der Himmel der Philosophen*, Nördlingen: Greno, pp. 93–187 (this text is usually attributed to Paracelsus)

Paracelsus (Theophrastus Bombastus von Hohenheim) (1978), 'The Art of Paracelsus', in: James B. Ross and Mary M. McLaughlin (eds.), *The Portable Renaissance Reader*, Harmondsworth: Penguin, pp. 552–557

Patinkin, Don (1969), 'The Chicago Tradition, the Quantity Theory, and Friedman', 1(1) *Journal of Money, Credit and Banking*, 46–70

Patinkin, Don (1972), 'Friedman on the Quantity Theory and Keynesian Economics', 80(5) *The Journal of Political Economy*, 883–905

Petrus Bonus of Ferrara (1894), *The New Pearl of Great Price*, A. E. Waite (trans.), London: J. Elliot

Pickering, Murray A. (1968), 'The Company as a Separate Legal Entity', 31(5) *Modern Law Review*, 481–511

Pilkington, Marc (2016), 'Blockchain Technology: Principles and Applications', in: F. Xavier Olleros and Majlinda Zhegu (eds.), *Research Handbook on Digital Transformations*, Cheltenham: Edward Elgar, pp. 225–253

Pilkington, Philip (2017), 'The Irish Sovereign Debt Crisis Post-2009', in: Juan Pablo Bohoslavsky and Kunibert Raffer (eds.), *Sovereign Debt Crises: What Have We Learned?*, Cambridge: Cambridge University Press, pp. 143–162

Polanyi, Karl (2001), *The Great Transformation: The Political and Economic Origins of Our Time*, Boston: Beacon Press

Polanyi, Karl (2014), *For a New West: Essays, 1919–1958*, Cambridge: Polity Press

Principe, Lawrence M. (2013), *The Secrets of Alchemy*, Chicago: University of Chicago Press

Proctor, Charles (2012), *Mann on the Legal Aspect of Money*, 7th ed., Oxford: Oxford University Press

Proudhon, Pierre-Joseph (2011), *Property Is Theft! A Pierre-Joseph Proudhon Anthology*, Iain McKay (ed.), Edinburgh and Oakland: AK Press

Prütting, Hanns (2008), *Sachenrecht*, 33rd ed., München: C. H. Beck

Quintilian (1969), *The Institutio Oratoria*, vol. 1 (books 1–3), H. E. Butler (trans.), London: William Heinemann; Cambridge, MA: Harvard University Press (Loeb)

Rahmatian, Andreas (2002), 'The Issue and Transfer of Shares Under English and German Law: An Outline', 23(8) *Company Lawyer*, 252–260

Rahmatian, Andreas (2005), 'Music and Creativity as Perceived by Copyright Law', 4 *Intellectual Property Quarterly*, 411–444

Rahmatian, Andreas (2008), 'A Comparison of German Moveable Property Law and English Personal Property Law', 3(1) *Journal of Comparative Law*, 197–248

Rahmatian, Andreas (2011a), *Copyright and Creativity: The Making of Property Rights in Creative Works*, Cheltenham: Edward Elgar Publishing

Rahmatian, Andreas (2011b), 'Intellectual Property and the Concept of Dematerialised Property', in: Sue Bright (ed.), *Modern Studies in Property Law*, vol. 6, Oxford: Hart Publishing, pp. 361–383

Rahmatian, Andreas (2012), 'The English Pound in an Independent Scotland', 27(9) *Journal of International Banking Law and Regulation*, 336–339

Rahmatian, Andreas (2013), 'A Fundamental Critique of the Law-and-Economics Analysis of Intellectual Property Rights', 17(2) *Marquette Intellectual Property Law Review*, 191–229

Rahmatian, Andreas (2014), 'Money as a Normative Text', 13 *Journal of International Business and Law*, 221–230

Rahmatian, Andreas (2015), *Lord Kames: Legal and Social Theorist*, Edinburgh: Edinburgh University Press

Rahmatian, Andreas (2017), 'The Nature of Laws in Law and in Economics', in: Giuseppe Longo (ed.), *Lois des dieux, des hommes et de la nature: Éléments pour une analyse transversale*, Paris: Spartacus-idh, pp. 109–147

Rahmatian, Andreas (2018a), 'Money as a Legally Enforceable Debt', 29(2) *European Business Law Review*, 205–236

Rahmatian, Andreas (2018b), 'Alchemistic Metaphors in Comparative Law: Mixed Legal Systems, Reception of Laws and Legal Transplants', 11 *Journal of Civil Law Studies*, 231–267

Rahmatian, Andreas (2019), 'Electronic Money and Cryptocurrencies (Bitcoin): Suggestions for Definitions', 34(3) *Journal of International Banking Law and Regulation*, 115–121

Rampling, Jennifer M. (2012), 'John Dee and the Alchemists: Practising and Promoting English Alchemy in the Holy Roman Empire', 43 *Studies in the History and Philosophy of Science*, 498–508

Raskin, Max and Yermack, David (2018), 'Digital Currencies, Decentralized Ledgers, and the Future of Central Banking', in: Peter Conti-Brown and Rosa Lastra (eds.), *Research Handbook on Central Banking*, Cheltenham: Edward Elgar, pp. 474–486

Reboul-Maupin, Nadège (2010), *Droit des biens*, 3ème éd., Paris: Éditions Dalloz

Reid, Kenneth G. C. (and contributors) (1996), *The Law of Property in Scotland*, Edinburgh: Butterworth

Reidy, John (1975), 'Introduction', in: John Reidy (ed.), *Thomas Norton's Ordinal of Alchemy*, London: Oxford University Press, pp. ix–lxxv

Reisberg, Arad (2015), 'The Role of Institutional Shareholders: Stewardship and the Long-/Short-Term Debate', in: Iris H.-Y. Chiu (ed.), *The Law on Corporate Governance in Banks*, Cheltenham: Edward Elgar, pp. 99–132

Renner, Karl (1949), *The Institutions of Private Law and Their Social Functions*, London: Routledge and Kegan Paul

Ricardo, David (2004), *The Principles of Political Economy and Taxation*, Mineola: Dover (1st ed. 1817)

Richards, Richard D. (1929), *The Early History of Banking in England*, London: P. S. King & Son

Rochat, Jean (2018), 'Change for Continuity: The Making of the *société anonyme* in Nineteenth Century France', in: Harwell Wells (ed.), *Research Handbook on the History of Corporate and Company Law*, Cheltenham: Edward Elgar, pp. 244–268

Rogers, J. E. Thorold (1887), *The First Nine Years of the Bank of England*, Oxford: Clarendon Press

Rognstad, Ole-Andreas (2018), *Property Aspects of Intellectual Property*, Cambridge: Cambridge University Press

Roob, Alexander (2016), *The Hermetic Museum: Alchemy & Mysticism*, Köln: Taschen

Ross, Ian Simpson (2010), *The Life of Adam Smith*, 2nd ed., Oxford: Oxford University Press

Rudden, Bernard (1987), 'Economic Theory v. Property Law: The *Numerus Clausus* Problem', in: John Eekelaar and John Bell (eds.), *Oxford Essays in Jurisprudence: Third Series*, Oxford: Clarendon Press, pp. 239–263

Sandys, John E. (1915), *A Short History of Classical Scholarship From the Sixth Century B.C. to the Present Day*, Cambridge: Cambridge University Press

Sapir, Jacques (2003), *Les trous noirs de la science économique. Essai sur l'impossibilité de penser le temps et l'argent*, Paris: Éditions Albin Michel

Savatier, René (1979), *La théorie des obligations en droit privé économique*, 4th ed., Paris: Dalloz

Savigny, Friedrich Carl von (1851), *Das Obligationenrecht als Theil des heutigen Römischen Rechts. Erster Band*, Berlin: Veit und Comp.

Say, Jean-Baptiste (1996), *Cours d'économie politique et autres essais*, Philippe Steiner (ed.), Paris: Flammarion (1st ed. 1815–20)

Schacht, Richard (1971), *Alienation: With an Introductory Essay by Walter Kaufmann*, London: Allen and Unwin

Schridde, Stefan et al. (2013), *Arge Regio: Geplante Obsoleszenz* (study commissioned by the German Green Party), Berlin: ARGE REGIO Stadt- und Regionalentwicklung GmbH

Schroeder, Ralph (2018), *Social Theory After the Internet: Media, Technology, and Globalization*, London: UCL Press

Schuler, Robert M. (1980), 'Some Spiritual Alchemies of Seventeenth-Century England', 41(2) *Journal of the History of Ideas*, 293–318

Schumpeter, Joseph A. (1954), *History of Economic Analysis*, New York: Oxford University Press

Schwarz, Fritz (2008), *Das Experiment von Wörgl*, Darmstadt: Synergia Verlag

Schwarz, Michael (2014), 'A Memorandum of Misunderstanding – The Doomed Road of the European Stability Mechanism and a Possible Way Out: Enhanced Cooperation', 51 *Common Market Law Review*, 389–423

Schwennicke, Andreas and Auerback, Dirk (2009), *Kreditwesengesetz (KWG). Kommentar*, München: C. H. Beck

Semenova, Alla (2011), 'Would You Barter With God? Why Holy Debts and Not Profane Markets Created Money', 70(2) *American Journal of Economics and Sociology*, 376–400

Shoemaker, Sydney (1995), 'Time Without Change', in: Robin Le Poidevin and Murray MacBeath (ed.), *The Philosophy of Time*, Oxford: Oxford University Press, pp. 63–79

Simmel, Georg (2011), *The Philosophy of Money*, David Frisby (trans. and ed.), London and New York: Routledge

Sinn, Hans-Werner and Wollmershäuser, Timo (2011), 'Target Loans, Current Account Balances and Capital Flows: The ECB's Rescue Facility', *CESifo Working Paper No. 3500, Category 7: Monetary Policy and International Finance*, Munich: CESIfo Group

Smith, Adam (2000), *The Wealth of Nations*, Robert Reich (ed.), New York: The Modern Library (1st ed. 1776)

Solinas, Matteo (2014), *Legal Evolution and Hybridisation: The Law of Shares Transfer in England*, Cambridge: Intersentia

Sparkes, Peter (2007), *European Land Law*, Oxford and Portland: Hart Publishing

Stambaugh, Joan (1964), 'Music as a Temporal Form', 61(9) *The Journal of Philosophy*, 265–280

Stein, Jerome L. (2014), 'The Diversity of Debt Crises in Europe', in: Daniel D ianu et al. (eds.), *The Eurozone Crisis and the Future of Europe: The Political Economy of Further Integration and Governance*, Basingstoke: Palgrave Macmillan, pp. 25–39

Stodder, James (2009), 'Complementary Credit Networks and Macroeconomic Stability: Switzerland's *Wirtschaftsring*', 72 *Journal of Economic Behavior and Organisation*, 79–95

Streissler, Erich (2012), '"i.i.d"? or: On So-called Precise Statements in Economics', in: Erich W. Streissler and Gunther Tichy (eds.), *How to Forecast Economic Developments During and After Crises*, Wien: Verlag der österreichischen Akademie der Wissenschaften, pp. 75–90

Streissler, Erich and Streissler, Monika (1984), *Grundzüge der Volkswirtschaftslehre für Juristen*, Wien: Manz

Sturm, Jan-Egbert et al. (2009), 'The Euro and Prices: Changeover-related Inflation and Price Convergence in the Euro Area', *Economic Papers 381*, Brussels: European Commission, Directorate-General for Economic and Financial Affairs

Stützel, Wolfgang (2011), *Volkswirtschaftliche Saldenmechanik. Ein Beitrag zur Geldtheorie*, 2nd ed., Tübingen: Mohr Siebeck

Supiot, Alain (2015), *La Gouvernance par les nombres. Cours au Collège de France (2012–2014)*, Paris: Institut d'études avancées de Nantes/Fayard

Tarnow, Fritz (1928), *Warum arm sein?*, Berlin: Verlagsgesellschaft des Allgemeinen Deutschen Gewerkschaftsbundes

Taylor, F. Sherwood (1976), *The Alchemists*, St. Albans: Paladin

Théret, Bruno (1998), 'De la dualité des dettes et de la monnaie dans les sociétés salariales', in: Michel Aglietta and André Orléan (eds.), *La monnaie souveraine*, Paris: Éditions Odile Jacob, pp. 253–287

Théret, Bruno (2011), 'Du keynésianisme au libertarianisme. La place de la monnaie dans les transformations du savoir économique autorisé', 10 *Revue de la regulation*, 1–25 (online, available at: http://regulation.revues.org/index9529.html)

Thompson, Edward P. (1967), 'Time, Work-Discipline, and Industrial Capitalism', 38 *Past and Present*, 56–97

Tillotson, John (1684), *A Discourse Against Transubstantiation*, London: M. Flesher, for Brabazon Aylmer

Tobin, James (1963), 'Commercial Banks as Creators of "Money"', *Cowles Foundation Discussion Paper No. 159*, New Haven: Cowles Foundation for Research in Economics at Yale University

Todeschini, Giacomo (2017), *Les Marchands et le Temple. La société chrétienne et le cercle vertueux de la richesse du Moyen Âge à l'Époque moderne*, Paris: Albin Michel

Tomkin, Jonathan (2013), 'Contradiction, Circumvention and Conceptual Gymnastics: The Impact of the Adoption of the ESM Treaty on the State of European Democracy', 14(1) *German Law Journal*, 169–189

Tortajada, Ramon (1987), 'M. de Malestroit et la théorie quantitative de la monnaie', 38(4) *Revue économique*, 853–876

Treitel, Guenther H. (2003), *The Law of Contract*, 11th ed., London: Thomson/Sweet and Maxwell

Turner, John D. (2018), 'The Development of English Company Law Before 1900', in: Harwell Wells (ed.), *Research Handbook on the History of Corporate and Company Law*, Cheltenham: Edward Elgar, pp. 121–141

Ugolini, Stefano (2017), *The Evolution of Central Banking: Theory and History*, London: Palgrave Macmillan

United States: Financial Crisis Inquiry Commission (2011), *The Financial Crisis: Inquiry Report: Final Report of the National Commission on the Causes of the Financial and Economic Crisis in the Unites States*, Seattle: Pacific Publishing Studio

Valéry, Paul (2008), *Tel Quel*, Paris: Éditions Gallimard

Van Houdt, Toon (1995), 'Money, Time and Labour: Leonardus Lessius and the Ethics of Lending and Interest Taking', 2(1) *Ethical Perspectives*, 11–27

Vickers, Douglas (1960), *Studies in the Theory of Money 1690–1776*, London: Peter Owen

Vilar, Pierre (1984), *A History of Gold and Money: 1450–1920*, London and New York: Verso

Vohs, Kathleen D. et al. (2006), 'The Psychological Consequences of Money', 314 *Science*, 1154–1156

Walker-Arnott, Edward (2015), 'Corporate Governance and Banks: The Role and Composition of the Board', in: Iris H.-Y. Chiu (ed.), *The Law on Corporate Governance in Banks*, Cheltenham: Edward Elgar, pp. 42–74

Walras, Léon (1886), *Théorie de la monnaie* (*extrait de la revue scientifique, numéros des 10 et 17 avril 1886*), Paris: Bureau des revues

Walras, Léon (1909), 'Économique et mécanique', 45 *Bulletin de la Société Vaudoise de Sciences Naturelles*, 313–327

Walras, Léon (1926), *Éléments d'économie politique pure ou Théorie de la Richesse sociale*, Paris: R. Pichon et R. Durant-Auzias, Lausanne: F. Rouge

Weber, Max (2001), *The Protestant Ethic and the Spirit of Capitalism*, T. Parsons (trans.), London and New York: Routledge

Webster, Pelatiah (1786), *An Essay on Credit, in Which the Doctrine of Banks Is Considered . . .*, Philadelphia: Printed by Eleazer Oswald

Werner, Richard A. (2014a), 'How Do Banks Create Money, and Why Can Other Firms Not Do the Same? An Explanation for the Coexistence of Lending and Deposit-Taking', 36 *International Review of Financial Analysis*, 71–77

Werner, Richard A. (2014b), 'Can Banks Individually Create Money Out of Nothing? – The Theories and the Empirical Evidence', 36 *International Review of Financial Analysis*, 1–19

Werner, Richard A. (2016), 'A Lost Century in Economics: Three Theories of Banking and the Conclusive Evidence', 46 *International Review of Financial Analysis*, 361–379

Willgerodt, Hans (2006), 'Der Neoliberalismus – Entstehung, Kampfbegriff und Meinungsstreit', in: *ORDO: Jahrbuch für die Ordnung von Wirtschaft und Gesellschaft*, vol. 57, Stuttgart: Lucius & Lucius, pp. 47–88

Windscheid, Bernhard (1963), *Lehrbuch des Pandektenrechts*, 9th ed., vol. 2, Theodor Kipp (ed.), Aalen: Scientia Verlag (reprint of the edition of 1906)

Witherspoon, John (1786), *Essay on Money as a Medium of Commerce; With Remarks on the Advantages and Disadvantages of Paper Admitted Into General Circulation*, Philadelphia: Young, Stewart and McCulloch

Yates, Frances (2002), *Giordano Bruno and the Hermetic Tradition*, London and New York: Routledge

Zimmermann, Reinhard (1996), *The Law of Obligations: Roman Foundations of the Civilian Tradition*, Oxford: Oxford University Press

Zinn, Howard (2005), *A People's History of the United States*, New York: Harper Perennial

Zöllner, Wolfgang (1987), *Wertpapierrecht*, 14th ed., München: C. H. Beck

Index